Psyche & the City

Analytical Psychology & Contemporary Culture Series

Series Editor: Thomas Singer

In our rapidly changing contemporary world, analytical psychology is confronted with the challenge of remaining relevant. To take on this challenge, Spring Journal Books has created a new series under the title Analytical Psychology & Contemporary Culture. The goal of the series is to bring analytical psychology into a cross-fertilizing dialogue with the fundamental issues of our time. The series will explore the multiple, interpenetrating relationships between history, mythology, politics, economics, sociology, and the arts as they express themselves in contemporary culture. At the heart of our mission is the creative exploration of the psyche's response to a world in rapid transition from the evolving perspectives of analytical psychology.

Psyche & the City

A Soul's Guide to the Modern Metropolis

Edited by
Thomas Singer

With contributions by

Paul Ashton, Gustavo Barcellos, John Beebe,
Nancy Furlotti, Jacqueline Gerson, Christopher Hauke,
Thomas Kelly, Thomas Kirsch, Antonio Karim Lanfranchi,
Charlotte Mathes, Elena Pourtova, Kusum Dhar Prabhu,
Joerg Rasche, Craig San Roque, Erel Shalit, Heyong Shen,
Thomas Singer, Murray Stein, Craig Stephenson,
Viviane Thibaudier, Beverley Zabriskie & Luigi Zoja

Spring Journal Books
New Orleans, Louisiana

Published by
Spring Journal, Inc.
627 Ursulines Street #7
New Orleans, Louisiana 70116
Tel.: (504) 524-5117
www.springjournalandbooks.com

Cover painting: *San Francisco Above Embarcadero*,
by Joseph Hartman
Back cover drawing of the *flâneur* and the tortoise:
Harry Weber

Cover & book design, typesetting: Michael Caplan
Globes: Northern Cartographic

Printed in Canada
Text printed on acid-free paper

ISBN 978-1-935528-03-6
Library of Congress Cataloging-in-Publication Data Pending

Table of Contents

PART TWO   Approaches to the City

This book is dedicated to the authors, whose individual urban rhapsodies have come together to create a most unique global hymn to the soul.

And to my children, Sarah, Molly, Eliza, & Jimmy, & their children—may the future let you, too, "leap for our Cities."

Acknowledgements

Many people helped put this complicated book together. Nancy Cater gave unwavering, good-humored support as our publisher, even as the project mushroomed. James Hillman paved the way by exploring both soul in the world and in the city. Iden Goodman, Baruch Gould, and Kyle Hunter were sensitive early readers of the material. Jean Kirsch helped me "dance" with my own material. Tom Kirsch guided in all sorts of ways, which he always does. John Beebe was unfailingly generous with his time and encyclopedic knowledge, as he always is. Michael Mendis, Sylvia Ruud, and Kate Babbitt were deft in the arts of copy-editing and production. Michael Caplan's work on the text, and his creative design and layout of text and images, have truly been done in the spirit of realizing the book's soul. And Harry Weber's drawing of the *flâneur* and tortoise "nailed it."

And, once again, my wife put up with my endless hours in front of the computer.

Foreword

THOMAS KIRSCH

What does a group of Jungian analysts have to say about "soul and the city"? Perhaps the most obvious answer is that the practice of Jungian analysis is of necessity an urban profession. For the most part, Jungian analysts live in and around urban areas. And Jungian analysts are prone to reflect on the nature of their environment in the same way that they think about analysands—where does the analysand's vitality express itself? Where is *soul* to be found, the sense of meaning, the shadow? Jungians tend to ask questions about the archetypal roots of the city in which they live, and like to osmose the mythology, history, anthropology, religions, and geography of their "place." In other words, Jungian analysts muse about their cities in the same way that they approach the rest of their world.

Many Jungian analysts also love to travel, to explore the art and cultural life that abounds in every city. And their travel is not necessarily in the most conventional of ways—Jungians often find their own unique approaches to a city. When my wife and I were in Paris, for instance, we toured its labyrinth of sewers. By studying the history of the flow and processing of water and sewage throughout the precincts, we obtained a unique view of the birth and growth of this magical city over centuries. My wife acquainted herself with Rome's 2,000-year-old system of aqueducts and the fountains they served before her first visit in 1977, thus gaining both an appreciation for how the city worked and also forming a plan for our later explorations by foot. It also amplified and enlivened her image of Rome as the "eternal city."

Each essay in this book tries to capture or evoke the spirit—even the "soul"—of a particular city. Cities are like organisms that grow and evolve over time to meet the needs and desires of their inhabitants, or to help them accommodate to the vicissitudes of chance and nature. One might venture to say that the relationship of a city to a civilization is analogous to that of ego to one's field of consciousness.

Jung himself was drawn to cities. Like many Swiss, he was fascinated by New York and its skyscrapers. In a letter to his wife Emma dated September 6, 1909, he described going on a steamer around the point of Manhattan; everything— the bridges, the bustle of harbor life—was bigger and grander than anything he had ever before experienced.

> There we boarded a fantastically huge structure of a steamer that had some five white decks. We took cabins, and our vessel set sail from the West River around the point of Manhattan with all its tremendous skyscrapers, and then up the East River under the Brooklyn and Manhattan Bridges, right through the endless tangle of tugs, ferry boats, etc. and through the sound behind Long Island. [1]

The image of "the city" is also used by Jung to describe the split in modern man's psyche. "Our world is, so to speak, dissociated like a neurotic, with the Iron Curtain marking the symbolic line of division." [2] For the editors of Jung's writings gathered under the title, *Man and His Symbols*, a photo of the Berlin Wall illustrated this psychic split of which Jung speaks. [2]

I have had more than a passing acquaintance with most of the cities featured in this book. I was born in one of the great "old world" cities, London, and grew up in what to many became the "mecca" of the "new world," Los Angeles. Los Angeles wasn't really a city then; it was more of a loose collection of suburban villages. For the past 44 years, I have lived near one of the most beautiful cities in the world, San Francisco. In addition, I traveled the cities of the globe for eighteen years on behalf of the International Association for Analytical Psychology (IAAP). Visits with colleagues gave me a wonderful introduction to the soul of many magnificent cities.

Through living in and visiting many cities, I have learned to appreciate how different they all are. This book is a study in the *individuality of the soul of each city*—and the individuality of each author who introduces us to one of these varied urban psyches.

Notes

1   C.G. Jung, *Memory, Dreams, Reflections* (New York: Vintage Books, 1965), p. 365.
2   C.G. Jung, "Approaching the Unconscious," in Jung, von Franz et al. (eds.), *Man and His Symbols* (New York: Doubleday/Anchor Books,), p. 84. On page 100, a photo of New York on the top half of the page shows the liveliness of a city, while the bottom half of the page is a photo of Hiroshima after the A-bomb. Again, the split in modern man.

Introduction

*Leap for our Cities, and leap for our sea-borne ships and leap for our young
citizens and for goodly Themis.* —"The Hymn of the Kouretes"[1]

A few years ago, Nancy Cater and I envisioned a book project that would focus
on the experience of soul in some of the great cities of the world. Cities can
delight us with their varied, unique characters, yet we are also confronted with
a deep worry for the state of their souls and those of their peoples. As global
citizens jet from one continent to another and rural citizens flock to the city
hoping for a better life, local neighborhoods are carved up and the horizon of
the urban landscape is filled with cement freeways and glistening towers. The
cities of the world are undergoing rapid and profound transformation, reeling
under the weight of postmodern development and challenging us with enormous
problems. Are the souls of world travelers left behind, unable to keep up with the
speed of their bodies? Are the souls of our cities' inhabitants lost or dehuman-
ized in the overwhelming scale and complexity of urban life? What of a city's
own soul? Is it overlooked and buried, along with its neighborhoods and their
histories? From these questions, it is clear that we are simultaneously inquiring
about individual soul, collective soul, the soul of a city itself, and the intersection
of individual and collective soul with the soul of a city.

In 1967, while I was studying medicine, I came across a remarkable series of
paintings by one of C. G. Jung's patients in Volume 9, Part 1 of his *Collected
Works*. I was particularly taken—indeed, stunned—by what I took to be a Self
portrait of the patient in New York City.[2]

I had never seen anything quite like it before. Is it the patient's own soul or the
soul of the city or both, hovering in the center of the image? I found the painting
numinous, lighting up something inside me of which I was hardly aware, yet
which seemed at the same time immediately familiar, deeply known. The image
of a centered presence in the city spoke to me of psychological integrity and
natural ease in the urban environment.

Soul and City

More than forty years later, the numinous effect of the image has continued to fascinate me because it suggests a subtle interface between the soul of an individual and the soul of a city. It feels both elusive and so absolutely real at the same time. Most of us have had glimpses of this phenomenon in ourselves, whether the city is our home town or someplace foreign and mysterious.

But this was the portrait of a soul in the early part of the twentieth century, in the New York City of that era. Each of us paints our own city portraits differently, depending on what is soulful to us and the time in which we live. For instance, my New York City soul portrait in the 1960s would have been much less differentiated than this elegant portrait. For most of those years, first as a college student and then a medical student, I traveled frequently to New York from nearby university towns. My first response on disembarking into Manhattan's busy streets from a bus, train, plane, or car was immediately and instinctively to spit on the ground. New York City overwhelmed me, and I needed to make my primitive mark on its pavement, to establish, dog-like, that I too had a place in this complex maze. I have never achieved the graceful, soulful hovering between inner and outer pictured in Jung's patient's image of New York.

The closest I got to some sort of meeting of individual and collective soul in New York City was walking out of a movie theatre in 1969, where I had just seen *Fellini Satyricon*, and finding myself in a swirling, angry mob of anti-Vietnam war protestors parading down Fifth Avenue. What we experience of soul and city is highly relative to our own life circumstances and perspective.

If you haven't asked the question already, you might now be wondering what I even mean by "soul." Ron Shenck, a Jungian in Dallas, Texas, wrote this to me of soul and cities:

> Soul envelops and includes spirit and matter together, seeing one in the other and bridging dualistic conceptualization. Soul invites reflection as opposed to action, tends toward depth as opposed to heights, circularity as opposed to linearity. Soul is more interested in guts than sentimental charm, more interested in breath and vapors, as well as concrete forms than in abstract concepts and reasoning. Soul animates ... stimulates imagination ... moves one, often to unlikely places ... And cities provide the arena, the place, for all of these aspects of soul to come alive.[3]

For a stunning imaginative flight that may serve as a parable of the soul's work, the section "Dante's Nest" in Craig San Roque's chapter provides a poetic companion to Shenck's definition (see Chapter 2, pages 47-49).

Taking these initial reflections about a book on soul and cities into account, Nancy Cater and I sent the following letter of invitation to prospective authors:

> *Psyche and The City: A Soul's Guide to the Modern Metropolis* will be a collection of depth psychology-oriented articles about several of the great cities of the world. We would like to explore in this work what makes different cities unique in terms of such hard-to-define qualities as psyche, soul, and spirit. What archetypal patterns characterize a city? How do the history, geography, and psyches of a city's past and current inhabitants unite to create each city's own special identity—both its positive aspects and its shadow qualities?
>
> These kinds of questions can be addressed in myriad ways—through personal anecdote as well through descriptions and depth psychological analyses of a city's collective history, local geography, and ethnic and religious compositions.

The responses we received to this letter of invitation were enthusiastic in their embrace of the idea, and writers were eager to participate. It seemed like a ripe moment for such a project, and it took little time to create an outline of the book's chapters. We had no idea, however, how the authors would interpret our invitation to best suit their own temperaments and interests. As the various chapters began to appear on my computer through the miracle of e-mail, the project began to feel like an international Easter egg hunt! No two authors chose the same approach or style. Some kept themselves out of the story altogether, focusing instead on a more objective, straightforward historical narrative to reveal underlying patterns of development. Others chose much more personal and subjective narratives as vehicles for their reflections. Each is poetic in its evocation of a city, and each reveals a fine eye for place and a fine ear for story.

A few words about the structure of the book: Chapters 1-18 form Part One and each focuses on an individual city. The chapters of Part Two consider more general approaches to cities, rather than one particular city. Chapter 19 is a tribute to the pioneering work of the renowned city activist Jane Jacobs and her connection to the ancient Greek goddess Themis. Chapter 20 presents the *flâneur* as a soulful stroller, one who experiences a city and its essence through meandering. The final chapter, the Afterword, is a hybrid that combines reflections on my hometown, St. Louis, as well as a few general comments that were stimulated by my reading of all the chapters.

All of the authors undertook a most difficult assignment, as personal and historical soul circles around and meets the soul of living cities. What has emerged is not a conventional guidebook: the authors did not seek the soul of the city in its restaurants, hotels, and museums (although the "soul" of New Orleans could not be touched without mentioning a restaurant or two). Rather, the daunting task of mapping the intersection of the soul's encounter with itself in the mirror of the city has taken each of our authors on such individual journeys that we elected to reverse the alphabet in establishing the order of the book's chapters. We follow the lead of Luigi Zoja's *flâneur* (see Chapter 20), who allows himself to be led through the city by a tortoise on a leash. We are hoping that the Self, too, has led the ego of this book; we therefore place the last, first. But whichever city is first or last, all of our authors are citizens and, as the ancient Cretan hymn sings it, they are all leaping for their cities. This book is a modern, urban, global hymn to the soul.

Thomas Singer
Editor, Analytical Psychology & Contemporary Culture Series

Notes

1   "The Hymn of the Kouretes," Crete, Greece, 1,500 BCE, quoted in Jane Ellen Harrison, *Themis: A Study of the Social Origins of Greek Religion* (1912; repr., Glouchester, MA: Peter Smith, 1974), p. 8.

2   Soul and City, Picture 14, in *The Collected Works of C. G. Jung*, vol. 9.1., *The Archetypes and the Collective Unconscious*, Bollingen Series XX (New York: Pantheon Books, 1959), between p. 292 and p. 293.

3   Ron Shenck to author, 7 February 2010.

PART ONE

The Cities

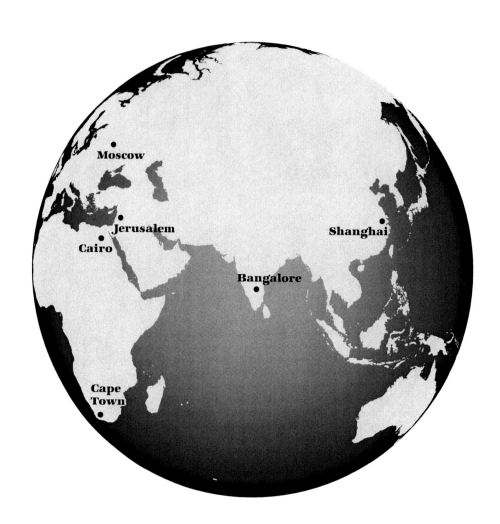

1

Searching for Soul & Jung in Zurich: A Psychological Essay

MURRAY STEIN

It would be foolish of me, indeed presumptuous, to speak about the city of Zurich as though I were an expert. I am but a recent transplant in this richly textured, historically multilayered, and today obviously cosmopolitan city—a stranger really!—and I cannot understand very well the lilting German dialect of the people who live here. To know this city in all its complexity would require a long life spent in careful observation of its numerous cultural layers, its diverse activities, and its people. It would help to know as well plenty of historical depth of experience in one's family heritage. Beyond the evident bustle of life in the businesses, banks, shops, and restaurants, it would be important, too, to know firsthand about its lunar life, its semi-lighted world—the nighttime workers like the bakers who prepare the fresh bread for the breakfast tables and for daily consumption, its nightclub denizens and illegal aliens, its tax collectors and harlots (to use a biblical phrase). With these I have little familiarity. Other far more secret places, such as the city's many bank vaults, which it is claimed contain a considerable amount of the world's wealth, are completely impenetrable to people like me.

I can therefore speak only of "my Zurich," of the city as it has presented itself to me and of what my imagination, dreams, and reflections have created out of the bits and pieces I have collected in the past forty years. From my exposure to its architectural treasures, its colorful variety of inhabitants, its legends and history, and its clean and mostly sober streets I have assembled some observations that I can venture to share. I structure them on a Jungian framework, starting with the city's persona—its self-presentation to the world in stories, facades, and monuments—and offering some impressions of its shadow. Then I consider its soul, a more subtle and mysterious dimension that might elude the observer but is intuitively available if one chooses to reflect psychologically on what one sees and what one does not see at the manifest level. I understand persona and soul to form a pair of counter positions whose dynamic interplay generates the city's paradoxes, its uneven developments, and its nervous "buzz."

In Search of Jung

I begin by recalling my distress when I first arrived in Zurich in 1969 to study at the old Jung Institute at Gemeindestrasse 27. At that time, I was completely unfamiliar with the city and its culture. Since Zurich was not a major world center like Paris, London, Rome or other great cities that have formed the hub of vast world empires, it is not especially well known outside of Europe. To me it seemed like a small out-of-the-way city with little to recommend it other than its illustrious late citizen, Carl Gustav Jung. So I was astonished to discover that the man on the street seemed never to have heard of Jung or the city's (to me) illustrious C. G. Jung Institute. Equally upsetting to me was that Zurich had named no street, no Platz, no statue in honor of a man who was arguably the most internationally famous Swiss citizen of his generation, if not of all generations. Not a sign of Jung in the public spaces of the city! What else was there to know about here? Who but Jung to celebrate? Needless to say, I was starting from scratch and had much to learn about Zurich the city.

I was told by some people that Zürchers (the name commonly used to designate the city's inhabitants) are exceedingly private and discrete people and therefore shy away from creating monuments for their more outstanding personalities or naming streets after them. But this is not altogether true, as I discovered by walking through the town and looking around. The people may guard their privacy jealously, but even so there are quite a few streets, bridges, and statues named in honor of people who have lived in Zurich or were born here. To me, though, none of them remotely approached the stature of Jung. Most of them were unfamiliar to me and seemed extremely local. Why was Jung not up there among them, I wondered. Something was missing here, something not right.

Ulrich Zwingli
at the
Wasserkirche.

*Photograph
by the author*

Monuments to the City's Persona

A city's monuments display its persona. They are like a showroom window. They create a city's face to the world around, and they represent its (more or less ideal) self-image. They may also serve to conceal what the city wants to hide from itself and from others, including its soul. They can tell one about a city's cultural identity, about its cherished public values, and about how it puts itself into play with other cities. The monuments display its conscious self-awareness, and they tell the citizen and the visitor what a city wants to project to its present and future inhabitants, to other cities, and to casual tourists passing through. If one looks into the stories behind these images, however, one often finds some fascinating and sometimes curiously discordant information, a shadow dimension concealed by the persona. In and behind the persona there are hints of what a city consciously is about and stands for and of what perhaps unconsciously it wants to reveal but cannot do so directly or officially.

With that notion in mind, I turn to what is arguably the most impressive statue in all of Zurich, the one of the Protestant Reformer Ulrich Zwingli who revolutionized the city in the sixteenth century and put his stamp on its culture indelibly.

The statue of the militant visionary Reformer is placed next to a stately pine and behind the Wasserkirche on the left bank of the Limmat River, just down the hill from the twin-towered Grossmünster church, where he preached Zurich into accepting the Protestant Reformation. It announces Zurich's proud and unflinching Protestant identity. In his right hand Zwingli holds the Bible, while his left hand rests on the handle of a long sword. The Zwingli statue tells us that Protestantism is an essential feature of Zurich's identity. Protestantism is as foundational to Zurich as Catholicism is to Rome.

The story of Zwingli in Zurich is fascinating. Beginning on 1 January 1519, when he gave his first sermon at the Grossmünster church, Zwingli hammered home with fiery zeal the revolutionary ideas that would establish a Protestant mood, style, and tone in the city. The characteristic features of Reformed religious practice, as instituted by Zwingli and his followers—austerity, simplicity, modesty, piety, unfailing cleanliness, strict order—would in turn become hallmarks of the Zurich aesthetic. To a degree this remains in place today, although the effects of modernization and globalization in the last decades have turned the city into a much more open and free international city. But Zurich remains a place where even today the trains and trams run predictably on time, and with clean windows!

The Zurich Reformation featured the strict abolition of images and statues from the churches, and color was removed from all its church windows. Zwingli denounced religious statues as leading to the worship of idols, and this may account for the relative paucity of statues in the streets of the city. As well, Zwingli normalized the life of the clergy and encouraged them to get married and raise families. In 1524, he himself married Anna, a widow, and they proceeded to have a batch of children. In Zurich, family life and the heavy responsibilities it entails took on a pious and religious quality. Zwingli also emphasized the importance of literacy in the population and scholarship among the clergy— he had been a student at the University of Basel, where Erasmus, known as the Prince of the Humanists, was then in residence and was strongly influencing the thinking of future Reformers. In the services of the church he insisted on preaching from the Scriptures (he was perfectly versed in Greek and Hebrew), and the Word from the pulpit was honored above liturgical parades and other Catholic "hocus-pocus." There would be no magic in Swiss Protestant religion. Education and learning became exceptionally important, and citizens were expected to take their trades, their crafts, and their professional occupations seriously. The spirit of religion thus entered into daily life as a type of serious and earnest engagement with work. Thus the work ethic was born, which Max Weber wrote about in his masterful *The Protestant Ethic and the Spirit of Capitalism*. So Zurich grew and prospered.

On 13 April 1525, a Maundy Thursday, Zwingli celebrated for the first time a communion liturgy in the Grossmünster with simple wooden cups and plates and no music. Here he sounded perfectly the note of austerity that would become the hallmark of Zurich's Protestant lifestyle. The City Council for its own political reasons went along with plans to sever all links with the Roman Catholic Church and claimed Church properties for the city. Zurich thus became one of the first of Europe's cities to become officially Reformed, and so it has remained inflexibly ever since. The spirit of the Reformation—at the time a revolutionary fire that was burning away the shackles of centuries of foreign religious authority—entered into politics as well. Zurich assumed a hot brand of political leadership in the new world that was being born. One historic consequence of this was that Zwingli, Zurich's leading citizen at the time, took part in an armed conflict with the Catholic forces from Luzerne at Kappel and died there in defense of his faith. His body was quartered and burned with dung by the soldiers of the other side. He thus became a celebrated and honored martyr for Zurich's convictions. Today the statue of Zwingli stands tall in the heart of old Zurich and declares the city's stubbornly entrenched Protestant persona.

Zurich's fighting spirit, suggested by the long sword in Zwingli's left hand, is even more explicitly on display in a statue just across the Limmat from the Grossmünster. If one walks across the Munsterbrücke toward the Fraumünster church on the other side, one sees rising high above the pavement into the sky the figure of a bearded soldier mounted on a horse and holding an ax in his right hand.

This statue honors Hans Waldmann (1435–1489), Zurich's third mayor. Before winning the office of mayor of the city, Waldmann had been a highly successful mercenary soldier and was reputed to have become the richest man in Zurich. While in office he was accused of financial corruption, foreign connections, and sodomy, and an angry citizenry threw him out of office and beheaded him in 1489. In the twentieth century, this act of capital punishment was declared illicit, and Waldmann was declared to be a victim of "Judicial Murder." The Zunft zum Kämbel (originally a guild of food dealers) sought to rehabilitate him in the 1930s by setting in place this controversial statue.[1] What this statue adds to Zurich's persona is a statement about its distinct flair for brash aggressiveness. Today Zürchers are known among the Swiss for this feature.

Hans
Waldmann
at the
Munster-
brücke.

*Photograph
by the author*

Hans
Waldmann
at the
Munster-
brücke.

*Photograph
by the author*

In Recognition of Its Shadow

A slender monument sits a short distance up the Limmat from the Hans Waldmann statue. It was placed there in recognition of the unsavory shadow aspect
in the Zürcher character. A visitor to the city would have to be very observant
indeed to spot it, however. It does not call much attention to itself. It is an
inscribed metal tablet placed on the river wall near the spot where the Anabap-
tist leader Felix Manz was murdered by city officials in January 1527. Manx
was a leader among the left-wing Reformers in Zurich called Re-Baptizers
(Anabaptists) who were bent on taking change some steps further than Zwingli
and his fellow Reformers at the Grossmünster wanted to go. Since these fellow
assiduous scholars of the Bible could not find any backing for infant baptism
in the Holy Scriptures, they became stubbornly committed to adult baptism
alone. This position was severely rejected by the Zurich authorities after several
public debates. When Manz was given a last chance to recant but refused, city
officials took him to a platform in the icy Limmat, bound him hand and foot,

18

Commemorative plaque on the Limmat.

Photograph by the author

and plunged him into the river. Six other co-religionists were to follow him into the same watery grave in subsequent years. In 2004, the city of Zurich and the Reformed Church of the Canton of Zurich expressed their regrets and accepted accountability for these murders. In recognition of the martyrdom of Manz and the other victims of this Protestant intolerance toward its own, a marker was put in place as an acknowledgment and confession of sins of the past and an attempt on the part of the living to provide restitution.

The descendants of the persecuted Rebaptizers—Mennonites, Amish, and some other Protestant denominations—received invitations to the Service of Apology held at the Grossmünster on 26 June 2004. The plaque here at the riverside represents Zurich's recognition of this bit of shadow from its history. I take it as a sign of the city's individuation, a move toward acceptance of responsibility for its past and present acts of intolerance and brutality.

The Protestant spirit was not ever a tolerant one. It draws sharp, hard lines and distinctions. In its heyday, it was famous for persecuting and banning heretics. The Catholic Counterreformation with its grand inquisitors mimicked this style and perhaps even took it a step or two further. In its present secular incarnation in Zurich, this characteristic of intolerance among Zürchers has been responsible for putting many people off when they come here and experience the city's attitudes. The rigidity of Swiss Protestant rectitude and its tendency toward harsh condemnation of differences of taste have given Zürchers a reputation for being excessively judgmental. You can see this attitude etched into the faces of some of the older folk when they meet up with someone who is strange to them or is exotically dressed. My daughter used to complain about the nasty looks she would get on the streets of Zurich because of the sexy shoes she was wearing. She was out of line with Zurich's sober dress code for young women. In the background one feels the chilly resonance of history. Zurich is upholding its puritanical persona.

More of the Persona

After living in Zurich for quite some time and visiting it for many years more, I was still wondering why the city had failed to put up a public marker for Jung. Then it began to dawn on me that Jung did not fit in here. In fact, he lived on the outer margins of the city, in the village of Küsnacht. From the start, he was an outsider to Zurich. Because this was not his city of origin—he was born in the village of Kesswil, which belongs to the neighboring Canton of Thurgau, and he spent his youth and university years in Basel—he was looked upon as a foreigner. His paternal grandfather was not even Swiss but German, and C. G. would mention from time to time with feigned modesty the rumor that he was a descendant of an illegitimate offspring of Goethe's. To be a true Zürcher you have to be born and reared here by parents who were likewise natives of the city. The more generations back that family lineage, the better. What is more, Jung never came to occupy a central place in the cultural life of Zurich, even though he became an extremely well-known figure in the city. He was an "alienist" (the name for psychiatrist in earlier times) and therefore a bit suspect on that account as well. He was also marginal in the university and intellectual life of the city of his day, having resigned his position at the University of Zurich in 1913 and thereafter creating for himself a private universe of students and followers whose headquarters were located in the Psychological Club.

It makes considerable sense, then, that Zurich would be reluctant to own him as one of its own and to erect a statue in his honor or name a street after him. His image would be out of place in Zurich's persona.

Much more on the point of persona is the figure of Alfred Escher (1819–1882), the dynamic modernizer of business in Zurich and in Switzerland, whose towering statue—next only to Zwingli's in size and importance for official Zurich—graces the top of Bahnhofstrasse and gazes down that opulent street so richly laced with stores filled with gold watches and bejeweled baubles, delicious things to eat, and elegant designer clothes, rising to an apex of grandeur in the monumental Swiss banks at the other end.

Alfred Escher
at the Zurich
Hauptbahnhof.

*Photograph
by the author*

Three times president of the Swiss National Council, a railway magnate whose statue therefore stands squarely in front of the Zurich Hauptbahnhof (Main Train Station), a founder of the Swiss Technical High School (ETH), and a founder of two of the great financial institutions of Switzerland, Credit Suisse and Swiss Life, Alfred Escher represents the political and commercial centrality of Zurich in Switzerland. He was a colossal power figure in Zurich and indeed in Swiss history. The spirit of Escher lingers palpably on in modern Zurich.

If Zurich's persona is indelibly marked by the Protestant Reformer, it is equally stamped by the business magnate. Zurich is deeply dedicated to commerce and money-making and to the political influence this brings with it. In the Zurich persona there is no felt contradiction between Protestant religion and personal wealth and social prestige. The life of the sober, pious Zurich Protestant is routinely blessed with rich bank accounts and well-appointed offices, with private homes on the Zürichberg or on the Gold Coast, where stately villas dot the shores of the lake. Zürchers tend to be extremely private about their wealth, so it is not so much on display in public, but annual surveys consistently rank Zurich as one of the richest cities in Europe. It is also frequently voted the world's most comfortable city to live in. A neighbor of mine who owns a nice house in the old town of Zurich once told me: "You know that God loves you if you inherit a house in Zurich." Escher's face lends Zurich's persona the features of financial muscle.

Surprisingly, it is precisely this mercantile attitude that Jung celebrates when he contrasts Zurich with his hometown of Basel in his autobiography: "The intellectual atmosphere of Basel seemed to me enviably cosmopolitan, but the pressure of tradition was too much for me. When I came to Zurich I felt the difference at once. Zurich relates to the world not by the intellect but by commerce. Yet here the air was free, and I had always valued that. Here you were not weighed down by the brown fog of the centuries." [2]

Jung enjoyed the pervading influence of great business tycoons such as Alfred Escher because for him Zurich's commitment to commerce and business was liberating. Zürchers are not much burdened by philosophical niceties and the baggage of learned ancestors. Zurich is considered the most up-to-date city in Switzerland when it comes to fashion and popular culture. This is where the money is today. Its museums and music halls (the splendid Opera House, the elegant Tonhalle) and theaters are held lightly in its hands as the appropriate jewels in the crown of a first world city. They are enjoyed as opportunities for fine entertainment. The feeling of lightness about the city stands in paradoxical contrast to its staid Protestant Puritanism and the jealously guarded and protected tradition of medieval architecture that can sometimes feel dark and foreboding. Commerce after all defines the modern spirit throughout the world, and in Zurich one can feel happily modern even in a most traditional setting.

Walking down the Bahnhofstrasse from the Escher statue toward the Lake of Zurich, one may find a charming (as distinct from imposingly important) statue of a man caring tenderly for a child. This sculpture is set back from the street in a large park and is surrounded by busy department stores. It is easy to miss unless one is looking for it.

It is a monument to the Zurich-born educator Johann Heinrich Pestalozzi (1746–1827), a much-loved and admired figure whose works on elementary education were read by intellectuals throughout Europe and North America in the late eighteenth and early nineteenth centuries and whose methods revolutionized elementary education in Zurich and throughout much of Europe. His big idea was to build on a child's consciousness as it emerges in the course of development, starting with the most basic elements and advancing from those into greater complexity as the child grows and expands its cognitive abilities. What this monument to Pestalozzi contributes to Zurich's persona is the grace note of humanism. It underscores the value the inhabitants of this city place on basic education. The presence of Pestalozzi also introduces the importance of psychological attunement and sensitivity to the young into the city's otherwise stony patriarchal persona. One could almost take this statue as a stand-in for Jung, the psychologist. Pestalozzi is reputed to have said, for instance, that "the greatest victory a man can win is a victory over himself," a thoroughly Jungian sentiment and one uttered (remarkably) in the time of Napoleon.[3] I see it as an important addition to the persona Zurich has created with its dominating images of Zwingli, Walder, and Escher, a feature that speaks of something a bit more maternal.

Johann Heinrich Pestalozzi on the Bahnhofstrasse.

Photograph by the author

23

Some Intimations of Soul in the City

If one wants to look beyond the persona and the shadow, which I have now touched upon, and discover the *soul* of this city, where does one go? The soul of a city compensates, or contradicts, its persona. It is the city seen at dawn or dusk, when it shows itself in its less official garb, with matters of the public world less actively on its mind, in more intimate, even secret, locales. To follow the lead of Jung's depth psychology, the soul is a level of psyche that is set apart from the persona, though it is related to it in many subtle and obscure ways, sometimes contradicting it, sometimes supplementing it, sometimes just plain foreign to it.[4] Like people, cities are multilayered and complex. The persona and the soul of a city form a pair in a dialectical play of opposites, and the push and pull between them creates the dynamic life of a city.

Zurich's contemporary persona is founded on ancient historical images and attitudes that reach all the way back to Roman times and extend up through the early Middle Ages, when Charlemagne put his stamp on the city with the building of the Grossmünster, and the later Middle Ages, when the city's guilds and mayors assumed political power. During the Protestant Reformation and the emergence of modernity, of which the statues of Zwingli, Pestalozzi, and Escher are the chief representatives in the city today, it received further definition. These figures speak overwhelmingly of a strict patriarchal attitude in the dominant culture. Zurich's soul, on the other hand, is less evident on its streets and more difficult to locate. In contrast to the masculine and patriarchal persona of the city, its soul is feminine. She is elusive and mysterious. Yet she is a vital aspect of Zurich, and she contributes vital energy that flows into its evident creativity and liveliness. She gives the city its color, its charm, its sly wit, and its zest for transformation. I also see her face shimmering on the waters and in the city's breathtaking beauty. In contrast to the stone faces of patriarchy, she is utterly fluid and serpentine. Take a walk in the evening through the winding streets of the old town, stand on the bridges and look up and down the river graced by swans, listen to the flowing water, and you will feel her presence.

I suggest three places to look for Zurich's soul—in its waters, in the late writings of Carl Jung, and in some of its old legends. The waters suggest the city-soul's fluidity and its processes of transformation, which burble up in the arts and in offbeat places; the writings of Jung spell out in more literate and intellectual terms the dynamic soul life of Zurich; and the legends offer some striking images and symbols that reach more deeply into its personality and below the level of today's collective consciousness among Zurich's inhabitants.

Winzer-
brunnen
at the Hotel
zum Storchen.

*Photograph
by the author*

It is well known that Jung loved to be near water. His house in Küsnacht is built right on the side of Lake Zurich, and his Tower in Bollingen likewise is situated immediately on the water. In the city of Zurich, too, he found plenty of it.

The city is built around two bodies of water, Lake Zurich and the Limmat River, which flows out of the lake northward and joins up after fifty miles or so with the Rhine. The ancient beginning of the city, named Turicum by the Romans, was a military encampment erected on a hill, now called the Lindenhof, which rises above the Limmat River. Around it there were a number of temples dedicated to the gods and goddesses of Rome, some cemeteries, and a bath. Turicum was originally a tax-collection station for traffic moving up and down the Limmat. The city expanded outward from this center, and in the Middle Ages it became a significant town surrounded by a wall with a bridge across the Limmat at the Weinplatz, the present location of the Zurich Rathaus (City Hall). Today there are six bridges over the Limmat connecting the two sides of the city, one for pedestrians only.

The modern city is therefore squarely situated on water, and on clear days the Alps are visible on the horizon to the south. The Limmat runs right through the middle of it, dividing it into a left and a right bank. On the left side is the Grossmünster, Zwingli's home base, and on the right side facing that imposing double-towered edifice is the Fraumünster, formerly an abbey. So there is water to the front of Zurich and water running right through it and dividing it in half.

Moreover, the city is full of fountains. It is easy to overlook them as one stares at the impressive statues of the great power figures of Zurich, but as soon as one begins noticing them they appear everywhere. They are in fact ubiquitous in Zurich, which is sometimes in tourist guides called a city of fountains. They are truly stunning in their uniqueness, their originality, and their sometimes colorful ornamentation. One of my favorites is in the Weinplatz near the Hotel zum Storchen, the inn favored by the sixteenth-century Swiss alchemist and physician Paracelsus when he traveled to the city from his home in Einsiedeln.

The fountain, named Winzerbrunnen (Winemaker Fountain), shows a simple working man carrying an empty basket on his back and leaving the Weinplatz, to which he has just brought a load of grapes for pressing from a vineyard beyond the city walls. He is standing on a container that houses the fountain's water spouts. Above him there is an elegant and highly decorative canopy. The fountain is inscribed with a witty saying by the craftsman who built it, Hans Prasser: "Ich, Hans Prasser, trink lieber Wein als Wasser. / Tränk ich das Wasser so gern wie den Wein, könnt ich ein reicher Prasser sein" ("I, Hans Prasser, drink rather wine than water. / If I drank water as much as wine, I would a rich Prasser be"). In the sunshine, everything sparkles. Nearby, the Limmat flows briskly under and past the classic eighteenth-century Rathaus, the City Council building. The councilors, if they are quiet for a moment, can perhaps hear the water passing under their feet, "the sloothering slide of her, giddygaddy, grannyma, gossipaceous," as James Joyce, an inhabitant of Zurich from time to time, said about the River Liffey in Dublin in *Finnegan's Wake*. According to a saying in the nearby Canton of Appenzell, if one gazes into moving water long enough one can look the Godhead in the eye.[5] The water opens to another dimension.

From alchemy we learn that the fountain is a vessel for transformation. Its waters dissolve solid substances, such as personae, and in the bath those dissolved solids may merge and blend into new forms of being. Since ancient times fountains have been places of refreshment for people and animals, like wells in the wilderness and oases in the desert. According to tradition, some fountains and wells offer healing and fertility. The Felix and Regula spring in the city, for example, was reputed to be such a place of healing.[6]

In Zurich, Jung found a city where transformational powers and processes were active in the soul. If a person wants to learn about Zurich's soul, I suggest reading the works of the mature Jung, especially the alchemical writings. They are all about transformation.

Jung once claimed that he could see the influence of the North American continent in the faces of the inhabitants who had originated in Europe but had lived in the New World for a time. Their faces, he observed, had taken on the features of Native Americans, and he attributed this to the effect of the soil on their physical form. The spirits of the earth were molding their features. He believed that the longer one lived in a place, the more one's features would be affected by the landscape. Having lived most of my life in North America, I found this observation hard to accept. The overwhelming majority of people I knew there bore little physical resemblance to Native Americans. But it is possible that an indigenous culture can have profound effects on the psyche of a person who takes up residence there and that this influence is very subtle and mostly channeled by unconscious networks. I have seen this kind of influence on friends and colleagues in North America who have come under the spell of Native American teachings, rituals, and wisdom.

I would apply the same notion to Jung. I believe Zurich drew him subtly and unconsciously into its soul and exerted a profound influence on his conscious thinking and attitudes. Since he wrote mostly out of unconscious inspiration in his later years—following his dreams, visions, and intuitions, which led him to alchemy and its profound symbolism of transformation—Jung can be seen as expressing the native psychology of the locus in which he lived. As Walt Whitman did for America, Jung created in his writings a poem that expresses Zurich's soul.

In his persona, Jung conformed somewhat to the Swiss Protestant image, but this suit of clothing never fit him comfortably, and he was not at home in the collective settings the city offered. The Zurich guilds, for example, which are private men's clubs that meet several times a year and celebrate the patriarchal heritage of the ancestors and to which nearly all the prominent male burghers belong, did not appeal to Jung. He preferred the Psychological Club and his remote tower in Bollingen. In his soul, however, he could come close to Zurich, since its soul too is of the water and is about transformation and deeply connected to nature.

A foundational legend in Zurich speaks of this connection to the unconscious. It is about Charlemagne and a snake. Charlemagne spent some time in Zurich in the late eighth century, where he lived in a house near the Grossmünster church

Charlemagne's serpent at the Haus zum Loch.

Photograph by the author

(the Haus zum Loch). He commissioned the building of this church on the holy ground where the famous Christian martyrs of the second century, Felix and Regula, were buried.[7] His statue sits in a niche of the west tower of the Gross-münster and overlooks the city. There are several legends surrounding Charlemagne's role in the city's history. One day, it is told, a serpent was found ringing the bell nearby that signaled a request for Charlemagne's judicious attention. Of course everyone was astonished and became fearful of harmful magic, but Charlemagne the wise ruler paid attention to the snake and followed it to its nest. There he saw a large toad threatening to eat the serpent's eggs. Charlemagne ruled the toad's actions unjust and had it executed, thereby preserving the snake's young. Some days later the door to Charlemagne's house mysteriously opened and in slithered the snake and made its way up to the table where Charlemagne was seated. It climbed up the leg of the table and proceeded to Charlemagne's goblet, where it deposited a brilliant precious gem from its mouth. This moment is represented on a frieze over a door at the Haus zum Loch.

She gave him the gemstone in gratitude for his help. Charlemagne considered it one of his most prized possessions and gave it to his wife, who wore it in a setting. In honor of the serpent, in turn, he commissioned the Wasserkirche to be built on the place where he had seen the serpent's nest.[8] Today this is very close to the exact spot where Zwingli's statue is placed. This legend speaks of the underground animal soul of Zurich and expresses the vital importance of listening to it. The intelligent female serpent is symbolic of the transformational energies that reside primordially in the earth on which Zurich is constructed. She is its genius loci. Jung picks up on this theme in his writings about Mercurius, a symbol of the transformational force continuously at work in the psyche. I imagine that Jung listened carefully and respectfully to the serpentine element in Zurich's earth just as Charlemagne had done some twelve hundred years before him.

Zurich is a city in constant self-renewal, forever under construction and reinventing itself as it adjusts and changes with the times. Yet it appears to remain the same as it always was. This is part of the city's allure. The external features of the buildings do not change from century to century, but the interiors transform dramatically from one generation to the next.

I live in a building in Zurich whose foundations date back to Roman times in the first and second centuries CE and whose first two stories with their meter-thick walls have been in place since at least the twelfth century. The house has been known since the Middle Ages as the Haus zum Schwanen (House of the Swans). The upper stories were constructed in the sixteenth century to the loud complaint of neighbors who felt the house was rising too high. In the eighteenth century, the house came into the possession of Solomon Gessner, the artist, poet, and publisher. Mozart and Goethe visited Gessner here when they passed through Zurich. Today the exterior of the house and garden look more or less as they did were when the ten-year-old Mozart attended a Gessner soirée in 1763 and played his violin here, but we live in a freshly renovated apartment with modern up-to-date appliances and bathrooms.[9] The house's exterior, its persona, has not changed much over recent centuries, but its inner world and structures have undergone several significant transformations in that time. Some of the wall paintings are retained from the fifteenth century and onward, and a graceful Apollo statue done by Valentin Sonnenschein in 1780 adorns the wall of our living room.

There is, however, one highly visible recent transformation in Zurich that is of critical importance. From my workroom, I can see the clock face of the Fraumünster church, which is located directly across the Limmat from the Grossmünster and which, like its male counterpart, dates back to the early

Middle Ages. The grandson of Charlemagne, Louis the German, founded the Fraumünster Abbey in 853 for his daughter, Hildegard, and endowed it with vast property holdings. By the eleventh century, the abbess had effectively become the ruler of Zurich, with rights to collect taxes, assign the mayor, and mint money. During this period, it appears that the Feminine was in control of the city, and the Fraumünster was her home. When the guilds took control of the city in the thirteenth century, Zurich underwent a powerful political and psychological transformation. In this revolution, many ancient privileges and titles were abolished or discounted, and the city's persona changed dramatically as a result. With the Reformation, the influence of the Fraumünster was scaled back even further, and Zwingli dissolved the cloister altogether in 1524. The abbess got married a year later. The Fraumünster functioned thereafter simply as a Protestant parish church, as it does still today.

Late in the twentieth century, however, a remarkable turn of events took place. The feminine soul of the city reasserted itself and threw at least one important aspect of the Zwingli Reformation and the Enlightenment's insistence on rational clarity into reverse. This corresponds in some features to a nearly contemporary event celebrated by Jung, when he declared that Pope Pius XII's 1950 dogmatization of the Assumption of the Virgin Mary was the most important religious event since the Reformation.[10] In 1967–1968, the Fraumünster church-wardens commissioned the Russian Jewish artist Marc Chagall to create and install a set of brilliantly colored stained-glass windows that would tell the story of salvation according to the biblical tradition. A revocation of the Protestant ban on color and images in churches was taking place and with great flair, for as Picasso said about Chagall, "When Matisse dies, Chagall will be the only painter left who understands what color really is."[11] Chagall brought radiant color back to the Fraumünster. In a flood of color and bright gem-like images, a veritable *cauda pavonis* (peacock's tail), to use the alchemical expression for a stage of transformation following the bleakness of *nigredo,* the five windows tell the story of God's creative and redemptive work in history: windows for the Prophets, the Law, the Patriarch Jacob, Zion and the New Jerusalem, and Christ. The central panel, with Joseph at the bottom and rising through the life of Jesus and the ascending to the crucifixion and the resurrection, confronts the onlooker directly upon entry into the chancel. If people want to catch a glimpse of Zurich's soul—a Biblical soul grounded in transcendence—and if they care to study it in a full display of emotion, let them sit quietly in the chancel of the Fraumünster on a sunny morning and open themselves to the flood of colorful light streaming into this space through these storied windows. They were set in place there by an old *maître* (Chagall was in his eighties when the windows were commissioned) who all his long life served the Feminine and Lady Soul in his works of art. The guide to the windows, which is sold at a counter in the church, says that if "the theme is love in his 'profane' pictures, in the religious ones it is the source of love."[12]

The stunning effect of these windows can of course be experienced only from within the church's interior. I take this church, dedicated from its founding in the eighth century to the Feminine, to be the city's boldest expression of its ancient and modern, and indeed eternal, soul. And with these windows now fixed in its soaring face to the East, the Fraumünster resumes its proper stature in the city's heart.

One thing more: the Fraumünster, a most gracious and beautiful statement of the Feminine in Zurich, looks across the Limmat directly at the impressive grey stone statue of Zwingli. Seen together, they create a moving rendition of a *Mysterium Coniunctionis* in a modern city.

Jung Found

I did eventually find a statue of Jung in Zurich. Actually, it is only a large bust, but it will serve. However, it is not in a public place. It stands in a prominent corner in the lecture room at the Psychological Club on Gemeindestrasse. It is a very impressive image perhaps half again the size of the real-life head, and it shows Jung's features in a moment of intense contemplation. I sometimes imagine him to be studying the members of the club as they listen attentively to lectures on analytical psychology and related topics, sometimes pleased with what he sees out there, sometimes not so much. When I look at him, I remember the first time I came to this building, now forty years ago, and how I was wondering why Jung was not more visible on the streets of Zurich. Now I think I understand. Jung does not belong to the city's persona. Zwingli and Escher and to some degree also Pestalozzi play that role. But Jung belongs instead to their counterweight, to the city's soul, and therefore his image is reserved for the inner spaces that are not visible in the streets and yet give the city its deepest contact with nature and its strongest vitality. Jung's life and work have actually made Zurich into a capital of depth psychology in the world of our time, but this is not widely recognized by the collective at large and certainly not in Zurich. I think now that this is as it should be. To quote the favored expression of my dear late friend, Arwind Vasavada, who trained in Zurich in the 1950s and had some memorable sessions there with the aged Jung: "Everything is just right."

Notes

1   Wikipedia article on Hans Waldmann, available at http://en.wikipedia.org/wiki/Hans_Waldmann.

2   C. G. Jung, *Memories, Dreams, Reflections* (New York: Vintage Books, 1989), p. 111.

3   Compare Jung's statement: "We must recognize that nothing is more difficult to bear than oneself." Carl Jung, *Collected Works of C. G. Jung*, vol. 7, *Two Essays on Analytical Psychology* (Princeton, N.J.: Princeton University Press, 1972), § 373.

4   C. G. Jung, *Collected Works of C. G. Jung*, vol. 6, *Psychological Types* (Princeton, N.J.: Princeton University Press, 1971), § 803ff.

5   Heinrich Runge, "Wasserkult in der Schwiz," in *Mythologische Landschaft Schweiz*, ed. Kurt Derungs (Bern: Edition Amalia, 1997), p. 21.

6   *Ibid.*, p. 18.

7   For a detailed account of the legends of Felix and Regula and recent historical and archeological researches into their identities and relics, see Hansueli Etter, Urs Baur, and Jürg Hanser, eds., *Die Zürcher Stadttheiligen Felix und Regula. Legenden, Reliquien, Geschicte und ihre Botschaft im Lich moderner Forschung* (Zurich: Hochbauamt der Stadt Zürich/Büro für Archäologie, 1988).

8   Meinrad Lienert, *Sagen und Legenden der Schweiz*, herausgageben von Stefan Ineichen (Munich and Vienna: Nagel & Kimche im Carl Hanser Verlag, 2006), pp. 106-110.

9   See "Ein Wunderkind auf Reisen," *Neue Zürcher Zeitung*, December 27-28, 2008, p. 13.

10   C. G. Jung, "Answer to Job," in *Collected Works of C. G. Jung*, vol. 11, *Psychology and Religion: West and East* (Princeton: Princeton University Press, 1969), § 752.

11   Quoted in Jackie Wullschlager, *Chagall: A Biography* (New York: Knopf, 2008), p. 456.

12   Irmgard Vogelsanger-de Roche, *Marc Chagall's Windows in the Zürich Fraumünster: Origins, Content and Significance* (Zürich: Orell Füssli Verlag, 2002), p. 9.

Sydney / Purgatorio

Craig San Roque

To peer deeply into this ghost city, the one lying beneath the surface, is to understand that Sydney has a soul and that it is a very dark place indeed.
—John Birmingham[1]

The history of Sydney, to borrow Mark Twain's marvellous phrase "does not read like history, but like the most beautiful lies." And all of a fresh new sort, no mouldy old stale ones. It is full of surprises, and adventures, and incongruities, and contradictions and incredibilities; but they are all true, they all happened.
—Tim Flannery[2]

⟨ A GUIDE ⟩

This layered portrait of Sydney, in four sections, offers a perspective on Sydney's colonial history and cultural maturation; then focuses on characters and circumstances in the city sector where the writer, a psychotherapist, practices. In part three, there is a style change into an obscure crime of historical implication; then, in part four, a psychological "romance." The fictionalized "case stories" reveal inner experiences of Sydney. The underlying metaphor is borrowed from Dante's *Divine Comedy*, in particular *Purgatorio*, and relocated to Sydney—a city of potential, creativity, and liberation perilously balanced upon a foundation of complex vice. Dante's story is structured as an ascent of Mt. Purgatory, set as an island in a southern ocean. Dante travels with his guide, Virgil, over four days. The night breaks occur at Cantos 9, 19, and 27, where Dante dreams. This essay follows that four-part form, including city-borne dreams and section transitions marked with a quotation from the relevant Canto from Dante's *Purgatorio*.

DAY ONE

Dante's cinematic *Divine Comedy*[3] is set in three locations: *Inferno, Purgatorio, Paradiso*. After leaving the cruel torments of hell, Dante's opening lines to *Purgatorio* run thus:

> To run on better water now, the boat of my invention hoists its sails and leaves away to stern that cruel stretch of sea;
> And I will sing of this second Kingdom in which the human spirit cures itself and becomes fit to leap up into heaven.

Purgatory, an imagined place of spiritual purification, is sited by Dante on an island peak in the southern hemisphere. The peak is the reverse image of the deep pit of *Inferno*, which Dante locates beneath Jerusalem. After doing their time in hell (under Jerusalem), Dante and his guiding spirit, Virgil, emerge at the end of a long, dark undersea tunnel. They emerge in a state of shock upon an unfamiliar shore. Dante recognizes the morning star, Venus, and then this poet of the thirteenth century, who could never have seen the Pacific, marks well the defining constellation of the South, the Southern Cross. These four stars symbolize for Dante the cardinal virtues of Justice, Temperance, Fortitude, and Prudence.

> ...and there I saw four stars never yet seen except by the first people.
> The sky seemed to be glad in their sparkling: O northern hemisphere you are a widow to be deprived of any sight of them!

Dawn approaches. As the darkness clears, he discovers, standing near him, a dignified old man, a kind of immigration officer who, assuming that the two men are refugees, questions how they have landed. Virgil intercedes, explaining their purpose: that a lady from heaven (Beatrice) had, because of Dante Alighieri's state of madness close unto death, instructed Virgil to guide her mortal friend through the three spheres. The visa is for Dante's instruction and spiritual rescue. The old man generously indicates the possible way through the daunting terrain confronting them. Over the next four days, we follow Dante and Virgil—climbing the peak, meeting with remarkable departed men and women, characters of political or spiritual consequence who Dante, as poet, locates for cure in Purgatory. The trek—interspersed by dreams, visions, and instruction in music and philosophy—finally brings Dante, on the fourth day, to the borders of earthly paradise. Beatrice, colored like fire, presents herself and assumes visible command of his transformation in preparation for the entry to Paradise. This after-death location, Purgatory, is not Hell; though souls suffer in Purgatory, the suffering is deemed essential for purification and liberation. Purgatory is a place on the way to somewhere (for most souls) and Dante works this theme with spiritual acuity and humor. His dedication to love and to his anima/ Beatrice is exquisitely serious, yet the politics of *Purgatorio* are depicted with gently sardonic irony.

For the allegory's sake, I remind you of the design of the island. Mt. Purgatory is constructed of nine cliff-hanging ascending terraces that repeat, in mirror image, the shape of the pit made by Lucifer's fall from heaven. The pit resembles a meteor crater or an open-cut mine. If Lucifer's pit presents the descent of man and all our depressive paranoid depravity, Purgatory's mount offers a guiding image of a potential space between heaven and hell where things might be reconciled and mended. If some souls in Purgatory suffer, the psychic pain is nevertheless purposive, since each soul, in their own time, has the opportunity to reach a maturational stage of concern for others. The sign over Dante's gate into Hell is: "Abandon hope, all ye who enter here"; perhaps *Purgatorio*'s sign might read: "Do not abandon love, ye who enter here."

The radical hope implanted in Purgatory is that we can get better at the capacity for loving co-dwelling in the city of God (I sometimes wonder who God contracts as personal architect—an Italian, perhaps, those makers of perfect cities).

Along the lower cliff shore, Dante's design placed the refugee camps of the excluded and castaway. Above them, with permanent sea views, dwell the "unforgiven," identified mostly as negligent, indolent politician/prince/ bankers—neither bad enough for permanent hell nor good enough for salvation. Then comes the true gate into Purgatory and the seven ascending terraces where it is possible for a soul to undergo reformation. In Dante's compassionate view, these souls suffer from various failures of love, hence the notion of this island as the location for progressive transformations in the capacity for relationship.

The first three terraces are the hangout for souls of "misdirected love"—the Proud, the Envious, and the Angry. On the ridge above, on Terrace Four, are those "deficient in love"—especially the lazy and slothful. Higher still, on Terraces Five, Six, and Seven, are those of us condemned for "excessive love"— the Avaricious, the Gluttonous, and the lustfully Promiscuous. On the summit of Dante's imagined Purgatory is, let us call it, "Café Beatrice," or maybe, "Helipad Before Paradise," for it is here that Beatrice and her beloved poet meet and ascend into heaven and another set of Mysteries.

This is the map of Purgatory, and this is an implicit map of emerald city Sydney—from Palm Beach on the northern shore, to Sylvania Waters in the south, our mansions clutch greedily at the gates of Paradise.

Charles Darwin: The Voyage of the Beagle

❦ SYDNEY HARBOUR / PORT JACKSON, 1836 ❦

By now, Captain FitzRoy and the exploration crew had coasted Patagonia, Tierra del Fuego, Chile, the Galapagos, Tahiti, Maori New Zealand, and Australia. The sailing ship was the *Beagle*, with a cargo of thousands of Conrad Marten's landscapes and sketches; samples of plant, insect, fish, bird, animal exotica; Darwin's collections of southern geology, biology, maritime measurements— incremental observations that would gather at last in the dawning evolutionary realization.

All those items swinging at anchor in Sydney's harbor, awaiting Darwin's slow revelation—the long gathered, staring facts of the evolution of species— that man and woman belong in a long chain of being.

The cumulative voyage of the *Beagle* transported home the detail that finally freed God from the burden of being the lonely, monochrome creator. The *Beagle* allowed the divine to settle back into being continuously complicit with creation. Things evolve slowly over a long lunch.

Darwin's entry for his Journal, 12 January 1836, opens with these lines:

Early in the morning a light air carried us towards the entrance of Port Jackson. Instead of beholding a verdant country, interspersed with fine houses, a straight line of yellowish cliff brought to our minds the coast of Patagonia. A solitary lighthouse, built of white stone, alone told us that we were near a great and populous city ...

At last we anchored in Sydney Cove. We found the little basin occupied by many large ships, and surrounded by warehouses. In the evening I walked through the town and returned full of admiration at the whole scene. It is a most magnificent testimony to the power of the British nation. Here in a less promising country, scores of years have done many times more than an equal number of centuries have effected in South America. My first feeling was to congratulate myself that I was born an Englishman. Upon seeing more of the town afterwards, perhaps my admiration fell a little; but yet it is a fine town.[4]

Ships in
Sydney harbor.

*From an
18th-century
drawing,
photographed
by Erica Cordell
from TV screen*

❴ A MARITIME TOWN ❵

It is a fine town still; yet, the case of Sydney is that of an aggravated, grievous, northern people who asserted British domination over native bark canoes and fishing camps along the shore—a "fatal shore," as Robert Hughes elucidates in his distinctive account of the history of the transportation of convicts to Australia from 1787 until 1868.[5] By all accounts, Sydney's conception was peculiarly British, somewhat careless. Hughes gives vivid unsentimental glimpses of the founding of the colonial camp, developing in an anxiety of contrary ambitions and confusions. It was no liberation fantasy, such as helped make America.

The Anglican Government in its soberly cruel incarnation of an imperial force, specializing in slavery and guns, circa 1770, gestated the intent to make a prison outpost as far from home as possible. Its not really clear why the English lords-of-thought considered that southeastern Australia was a profitable move, even though it is clear that, in those troubled times, the British king, government, and financiers did have worries about expanding and sustaining the white man's Empire. They worried about protection of trade routes, slavery, the destabilization of British possessions by the American revolutionary wars of

Independence (Boston Tea Party, 1773); the French working up to their revolution (Bastille, 1788); and an irritating number of hungry Irish, Scots, and Anglo peasant dependents who would not conform to clumsy, desperate social controls. As cities densified, so did fear of insurgency among the "criminal classes." Prisons and prison hulks were full, so one supposes that the Lords were looking for a release valve, or a place to keep an eye on Asia, or further experiments with cheap labor if the slavery ran out. So maybe, on a dark night, a king's minister read Dante's *Purgatorio* and thought: Now there is a good idea—imagine the southern hemisphere and *Terra Australis Incognita* as a possible final solution.

Anyhow, whatever anyone imagined and however quixotic the planning, that seminal flotilla of eleven ships left Portsmouth May 13, 1787, under the astute guidance of Captain Arthur Phillip of the *Sirius*, with maybe 1,403 souls packed into small leaky boats. By way of Rio de Janeiro and Cape Town, South Africa, then east across the Indian, they arrived in the uterine harbor that was to become Sydney—January 25, 1788. It's worth noting the success of Phillip's management; seven children were born on the voyage and only sixty-nine persons perished or were discharged. Having arrived that day, on that shore (in a state of shock?), the rum and the women were released into a night of drunken derangement. In the morning, the controls came down; the prison outpost began its life. They set about sorting things, and a mythic pattern for Sydney was initiated. Arrival, shock, derangement. Adaptation, survival, domination.

From 1788, following the Dog Star (*Sirius*), the rest of the world progressively spewed into these refined indigenous sites that are now the fine and luscious coastal suburbs. Sydney swoops and dives in a convolution of hills, bays, sandy coves, and sandstone escarpments; an eastward-gazing, azure, gracious, grubby, wharf-side historical opera set; the sweep of Sydney Quay … a maritime town.

A place of boats, more boats, "boat people"—and I and all my family members and conjugal partners are mongrelly among them; arriving still, unsure what it is to arrive and to belong in a place like this. A dream, perhaps, a nightmare not quite awoken from; not yet, to satisfaction, understood.

In 1836, Darwin made charming naturalist's observations of eucalyptus, mountains, sandstone valleys. He also concisely noted the depressed, plaintive condition of indigenous people haunting the town. In a sharp observation on the drama of survival, he noted: "Wherever the European has trod, death seems to pursue the aboriginal."[6] This is the nightmare from which we have not yet awoken.

Darwin enquired into three items of interest to him: the state of higher class society, the conditions of the convicts, and "the degree of attraction sufficient to induce persons to emigrate." He notes that "the whole population, poor and rich, are bent on acquiring wealth...the number of large houses and other buildings just finished is truly surprising; nevertheless everyone complains of the high rents and difficulty of procuring a home." He would note the same acquisitive frenzy today. Darwin worries about the social impact and moral consequences of the convict mentality, adding that "the children learn the vilest expressions ... and equally vile ideas." Our beloved evolutionist passes sentence thus: "I am not aware that the tone of society has assumed any peculiar character; but with such habits and without intellectual pursuits, it can hardly fail to deteriorate. My opinion is such that nothing but rather sharp necessity should compel me to emigrate." Darwin's last word on Australia goes—"Farewell Australia? You are a rising child, and doubtless some day will reign a great princess in the South; but you are too great and ambitious for affection, yet not great enough for respect. I leave your shores without sorrow or regret."[7]

But some of us did emigrate. This now our place—a brief, richly layered history; frenzy of aspiration and refuge; tribally inflicted wounds licked, maybe forgotten, maybe not; a place of obscure genealogies, degrees of separation, mourning and melancholia, envy and gratitude: opportunity.

⟨ CHARACTER ⟩

I might introduce you now to D'Arcy Wentworth, ambiguously recruited to the Australian project, arriving with the second fleet of convicts in June, 1790. He entered the scene—a wild, well-connected young man of energy— "volunteering" for the penal colony as a surgeon. In fact, his offer of exile was a plea bargain to avoid likely execution following charges for (alleged) highway robbery. Not quite convict, not quite free, D'Arcy made something of his ambiguous condition and his sporadic medical training in London. His son, conceived on board the *Neptune* with Catherine Crowley (convict), became, not "a convict bastard," as could have been the case, but, by force of character, father and son became initiators of an enterprise of (unsteady) gravity, becoming provocative patriarchal ballast to an emergent nation. Doctor D'Arcy, over twenty-five years, argued or colluded with each successive governor and came to possess the largest landholdings in the colony, and was simultaneously and paradoxically Principal Surgeon, Superintendent of Police, magistrate, dealer in rum, and director of the fledgling Bank of New South Wales. After Catherine died, he was blessed with two *de facto* spouses living (amicably?) in separate establishments. He sired many children. The first and native son, William Charles—explorer, poet, lawyer, and political dealer—stimulated, during turbulent early years, the establishment of the independent newspaper, the Constitution, the Parliament, Convict Emancipation and the University—all accomplished through bold confrontation, a long view, and seizure of opportune moments. William Charles married Sarah Cox, daughter of convict blacksmiths. Their descendents have irascibly stirred and tempered politico-social and environmental action throughout the nineteenth and twentieth centuries. These iconic folk of canny Irish/Anglo stockiness, refusing to be put down, demonstrate an intelligent yet controversial line through Australia's story from beginning to the present.

I came to know D'Arcy's fourth descendant, William Charles, known as "Bill." This Wentworth was a Member of Parliament (1949-1977) in the conservative Liberal Party, which he helped found. An eccentrically visioned man, Bill "crossed the floor" on nineteen occasions to vote with the Labor opposition party. Such rebellious bilateral behavior is entirely consistent with the behavior of D'Arcy and the anarchic matrix of the colony that D'Arcy so ably exploited; an exploitation in which all Australians, one way or another, become involved or complicit. My uncle, Barrie Dexter—a steady, inventive diplomat—worked with querulous Wentworth and tireless indigenous activist Charles Perkins, and other persons of fiber, to lay foundations for the historic 1967 national referendum addressing racial discrimination, bringing recognition of Aboriginal citizenship.[8] This event was ideologically twinned with the end of segregation in the USA. Barrie, Bill, Charlie, and their kin and "mates" helped advocate, develop, and manage the first Federal Ministry responsible for Aboriginal Affairs, making formative policy addressing the conditions of Australia's own displaced people. ("Displacement" as a psychological condition is a complex matter in this country of unsettled indigenous people and resettling immigrants.)

An idealist and rhetorician himself, Bill Wentworth was not seduced by the Stalinist/Maoist rhetoric of the '50s and '60s, and forcefully opposed Communism as a threat to economic emancipation. This archetypical Anglo-Celtic Sydney character was a difficult, endearing man, whose vision both formed and disturbed my own view of Australia's story. Inclusion in the family dynamics of these three illuminating men—Bill, Barrie, Charlie—helped me grasp close-up the character of my country's disconsolate formation and the consequent "cultural complex" systems played out in the theaters of successive intersecting families. As I write about Sydney, I discover, for better for worse, my own ambiguous place in this beautiful terrain. If Darwin is right that "wherever the European has trod, death seems to pursue the aboriginal," then in my own footsteps also, the presence of that death follows—as Virgil follows Dante.

Belonging and Degrees of Separation

In a country of small population, one finds oneself surprisingly interconnected. There are few "degrees of separation." As a psychotherapist, one's own patients may, at one generation removed, have been acquainted with one's own kin, lived in the same town, arrived on the same ship. Intersections are close, boundary management intricate. Kinship also means implication in foundational acts of enculturated crime, whether crimes from Britain, crimes against the indigenous, crimes of establishment, or later neglectful abuses of environment. This is a city-state forged by brutality and endurance, and everything done has been done by one's own kin and classmates. (No man is an island.) This is an island nation forged by folk from one's own village—villages of Devon, Galway, Calabria, the Aegean, Lebanon, southern China, and Vietnam ... Belonging may be a matter of honoring that memory, resignation to a southern fate, and having the audacity to dare a self-creation, as D'Arcy did. Belonging here has something to do with recognizing the truth of our polyphonous psychic inheritance and making (good) use of it. But belonging brings with it a peculiar detachment—indifference—an attachment disorder perhaps; because the founding has been so forthright, so violent, so indolently harmful, so exuberant, so clumsy. It is for this reason that I fell into psychoanalysis. It was in order to get a purchase on the troubled unconscious psyche of the place that had grown up within me. It was as though, also, there was no inherent interiority to Australia—or the interior life had to be found or created all over again. Psychoanalytic process does help discover and respect the interior relational life of the human being, but in Australia such psychic maturation is a long time coming. In Sydney, I have been embarrassed because I could not brazenly "seize the city" (as though it were a "right" to do so). Only certain kinds of people seem to seize this city; the victors of Sydney are the innocent hedonists, the arrogant and privileged "sons and daughters"—and those with criminal minds. I am not a criminal, yet somehow I deserve *Purgatorio*, not as punishment but as process by which interiority can be consolidated.

> The southern hemisphere; the light shifts and the heat edges in. "Tell me, Virgil, is hell following us down from the northern world; or are we here at last undergoing our cure?" *(after Dante)*

DAY TWO

Terrible as lightning it descended and carried me aloft into the fire.

— Canto 9.28

A city can be loved, knowing all the time that beneath the city there is a hook on a wall where the body of Inanna hangs, desecrated continually[9]—last year in Baghdad, this year in Harare, Zimbabwe. There are cities of reverie; cities that sing, hum, vibrate; places that once were nightmares carried aloft into the fire, yet now instruct in how to rebuild annihilated places so that they do sing, hum, vibrate again in physical body (Warsaw). The subtle body of a city is the thing to watch. A city embodied in the imagination of millions can endure, live through the nightmare, regenerate. Sydney, which has not yet been destroyed, is maybe slowly attaining its subtle body. In Sydney also, women are hung in basements. Or silenced, like Antigone, in caves—until the feminine uprising can stand it no longer. The complexity is the thing—the richness, the layering of pain—all cities induce mania and are sustained by corruption, lassitude, anxiety. In great cities, the divine comes to nest, continuously interweaving love, imagination, and creation with its own special traffic of darkness. Sydney, perhaps, is slowly acquiring an inner design and character that may enable it to survive its own apocalypse. What did Dante say in the opening lines of *Purgatorio*? "I will sing of this second kingdom in which the human spirit cures itself … "

I honestly believe that this line does mark the secret hope of nearly every person who has migrated here—to a country where a human spirit might find purpose, cure, new life. But how do you make a city work as cure for restless, displaced, ill-disposed, ambitious, and bewildered spirits? This is partly an urban planning problem that Governor Macquarie and his wife addressed (circa 1815), bravely laying Georgian architectural simplicity into the haphazard ground plan.[10] It is also a personal commitment, asking for patient attention to the ground beneath one's feet. The layering of poignant histories greets the one who steadily searches. There are those who put their ear to the pavement, seeking sign of a pulse, a heart.

Woolloomooloo

The place where I work is on the third floor of a discreetly satisfying, neoclassical 1890s building, not far from the old wharves in a curve of harbor known as Woolloomooloo Bay. Here is a landing site of timber and steel shipping for two

The date
set into the
roundel at
Circular Quay
refers to the
establishment
of the colony.

*Photograph by
Erica Cordell*

hundred vibrant years; wool trade, immigrant arrivals; the Navy. Here, in 1788, were speared the first white men, straying over the hill to the little stream in the valley. Now the stream is gone. Nearby are the sailors' hotels—the old Shamrock, the Tilbury, Frisco, The Bells—along this liquid green curve, the Navy and WWII American sailors flooded our girls in an epiphany of white uniforms. Here on the slopes above the protected bay are ochred wharf-worker's cottages, resistant remnants of Depression Sydney. Here was an Aboriginal men's ceremonial ground, now obliterated, or so it would seem, for this very same area is occupied at nights by gatherings of homeless, displaced men.

This city village—Woolloomooloo, East Sydney—has survived; its current shape rescued from that ravaging period during the 1970s when certain badly dressed Sydney men, who frequented strip clubs, insisted it best for all of us to strip everything "old" they could lay their hammers on and re-dress the girl with lucrative new bricks and glass. The "slums" were to be cleared, and the crumbling, century-old mansions on Potts Point/Kings Cross cliff overlooking Woolloomooloo Bay were to be replaced by brutally terraced apartments offering the paradisical "water views." Something about this rapacious messing with our city, at that time, hit a raw nerve. It really upset some people. It upset, most surprisingly, some adamant working-class men from ships, buildings sites, and the Unions—a tale evocatively told by John Birmingham in his history, *Leviathan*.[11] In the course of these Union-led "property wars," a courageous journalist, Juanita Nielsen, disappeared (July 4, 1975). Her house is still there, up the cliff, but she herself may be buried under tons of builder's concrete or dismembered in the harbor. Juanita (of a well-connected family) supported the Unions in their unexpected disdain for shit-heavy property millionaires. Nielsen, an articulate woman, perhaps also said too much about local police collusion with drug and prostitution scams, for this area, Kings Cross/Palmer Street, was/is still the brothel/erotica sector. But then again, everyone local knew the deal about "protection"; Australians, like Sicilians, have a code of silence. Nielsen is still a "cold case." It seems she was last seen entering or maybe leaving the basement of a well-known nightclub. One does not, if one is locked in a strip club basement, tell worried men with friends-in-high-places to "get fucked." A journalist who investigated her case sums it up: "she encapsulates the never ending battle between developers and those who want to maintain communities."[12] What is the skill of maintaining communities? Perhaps care with the virtues according to Dante—justice, temperance, fortitude, and prudence. Juanita Nielsen was a woman of virtue; she had everything but prudence. Alas, requesting heavy-balled men of property to reflect a little does get you a result. Without a trace.

{ THE WOOLLOOMOOLOO WASHHOUSE }

Across the street from my building is a little row of shops sheltered by a Demeter-like tree. The first green shoots are returning, shading intimately the old corner store, updated with anti-vandal protective shutters. You will see the office of the First Fleet Society, which holds archives of convict history from 1787. In the window, there is a list of all who sailed in that first and famous fleet—the eleven ships: *Sirius*, *Supply*, *Scarborough*, *Lady Penrhyn* (the women's ship) ... —all in all carrying 1400-1500 souls (accounts seem to vary). The convicted numbered 756; the rest are crew, guards, administrators, family members, children— all on an eight-month epic voyage to a penal colony. You might glance next door to the Woolloomooloo Washhouse, operated by dark-haired, long-haired John and his aged mother, dressed always in widow black. She courteously receives the local laundry and thus she knows most of the inner-sheeted intimate secrets of the neighborhood. She speaks very little English. Dark John has a sense of humor and an eye for blonde women from Aryan countries who now flock south for Sydney's Bondi beach fantasia.

"John," I say one day, making conversation, "is your mother … from Russia?" He blanches. " … Maybe white Russian?" He growls, succinct, "Belarus." I get the idea there must be some tension between Belarus and Russia and leave well enough alone. Belarus John has a sharp way with slightly uncomforting men who visit him from time to time. Another day, their car is just pulling away. "John"— I say with a teasing smile—"These men … friends of yours?" He says distract-edly, "I am thinking of buying a motel in Bondi. I've gotta get out of this place."

Another morning, dropping off laundry, Belarus is looking wistfully across the street at the French woman who has taken the shop-front below me and beside Edo, the cool and charming hairdresser. The Frenchwoman's setup is a studio gallery where she paints and displays her gaudy, postmodern, retro-bohemian wares. She is local color. John asks my advice on redecorating the laundry. I say, "Sure, but why ask me?" John says, "I ask you; I ask an artist." "What about the Frenchwoman?" John replies, "She don't sell, but you, you sell." "John," I say, accustomed to his dry wit. "What do I sell?" He says, "Art— interesting people ring your bell. They go inside. They come out after an hour. Some smile, some cry, but they come back. You're not a dealer, so we say, he is a portrait painter—Who is coming to sit for him today?—we say—these people they sit for you. You see, we know." He is right. People do sit. "Alright, John, let's talk about the colors."

❧ EAST SYDNEY HOTEL ❧

You could learn a lot about what goes down around the city from the people who visit my room for "portraits." But alas, these are secrets I cannot tell. You also could get at the guts of this place if you holed up for a while in the East Sydney Hotel, just across the corner. The hoteliers have presided over the bar for thirty years, host to men of criminal mind and intent, barristers from the Supreme Court just up the hill, film writers, wanderers, refugees, serious drink-ers up from the wharves, a shrink or two, and some habitual souls whose cure or conviction they serve. Many souls have spilled the beans at that bar. It was Dr. Anne Noonan, a Sydney Jungian analyst, who put the idea that if I wanted to get into the obscure soul of this bit of Sydney the best way would be to get such a bunch upstairs, sleeping in the hotel, incubating local dreams—and on that basis compose a dreaming novel of the place. And Anne is right, for the place seeps with narrative in past and present tense. Almost everything seminal that happened in early Sydney history happened within walkable distance of this specific, once Irish, hotel—a handy place; history distils in places like this.[13]

Just over there is the old Atalanta café, begun by Italian fishermen who once kept their boats down on the cove. The Atalanta, like the mythic athlete after whom it is named, was a trim, independently-minded place—formica tables, fish, calamari, and simple wine. That convivial presence still infuses the updated version, known as Puntino's Tratorria—courtyard, lime green and terra cotta, scattered with broken mosaic hinting at Pompeii. Good pasta, old landmarks. And now the landmarks are the dealers on certain corners, the Soho Gallery, the Police club, fight gym, Toby Barista's, Infinite Bliss Patisserie, the Harbour Tunnel freeway exit, and always the endearingly assorted paranoids who wander in and out of the Woolloomooloo late-night shop and liquor store—and god bless the shopkeeper there who makes all of us feel at home, including, without offence, the gently agitated men who walk the street every night and morning, to and from the homeless hostel with blankets, seeking their "quantum of solace."

One night in the Atalanta, over the formica table, I recounted a dream to Anne Noonan and a few others after a seminar up in my room. It was summer, January 1988, the bicentenary of the settlement of Australia. (I am not all that keen on public reporting of private dreaming; dream predators are always out to get an analyst who lives so dangerously as to wear a dream on his sleeve. But it can't be helped; the imagery is pertinent to the theme.) The dream scene featured two mosaic-encrusted, gigantic female figures that had been dredged up from Sydney harbor and laid out on Circular Quay. No one in Sydney could explain how ancient female statues could have come to rest at the bottom of the harbor. The city government did not want to take responsibility for this enigmatic find. At the time, Middle Eastern artifacts seemed irrelevant to Australian interests. Anne commented, wryly, that it made sense to her, since over the past two hundred years lots of women have been dumped in the bottom of the harbor—besides, she added with a beady eye, most Australian men won't take responsibility for the women they've buried under tons of concrete thinking.

What Anne says is true; but there is more. The detail of those faces was mesmeric, and in fact, surreptitiously, those two ancient submerged dream figures became tutelary spirits for me. Anne was right also that the urge of feminism was (1988) maybe raising the psychological consciousness of women in Sydney. In retrospect, I can see that the stimulus of this dream set a pattern of investigations into the archeo-mythology of the feminine, which Anne, I, and others had begun obediently to facilitate, congruent with the rise in archetypal mythopoeic impulses in international centers of Jungian enthusiasm.[14]

In the dream, it transpired that an Arabic archaeologist had entered Sydney harbor in a reed raft, like those used on the delta of the Nile or the Euphrates. I can see internally, even now, the incongruous sight of a reed boat bumping against the wooden pylons of the Quay. The archaeologist deferentially offered to take the women home on the reed rafts. He explained that they had been sunk in the harbor ages ago to preserve them, to keep them safe from a catastrophe that would engulf his homeland. He was grateful that Sydney had innocently preserved his heritage. Two mysterious, encrusted female figures rising from beneath the waves, laid out on the foreshore—the archaeologist patiently removing mud and debris, revealing their original vibrancy.

That influence is here now as I walk alone back through Surry Hills, along Crown Street, darkened artery to Woolloomooloo. It is raining. I confess I am walking with Dionysos after a celebration for our resident philosopher/analyst, Giles Clark. I mention this pleasant event because Giles has developed a notion, influenced perhaps by Spinoza, of the "animating body" (psyche/body in reciprocal animation). Walking through these streets, I wonder how an environment, a city, might acquire its own polyvalent "animating body."[15] I cross Oxford St. near the Colombian Hotel, a site of homoerotic action, and I continue across William St., an artery to streetwalking femo-erotic action, favored by men who slide past in darkened vehicles. I have a habit of entering liminal spaces. I am musing about the town of Eleusis, the site of old mysteries on the outskirts of Athens.[16] These two districts are a long way apart, and yet, somehow, cities make the ancient things of civilization feel closer. Perhaps it's the prospect of ruin. Tonight I am not thinking of ruin; I am musing on the task of making this city visible to you. At the celebration, a friend had muttered, "No mystery makes itself visible without pain." I am under the influence of mosaic-encrusted faces. I present you with flickers of this present humming city and acknowledge the somber chiaroscuro of immigrant memories, indigenous footprints. The present is backed by old mysteries—some lost, some ruined, some recovering. It is very late. One has to keep one's wits about one, but I fall into a cantor rhythm, oblivious of the light rain and loitering men. Words come to my mind. A story begins, thus—

Dante's Nest

There is a place known as Dante's Nest. It is there, every evening, no matter the weather, that a small and delicate bird folds its wings. In the folding, the bird draws into itself certain things. Every evening, the roving imagination of Dante Dioniso Dileusis takes the shape of a bird arriving in a quiet place. There

47

From the
author's
consulting
room.

*Photograph by
Erica Cordell*

it settles itself—ruffling, preening, breathing and cooing, gathering memories of fruit, observation of almond, glint of fig, lemon, ancient tree, stone walls. Gathering every sight and sense discovered during the day's flights, the delicate bird collects for Dante's human being the sights and scents of the day's subtle hunt.

The imagination of Dante Dioniso Dileusis is not particularly human; it is not bound by human perception, human constriction. In its unbounded mode it wheels through many worlds; it collects flocks of birds, currents of insect, flying shapes, delicious color, fish leaping, skin, musical note, animal call; chatter.

With all this gathering, lest all be lost, there is a place known as Dante's Nest. It is here every evening, regardless of the weather—a small and delicate bird folds its wings. And there, in the nest, the bird sits and broods. Somewhere thus, in the pulsating subtle body of Dioniso Dante, the gathered day becomes, in the warm body of the bird, a collection of eggs, speckled blue and black.

Incubating, these fruitful fertile eggs, words gather. They shimmer through the brain, they nestle in the throat, they draw up breath from the deep well of the lungs, they roll along the tongue, they spit, glowing. It is from Dante's Nest that the sung poetry of the human world has emerged—since the very beginning of human time.

The nest of Dioniso Dileusis is hidden in a very obscure place. It is, however, a place upon which the salvation of the intelligent world depends. It is here where a small fire is saved every day for the continuing purpose of humanity. The end of the real world will be on the day when Dante's Nest is crushed in the hands of a brutal boy, a boy too naïve to comprehend the age and destiny of the world. The nest, that delicate thing which allows all things to gather.

The wise and clever say that the future of the world depends upon wise and clever things, which only they can carry out according to the will of the people, or against the will of the people. This might be true—but I say this: The destiny of the world depends upon Dante's Nest and the small bird who, folding her wings every evening, begins the brooding.

DAY THREE

There came to me in a dream, a stuttering woman, cross-eyed and lopsided on her feet with maimed hands and all her color washed out ...
— Canto 19.7

In India, they have a phrase, "this is my station." "Station" denotes the functional location that a person takes up in life. Here one is psychically available to those whom one serves, spiritually/practically. The publicans of the East Sydney Hotel take up their station there. Slowly I assumed a station here in Cathedral Street, Woolloomooloo, having returned to vertical Sydney after many years at my other station in the horizontal lands of the central Australian plateau; my station there within the existential apocalypse of indigenous substance abuse. I confess that, back in Sydney, I felt I had lost refinement and orientation. I stumbled in the gentility needed to find a way of doing psychological work again within a city ethos. But then, I became aware of a gently chiding internal presence. Let me say that this in-tuition assumed a personification known to me as "Charlie Wong" (a friend says he is probably a Taoist immortal, incognito). Wong's gentility helped settle me down in town. Contemplating Dr. Charles Wong helped integrate the grievousness of years in the destroyed stations of indigenous Australia.[17] His character helped the transition in a manner similar to that of indigenous tutelary guides who helped settle me down in Aboriginal territory. It is a curious thing, this operation of the tutelary spirit (though the phenomenon is no stranger to Jung). In strange terrain, the wise traveller accepts a guide.

The author, assuming a station in Cathedral St.

Photograph by Erica Cordell

It's about here somewhere, in this mood, that I might lead you into a curious dream which came to me in Woolloomooloo.

A doctor is summoned to a barrister's residence bearing the name "Nigeria House." There has been a death. There are women in the basement. The doctor begins to unravel the true cause of death. It is not as expected. A house is discovered as responsible for the crime. The key phrase of the voice in the dream is "the house itself is the murderer."

This dream did apply to a patient's situation—yet, in reverie, for months puzzled by this unexpected dream, I contemplated what Nigeria had to do with myself, Sydney, and what crime? I walked where, historically, the lucidly shown house might have been located—Glebe, Paddington, Potts Point? And then the invitation to write this essay arrived, and in the course of colonial research I discovered reference to the "Africa Company." And thus a story for you in crime genre emerges, a story based exactly in content on the Nigeria House dream. Perhaps, reverie is how the city spirit communicates. This idea is based on a notion of geographic transference, but let's not spoil a good story with theory; let us rather deal in "Fact and beautiful lies, all of which are true" …

Nigeria House

Dr. Charles Wong took the call at 11:30 on a Thursday night. It was not convenient. He apologized to friends gathered at the card table, and left for Nigeria House. The call from Michael Ramsay Camden, agitated, breathless, a little drunk: "Charles—Caroline ... she's passed out. I fear ... she might be dead—please come."

The doctor parked discreetly, allowing for unobtrusive exit, as was his custom, and walked with care through Victoria Street's shadowy plane tree arcade, approaching the barrister's residence. The nameplate, "Nigeria House," starkly displayed by porch light. The house—sandstone grace, iron gate, entrance path tiled; black and white ceramics from China, palm foliage, broad veranda; a gentleman's residence from when the viewing hill above Woolloomooloo was cleared for the villas of an exclusive class. At that time, nostalgic families might have looked northeast over masts and shimmering transparencies, mentally skimming the Pacific, America, the Atlantic toward the blessed isles of home.

Caroline was indeed dead, lying on her back, flung across a substantial red cedar dining table. Asphyxiated, choked, or poisoned. Dr. Wong attended to Caroline. There was little to be done until the police determined to their satisfaction a cause of death. Matters would have taken their predictable course had not Wong been called—or, should I say, had a more conventional doctor been called.

In Singapore, Camden had defended an intricate matter for a clan relative of Charles Wong; their mutual obligations were strong enough for the doctor to take considerable care in the situation. He had never entered Nigeria House before that night. You need to know about the house. It is an ambience familiar to old Sydney—genteel darkened halls, ceiling heights of the period; the furnishing, the robustness of a subtropical colony, a bohemian richly antique casualness; artifacts of Oceania and Africa: the house of the travelled, the hunters and collectors of the Southern Hemisphere. The moment the doctor stepped onto the blackened polished floor he said, to no one in particular, "This is a house of crime."

Michael gave explanations. His wife had choked on something. She had been sick for weeks with a flu. She had been weakening and distracted, she hardly slept, she muttered at night, she was depressed, almost demented. Given her age, dementia was just possible. But dementia is not a cause of such a death. Wong was equally certain that Michael Ramsay was not, himself, directly, the cause of death.

Wong asked Michael permission to look over the house. He took care in the kitchen, sniffing and occasionally tasting salt, coffee, spices. The stairway, the upstairs rooms, a dishevelled master bedroom telling tales; bathrooms, portraits, and the artifacts. For a brief moment Wong glanced obliquely in the antique mirror, glimpsing parallel streams of Chinese and European lines pervading *Terra Australis* from the moment gold had been announced. Wong was ashamed to admit he had had little interest in European history before the 1851 gold rush brought his clan southward. Wong fastidiously ran a finger over the most ancient of the artifacts and furnishings. He gave careful attention to the floor, the dark stained wooden boards that resonated throughout the house. Artifacts from Africa. Mariner's items. Charts. A map of the 1896 Calvert Exploration expedition. The array of Bokhara carpets favored by Camden's class. A cabinet held a set of chains and manacles—convict era material. These objects and their history simmered in the doctor's brain. He went almost obediently downstairs into the basement areas. The service working areas opened onto a kitchen garden that once would have run to the cliff edge, overlooking the bay and the wharves. "The ships," said Wong curiously to himself. "The ships ... "

There were two women in the basement rooms, working at the big table, folding laundry. They were talking. Wong politely introduced himself, a small bow, deferential. A custom.

"Mrs. Camden?" said Wong, pausing while the two women turned solemn eyes upon him. "Can you tell me what happened to Mrs. Camden?"

"Miss Caroline?" said the one, in accents not familiar to Charles. "Miss Caroline, yes"—and the women nodded, folding laundry in obscurity but aware of all that passed above in Nigeria House. Folding, but saying nothing.

"The police will be coming," said Charles. "They will want to see you." "They will not see us," the women replied gravely, folding the sheets. "They will see you ... they will not see us." They smiled a little cheekily. Wong suddenly felt ashamed, remiss at his impoliteness; he was used to such shifts of perception, and here was one now.

He paused, letting a silence alter his orientation to another and earlier time. To a different configuration of human body. Wong spoke quietly to the presence at the scrubbed pine table, "The ships. It came from the ships?"

"Yes," said the woman of Irish accent. "It came from the slavers. It came because of the slavers ... it was a terrible thing." The women folding the laundry; the doctor unfolding the cause of death. "Something from Nigeria?" ... tentatively. "It's everywhere," said the other woman with the east London voice. "It's soaked in. Like arsenic in the paint, in the oil, but it's not arsenic; something from the black people ... they got her." The Chinese doctor looked carefully through and into the iris of her eyes—"Why Caroline?" "And why Mr. Ramsay

Camden?" echoed the East London voice. "It runs in the family, as well you know"—the Irish voice, fading.

"Please," said Wong, who by now could hear the police arriving. "It is because of the ships, sir," said the East London woman. "The fleets and that Captain Traille ... it's because of what happened on the *Scarborough* ... " The other woman nodding, clothed in the cloth of convict women, quietly poised while the doctor looked carefully within her being, her memory—fragile as it was.

Wong went up. Michael Ramsay Camden was questioned, and by 2 A.M. arrested and charged for the murder of Caroline Camden née Calvert. The doctor did what he could for the barrister; but the thing had been arranged so definitively. There looked to be little chance of convincing the police that this was a case of reasonable doubt, though later Wong said as much to the forensic specialist: "Not Ramsay Camden, doctor, the house is the murderer. I suggest you examine the history. You will find objects of an age with the original house contaminated. A pervasion through the body of Mrs. Camden. Examine the hair. The cause of death—by intent, accident, or sorcery—is the house. Examine the floor stain, most of all the Japan Black." This, Wong said deliberately, confidentially—departing, poised on the veranda beneath the porch light of Nigeria House.

In the following weeks, while the prosecution prepared a case, Charles began his researches. He arranged to visit Ramsay Camden's defense counsel. They met in Bambino's, the ground-floor restaurant of the St. James Trust Building on Elizabeth Street, where Ramsay had his chambers, as did his friend and Counsel. Wong was direct, in a manner unusual for him. He said, "You will need some history, most of which will be known to you. I regret I have not, until now, interested myself in the detail of your people and how you managed your immigration."

The Counsel calmly entreated Wong to speak freely, frankly. Wong began, laying certain notes on the table. "The Second Fleet—*Lady Juliana, Justinian, Surprise, Neptune, Scarborough*—reached Sydney, June 1789. The store ship *Guardian* foundered off South Africa. The British Government contract for the 1789 convict transport was offered to the lowest tender, specifying a fixed price to carry convicted Britons, whether they arrived alive or not; giving the contractors the right to sell off unused food supplies. The Africa Company became the contractors, their ships already outfitted as transports for the Africa-America slave trade.

"On those ships there were fixed, pinioned leg irons preventing movement during the entire voyage. These were brutal forms of so-called maximum security in soaked dark containment. 'Negroids' were not credited with human feeling."

The barrister nodded, adding, "Wilberforce and Darwin changed all that." Wong continued, "Many died on the slavers, just as they did on the convict voyage. No sanitation, no fresh air, minimal food, no medical treatment on a voyage of ten months. Suffice it to say that the conditions into which these people were taken by the Africa Company reveals sadistic cruelty and enforced stoicism, familiar to those of us who have suffered British ventures." Wong sat back, gazing thoughtfully at the groomed occupants of Bambino's. The barrister had ordered Wong an indelible Hunter Valley red, Brokenwood Cricket Pitch 1989. It remained untouched. "Certain things become interesting. It turns around the contract. In the First Fleet under Phillip, with a contract based on *alive* arrivals, about 60 lives were lost from the 1,400 who set out. In the second voyage, the contract was fixed payment for the embarked numbers—it did not matter whether there was an arrival or not. In fact, the more passengers who died, the more spare stores would be available to the contractors to sell off. On that second voyage, 1,006 male and female prisoners left Portsmouth. But how many people perished at sea? 267, or thereabouts." Placing a note before the barrister, the doctor said, "Kindly begin with reexamining *The Fatal Shore*. I quote: 'The starving prisoners, chilled to the bone on soaked bedding, unexercised, crusted with salt, shit and vomit, festering with scurvy and boils ... ' Such first-hand accounts indicate deliberate and conscious depravity—by the contractors, complicit with the government. Hughes reports a Thomas Milburn, who frankly recounts being chained to a dead companion for a week so he could claim the extra ration share.[18] It appears that those who arrived were sick, malnourished, a burden on the already starved colonists. It seems that another 150 prisoners died on arrival, many dragged up from the dank holds unable to function as humans. Some were thrown overboard as the ships advanced through your Sydney harbor. In all, on this voyage it appears that 417 convicted souls out of 1,026 are documented as lost. Captain Phillip indicates that the Second Fleet was a device to clear the gaols of 'the disordered and the helpless'; in that sense it succeeded." He paused, considered the Hunter wine, met the barrister's eye, and continued.

"The contract is the thing. The 'Africa Company' might plead that they had fulfilled their contracts as required by the British government; it was not their business as to how many disembarked in Sydney Cove. Lieutenant MacArthur, on the *Neptune* with Elizabeth, his wife, protested. The *Neptune* has the worst record of passenger debilitation and deaths. Concerns were dismissed by the

Neptune's Captain Traille." Wong momentarily paused, remembering the name in the soft voice of the convict presence folding clothes in the laundry.

"We press on. In any case, despite a murder charge in 1792, the shipmasters and the master surgeons were acquitted of responsibility. The details are very interesting; I merely sketch you the picture. D'Arcy Wentworth was assistant to the surgeon on the *Neptune*, entrusted with care of the passengers, but Wentworth made no record of these events—he was in any case almost a convict himself, under probation, unlike MacArthur. There appears to have been much contention on the voyage, as we might expect. Now we come to the detail that may interest you."

"We do indeed," said the barrister. "The Africa Company?"

"Camden, Calvert & King of 11 Crescent, The Minories, East London held the contract for that voyage. This appears to be the Africa Company."

"A British slaving enterprise."

Wong nodded. "Despite the loss of 417 out of 1,406 lives, never mind the continued weakness and debilitation and impact of illness on the original colony, let's say 30–40 per cent of the second influx were lost by neglect. Yet the Africa Company or the slave contractors, Camden, Calvert & King, retained the contract for the next—the 1791 Third Fleet. Would there not be consequences for the masters and owners of certain ships had this occurred today?" The barrister, knowing his history, prodded his companion to be explicit as to where the line was leading.

"Well," said Wong, "Some lines of enquiry deserve pursuing: the conditions to which Africans were subjected under the slave trade. Secondly, the conditions of transported prisoners to Australia, and by whom this transportation was managed. And third, the character of governance, favor, and justice, in Britain and in Sydney during the first twenty years or so. This might interest us—and what interests me in the psychiatric sense is the impact of such events upon the psychological evolution of British and African persons in this colony."

"What must interest us," interrupted the barrister, "is the impact of these events upon the case of Caroline and Michael Camden."

"Caroline *Calvert* and Michael Camden," countered Wong. "In all of this," Wong continued, "the Camden and the Calvert families become persons of interest. It would appear that the unfortunate Caroline's ancestors operated a long-term trade in slave and convict transportation. Her ancestors, who kept a house in Blackheath, England, were a part of maritime services in association with the Africa Company and then the East India Company. This family's involvement does bear inquiry, for reasons that may influence the manner of your defense. You might forgive a Chinese whisper, but this I have heard," muttered Wong, now feeling a little tired of the affair, "from an account of an eyewitness at the time—an Irish woman of, shall we say, convict lineage. It seems that a Captain Calvert landed in Sydney around 1810, and was recognized by a 'Negro' convict who operated a ferryboat. The captain was given a present of an African artifact." Wong sketched it deftly. "It seems there were ten African convicts on the First Fleet, joined by more who survived the *Neptune* and *Scarborough* on the second voyage. You knew that? The artifact was courteously presented to Calvert by a dark man who had survived a Camden-Calvert ship. Calvert, and perhaps his son, for a younger man was with him, made Sydney a link in the Calcutta-East Indies trade. He bought a store near the Quay where he camped between voyages. Handily, nearby was a marine blacksmith, Francis Cox, and the rum store of Dr. D'Arcy Wentworth. There is no evidence to connect Wentworth and Calvert except for Wentworth's presence on the Calvert ship, *Neptune*. And the fact that Wentworth traded as a side business when he wasn't on duty in the hospital, or the courts.

"What might matter is this. Cox, an artisan, became acquainted with Wentworth. The Sydney hospital construction began on Macquarie Street. Wentworth was chief surgeon and a financial partner. I am not interested in those dealings. I am interested in the chemistry. Builders and blacksmiths take an interest in preservatives, as do medical men. Some few years later the man we know as Captain Calvert built a house for his new wife on the cliff above Woolloomooloo. I believe he asked Cox to handle the metalwork, the paint, the oil staining. Calvert demolished his store, using the stone for his elegant house. The house became a location of colonial arts, of exploration and development. Francis Cox, in 1823, built himself two cottages near the quay; his daughter, Sarah, married D'Arcy Wentworth's son, William. These are circumstantial matters. Perhaps. What matters is the nature of Caroline Calvert's illness.

"Caroline Calvert was a direct descendent of the man who named his house after Nigeria, source of 3.5 million slaves—a basis of American industry, of ubiquitous English financial empire. The Australian branch of the Calvert family had good luck in trade and bad luck in health. In each of the generations, records indicate that they suffered pneumonia, migraine, a wasting disease, chronic fatigue and immune system disorders, masked by alcoholism. Breathing troubles were common. Caroline is not the only one in that house who has passed away under indefinable conditions or causes. I am giving you a case of reasonable doubt."

The barrister had begun a slow nod, his glass now emptied.

"Now," smiled the doctor, "I must tell you about your friend and client, Michael Ramsay Camden, who by coincidence of breeding is himself descended from the Africa Company Camdens. Yes, partner of Calvert. And, by the way, a former director of the East India Company carries the name Ramsay. Michael emigrated in 1968, also from Blackheath, England. In due course, making use of his connections, Camden became a partner in a law practice here in the St. James building. He was expert, I believe, in ambiguous criminal cases.

"And this you know. The inherited Victoria Street house was neglected by Caroline's father, not a captain but a risk assessor in the Colonial Mutual Assurance Company. He suffered from depression, an alcoholic. His wife left him. He took in boarders, mostly retired seamen. In 1974, he offered the decaying building for sale, expecting it to be demolished by a drinking associate who knew some property developers. I am told that in 1975, the Building Labourers Federation actions, and those of a Juanita Nielsen, saved this unfortunate heritage item, which would have been better left to die. Caroline's father, instead, died of a stroke."

The barrister added, "Caroline and Michael were inspired by heritage-renovation remorse. She restored the house to period, stripping the '40s linoleum from the floors, putting back the family heirlooms. The deep structure remained."

"Yes," said Wong. "Renovation did not save Michael Ramsay Camden nor Caroline Calvert. What remained in the deep structure was the chemical infusion absorbed into the fabric of the building around 1820. What remained was the artifact given to Calvert by the African, on behalf of 'grateful' passengers."

"And in the artifact, Charles?"

"In the artifact was embedded the first shot of the revenge cycle. You could read up on West African sorcery. We can talk sorcery, but I would say the first shot was projected from the compressed despair of Africans from Nigeria and the western coast transported from home to the eastern coast of America. And how many bodies were transported in the ships of the Africa Company? This is a despair, my dear barrister, that can take an indelible psychic form, which, when taken in by a descendent of Camden, Calvert & King will infiltrate body chemistry and sicken in the interior. Imagine a heavy metal, a spiritualized cadmium, perhaps. Sorcery is sometimes a matter of chemistry. Add this, my dear barrister, to the substance mixed into the oils, the floor stains, the metalwork of Nigeria House by men who knew they were outfoxed by British contract systems, but found a way to quietly pay back the men who transported and abandoned so many souls on the voyages from Portsmouth to Sydney Cove.

"Thus I have been informed; the death of Caroline came from the ships. And from the house. It did not come directly from her husband."

The barrister summed up, inviting Wong now to sample the Brokenwood. He took up the red, glowing glass with a small smile of completion. "And so you would say, Wong, that Calvert was recognized by convicts or ex-slaves in Sydney, and dealt with. He was recognized by convicts or their supporters and dealt with. You suggest a collusion between builders and people with access to chemicals or toxic materials. You cannot prove it was Cox and Wentworth, but you assume that their sense of injustice at the Camden-Calvert trauma may have prevailed. The mode of operation was indirect, surreptitious, but can be proved partially, if the house is toxic from identifiable substances. Whether we can prove intent or not, we can show circumstantial factors."

The barrister arranged a forensic analysis of the house, and the hair of Caroline Calvert-Camden. The results were indicative of a significant presence of lead, arsenic, cadmium, and an unidentifiable toxin. The jury were asked to consider the suggestion that Michael was not directly responsible for the death by asphyxiation or poison of his wife; on the contrary, Ramsay Camden was himself a victim. There is sufficient doubt, pleaded the barrister.

Dr. Wong, under examination, proposed simply that "revenge is a dish best served cold." It was served cold, over four generations. The cause was accumulated vengeance, or justice—progressive, inexorable—accomplished through people shipped in chains from Africa to America, and by the artisan skill of certain pragmatic British men and women shipped in the same chains to a southern hell. This became clear to Camden, though the jury had trouble with it. The good barrister proposed that the exact origins of Caroline Calvert's asphyxiation would require a meticulous investigation; an investigation that was possibly beyond the pale of the New South Wales Government interest. Sometimes, he suggested, it is better to blame someone else, rather than accept one's own complicity in an unfathomable crime.

Sometimes, thought Wong, one can do nothing of consequence to prevent a nemesis. The psychogenesis of an illness can begin in the hold of a ship on the high seas and continue through several generations unabated. Charles left the court and walked along Macquarie Street, gazing meditatively at the remains of the Sydney Hospital.

DAY FOUR

There is no going further, without the fire biting you, you holy souls; so enter into it, and do not be deaf to the singing from beyond … and there were in my mind's eye human bodies which I had seen burnt.

—Canto 27.10

The Subtle Body of a City

There is a place in the mind that collects things. It has an essential place in the survival of humans. In any settlement, a few achieve the skill of the collection of thoughts. A city is a place of gathering. Eventually, perhaps, a city acquires its subtle body. A city that has attained an animating subtle body will live forever, and go on being defended and remembered. A city that has attained a subtle body will have continuity of presence; if destroyed it can rebuild itself from the held experiences of those who dwelt in her. A city that fails is a city that has not attained an autonomous subtle body. The subtle body of the city is composed incrementally by a myriad restorative actions of people who have been burnt, by people who yet retain the whim to create, retain the urge to live. With this in mind, I come finally to Hannah's story.

❦ THE MEMORY TABLE ❦

She was seated, as she often was, at the corner table. She chose it for the circular marble top, the view of the street, and the quick access through the door. She came always at five in the afternoon. She placed the violin case on the bare boards at her feet. She always looked for the row of old copper nails, bright burnished in the floor, counting them quickly. The woman at the bar would smile and bring her tonic water. At this table Hannah kept her memory. The table was her transition point in the movement between two men, the one in the musician's studio and the one in her husband's apartment. Here at this table, she stopped to recover the memory of the body she inhabited when in her husband's domain. The one she left behind each time she walked toward the musician's room. It took her approximately thirty-five minutes to complete the transformation, though she knew it could be done instantly, at the door if necessary. In an emergency.

She had perfected dissolving herself on the walk up the hill so that by the time she reached the musician's door she was almost melted into the specific string piece she was due to play with him. It was the return that troubled her. The return to the carefully constructed body that her husband never really touched and perhaps never saw, intent as he was on engineering the bridges of the city and focussed, as his mind had to be, on tensile strengths, structural reliabilities, sub-city traffic, tunnel infrastructure. He was good man, but had little idea of how to support the tensile strength of the woman who supported his tender and fragile passages. He had a refined sensate grasp of the interior of the city, but not of the interior of a human woman. And for this, Hannah ascended the worn sandstone stairways to MacLeay Street and the music room, carrying the violin case as though it were the coin to give the ferryman.

It is possible that on the return, if she failed to stop somewhere specific, between one man and the other, she would forget who she had to become in the company of a husband. Her husband, from Budapest, as a ten-year-old boy had been dragged out of Hungary one night in 1956, while Russian tanks crushed the scarred stone pavements above where he played and hid in damp tunnels near the Danube. He liked tunnels; tunnels get you to security. He would often quip, "Tunnels maketh the city." This Hannah understood; but a tunnel is not enough.

There was a time, between the hour with the violinist and the return to her apartment on Crown Street, that Hannah would affectionately inject her body with heroin. There is an obscure place where this can be done, especially in the gloom of winter, near the sandstone steps below Victoria Street. If anyone saw her, they would think she was a street worker having a break. The rite of the heroin did something—a kind of secret place of feeling where she could go, somewhere between one man's body and the next, or perhaps something to consolidate the feel of the music and his delicate touch, sending liquid transformations along the veins. Hannah had set herself a project of acquiring reliable access to her internal psychic fluidity.

One day Hannah realized that she did not want the gift of the particular oblivion that heroin offered; she wanted metamorphosis. On that day she went into the hotel and sat at the corner table. There was a nice woman there, an experienced publican who welcomed her with wryly compassionate understanding. From then on, the woman at the bar would smile at Hannah, allowing her the protection she needed.

Hannah gave up heroin and took on the table procedure—the repetition of transformation at the memory table. It gave her security. A landing place. Each period she spent with the musician, the deeper she fell and the further she had to travel back.

Today Hannah realizes that the state into which she falls at the table is *her* moment, not only of security, not only of transformation into her husband's wife, but in fact her liberation. At first she thought that she sat at the table to recover herself after having been so dissolved. But gradually, without the heroin, and with the time to be alone, she felt free from the husband, whom she loves in his way, and she felt free from the musician, whom she loves also. She drew triangles in water on the marble. Two men as two points—and herself at the peak. She imagined herself rising above the tension of the two men. Then the triangle reversed, with herself at the point below, because there was something else below from which Hannah wanted liberation; this was far down beneath the latitudes of her memory. Suffice it to say that some music has the capacity to take us into ancestry, and today with the musician she had felt the touch of an ancestry; then recoiled, cried, and left in shock. Hannah's forgotten history of bleak poverty, then terror, then the shock of annihilation, like a blow, came in upon her at the memory table. Who would not want liberation from such things? Now, at the table, doing her secret work, Hannah could sense, below the bleaching terror and the shock—a long, long way down—the comforting essence of the coasts of a sea that would occasionally, as in a lullaby, murmur forgotten names of the cities of Armenia.

In the musician's room the eastern wall gives a lucid view of harbor. On the north wall, photographed locations of Vienna, from before his parents disappeared. Above the music shelves, a drawing entitled *Kant's Dove*. When she asked what it meant, he told her that Kant said that a bird cannot fly in a vacuum. Wings need resistance, someone to beat against. Hannah realized that the musician took pleasure in the resistances that she brought to him. Her body was like gravity to him. Once, when they fought, he declared his intention, as always, to find the liberation in a situation. "This is the basis of my discipline. Two bodies can meet and recreate havoc, or two bodies, aware of terror, may yet find a way, with care, to a liberation." He told her then, without malice, the events of his parents' timely escape from Vienna in 1936, their ordeals after Vienna, and the reunion that brought him into life and into this room. And to Hannah.

One day, at the memory table, she accepted that her husband's life task was "security," and the musician's, "liberation." This was their gift. It was her task to create a harmony between security and liberation, but how, she did not know— until her memory once again took her somewhere. In memory she felt herself as a small child, clinging to her father's back, then suddenly dropped, wrapped in a black coat, and thrown among trees. This was part of the terror and the shock suddenly given context, something solid to beat against. Then her father in a circle of men. Passionate music from somewhere; then his death, very bluntly done, on a road in Croatia. Always she felt his moment of oblivion. The shock in her own body. Then nothing. Today, in the music room, with the Piazolla tango *Oblivion*, she seared the horsehair and gut of the instrument. The rise and fall, the sustained moment, the silence and coda; the desire that he could elicit from her pulsating, subtle hands. On an occasion such as this, the musician only had to hold her to task—to incarnate the depth of pain, hold her in the trees with the black coat, persuade her not to run with guilt, watch the circle of men, feel the shock and reach a resignation and compassion. With each beat of the wings of Kant's dove, a rush and range of interior and remembered feelings flooded her wrists, her blood, the horsehair and the gut. Today she accomplished this. She descended to the point of her father's death. The loss, her oblivion, their love. In this condition, at the memory table, she began scanning her body, centimeter by centimeter, locating all sexual and infantile psychoneuronic patterns of her long obscured love affair with that oblivion. Today she could actually feel the changes in her limbic system, so sensitive had she become.

And tonight, having sat at the table for a very long time, she is caught by an unfamiliar couple at a nearby table—a slim, dark woman, perhaps Eurasian, with one earring, a black coat slung over her chair, her black leather handbag open at his feet in such a way as to catch attention. The man may have been Magyar; there was a hawkness in his demeanor that held a tautness of space. Their words had precision. Hannah caught the terms "transformational renovation," "synaptic plasticity," "libidinal intent," "enigmatic signifier," and concluded that this unfamiliar couple were neurologists from the hospital. Hannah was caught by the steadiness of gaze between them. It emanated a feeling state that Hannah, even at her table, began to feel tingling in her own skin. It suffused her. It was at that table and at that hour, in the presence of the couple, that a completely different change in her self began. She felt, and allowed, each incremental sensation of her bicameral self to loosen, to loosen as she might systematically relax her finer muscles before she took up her bow and violin.

For years now—between one street and another, one apartment or another, one lover or another—Hannah had been practicing crossing, relocating her self in alternate chambers. Today, the crossing gave way to a steady state at the junction. The steady state became a movement toward lightness and relief. The transformation continued, and Hannah was suddenly, really, alone. There was neither panic nor ecstasy, but rather a quiet jubilation as she sat there listening to every word of the slim, dark woman's quiet suggestive encouragement, reverberating.

Inner-city
Sydney
streetscape.

*Photograph by
Erica Cordell*

It occurred to Hannah only gradually that the woman was speaking within Hannah's body, while of course, at the same time, she sat there with her gaze fixed silently upon the man. The span of Hannah's attention altered, spread itself into the movement between their three bodies. Hannah began witnessing a strangely beautiful negotiation of hope—the creating of love, the love itself, the loss of love, an obliteration that she knew well—and then a tranquillity, a continuously moving river of continuity. Hannah liquefied, slipping between those two instructive beings seated so silently, astutely reorganizing the matter of herself into an entirely new, though nostalgically recognized, matrix of being. Hannah accepted this. The blunt annihilation of her father was laid enough to rest; the terrors of her mother's departure, leaving Hannah among the trees, ceased.

The voice of the woman ceased, though she and the man continued seated at the table, as though composed in a photograph—darkened shadow and a circulation of light. Hannah saw the small, delicate yellow flower and the two glasses of cognac. A small detail in recollection.

She rose from her table, leaving the two doctors at their work, stepping into the street, turning in her husband's direction. She met the familiar sudden fear. She felt remnants of the familiar catch of her throat. But this time the fear slid away. Nothing remained of the trauma of old and broken cities; nothing remained of her subservience to the husband who had done the best he could; nothing remained but a gratitude for the ferocious love of the musician; nothing remained but her own hands on the grave lightness of the violin as she approached the door of the apartment. No, not even the dread of comfort, but the joyful anticipation that on this occasion the person who opened the door to her would be herself, in her own dark and enigmatic grandeur.

It is a wonderful thing to come upon a woman of history recomposed. To come upon a woman who has taken courage, taken time to come alive in the nerves of her body. It is a liberating thing to come into an entirely different composition of the past, utterly connected and utterly grateful for the corner table between worlds, suspended there while two doctors, subtle tutelary spirits, hold their breath, sensing every move Hannah makes as she steps tentatively into her recovered and repossessed being.

Adding Up The Bill

As an individual is not just a single separate being, but by his very existence presupposes a collective relationship, it follows that the process of individuation must lead to more intense and broader collective relationships and not to isolation.

—C.G. JUNG[19]

Things have come to me here at the marble table. Tutelary spirits walk the streets, their faces encrusted with pipe clay, ochre stripes, lapis lazuli. They search out men who walk late at night, women who sit in a corner. Languages overheard from the subtle world.

You sit at a place in this city or that—each city spells a history, each a music—and this, today, is mine. A city may transform, compose, decompose. A city breathes as it can.

From time to time, someone opens their skin and the city of God slips in. John Donne says, "No man is an island, entire of itself—if a clod be washed away by the sea, Europe is the less,"[20] and I say, "Because Dante was washed to the south, Australia is the more."

Hannah, inheriting successive devastations of her homelands, sought hope on this island. There are crimes in this city that go on and on, the consequence of contracts made by men who once ran convict ships. Simple things happen. A woman serves a cognac to a woman and she is grateful. A man teaches violin and a great tradition continues. A small bird gathers itself into a nest at nightfall. Sea levels rise. Fires burn. Our city is surrounded. Rain falls.

END

DISCLAIMER   *Hannah's story is fiction, derived from truth. The hypothetical death of a Caroline Calvert is an invention. The existence and events of Nigeria House are based on a dream. Dr. Wong is a fiction.*

DEDICATION   *Hilde Halpern ex Prague, Anita Bulan ex Armenia, Anna Pollak ex Vienna. Grateful acknowledgments to Erica Cordell, Anne Noonan, Freya Mathews, Jeanette Bourke, Judith Pickering, and to Helen Norton for her painting series on Sydney/Purgatorio; with thanks to Woolloomooloo denizens and the ever gracious proprietors of the East Sydney Hotel.*

Notes

1   John Birmingham, *Leviathan: The Unauthorised Biography of Sydney* (Sydney: Random House, 2000).
2   Tim Flannery, *The Birth of Sydney* (Melbourne: Text, 1999). See page 42, as well as page 319 for Twain's account.
3   Dante, *Divine Comedy*, trans. C. H. Sisson, with an introduction, maps, and the Plan of the Comedy by D. Higgins (Oxford and New York: Oxford World Classics, 1992; reprinted 1998).
4   Charles Darwin, *The Voyage of the Beagle Round the World under Captain Fitzroy R. N.* (London: Folio Society reprint of 1860 text, 2003). Australia section, Chapter 19, pp. 430-450.
5   Robert Hughes, *The Fatal Shore: A History of the Transportation of Convicts to Australia 1787–1868* (London: Pan/Collins, 1988).
6   Darwin, *Voyage of the Beagle*, p. 434.
7   *Ibid.*, p. 450.
8   On Perkins, see book and television series by Rachel Perkins, *The First Australians*: www.sbs.com.au/firstaustralians; on W. C. Wentworth IV, see Australian Institute of Aboriginal and Torres Strait Islander Studies, Canberra (AIATSIS), website www.aiatsis.gov.au/.webloc and links to Wentworth and W. C. Wentworth Obituary by Ward and Dodson, June 2003; on D'Arcy Wentworth, see John Ritchie's biography *The Wentworths, Father and Son* (Melbourne University Press, 1997); on Dexter, see MS 4167 Papers of Barrie #189914, www1.aiatsis.gov.au/finding_aids/MS4167.htm. On Charles Perkins, see www.australianbiography.#189915.
9   Prototypic Sumerian myth of Inanna, left to rot on a hook in the underworld by her sister, Ereshkigal. See Diane Wolkstein and Samuel Noah Kramer, *Inanna, Queen of Heaven and Earth* (New York: Harper & Row, 1983).

10 Susanna De Vries, *Historic Sydney: The Founding of Australia* (Brisbane: Pandanus, 1983). This is a clear sample of the architectural development of the early city. John Birmingham's book *Leviathan* writes another chapter on the callous demolition of the heritage. And then came the more recent (2000) pre-Olympic efforts to redress the balance. See historian Shirley Fitzgerald in Debra Jopson's "Living in the Past," *Sydney Morning Herald*, weekend edition, August 23, 2008, p. 27: www.smh.com.au.

11 See Birmingham, *Leviathan*, on Juanita Nielsen events.

12 Peter Rees, author of *Killing Juanita* (Sydney: Allen & Unwin, 2004), quoted in *Central Sydney*, July 9, 2008, p. 4.

13 For example, Ruth Park's *A Harp in the South*, classic novel of 1930-1940 Irish life in the east Sydney sector.

14 See Glenda Cloughley and development of Gimbutas archeomythos: www.chorusofwomen. org and "Gifts of the Furies."

15 See Giles Clark, "The Animating Body," in *Landmarks: Papers by Jungian Analysts from Australia and New Zealand* (Sydney: ANZSJA, 2001). "Dante's Nest" appears in full in *PAN Journal*, 2009 (online), ed. Freya Mathews.

16 A reference to the ancient generative mysteries associated with Demeter/Persephone, sited at Eleusis, near Athens.

17 Craig San Roque, "A Long Weekend in Alice Springs," in *The Cultural Complex*, ed. Thomas Singer and Samuel L. Kimbles (Hove and New York: Brunner- Routledge, 2004).

18 Hughes, *The Fatal Shore*, pp. 143-147.

19 C. G. Jung, in vol. 6 of *The Collected Works of C. G. Jung*, trans. R. F. C. Hull, ed. H. Read, M. Fordham, G. Adler, Wm. McGuire, 20 vols. (Princeton, NJ: Princeton University Press, 1953-1979), §758.

20 John Donne, from his *Devotions upon emergent occasions* (1624), cited in *Oxford Dictionary of Quotations* (Oxford University Press, 2004), p. 282.

3 Heart and Soul in Shanghai

HEYONG SHEN

Shanghai, one of the world's largest and most famous harbor cities, sits on the Yangtze River Delta on China's eastern coast.[1] Long known to Western travelers as the "Pearl of the Orient," Shanghai has attained symbolic meaning as the gateway to China, an idea embedded in its other, shorter Chinese name, Hu. When people in China listen to someone say "Hu," they hear a word that has the same meaning as door and gate. But this is not just any gate: Shanghai also bears the nickname "Shen," and when people say "Shen" in Chinese, the word they hear has the same meaning as "god" or "divine." Shanghai is therefore not only the way into China for many people, it is also the *godly* way to enter our Asian country—a pearl marking the ideal way to first enter our unique land.

In the year this book is being published, the 2010 World Expo is taking place in Shanghai, its theme the promise that has always attached to the city, especially for those who arrive here from another place in China: "Better City, Better Life." Let us try to understand how Shanghai city has acquired such a reputation.

For one thing, Shanghai, though an elegant metropolis, is a very straightforward one. Its name—a pair of syllable-signs easily expressed in English through eight perfect letters that, when voiced aloud, immediately convey an essential "Chineseness"—is like a mantra for those who pronounce it as their destination. It is one of the few places that conveys, in a primal way to people all over the world, the impression of a great city, a haven of stable cosmopolitanism in the midst of world-wide changes.

The characters that make up the city's name can be rendered in English as City on the Sea, which is a simple enough image. In Chinese, the name is simpler still: the first character, *shang*, literally means not city but "up, on, or above," while the second character *hai,* means "sea." So the city's real name is "On the

滬
hu

申
shen

上海
Shanghai

67

Sea"—about as primal a designation as one could give to any human location. A less terse translation might be, "A place on the upper reaches of the sea," which carries the ancient idea of commerce as a descent to the sea in ships, one that all high cultures have practiced to remain prosperous.

There is yet another idea concealed in the name "Shanghai," however, one that can be accessed if we look and listen more closely to the individual characters that make up the Chinese compound word. The Chinese character for "sea" is made by adding to the pictograph on the right side, *mu*, which indicates "mother," three additional points on the left side to suggest water. The implied meaning is that this gateway city, Shanghai, is not just on the sea but is also contained and nourished by the sea, which has always gestated and supported the city's life. Likewise, *shang,* the character that would signify being "on" (or "built above") this maternal source, also carries fertile associations, for it shares the same pronunciation with another Chinese character, which means "respect," "noble," or "esteem." And indeed Shanghai, the favored son of a great mother culture, has long taken advantage of this special position.

mu

There is no certainty about how long ago Shanghai achieved its privileged status—our knowledge is too shrouded by the interpenetration of archeology and archaic myth that typically encodes Chinese history. But here is what it is possible to say about this undoubtedly rich past. Some relics were left in the area about 6,000 years ago, the most recent period of the Stone Age, and there are several layers showing evidence of ancient civilizations in the Song Zhe and Ma Qiao sites. People at one time seem to have called the place Hu Du, which means "in ancient times." Somewhat nearer to the present day, during the Era of Warring States (476–221 BCE), a legend took hold about the dredging of the Huangpu River by an engineer named Shen, who is supposed to have accomplished this feat around 262 BCE. For a long time, the Huangpu was actually called Shen's River, and the village on its banks, Shen's City. Given the actual size of Shanghai at that time, "City" was honorific: it was only during the elegant, ever-gentrifying Song Dynasty (960–1279 CE) that Shanghai was actually upgraded in both fact and designation from village to market town, and finally obtained its present name. Only then, with its importance as a trade hub fully recognized by the imperial court, did it begin to play an important role in the economy of China. The city proceeded to gain its reputation as the key post at the junction of the river and the sea, and as capital of the southeast.

The Song Dynasty was also the period that inaugurated China's burst of maritime development, which continued unabated through the following centuries up to the mighty navies of the Ming Dynasty (1368–1644 CE). A great number of merchant ships were consequently harbored in Shanghai, which became the major shipbuilding center. As a sign of the importance it had achieved by 1553 CE, the thirty-second year of the reign of Ming emperor, Jiajing, work began on the building of city walls.

Shanghai's prominence did not escape the notice of the major Western powers, which began to demand that it open itself to trade with them. This is the main reason Shanghai became the cosmopolitan city we know today. Nevertheless, it was not until 1843, after the first Opium War, that Shanghai really opened itself to foreign commerce, setting the stage for its evolution into a hub of modern international trade. Today, with a permanent population that has been counted as high as 19.21 million in the city proper,[2] it is truly one of the world's greatest cities. The cosmopolitan quality of its commercial life helps explain how it has managed to establish such an elegant standard of urbane sophistication.

The Chinese way of entering the complex phenomenon that is Shanghai, however, is not through such an entity's worldly status, but by examining its power to affect the heart. The Chinese word *hsin,* often given in English as "heart," is better translated as "the heart-mind." This more clearly conveys the psychological "instrument" used by the Chinese to understand aspects of things that would be barely comprehensible if approached any other way than *heart-fully. Hsin* designates what Jungian analytical psychology would term *the psyche.* It should be understood by people in the West as the involuntary but reliable registrar of experience, the same organ of information that a psychoanalyst relies upon to do deep therapeutic work. *Hsin* suits our approach to Shanghai here because, like an analytic patient immersed in the process of becoming him- or herself, the city is actively engaged in a process of individuation.

The analogue in Chinese culture to individuation is *civilization.* Interestingly, the original pictographic character that became China's basic word for the astonishing phenomenon of civilization literally signified "contained the heart." This is in marked contrast to the Western notion of civilization, which leaves the idea of individual heart out (to return in occasional phrases such as "the heart of the city"). The Western city is a pragmatic reality, built up simply on a geographical and historical notion of what cities have been and presumably will continue to be. This conception is codified in the Roman term *civis,* from which words such as "civil," "civilian," and "civilized" derive. The Chinese notion, by contrast, goes much further than a tradition of courtesy based on sharing common space with others toward the notion of a "same-heart" connection when relating to others. Along with this comes the associated idea of an internal circulation of life-giving energy, based on the city itself having a functioning "heart."

"contained the heart"

What, then, we might ask, is the heart of Shanghai like? Where does its emotional genius reside? At the most basic and fundamental level, as any tourist who consults a decent guidebook will be advised, Shanghai's civic "heart" is the central area comprised of the City God Temple and Yu Yuan Park. This preserve of Shanghai's individuation, containing the primary spirit of the city's humanity, is a throbbing center, always full of people showing uncanny respect for each other as they share this treasured spiritual enclave. There is a local saying that you are not in Shanghai without going to the City God Temple, so let us begin our psychological visit to Shanghai there.

A view of the City God Temple, showing Yu Yuan Park.

Photograph by Liu Zhengjun

Cheng Huang Miao (the City God Temple) was originally called the Jinshan (Gold Mountain) Temple. It was built by Sun Hao (242–284 CE)—the fourth and final emperor of Eastern Wu during the Three Kingdoms period—to honor the spirit of Jinshan, or Gold Mountain, an island off the coast. It did not become the City God Temple of Shanghai until the Ming Dynasty, under its greatest emperor, Yong Le (1402–1424 CE). Cheng Huang literally means City God, and the consecration of this venerable Taoist temple to one "Huang" is meant to convey something analogous to the Western notion of a *genius loci*. In the term "Cheng," however, there is the additional idea of *temenos,* or place of sacred containment. The Chinese character *cheng* means both city and wall. The cultural meaning is therefore "protecting the land," and *huang* refers more concretely to the dry moat that often lay outside city walls in China. This precinct refers to a protection of the city itself, and thus to a god. The ritual and worship of such protective city gods has a long history in China, dating back to the Zhou dynasty, which assumed general state rulership in 1046 BCE.

Two thousand years later, by the time of the Ming dynasty (1368–1644 CE), which succeeded in restoring a remarkable order to China, almost every city in China had erected such a temple precinct for its particular god, with the temple serving as the symbolic microcosm of civic order. It was a place where the harmonious behavior of citizens toward each other would become the model for the way people ought to behave in relation to each other everywhere else in the city, a standard of civility based on *hsin* that everyone could implicitly understand.

The worship of this God of the City in Shanghai reflected the clarity with which the Ming emperors saw that every part of the empire had a deep need for protection and that such protection always starts with the self-restraint of its people and their courtesy toward each other. (A related concept from Jung's analytical psychology would be "introverted feeling.") As avatars of this humanistic, civilized standard, the city deities were frequently conceived to have been originally real persons—heroes and warriors who by dint of their own stature within Chinese civilization had achieved mythic and finally divine status. Three such figures actually have statues in the City God Temple: Qin Yubo (1295–1373 CE), Huo Guang (d. 68 BCE), and Chen Huachen (1776–1842 CE). Each is meant to personify the noble relationship between the city and inhabitants, again conceived as a harmony of *hsin* intent between the inhabitants and this god-ideal, whose spirit has imbued the city's prestigious heroes, now elevated into images of the transcendent God of the City.

Within the grounds of the City God Temple is a winding path. A relatively short walk across the Nine-Winding Bridge, which is surrounded by lotuses, past a special kiosk with eight windows placed in the lotus lake itself, takes the traveler to Yu Yuan Park, the true heart of the city.

Yu Yuan originally designated only an important Temple garden that was established in 1559 CE. The name conveys the Confucian meanings of "pleasing old parents" and "joyous relatives." It is laid out in a typical Chinese garden style. The pavilions, terraces, ponds, and rockery would indeed be something a citizen of Shanghai could show parents and relatives on a visit: the urban landscape architecture is superb, and ranks first among that to be found in the city's gardens. Many traditional stores and shops, with many different kinds of trade and business chambers, are gathered here. It is the typical old-style Chinese market—various, busy, and happy. For a long time, it was the most important marketplace in Shanghai, and one of the most important public places in China.

城市
chen shi

The usual Chinese word for city, *chen shi*, has a character for protected land (*chen*) first and the one for market (*shi*) second. Shanghai's history developed the other way around: the market came first, then the city and wall were built to protect this important site of commerce.

Taken together, the City God Temple and Yu Yuan Park make up the true center of Shanghai, at least from the standpoint of *hsin*. Every time you come here, the first impression will be the people of Shanghai gathered to conduct the important business of their lives, standing in long curving, lines—perhaps waiting to buy the delicious and ever-available *xiao-long-bao*, a special dumpling made in a bamboo steamer, long the traditionally favored "fast food" of the Chinese. Such queues are colorfully described as *ren long*, "people dragon line" (the pronunciation of "bamboo steamer" sounds similar to "dragon" in Chinese). Since the Chinese are accustomed to relating themselves to legends of dragons (for instance, in their New Year's parades), when they queue up for *xiao-long-bao* they are meeting a need not only of the stomach, but also of the soul—the need for a satisfying archetypal image of their great feeling for their culture. The importance of food in Chinese culture hardly needs emphasis, but there is an old Chinese saying that speaks to the spiritual significance of feeding oneself well: "People take food as their heaven."

Nearby, the city's custom takes other forms: the stalls of dressmakers, cobblers, bootblacks, and fortune-tellers, and the old house used for storytelling performances. The streets here are bustling with life, lined with vermeil-colored wooden shop-fronts, with bluestone broad-brushed ground and people coming and going. The ancient part of Shanghai is like a living version of the famous painting in the Beijing Museum, *Qing Ming Shang He Tu* (*Along the River during Qing Ming Festival*),[3] which classically evokes Chinese people carrying out their transactions. Lewis Mumford—the first cultural historian to recognize that a successful city is an extraverted embodiment of the archetype Jung calls the Self—ended his landmark book, *The City in History: Its Origins, Its Transformations, and Its Prospects*, with an image of this painting.[4] An ideal example of what a city can be, it invites us into a place where humanity prevails, informing peoples' everyday lives with the sense of belonging to a greater and wholesome whole. The same idea is epitomized just as unforgettably in real life by the streets of present-day Shanghai, where business is continuously and cheerfully conducted, as if emerging only by the will of its citizens, even the humblest.

Walking Along the Bund

{ FEELING AND COMPASSION }

The three main rivers of Shanghai—the Suzhou, Zhaojia, and Yunzhao—all run into the Huangpu. Since the Huangpu River is connected with the sea as well, it is extraordinarily well positioned to command commerce. At one time, after Shanghai had assumed its status as China's master commercial center, there were three gates to the city, representing the openness of Shanghai's citizens to trade and business.

This attitude survived foreign challenges with a grace born from Shanghai's confidence in its own cultural autonomy. After the First Opium War ended in 1842 with the Treaty of Nanking, and under the impact of the most powerful Western countries of the time, the defeated Chinese were forced to open the country's maritime cities to essentially unlimited trade with the West. Guangzhou, Fuzhou, Xiamen, Ningbo, and Shanghai were all declared international ports that would be wholly open to the outside world. Shanghai, so conveniently located in the middle of the Chinese coastline, was a natural choice to become, in 1843, one of the first open ports. As an English observer put it at the time, speaking for many of his contemporaries:

> Shanghai has occupied the most important place in China's coast for foreign trade; therefore it has attracted public attention. None of the cities familiar to us has had such superiority. In fact, it is the gateway and main entrance of the Chinese Empire.[5]

That gateway to the West was given visible body in Shanghai by the Bund, an area which remains a must-see destination on any first visit to the city. If the City God Temple and Yu Yuan Park carry forward deeply loved traditions rooted in the history of Chinese civilization, the ten-mile-long Bund, facing with confidence the majestic Huangpu River, epitomizes the other vector of Shanghai life. Experiencing the Bund always leaves people with a vivid impression of the elegance with which Shanghai conducts business.

Soon after the British, French, and Americans arrived with their naval forces, they seized the Bund as one of their "leased territories," or Concessions.[6] But because of the way the West treated this new "territory," particularly during the earlier years of Shanghai's recent history, the "Pearl of the Orient" became for a period the shady haven of diligent exploiters. By the beginning of the twentieth century, the city had ironically acquired the reputation of harboring kidnappers (think of the term "Shanghaied"). This "exotic" history must, however, be put into perspective with Shanghai's overall economic success, which for the most part has been spectacular, showing a continuous increase in manpower, material resources, and property values.

A view of the Bund at night, showing new developments alongside the famous old buildings.

Photograph by Liu Zhengjun

Stretching from the Bund to Yangjing Creek (the boundary river of the territories "leased" by the Western powers) is the Shi-Li Yang Chang, a stretch of ten miles of foreign businesses familiarly called the Yang Chang. Nanjing Road, its most well-known street, was first created by British merchants as Paike Lane, a horse trail (to Chinese ears, "Paike" was a homonym of the English "park"). There the British opened the Shanghai Horse Racing Club in 1848, and for a time Nanjing was Ma Lu, the "Horse Road." The district quickly became a showcase for the possibilities of commerce; its stores dazzled the eye with products from abroad, the fantastic array of commodities that Victorian-era trade could assemble. It remains the major shopping street in Shanghai today.

Before the Cultural Revolution, famous shops and well-known traditional stores were gathered into the Yan Chang, including the Wang Yutai Tea House and the Shao Wangshen shop, with its 100-year history of importing from the cities of Ningbo and Shaoxing. During this phase of the city's development, some of its street names and its local brand names became recognized all over the country. Shanghai was a metropolis for foreign adventurers—the city with the best clothes, queen of the material world, with the "number one" downtown of all cities.

Because of their extensive links with international markets, the "leased territories" in China made big strides toward prosperity, which of course encouraged the Western powers to rationalize their intrusions upon China's traditional autonomy. Shanghai, however, really did thrive as an international city. New developments and undertakings made Shanghai the leader among Chinese cities in acquiring modern advantages. As its chronicler, Ye Shuping, has noted, Shanghai was the first Chinese city to introduce the use of gas, electric lights, running water, motor cars and trams; to import telephones and telegrams; and to have modern newspapers, radio stations, educational organizations, and publishing houses. As he points out, "Most of the new things of modern times were first born [in the Leased Territories of Shanghai] and then spread to the whole country."[7]

In the formation of any city's appearance, the look of streets, roads, and buildings are all decisive. Around 1870, a new kind of brick and wood residence, known as the Shikumen house, began to appear in the Shanghai Concessions. The layout, which lined many Chinese lanes, followed the example of joined European row houses, but its structure of separate units evolved out of the traditional Chinese Siheyuan courtyard, with houses on four sides. The style of the Shikumen house was also influenced by the architecture of city dwellings south of the Yangtze River.

On the other side of Shanghai, along the Suzhou River, one would have encountered a totally different situation—a large, depressing slum. Poor people, who during the day toiled as laborers and rickshaw men in the Yang Chang and other leased territories, lived there with their families in appalling conditions.

The Bund and Nanjing Road are not leased territories anymore, and with so many of their buildings having been torn down, the evidence they once bore of the consequences of Western domination of Chinese commercial life is itself now a historical memory. Today we can no longer see Yangjing Creek; the waterway was filled and it became Yanan Road. But some of the colorful language of those years, the Pidgin dialect known as Yangjing Bang English (meaning "English spoken around Yanjing Creek") is still in use, even internationally—including the familiar greeting "long time no see."

George Bernard Shaw visited Shanghai in 1933 and was warmly welcomed. He seems to have experienced the city as a repository of all the archetypes. When someone gave him as a gift a set of clay figures showing the faces of different characters from the Chinese opera, he looked at the images of the warrior, the vivacious woman, and the evil man and noted that these were eternal human roles that we all carry deep within our minds.[8] But another famous westerner, Albert Einstein—who came to Shanghai twice in the course of his travels to Japan in 1922[9]—found himself focusing on how difficult the lives of the people were, how hard they worked for very little money. The shadow side of the glory of the Bund was clearly not lost on the creator of the theory of relativity.

Such negative developments had not escaped notice within the country, where there were active movements to take back China for the Chinese. In October 10, 1919, Sun Yat-sen and his followers founded the Kuomintang (the Nationalist Party) in Shanghai. Two years later, the Communist Party had its first conference at Wangzhi Road 106, in the French-leased territory of Shanghai, with twenty-one members in attendance, including Chen Duxiu (often described as the founder of the Chinese Communist Party) and Mao Tse-Tung. Both of the political parties that would dominate the fate of modern China in the twentieth century were thus founded in Shanghai in the shadow of the Bund.

Under the powerful influence of the West, however, Shanghai had embraced a third ideology, modernism itself, and today it is also heralded as a postmodern masterpiece. Its impressive buildings constitute a rich collection that evokes the history of Western architecture—from Renaissance and Baroque, to New Classicism, Eclecticism, and modern skyscraping. (Most of the buildings house world-famous international firms and banks, and Westerners have long called its Bund "the Wall Street of the East," though in truth this slights it, for the Bund is far grander than its New York counterpart.) This kind of openness is perhaps the most enduring aspect of the city, and may be a spiritual outgrowth of its geography and history. Once again, we can find anticipations in the Chinese names for the places we have been describing. For instance, Wai Tan, the Chinese name for the Bund, contains the embodied meaning "outside shoal." It suggests for me the way this part of Shanghai has always been open to currents from outside China.

For the Chinese today, the Bund represents the checkered history of Shanghai's dealings with foreign powers, and its buildings concretize both the honor and dishonor of contending commercially with Western influences for more than 150 years. Over the course of its history since 1843, Shanghai has survived by becoming an international metropolis, one that has absorbed but has not been conquered by its influences, and that has finally surmounted their spheres of authority over it.

Shanghai, like New York, has perennially been a community of immigrants from other places. Its present-day inhabitants are mostly from other provinces and areas of China, but as in the past, citizens from many countries and all continents still come to Shanghai to live and work. Those who stay for long enough start to call themselves "Shanghailanders." In the 1920s and 1930s, for example, almost 20,000 Russian Jews and so-called White Russians fled the newly established Soviet Union to take up residence here. Russian-born people at one time constituted the second-largest foreign community in the city.

One consequence of fostering the development of an immigrant society is the inevitable amalgamation of foreign customs into the traditions by which a city lives. To form its own spirit, a city must have a process of inner cohesion as well as an ability to allow influences from the rest of the world without cultural injury. In the present-day downtown, we can take the Xujiahui district, the site of an impressive metro station, as the symbol of this quality of Shanghai.

Xujiahui was originally the joining place of the Fahua and Zhaojia rivers, but the name given it means "Xu Family Gathering"—after a particularly important family in the development of this aspect of Shanghai's cosmopolitanism—while the character *xu* carries as well the meaning of proceeding gently, with slow steps, so as to allow or permit promise and hope. Today, Xujiahui Cathedral is the biggest church in Shanghai, and from it one can walk to the cemetery of Xu Guangqi, which today is a public park. Nearby, located right on the meridian line, is the old Shanghai observatory.

Xu Guangqi (1562–1633), a Chinese scientist of the Ming Dynasty, lived and was buried here after his death. The first to learn western sciences systematically, and together with the pioneering Jesuit missionary, Matteo Ricci (1552–1610), who had managed to gain acceptance at the court of the emperor, he translated Euclid's *Elements of Geometry* into Chinese in 1607. Xu also wrote the sixty volumes of *Nong Zheng Quan Shu*, one of the earliest and most comprehensive texts of agriculture in China. We cannot overstate his importance in facilitating communication between East and West, which led to Leibniz's eventual introduction to the *I Ching* by Father Jouvet—a decisive factor in C. G. Jung's later reception of this book into his psychology.[10]

Xu Guangqi's name—of which, as a culture-bringer to Shanghai, he was fully worthy—means "beginning with light." His nickname, however, was Yuanhu, which holds the meaning of "beginning of Shanghai" as well, since *hu* is the short name for Shanghai. Derived from a classical Chinese character, *hu* refers to a kind of bamboo paling joined by rope that local fishermen used to catch fish and shrimp in the river, a simple and natural tool. The three main components of this character are the traditional pictographs for water, bamboo, and fish. "Water" can be related to the unconscious aspect of commerce, the flow of water being like the unpredictable flow of trade. As a tool for fishing in the water, *hu* is made of flexible bamboo, and of course bamboo is an important Chinese symbol. Empty inside, this wood is often described by Daoist philosophy as "empty at heart," which summons the Buddhist notion of emptiness as well as the recognition of the reliable interdependence of things when we do not become attached to their separate forms. *Hu* is thus an open culture structure, renewed not by will or "intention" but by the natural tides of existence itself. Since bamboo is used a fishing rod and fish are caught unpredictably, *hu* also has the symbolic meaning of chance, chance meeting, and abundance. Finally, the character *hu* contains the pictographs for gate and city, once again implying Shanghai's ability to attract and catch such chances, for as the gateway of China, it is open to people's coming and going.

hu

"gate" "city"

Looking at Pudong

{ THE CHANGES AND THE CHANCE }

There is an ambivalence that attends the excitement of arriving on the doorstep of a great city. Well before Shanghai reached its present eminence, this was captured by a T'ang poet writing about another city, then the imperial capital. His lines speaks to the experience of a visitor to Shanghai today, who, while sipping fine wine in an elegant hotel lobby, may withdraw into fantasies of a simpler, more natural life than that promised by the gentrified Shanghai:

> Red leaves are fluttering down the twilight
> Past this arbour where I take my wine;
> Cloud-rifts are blowing toward Great Flower Mountain,
> And a shower is crossing the Middle Ridge.
> I can see trees colouring a distant wall.
> I can hear the river seeking the sea,
> As I the Imperial City tomorrow— [*sic*]
> But I dream of woodsmen and fishermen.[11]

Walking through the Bund, one can appreciate how the many years that Shanghai flourished as a world financial capital, a time marked also by its exploitation by the West, have given the city a foreign flavor and feeling-tone. But to gain a perspective on Shanghai as China's greatest city today, one must stand at the center of the Bund and look east; from this perspective, the whole Pudong district is visible.

Pudong displays an amazingly wide range of super-tall skyscrapers, fully poised to challenge any arrangement of buildings in the West. The most prominent examples include the Jin Mao Tower and the Shanghai World Financial Center, which at 492 meters is the tallest skyscraper in the mainland of China and the second-tallest manmade structure in the world (the tallest, presently, is a tower in Dubai). The Oriental Pearl Tower, the Jin Mao Building, and the Shanghai World Financial Center form Shanghai's Pudong skyline, whose unusual yet interlocking shapes make it clear why this new financial district has already attained global recognition as a center of culture and design. It is the face of the new development of Shanghai, which only began in 1990.

In preparation for the World Expo in 2010, Shanghai has for over a decade been engaged in continuous improvement. Present-day Shanghai is the very

A view of
Shanghai's
new Pudong
district.
*Photograph by
Liu Zhengjun*

heart of commerce and finance in China, the "showpiece" of the world's fastest-growing economy. The Chinese expression for the theme of the World Expo held in Shanghai is *Chenshi, rang shenghuo geng meihao*: "City, let life be more beautiful." What is meant by this phrase is best conveyed in a sentence from the Istanbul Declaration on Human Settlements, issued at the United Nations Conference on Human Settlements (Habitat II): "Our cities must be places where human beings lead fulfilling lives in dignity, good health, safety, happiness and hope."[12]

As with most cities today, Shanghai has many problems that affect the chances for a better life: congestion, pollution, the wealth gap, housing price inflation, the difficulty and high cost of accessing medical services, corruption, crime, and social conflict. It is because of such problems and related disorders that Expo 2010 proposes—and would like Shanghai to potentially symbolize—the concept of a City of Harmony.

He xie (harmony) is a core proposition of Chinese philosophy, based on such spiritual principles as *zhong sheng* (centered and straight) from the *I Ching* and *zong jie* (attained in due measure and degree) from the Confucian classic *The Doctrine of the Mean*. Chinese philosophy has always understood that harmony is multidimensional, something that happens not only between people and not only between the human being and heaven, but also within the individual—in the way that heart-mind establishes a link between body and soul.

In the first chapter of *The Doctrine of the Mean*, we read:

> While there are no stirrings of pleasure, anger, sorrow, or joy, the mind may be said to be in the state of equilibrium. When those feelings have been stirred, and they act in their due degree, there ensues what may be called the state of harmony. This equilibrium is the great roof from which grow all the human actings in the world, and this harmony is the universal path which they all should pursue. [13]

Again we come back to the central idea informing Shanghai's ambition as a city, that the starting and crucial point of civic harmony lies in the human heart. Only the people, with their hearts, can make a great city a place of human betterment.

The Chinese in Beijing like to refer to themselves as "living at the foot of emperor," but the people of Shanghai like to say that "we are close to the world." The city and its people have long cultivated an attitude of openness to others, and have embraced the open-heartedness that is created in everyone around them as a result.

Gu Hongming (Thomson, 1857–1928), who was the supervisor of Huangpu River Authority and supervisor of Shanghai's Nanyang University (Shanghai Jiaotong University today) from 1905 to 1910, summarized the characteristics of the Chinese character and Chinese civilization in his paper "The Spirit of the Chinese People" (1914): depth, broadness, and simplicity. [14] These core principles have informed Chinese civilization throughout its history, and they are not absent in Shanghai. But among the people of Shanghai, delicacy and gentleness have been added, and to attain these qualities and employ them in daily life is the goal of the civic individuation of our city.

Our nickname, Shen, is related to *kun*, the second hexagram of the *I Ching*, which carries the symbolic meaning of the feminine principle of receptivity, as imaged by earth, living place, and gate. As ever, though, Chinese language is paradoxical and suggests its own opposite meanings. The original form of the character of *shen* was made from a pictographic image for lightning. Lightning, often conceived as masculine, was the symbol for the ancient people of a god. So in the Chinese language, Shen, the nickname of Shanghai, though related to feminine receptivity, also accepts the intervention of a masculine god in human affairs—suggesting that Shanghai is a place where the people are ready for new spirit to strike. Within the symbol system of the *I Ching*, *shen* is related to thunder and *kun* to the earth. When combined, these two image-concepts create the Fu hexagram, 24, which Richard Wilhelm, who made his translation in the first years of the century while living in Tsingtao, renders as "return" or "the turning point." The meaning of this moment in our lives, he thought, was that "Return leads to self-knowledge." As he put it:

> The hexagram of Return, applied to character formation, contains various suggestions. The light principle returns: thus the hexagram counsels turning away from the confusion of external things, turning back to one's inner light. There, in the depths of the soul, one sees the Divine, the One. It is indeed only germinal, no more than a beginning, a potentiality, but as such clearly to be distinguished from all objects. To know this One means to know oneself in relation to the cosmic forces. For this One is the ascending force of life in nature and in man. [15]

All of these overtones of *shen*—receptivity, thunder, and return—are related to one place in Shanghai that has always been open to intellectual currents but has also always returned to its own Chinese principles, Fudan University (founded in 1905). One of the oldest and most prestigious universities in China, Fudan preserves some of the intellectual implications of Shanghai's tradition of openness to fertilizing currents. The two characters that make up the name were chosen from the Confucian Classics: "Itinerant as the twilight, sun glows and moon luminesces." The university motto comes from *The Analects*: "*Buo xue er cu zhi, qie wen er jin si*," which means "to learn extensively and adhere to aspirations, to inquire earnestly and reflect with self application."

Fudan

In the Great Commentary to the *I Ching*, we read, "Fu indicates the free course and progress. ... He will return and repeat his proper course; in seven days comes his return—such is the movement of the heavenly revolution. ... Do we not see in Fu the heart of heaven and earth?" [16] The human being who has *realized* his or her humanness, in other words, is the heart of the heaven and earth. It is in just this spirit that Shanghai continues to develop as a human habitation.

Notes

1   The Yangtze River, which originates from the Qinghai-Tibet Plateau, rushes down for thousands of miles and finally opens into the Pacific Ocean.

2   "Shanghai's Permanent Population Approaches 20 Mln," *People's Daily Online*, 20 February 2010, available at http://english.peopledaily.com.cn/90001/90782/90872/6897139.html.

3   *Along the River during Qing Ming Festival* is a view of the Song Dynasty capital of Bianjing. It is attributed to Zhang Zeduan (1085–1145 CE).

4   (New York: Harcourt, Brace, and Jovanovich, 1961).

5   Quoted in Ye Shuping, *Old Fashions of Shanghai* (Beijing: Beijing Art Press, 1998), p. 121.

6   The term is itself a concession to the power realities of the colonizing impulse; under international law, it means "a territory within a country that is administered by another entity than the state which holds sovereignty over it," that state having "conceded" that right to a another power, usually after military intimidation. The English Concession was established in Shanghai in 1846, and the French Concession in 1849. See the useful Wikipedia article http://en.wikipedia.org/wiki/Concession_(territory) (accessed 18 June 2010).

7   Shuping, *Old Fashions of Shanghai*, p. 123.

8   Kay Li, "Globalization versus Nationalism: Shaw's Trip to Shanghai," *SHAW: The Annual of Bernard Shaw Studies* 22 (2002): 149-170.

9   Danian Hu, *China and Albert Einstein: The Reception of the Physicist and His Theory in China, 1917-1979* (Cambridge, MA: Harvard University Press, 2005).

10   Joe Cambray, "The Place of the 17th Century in Jung's Encounter with China," *Journal of Analytical Psychology* 50 (2007): 195-207.

11   Hsü Hun, "Inscribed in the Inn at T'ung Gate on an Autumn Trip to the Capital," in *The Jade Mountain (Three Hundred Tang Poems)*, trans. Witter Bynner from the texts of Kiang Kang-Hu (Garden City, NY: Anchor Books, 1964), p. 26.

12   United Nations Conference on Human Settlements (Habitat II), "Istanbul Declaration on Human Settlements," June 14, 1996, General Assembly document A/Conf.165/14, available at http://www.un-documents.net/ist-dec.htm.

13   Tsze-sze, *The Doctrine of the Mean*, trans. James Legge, in *Hanying Shishu (The Chinese/English Four Books)*, ed. Liu Chongde and Luo Zhiyu (Changsha: Hunan People's Press, 1992), pp. 25-26.

14   "The Spirit of the Chinese People" was written in English for the Oriental Society of Peking (1914). Available at http://en.wikisource.org/wiki/The_Spirit_of_the_Chinese_People/The_Spirit_of_the_Chinese_People (accessed 19 June 2010).

15   Richard Wilhelm, *The I Ching, or Book of Changes*, Bollingen Series XIX (Princeton, NJ: Princeton University Press, 1977), p. 505.

16   "Treatise on the Thwan," in *Zhou Yi, Book of Changes*, ed. Tai Yi and Tai Shi, English translation for this bilingual edition by James Legge (Changsha: Hunan People's Press, 1993), p. 111.

4

São Paulo: Harlequin City

GUSTAVO BARCELLOS

Historical sites, architecture, art, food, music, shopping, festivities, fashion, hotels—so says the front cover of a tourist guide to the city of São Paulo. Yes, but all of that can be found in every other big city in the world. The following pages are not a tourist guide at all; rather, they are a meditation on the city of São Paulo—its soul and spirit, old and new, past and present—a meditation that seeks to make us feel what it's like to be a big metropolis in the "deserts" of South America, as a Brazilian poet once said.

São Paulo is a city full of contradictions, difficulties, surprises, and peculiar ways of being. Big, gray, difficult to navigate, yet full of life and death, São Paulo is more than a sea of buildings and more than a spread-out car city. Metropolises are not merely bigger suburbs or "larger" small towns, said Jane Jacobs in the 1960s—they are a totally different organism. They are passion, inspiration, enthusiasm—and a lot of problems.

São Paulo is a metropolis: cosmopolitan, modern, chaotic. I was born here, and apart from some years long ago when I lived in New York, I have always lived, loved, and worked in São Paulo. It is a very complex place, full of poetic paradoxes: gigantic and small, beautiful and ugly, gray and colorful, rich and poor, sweet and sour, soul and spirit, nature and cement—but, above all, people: faces and languages from all over the world, and the energy of immigrant fantasies. São Paulo is dense fog, monotone drizzle, sinuous streets and alamedas, immense avenues, dark alleys, vibrations, noise, skyscrapers, bars, creatures that deal and sell everything in the downtown nights, including, of course, themselves. There is everything in São Paulo. São Paulo is like the whole world, says another poet.

Largo do
Paissandu.

*Photograph by
Carlos Moreira*

São Paulo is the heart of Brazil, the engine, the economic and cultural nerve center of the country, the source of its lifeblood, strength, deepest and fiercest lyricism—and the place where you find the best mirror of what anthropologists and artists call Brazilian civilization: the "avalanche of ethnicities," in the words of Roger Bastide; the amalgam of people, the poetics of miscegenation and mixing. Harlequin São Paulo—mosaic of peoples, mosaic of dreams, mosaic of construction. A whole that lacks cohesion. The common place of so many diverse people.

———

A song composed in 1978 by hugely popular Brazilian singer and songwriter Caetano Veloso, called Sampa, celebrates a mythic corner in the Old Center of the city, where Avenida São João meets Avenida Ipiranga. This intersection is famous for having been the epicenter of a downtown that, from the 1940s through the 1970s, was the meeting place for artists, bohemians, musicians, intellectuals, businessmen, and other very interesting people. Bar Brahma, for example, founded in 1948 right on that famous corner, used to attract those people, and is still today a favorite spot now that the whole area has been revitalized. These avenues were important arteries for shopping, cinema, and dining over a long period of time—and even today you can watch the sea of people of every kind strolling amid the stores, businesses, and cars; you can feel the intensity of both past and present. Visiting São Paulo, no one should miss that corner.

The song begins by singing that something happens in the composer's heart only when he crosses that symbolic corner. The song itself became a sort of popular hymn to the city of São Paulo. Everybody knows how to sing it, and the lyrics are a wonderful reflection of a deep feeling for São Paulo. At the same time, it is amazing and meaningful that this best-known song about São Paulo, the very one the *paulistanos* have chosen to be their perfect song, was in fact composed by someone not from São Paulo, but from Bahia. This already says a lot about São Paulo.

Something happens in my heart as well when I reflect on the city of São Paulo, my city—walking around it, recalling it or seeing its images. The important axis between city and soul, opened up by archetypal psychology—that profound intertwining of *anima* and *urbe*—can be felt by the experience of the soul as well as by the experience of the city. Soul leads me to the city, a place of encounters, a place of culture and history, and the city leads me back to soul, the place where all this becomes image. The city is a grand metaphor for the collective psyche. The city is simultaneously the place and image of the soul. Here I am following Caetano Veloso's suggestion in his famous song, and letting the heart open to the city and its soul. Thus, *anima* and *polis* can be perceived first of all as experiences of the heart, and heart then is a necessity for this approach to the theme of city. This indefinable (some)thing in the heart, the motive for these remarks, is then charged with emotion. I am seeking a reflection on the emotional experience of being and living in the city of São Paulo that is not a subjective report, but much broader.

———

What, then, is a possible poetic response to the city of São Paulo, where souls mix and merge, linked indecipherably, and only a poetic response can express it? How to grasp an identity so furtive, so fluid and multifaceted, so swift and mutating, and one that affirms and insinuates itself into every aspect of the mosaic of people and things, frozen in the daily dance on its corners? An identity that affirms its non-definability in every vortex, every human opening, every concrete subtlety. How else to express it except in a multifaceted mode— intermittent, vast, like a bursting noise, an uproar? Our eardrums endure it and cooperate with this city as much as our hands that make it—they continuously construct and deconstruct what the city creates, inside and outside—the noise of cars, people, speech, machines. São Paulo, city of conversation.

The image of the harlequin, character from the Italian *commedia dell'arte*— a figure dressed in multicolored diamonds; part animal, part rogue, part comedy, and part farce, a trickster—but this time a mestizo harlequin, was the choice of Mario de Andrade (1893–1945), the great poet, novelist, and essayist of São Paulo, for expressing the evolutions and textures of his city. The feeling of the harlequin runs throughout his verses, which run throughout the city and its mysteries, which run through his readers in all their commotion. The city's multiple angles find their complete translation in this image. It's not a patchwork, a mere agglomeration, amalgam, but a vestment—pieces of colored fabric, stage image, the harlequin mantle: costume and masquerade, pattern and pantomime, actor and soul. Shards of colored glass. We are all actors in São Paulo, a stage for various fantasies of being and becoming, playing out the fictions that the city elaborates for us.

But Mario de Andrade himself is really the most perfect translation of the city of São Paulo. The city follows him throughout his poetic course. It is he who emanates the "harlequin city," Baudelaire's *cité pleine de rêves* [dream-filled city]. It is he who spies the "tangled corrupt form / human that bellows and applauds itself / And acclaims itself and falsifies itself and hides itself. And dazzles..." ("Meditação sobre o Tietê," [Meditation on the Tietê], 1945).

It is impossible to comprehend Mario de Andrade without São Paulo; equally impossible to comprehend São Paulo without Mario, said Roger Bastide, the enlightened French anthropologist who lived among us (mostly in São Paulo), studied Mario's poetry, and contributed so much to our self-understanding. Bastide dared to say that the city's streets are kisses to mark Mario's lips—a dazzling image. The publication of *Pauliceia Desvairada*, Mario's first book of modernist poetry, for me marks the second "founding" of São Paulo—the modern São Paulo, the big city. Mario is as grand and scary as it is. It's no accident that a lovely, imposing building in the old downtown area pays due homage to the city's greatest poet: the Mario de Andrade Library. He, more than anyone, converts modern São Paulo into a living poem. In his poetry, the platitudes about the city unravel and we see the landscape as if for the first time.

———

Its amplitude, the dimension of the extraordinary, is the hallmark of São Paulo. The numbers, for example, go crazy in São Paulo: It is the largest city in Brazil and the entire southern hemisphere. It is the nineteenth-wealthiest city in the world, and it alone represents 15% of the Brazilian GDP and 36% of all goods and services produced in the state of São Paulo. It is headquarters to 63% of the multinational companies operating in Brazil. It has the largest fleet of taxis in Latin America, and the biggest fleet of helicopters in the world. It has six million vehicles—an average of one vehicle for every two residents. It is the third-largest city in the world in number of buildings. There are over 12,000 restaurants, of 52 different ethnic cuisines. There are 88 museums, 120 theaters, 39 cultural centers, 52 parks, and 60 shopping centers. São Paulo has the largest bus station in South America, where 90,000 people per day circulate.

It is the most multicultural city in the country, with the largest populations of those of Italian, Japanese, Spanish, and Lebanese origins outside their respective countries. Today, the city's Japanese community is the largest outside Japan, and 60% of São Paulo's inhabitants have some Italian ancestry, allowing it to count more people of Italian descent than any city in Italy, including Rome. The population of São Paulo is 11 million. The greater metropolitan region, which includes several cities, has 21 million inhabitants. Moreover, many of the regions close to São Paulo are in a process of merging with the capital to form the Extended Metropolitan Complex, whose population surpasses 29 million, comprising the first macro-metropolis in the southern hemisphere. Together, these 65 municipalities have 12% of Brazil's population. It's impossible to even imagine such enormities. And they are what we live.

São Paulo is in Brazil, but it can't be compared to any other city in the country. It isn't the official capital. It is not graced with the natural, exuberant landscape of many other places in Brazil, such as Rio de Janeiro, with its sumptuous topography and the imperial past impregnating its soul and mores. It is not like Manaus, in the midst of the Amazon forest, sitting on the margins of that immense and mysterious river. Not like Salvador, Bahia, where you find the key to understanding Brazil and its colonial roots, its African heritage, its polytheistic religious torment. Not like Brasilia, the political capital, with its architectural wonders by world-renowned Brazilian master Oscar Niemeyer and his light, mystical poetics of power. São Paulo is a human construction.

Some of my friends and acquaintances compare São Paulo to New York, Los Angeles, Paris, Tokyo, or Rome. This is common in the conversation of those from outside São Paulo. But this is a simplification. The mystery of São Paulo is in only appearing to be similar to all these cities, but not really being so; it is remembering all these mirrors at the same time and not really fitting into any of them. São Paulo is on the other side of the mirror of its vanity—the converse of the converse of the converse, as the song says.

The most interesting thing about this city is its cultural diversity. The whole world is here; the entire country is here. All the faces. People from everywhere make up this place. They come from elsewhere and lend São Paulo its particular cosmopolitan dimension.

One can eat anything one wants, for example. Food is very important in São Paulo, and the city itself is a major devourer. There is the best sushi outside Japan, the best pizza outside Italy, Asian, Slavic, Hungarian, French, Vietnamese, Indian, Arab, Greek, and regional cuisine from every corner of the country, better than at its origins—pieces of the world, pieces of Brazil. Fast food, sophisticated restaurants, bar food, luncheonettes, bakeries, bistros, barbecues, fried pastry at the outdoor market, cafes—all these are evident.

Viaduto Santa
Efigênia, 1984.
*Photograph by
Carlos Moreira*

But, in reality, the city devours itself—voluptuousness again. *Paulicéia*, the "large mouth of a thousand teeth," says Mario de Andrade. Building up and breaking down is what happens here. There is always a "new city" in the making—the centers move rapidly; new centers arise as the advancing of multiple dislocations of interest; houses are demolished and replaced by high-rises; streets change their personalities, their frequency, their ways of being—everything ages quickly or comes back years later with a new face. Urban renewal takes place destructively, and the city never stays the same. Every generation knows a new and different city.

———

As I write now, the city is celebrating 455 years of existence. New and old at the same time, *puer* and *senex*, there is a face looking to the past and to the very soil on which it was first dreamed and built; and a face constantly looking to the future, obsessed by where a modern metropolis can go with all its fascination and all its problems. Soul is on both sides, and that is the difficult thing: you need many eyes to see São Paulo on the level of the soul.

It all started with a very small settlement and a very big dream. Though it was a Christian dream, it had archetypal roots, and those are the ones that link us with the utopia of a new world, a heaven on earth, a New Jerusalem.

The primitive nucleus that gave birth to the city of São Paulo was a school, settled on the Piratininga plateau by Portuguese priests, members of the Society of Jesus of Ignacio de Loyola. They came to Brazil to introduce Catholicism to Indian soil. Among them, a highly gifted priest named Father Joseph Anchieta (1534-1597) played an important part. He had studied at Coimbra University, was an excellent Latinist, fluent in Portuguese, Castilian, and Latin, and years later managed to compile a grammar of the old Tupi linguistic family in order to communicate better and teach the Indians. He wrote famous poems to the Virgin Mary in the sands of a beach (another wonderful image). He and his colleague Father Manuel da Nobrega, with the help of the Indians and the Portuguese, traversed the steep cliffs that separate the inland from the coast—which took them days at that time; today it is a forty-minute drive—and celebrated a Mass upon their arrival, on January 25, 1554, on a hill they chose in between the Tietê, Anhangabaú, and Tamanduateí rivers. That is the official date for the foundation of the city. Two years later, they built a church and a school to catechize the Indians. Around that little construction of wattle-and-daub, that little school, the village of São Paulo de Piratininga sprang up. Fluidity has always permeated the nature of the city, since São Paulo was deliberately born on a hill between rivers, in the middle of waters, surrounded by fertile lowlands—and frogs.

São Paulo was not founded on the tumulus of a father of a family or a clan, on no heroic deed, no literal battle or heroic figure alone to be honored—although we can see some heroism in conquering the difficult mountains separating the shore from the plateau, and heroic too is the whole project of sailing the Atlantic in the mid-sixteenth century to a new, unexplored, and strange land to convert some millions of pagan Indian souls to Christian truth. This is called the mission.

But, more importantly, the city was not founded on the heroism of the mission alone, but upon the dream of education. On a deeper level, I believe the flowing imagination that founded the city of São Paulo had more to do with conversion and education, and we will see that years later it reappears with yet another important school. The very saint to whom the village was consecrated is Saint Paul, the apostle of conversion.

If an erotic imagination pervades great cities, as James Hillman says, in São Paulo I take that to mean that Eros, much more than Hero, is present when you feel the urge to bring people closer to your vision, closer to what you most love, to see things as you see them.

During its first three hundred years or so, due to historical, geographical, and economic reasons that are too many to list here, it was nothing other than a nearly invisible village. The situation began to change in 1828, when the Law School of the Largo São Francisco was founded. The importance of its founding is that it marks the inauguration of the oldest institution of higher legal education in the country, filling a gap in Brazil's higher education system at a time when young people normally had to go to Europe to study. This resulted in a radical change, due to the large influx of professors and students, cultured people, many with artistic temperaments. It marks a turning point in São Paulo's history. Various writers, painters, and even presidents came from there—José de Alencar, Bernardo Guimarães, Di Cavalcanti, Monteiro Lobato, for example—and, very importantly, Álvares de Azevedo, who, along with his colleagues at the academy, all bohemians and poets, invented the city of the taciturn romanticism of dim lights and unhealthy souls, venting their spleens in the tropics of the eighteenth century.

Well, but that's biography—and actually we want to escape biography, lest the soul become frozen in literal history. We want soul. History, anyway, or empirical anamnesis, tells us that there are two emblematic schools casting deci-

Anhangabaú,
1980.
Photograph by
Carlos Moreira

sive moments in the city's development, shaping its ancestral soul: the school of the Jesuits and the Law School in Largo de São Francisco. Education.

———

São Paulo is filled with an insatiable hunger. Hunger for what? It is said that "São Paulo cannot stop!"—almost a motto. But the city's official motto is *Non ducor, duco*—"I am not led, I lead"—which appears on its coat of arms. Everyone thinks that everyone is working in São Paulo. This is the most prevalent fantasy of its native residents, and is what attracts those who come here. Work. The city of work. As a matter of fact, I myself think everyone is dreaming in São Paulo, in one way or another.

São Paulo massacres us. It is extremely large, very dense, very tense, and has a lot of people and a lot going on at the same time: we end up exhausted, which is why we invariably have a love-hate relationship with it. This is our complaint, the complaint of everyone in São Paulo, but is also its charm. We always need to leave, to escape the stress, the pollution, excessive work and the commitments it brings. Escape the out-of-control pace, the lack of air, the noise and intensity. Escape to the dream of the beach, the mountains, nature, to another life. But always just to discover that most of us who live here can't go too far, that we are part of São Paulo's fabric, that it's in our blood and that we are lovers of the speed, of the hallucination, of the excess and the noise, of this intensity that challenges us to stay alive—all this becomes confused with the beating of our *paulistano* hearts. Everyone in São Paulo loves it, even those who have left. It doesn't expel anyone; it is ever-welcoming. Mother and lover, it deludes and delivers, ennobles and diminishes everyone who seeks it out.

———

The intense verticalization of the city occurring over the last century, the call to height simultaneous with its horizontal expansion, shows that the spirit and *raison d'être* of São Paulo is growth. Here everything wants to grow. It is a city launched toward the infinite.

There is still something to be said about the solitude of the grand masses of the metropolis—a humid solitude, millions of lights from apartment windows at night holding the secret lives that see these immensities; the paradoxical machine of the city that separates people horribly but is the source of the acquired taste for the cosmopolitan—for living with difference, with the strange, with the curious—that builds the discreet hospitality of São Paulo's people. Cosmopolitanism creates its own network of relationships, its own organicity, and continuously launches us into the challenge of the Other, the continual recognition of new and different subjectivities. This is the exercise of *paulistanos*—the most demanding, of course, but also the most natural and the most pleasurable. São Paulo's residents take pride in this reconciliation of such different languages, ethnicities, religions, education, culture, manners, traditions, and cuisines—all assimilating each other.

São Paulo is a city in continuous metamorphosis, always transforming itself into something else. It is constantly constructing, deconstructing, and reconstructing itself—"palimpsest city," as some historians call it. From an introverted Jesuit settlement with a mestizo population, at the beginning, it becomes a village of warrior pioneers dedicated to extending the limits of the colony in a quest for gold and precious stones from the general mines; it becomes a foggy, lugubrious burg of ultra-romantic and bohemian students with London airs; becomes a new city of immigrants full of impetus, the fervor of hope, and ideas of freedom; becomes a garden-festooned, French-like metropolitan capital of the coffee barons; becomes a chaotic modern industrial metropolis with an air of excitement and permanent challenges; becomes, today, a hybrid organism, a magnetic pole of commerce, services, and technology.

São Paulo has been the focal point at decisive moments in the history of the country. To cite several of these: The São Paulo pioneers (*bandeirantes*) confronted the interior of *terra incognita*, pushing back the lines established in the Treaty of Tordesillas to delineate the territories of Portugal and Spain, and lending Brazil its present geopolitical shape. Independence was conceived, pondered, counseled, and finally proclaimed in this city. The artists of Modern Art Week, in 1922, shook up the country esthetically, harmonizing it culturally with the century that was beginning, and opening the minds of countless people.

———

At a deeper, psychological level there are numerous archetypal energies that sustain and continuously construct the city of São Paulo. Of course, there are many gods in an indefinable, complex metropolis such as this, because the gods are never alone and never appear without their partners—Narcissus, Aphrodite,

Mars, and so many others, hiding in their corners, sought after at their unvisited altars or sometimes openly in the public square. Money, Victory, Work, Vanity, Competition, Voluptuousness, Fear, and Pleasure are some others. In the end, the gods meet in the city—a space for mediation, an intermediate space between the human and the divine, *mesocosmos*, as Joseph Campbell noted: the city as a mediator between the macrocosm of the universe and the microcosm of the individual.

There is the Narcissus of grey, humid, self-absorbed afternoons, when the metropolis believes itself to be the high point, a marvel of human endeavor, in love with its own diversity, monstrousness, appeal, and strength—projecting and reflecting itself, a hallucination in its thousands of glass-clad buildings, close-in and paranoid, the edifices of power of banks and companies that only further heat up this autoerotic fervor.

There is Aphrodite of the bonfire of the vanities, of the elegant shop windows and the not-so-elegant as well, of street vendors, of the passion for the shopping centers and the rush to consume everything. Aphrodite of the poetry of small gardens and squares, of grand architectural and engineering feats—beautiful bridges and avenues, the ancient and modern beauty of the houses, and of the multiple seductions of advertising and the harbingers of the pleasure, success, and ambition of the city.

Mars, of violence and war, is represented in the difficult and demanding day-to-day struggle in this stone and cement jungle, the occult war of vast social inequalities, the problems of living together—urban war, robberies, kidnappings, crimes both petty and serious.

Hestia extracts from this immense flame of ascending impulses and decadent vanities a rare intimacy, an intimacy that paradoxically derives from one's own experience of the extreme anonymity São Paulo offers or imposes. We see Hades when, despite its plutocratic wealth or maybe because of it, the city believes itself shadowy, the destroyer, vampire-like, filled with darkness, preying on our ingenuity at every corner of dreams.

As for Cronos-Saturn, time never stops in São Paulo, the twenty-four-hour city, a city that intertwines us with Time—the acceleration of ambition; time which is money; the constant challenge of obtaining free time, quality time; the ubiquitous, overwhelming sensation that "there isn't enough time!"—everyone running against time, the time of moving around in this city, as well as the multiple time zones of experience that make us see, simultaneously, people living in the precariousness of the nineteenth century and people living on the front lines of the twenty-first century.

But in the end, the city belongs to Hermes, there can be no doubt about that. It steals as much as it offers, hides and shows itself, open and closed at the same time. In São Paulo, the dominant archetypal energy that flows in its unconscious soul—from the dream of its founding through the dream of industrialization, of commerce, of services—is, in my view, that of Hermes. Commerce, education, communication, highways, the crossroads that are its main vocations—this mercurial enchantment catches those who are born here, those who settle here, or those who are attracted to this place.

———

The "chaotic-cosmetic" of São Paulo, its attraction, makes me think of the entire world. Everyone wants to "conquer" São Paulo, even those who were born here, like me. In the end, it is São Paulo that conquers the whole world, and no one can figure out exactly how or why.

In São Paulo, people learn to be a little bit Italian, a little bit French, a bit American, somewhat Lebanese, Belgian, African, German, *Gaúcho*, *Baiano*, Northeaster, and more. We learn to be tolerant even though there is so much intolerance in the city, so much hurry and anonymity. In the end, the immensity, the avaricious cruelty of life in the metropolis, the harsh demands of this reality, oblige us to be gentle with each other—anything else is suicide.

In São Paulo, we learn that the strength, the pride in being *paulistano*, is in being a pioneer, immigrant, or student—which means being an entrepreneur, a doer, an apprentice—in blood and soul. Sooner or later, everyone learns to look after themselves—bottled up inside cars or buses in traffic immobilized for hours, on the anonymous corner where no one sees you, in the shouting circus of the sidewalks, in the unexpected challenges moving against the flow of the dream of happiness.

The city teaches; it is the master. We are all in school.

5

San Francisco:
The Cool,
Grey City of Love

JOHN BEEBE

San Francisco, a harbor town, is also a psychological haven for many people, and there can be a betrayal of its secret in describing the city's peculiar containing power to those who do not depend on it so much. Indeed, even San Francisco's most celebrated upheaval, the great earthquake of 1906, was protective in that regard: it shook two famous visitors to Northern California, Enrico Caruso and William James, out of their beds, so that they could not possibly ever lift their formidable voices to reveal the city's ability to offer security to those within its precincts. That secret continues to be kept by the people who live here now. It is one we rarely reveal to our visitors, even when these are members of our own families, who often recall their visit to our city as a series of lovely views that do not really get them close to what it would be like to actually live here. It is never remembered as a place that really trusted them with the kind of homely, unpretentious close look that loved ones visited in other places automatically offer.

So, true to San Francisco's code of self-protection, I will start to introduce it from a vantage a tourist might get by stepping off the Hyde Street cable car before it descends to its most commercial destinations—Ghirardelli Square and the tourists-only Fisherman's Wharf—at a somewhat classier perch: the corner of Hyde and Lombard. Resisting as well the temptation to follow "San Francisco's crookedest street"—silly, s-curved Lombard—along its eastward serpentine plunge toward North Beach, the visitor I am guiding would walk west along Lombard to the corner of Larkin. There, surrounded by buildings on Russian Hill that are of every San Francisco type, it is possible to find the entrance to a small, tall park that bears a plaque containing lines from a poem by the glade's namesake, George Sterling, one of the city's immortal spirits—a would-be poet who understood the secret few who live here have ever thought to share:

> Tho the dark be cold and blind,
> Yet her sea-fog's touch is kind,
> And her mightier caress
> Is joy and the pain thereof;
> And great is thy tenderness,
> O cool, grey city of love![1]

Sterling is hardly known to the literary world today except as the great friend of his Bohemian Club buddy, Jack London,[2] but in his lifetime he was wreathed the unofficial poet laureate of the city.

He comes into his own as a poet by recognizing the "grey" of San Francisco. When the photographer Gabriele Basilico visited the city for the first time in 2007, the photographs he took (which were displayed at the San Francisco Museum of Modern Art the following year) showed us how much color the city contains,[3] but this was a naïve outsider's view, impossible for someone who actually lives here to sustain through days of the city's actual, fogbound variations of Sterling's grey, punctuated mostly by the intense dark of certain evergreen shrubs. Alfred Hitchcock was more knowing when he used black-and-white photography in his 1958 color film *Vertigo* to suggest the look of San Francisco from Midge's studio apartment on Telegraph Hill.

As his poem may perhaps convey in ways he did not intend, the slender level of George Sterling's actual poetic gifts made him vulnerable to what sensitive people often stay in San Francisco to avoid. Nearly half a century after Sterling had committed suicide, the Cockettes, a gay liberation troupe who held court at a movie theater in North Beach, just a few blocks away from George Sterling Park, found the rest of the world no less cruel. When they attempted to take their bearded drag show to the more recently liberated New York, the self-exposure of their homemade artistry received the same harsh verdict as Sterling's, this time from the avatar of worldliness, Gore Vidal: "Having no talent is not enough!"[4] It is from that sort of realist cynicism, welcome in almost all the other cities of the world, that the beautiful souls who turn up in San Francisco have usually decided to retreat, because they trust that this city will hold them in a different way.

If one climbs the steps up to the very top of the narrow Sterling Park, to the tennis courts surrounded by majestic Monterey cypresses, one gets a good

San Francisco's
Financial
District.

*Photograph by
David Martinez
(2010)*

view of San Francisco Bay's most famous holding environment, the island of
Alcatraz, where the convicted killer Robert Stroud—played so memorably by
Burt Lancaster in the 1962 movie of his life[5]—was able to transform his con-
finement apart from other prisoners, with only birds in the yard to keep him
company, into the chance to develop as an ornithologist. The relationships "the
Birdman of Alcatraz" created in the nonhuman realm bought him the same kind
of humane contentment that we associate with the Italian saint from whom San
Francisco gets its name, and his spiritual hobby mirrors the alternative realities
in which San Franciscans have so often elected to isolate themselves.

What is one to make of these characters that populate the city, when they
are one's mayor, one's barber, one's shoe repairman, and one's Jungian analyst?
If you live here long enough, you get to know them all, and they are all, in a

way, "San Francisco," because you never exactly get to know them. It would be unimaginable, however, to try to live here without them. Many, as I have indicated, are in service jobs. In the mid 1990s, before Union Square—a small, chic quadrangle faced by hotels and department stores at what for many is the heart of the city's only true downtown—had been remodeled in a way that seemed to strip-mall it of its charm, the great saloon singer Tony Bennett, wearing with his accustomed aplomb an improbably loud-colored jacket, sang his signature number, "I Left My Heart in San Francisco" (one of three songs that have served to immortalize the city in American popular culture, the other two being Jeanette MacDonald's "San Francisco," brilliantly revived and transcended through Judy Garland's Carnegie Hall rendition, and Otis Redding's "Sittin' on the Dock of the Bay"). It should not have been surprising to see Bennett's working-class turn-out, but the crowd was a bit astonishing to contemplate from the steps of the St. Francis Hotel because it broke a conspiracy of invisibility. I had gone to the great hotel for a haircut, surrounded by business patrons, and now it seemed that all the people who work at service jobs—the tailors, the waiters, the cooks, and the people behind counters of the lunchrooms and stores that make possible the illusion of elegance that has to be sustained in this part of San Francisco—had left their posts for the three minutes it took Bennett to deliver his song, to receive the imprimatur that only this old, extraverted feeling type could deliver to them, his hand extended to them to say, you count, because you make San Francisco happen. It was as if the event were generating its own newspaper copy even as it occurred, so caught up were we all in the myth of San Francisco that we didn't need Herb Caen, or Art Hoppe, or Allan Temko (to name the most authoritative columnists of *The San Francisco Chronicle*) to tell us where we were.

It would be a mistake, however, to assume—as someone complained who had heard me mention something I had read in one of Caen's characteristically nostalgic columns—that San Francisco is "a second rate city hung up on a trivial past." The city may attract all kinds of people to it who cannot match the ambience they have chosen, but it is not itself so disappointing. The year she died, the San Francisco novelist Alice Adams published a book of stories set here titled *The Last Lovely City*,[6] and there is much to that. Adams, who was born in Virginia, was not unused to charming places to live, and she fiercely adored San Francisco. Perhaps for that reason she deplored the venality that was overtaking it at the hands of the "yuppies," the young urban professionals who would move into neighborhoods that were fine as they were and aggressively gentrify them in unnecessarily expensive ways. Adams understood that the gentrification was supported by the prices they insisted on charging for their services. "Your

Doctor Loves You," one of the stories in another of her books,[7] has a knowing, autobiographical feel to it. It is about a woman, recently separated from an alcoholic husband, who allows a relationship to develop with her internist, who a friend intimates is smitten with her. She invites him to dinner, and a friendship begins that might become an affair. He won't, however, stop engaging himself with her medical problems, and after he makes an unbidden house call and follow-up visit to check out a brief flu, she decides he is hopelessly solicitous. That doesn't stop him from sending her a bill for the "house calls." Though set north of the city, across the Golden Gate Bridge, in the well-heeled Marin County town of Ross, the story is recognizable as a San Francisco one.

To live in San Francisco is constantly to think about the people who are ruining it. At the same time, it is the people who have just come here who see most clearly what it has to offer. Recently, I had dinner with a relatively new arrival, a friend who, like many people I know, spends part of the year in another city—in his case, St. Paul. I asked him to define for me what is unique about the city.

"Easy," he said. "First, the views."

It is often said that San Francisco, like Rome, is built on seven hills—these being Telegraph Hill, Nob Hill, Russian Hill, Rincon Hill, Mount Sutro, Twin Peaks, and Mount Davidson—but in fact there are at least forty-three named hills, according to the Wikipedia website[8] that I turned to. Everywhere one goes in the city, there is an amazing view corridor disclosing some of the loveliness that Alice Adams had feared could not last, if the developers of her adopted city kept having their way.

Over dinner, my friend and I amused ourselves describing the way we both feel driving north up Divisadero, with an impossibly tall, lone apartment house standing in the distance, marking the goal of Pacific Heights—an elegance of living that is gradually being replaced by more practical high-rises erected south of Market Street, buildings that remind me of Miami. I told him about the sixth-floor penthouse I had lived in soon after I had come to the city to pursue my medical internship and psychiatric residency. The apartment that framed my experience of the world around me in my late twenties faced Buena Vista Park, but was high enough up to have a different view from every window—on the east side of the building one could look across the Bay Bridge to Oakland and Berkeley, on the west side the eye crossed the Golden Gate Bridge to an unbroken view of spectacular sunsets. In those days, I would send friends and family in other parts of the country Christmas cards that showed Santa Claus, like the Wizard of Oz, in a balloon floating over the vista of the city itself that opened up from the central window, placed between the other two.

Telegraph Hill
and
Coit Tower
from
Russian Hill,
with Oakland
and its
hills in the
background.

*Photograph by
David Martinez
(2010)*

"What else?" I asked my friend.

I realize he would have gone on without being prompted, but he had paused, with the respect San Franciscans often give to each other's private reveries, until the complex recall of my own first recognition of the beauty of the city had begun to die down.

"The city's proximity to Muir Woods and Sonoma and Napa counties," he said, immediately summoning memories of day trips and marvelous drives north, and also a couple of long journeys south by car along the Pacific Coast, to Big Sur—all of it feeling like an extension of what San Francisco had to offer on the ground, as view became extension of self, an expansion of mind as close to hand as a steering wheel.

For many, especially if these journeys were made with other young adults, such memories are erotic as well. I pulled myself back to the conversation, and the polenta getting cold on my plate, with difficulty. We were drinking a good Italian wine from Apulia, and it reminded me that the friend I had taken to Big Sur, the highly travelled mother of a prep school buddy, had compared the drive to the one down the Amalfi Coast. It was every bit as good, she assured me. I was beginning to critique my memory's selective air of privilege—as if I'd never had to worry about money in San Francisco, or hadn't had to work so hard at building a career that trips like that had been, in my thirties, simply out of the question—when my friend from St. Paul continued his objective survey of what was still to be found here.

"Ethnic diversity," he was saying.

I mused about what that meant. The street I have lived on for the past thirty years, in the northwest section of the city known as the Richmond District, lies between Lincoln Park and Golden Gate Park, and there are citizens of every San Francisco description living behind facades painted to catch some of the light that falls especially brightly, when there isn't fog, on the apartment buildings and stucco-faced houses that make up our block. Once, I counted out our demographic diversity in identity-politics triads: Japanese, Chinese, Indian; Gay, Lesbian, Heterosexual; Jewish, Catholic, Russian; Unemployed, Employee, Retiree; Black, White, Hispanic; Young, Middle-aged, Old; Single, Married, Widowed or Divorced. All this on our block—which probably has fewer than forty buildings—I had thought with pride. And then I had become annoyed with myself for emphasizing the ethnic distinctions. Wasn't the point that all of us were lucky enough to live on the same street? What brought us all together, which my friend had not managed to think of, was the fact that three city buses stopped within a block of our home. All of us who live in San Francisco take one of the "Muni" buses sometimes, if only to remind ourselves that we are still San Franciscans.

Seeing that I wasn't biting on ethnic diversity (when I did speak, it was to ask him if he thought the people of the different ethnic groups actually reached out to each other much, or simply kept a respectful distance), he tried a different word: "Openness. *The San Franciscan is the person who is open to new things,*" he said, "and that's what outsiders see right away. You can always start a conversation with someone here."

That's true, I thought, and it usually doesn't mean that you are coming on to them—unless, of course, you are.

By now we had ordered dessert. I tried to get him to be more specific.

"Well, people can be exactly who they are, rather than approximations. You are not, for instance, just gay; you are in a relationship of twenty-five years, and why that is so, why it is appropriate for you, is perfectly clear to everyone. You have to work at not having an identity here."

I felt we were zeroing in on what the lovely setting is really about: it is a stage set for the flowering of individuation.

As an analyst, I have had to emotionally support many people who have found it hard to live in San Francisco, for reasons that range from the economic to the environmental. For some, the city is too expensive, or too cold—too gay, or (don't be surprised) too straight, at least in the circles the person has chosen to move in. It's notoriously hard to find a partner in a city of loners, yet San Franciscans resist any sustained attempt on a therapist's part to promote any particular relationship with gratuitous offers of couple counseling. People want to tough it out in their individual ways, and if a relationship comes, it's one between very idiosyncratic people who have chosen to foster each other's way of being individual.

It's particularly poignant to get to know San Franciscans with children, who have had to make room for their children's individuality as well as their own. San Francisco public schools are not easy to adjust to, for either parents or children, and so those who can possibly afford it usually elect to send their children to private schools. The children here are not *en bloc*, as I imagine children in Paris to be. They are peculiar, and let each other be so to a degree that one would not find in any other city I know.

Psychotherapy is a leitmotif of the city. Not far from each other are three analytic institutes: the San Francisco Psychoanalytic Institute, the C. G. Jung Institute of San Francisco, and the Psychoanalytic Institute of Northern California. Most of the psychotherapists in the city go sooner or later to get therapy for themselves from a graduate of one of those institutes. The method—long-term, analytically oriented therapy—is a process of gaining insight into one's own idiosyncratic way of being: it does not demand adaptation to any particular standard. And that permission to be idiosyncratic is passed on to the patients those therapists see. The beat poet Allen Ginsberg felt he got permission to live his homosexual life openly in the late 1950s from a psychiatrist in San Francisco, and it was at a meeting in San Francisco that the American Psychiatric Association decided in the early 1970s that homosexuality could no longer be regarded a mental disorder. More recently, it has been the site of one of the most widely publicized social experiments of our day, the granting of marriage licenses to gay couples in advance of any legalization of their right to marry in the State of California, simply because the Mayor of San Francisco decided it should happen. The issue is still hotly debated, but the point was made as soon as people happy to be affirming each other's individuality in close relationship started lining up at City Hall. *This is the place where you become yourself and people let you.*

The typical San Franciscan's freedom of identity is something many have sought to politicize, but the politics of the city is not as focused, or evolved, as the politics of, say, Chicago, which could produce Obama. Aside from Harvey Milk, no politician who has emphasized the identity of a group of constituents

(Milk was of course dubbed the "Mayor of Castro Street") has succeeded in galvanizing the imagination of the city. Rather, the Supervisors are most representative of San Francisco when they are, and act, peculiar—like the Chairperson of the Board of Supervisors who believed that AIDS might be the result of the fluoridated drinking water. It's hard to imagine a city that would be more tolerant of individual eccentricity in high office.

What is more interesting to me as a Jungian analyst is that this degree of individuality actually promotes individuation in the Jungian sense. The model San Francisco patient comes to me lamenting the loneliness that attends their individuality, but I have never yet succeeded in getting a San Francisco analysand to greatly modify his or her own peculiarity. My patients worry that their lives may fail as a result, but they have no intention of being anyone but themselves, and they make it clear they won't tolerate an effort on my part to make them adapt. By the same token, they are marvelously accepting of my own oddness, and it has dawned on me more than once that I am a very odd therapist. When I do peculiar things—like forget an appointment, or become so caught up in something the session is stirring up in me that I can no longer properly attend—they are usually interested to see how what is going on in me may be a mirror of something they need to see, too. San Francisco is almost never about "business as usual," and the superego is simply not the arbiter of what any ego should be doing with its life.

In my own case, the paradox of this atmosphere of extreme permissiveness is that it drives me to work hard to make myself correct the aspects of my individuality that do get in the way. If I forget an appointment, for instance, I give the patient the next one free. And I work hard to figure out what has led me to be so inconsiderate. I don't think I would want to take the trouble, except as lip service, in a city where the patients were keeping score.

What then of the people who can't stand San Francisco, seeing it as the terminal moraine of American narcissism (and would see me, based on what I've already said, as its rationalizing mouthpiece)? I would advise them to get to know San Francisco by walking around, by seeing how much the emptiness of the city that they so resent (the restaurants that close at 10, the lack of attention to detail that permeates just about every transaction, the absence of intellectual content in so many of the beliefs that guide the people here) comes into its own in the city's open spaces.

At different times in my life, I have walked alone in the city, exploring neighborhoods that are unfamiliar. What is interesting is how rarely I talk to anyone on such jaunts, unless I go indoors to take coffee, food, or alcohol into myself. At such times, the city speaks to me as a place that survives everything that can be said about it. My favorite evocation of the city is the strange circuitous path Jimmy Stewart's "Scottie" takes, the second time he follows "Madeleine" (Kim Novak) in the movie *Vertigo*. The first time, as Scottie's car follows Madeleine's in the sleuthing Madeleine's husband has hired him to do, there's no dialogue for over ten minutes of screen time. This time, the silent sequence is not as long, but in Scottie's mind it might be, and he grows more and more exasperated until he finally realizes that she has led him back to his own home. Hitchcock's meaning couldn't be clearer: San Francisco is a city where the pursuit of the other inevitably leads us back to the self.

That self that won't let one go is hauntingly conveyed in the paintings of the contemporary photo-realist painter Robert Bechtle, a longtime resident of San Francisco, some of whose paintings show a series of cars on a street not unlike the one I live on but steeper, with the lengthening shadows of the houses falling on them and nobody around even to feel the uncanny foreboding of the scene. If, drawing on traditional Jungian analytic symbology, the car is the ego and the house the transpersonal Self (capitalized to indicate the uncanny otherness of what we are), then San Francisco is a city where the very steepness of the climb toward individual realization forces the ego to live under the Self's shadow. This is a burden some of my patients learn to accept, and that others bitterly resent. I understand the split, because both sides of it are within my own identity as a San Franciscan. This city won't let me be anything but me, even when everything in me would give its eyeteeth to conform to a definite standard.

Robert Bechtle's *Mariposa I* (1999), oil on canvas, 36 x 66". Collection of Diane Johnson & John Murray. *Photo by David Martinez*

And so, in time, each of us who lives here develops those few friends who do not question the individuality that the Self imposes on us and support us in living up to it. It is not San Franciscan to question the choice someone else makes to be the only person he or she can be. As a consequence, it is rare for any of us to see each other too often. The patients I see once a week are far closer to me in that way than the friends of half a lifetime of living here, and by the time they really can let me be me and I them, our work is all but over and they become people that I see only occasionally too.

Not long ago, in some renewed wanderings through the city occasioned by the need to write this piece from the vantage of a fresh look, I found myself at Immigrant Point, where a stone plaza overlook has been built with the help of the Jewish Community Endowment Fund. The role of the Jewish community in developing San Francisco has rarely been told, but the city has often benefitted from Jewish philanthropy. This site was a gift to the city underwritten, in addition to the Fund's support, by George Sarlo, a Hungarian immigrant, and his wife Sejong, who is originally from Korea. They embody the various diasporas that have come together so frequently in San Francisco. Beautifully carved by a stone mason on the curved ledge of the overlook is a statement of President Woodrow Wilson, who was also a great historian: "We opened the gates to all the world and said: 'Let all men who want to be free come to us and they will be welcome.'"[9] It speaks, not to just the Sarlos of San Francisco, but to the people like myself who came here from other parts of our own country to be free of the constraints we had experienced against our individual identities.

Geographically, the overlook gives a glimpse of the Golden Gate Bridge just over one's right shoulder and, farther north, looks toward the Marin Headlands and the Point Reyes National Seashore. But it really draws one's attention straight ahead, to the Bay waters pouring into the Pacific Ocean on the western horizon. It's an astonishing evocation of the fluidity of the city of San Francisco itself, as a form emptying into the transcendent—not a form inviting us to attach to the emptiness beyond it (the greatest hazard of Buddhist practice), but rather a vehicle that we love to let do its job of emptying our minds. Standing at that place, one can understand how Zen took root in San Francisco in the 1950s, as it did centuries before in equally lovely Kyoto, and one can be angry that so much development here has threatened to efface the central mystery of its formlessness. The genius of San Francisco is that it enables one to experience emptiness both without attachment and without sacrifice of transcendence.

David Martinez, who took the pictures that accompany this chapter, told me when I asked him to take up this assignment that the soul of the city is in its northern part, along the ocean. The city, in fact, is like a head facing north, and the northwest of the city is where its eye is located (the Golden Gate Bridge, leading to Marin, is at what would be the bridge of the nose of the rather impassively gazing San Franciscan I am visualizing when reading the map of the city this way).

We all like to look at San Francisco, but what does San Francisco itself see, with this north-facing eye that is also its soul? We recall the moment in *Vertigo* in which, facing due north, Kim Novak's character, the false Madeleine, plays the love trick of pretending to commit suicide by jumping into the water beside the bridge. Once a patient of mine had a similar moment, when feeling suicidal he drove to the Golden Gate Bridge to get away from his lover, who had recently been driving him crazy. Parking close to the bridge, he met another gay man also walking to the bridge, also feeling semi-suicidal. Rather than kill themselves, these strangers decided their meeting was a reprieve, and they went home together to celebrate by making love—something the lover of my patient, who could be cynical, found hilarious when he heard about it. That chance bonding with the stranger not only saved my patient's life but, paradoxically, gave him the courage to go on with his primary relationship quite faithfully for many years after—which I regard as a sign the soul was present in the chance encounter. What does San Francisco's eye see, then, when it looks north?

Sometimes in my years in San Francisco, I have vacationed as far up as Humboldt County, where what are often described as the oldest living things on our planet, the Giant Redwoods, live in great forests with clean floors of clover and fern and wildflowers (one gets only a taste of their northern simplicity in Marin's lush Muir Woods, which are just across the Bridge from San Francisco). The Redwoods are some aspect of what San Francisco must be envisioning, but the city is looking at them—if it is—like an old Anasazi Indian in an eternal waking sleep. Sitting with analytic patients in my office in Laurel Heights, looking out my north window, I sometimes start musing about the majesty of individuation, what people manage to live through, and how their aloneness speaks to others who are alone—rather the way the individual trees in the Humboldt forests are able to "sing" to each other when the wind blows. At such times, I think I become like San Francisco itself, asleep with his eye open, facing true North in a spiritual dream. The direction of my vision, as I have experienced in such moments, is toward an integrity that is beyond identity—beyond even the falsifications of identity with which all of us flirt (the subject of *Vertigo*).

Such integrity is unwilling to give up the form of its knowing—San Francisco itself—because in San Francisco it finds a home that celebrates and lives its own emptiness without being especially attached to it. Rather, the true San Franciscan I am projecting accepts the emptiness of San Francisco as the only possible justification for the beauty San Francisco grants him. Indeed, this is his way of bearing witness to the city.

Notes

1   George Sterling, "The Cool, Grey City of Love," *The Bulletin*, 131/56 (December 11, 1920), p. 12.
2   Although they were both heterosexual, their intimacy made them the target of gossip among the first San Francisco generation that had read Freud.
3   Some of these are in *Gabriele Basilico, Silicon Valley, 07* (Milan: Skira, 2008). The show at SFMOMA, which ran from January 26 to June 15, 2008, was titled "From San Francisco to Silicon Valley."
4   http://www.brightlightsfilm.com/37/cockettes.php, consulted February 7, 2010.
5   *Birdman of Alcatraz*, directed by John Frankenheimer.
6   Alice Adams, *The Last Lovely City* (New York: Knopf, 1999).
7   It is collected in *The Stories of Alice Adams* (New York: Alfred A. Knopf, 2002), pp. 478-496.
8   List of hills of San Francisco, online: http://en.wikipedia.org/wiki/List_of_hills_in_San_Francisco, consulted March 14, 2010.
9   This text is as quoted in the press release of The Presidio Trust at the time of the carving, May 22, 2007. Online: http://www.presidio.gov/trust/press/pressreleases/stone.htm, consulted March 15, 2010.

6 Paris, Essence, and Soul

VIVIANE THIBAUDIER

The origins of Paris can be traced far back into antiquity. Its name is believed to derive from "Per-Isis"; that is, the "House of Isis."[1] Even though this belief is now disputed, everyone nevertheless agrees that from the first century BCE (and probably long before), there were many shrines dedicated to the goddess Isis in the region of Paris, particularly on the site of today's Saint-Germain-des-Prés church and on the Île de la Cité, the spiritual heart of the city. This islet, inhabited as early as the second millennium BCE by a seafaring tribe of Gauls, the Parisiis, was long dedicated to the worship of the goddess Isis. It was later devoted to the cult of the Virgin Mary, and still is.

In the fifth century, when Gaul was at the beginning of its Christianization, a 28-year-old woman named Geneviève encouraged the Parisians to resist the siege of Attila and the Huns. According to the legend, her fervent prayers and exhortations inspired those who were exhausted and ready to surrender: "Let the men who are no longer capable of fighting flee. We women will pray to God for as long as He will hear our pleas." The Huns, barbarians from the distant East, were ready to pillage the town and burn it to the ground, as they had done with so many other cities they had crossed in their devastating advance. But they say that, strange as it may seem, the horsemen were soon observed to turn around and go on their way without acting upon their deadly plans. This is why Geneviève became the patron saint of Paris.

Fifteen centuries later, in August 1944, Paris again escaped total destruction decreed by the folly of another barbarian from the East.[2] However, strangely, once again, General von Choltitz, the military governor of Gross-Paris, ignored orders from a delirious Hitler to burn the city to the ground "on the spot." Had von Choltitz been less "cautious,"[3] Paris would probably no longer be itself: a city of such unparalleled beauty that it invariably charms inhabitants and visitors.[4]

113

Thus, over twenty centuries of legend and history, the destiny of the city has been closely linked to the feminine, be it divine, human, or the result of a soldier's "surrender."[5] The goddess Isis, the Virgin Mary, Saint Genevieve, and the amazing "restraint" of a German army general have all, over the ages, intervened to save the city.

Moreover, although astrologers claim that the country of France is a Leo, a sign associated with masculine power, Paris is ruled by Virgo, the quintessence of femininity and delicacy. This female divinity that has watched over Paris has made it a place where under various guises the masculine and feminine are destined to meet and cross-fertilize. This cross-fertilization brings about the humanization of the primitive warlike masculine and the sublimation of the woman and the feminine. It is therefore no accident that since the seventeenth century, Paris has been the capital of elegance and fashion and since the beginning of the twentieth, that of haute couture, where great designers like Chanel, Dior, Givenchy, Yves St Laurent, and so on dedicated their lives and talent to the exaltation of the woman's body.

Since its founding as a veritable city by the Romans in the first century BCE (before, it had been a village), Paris has been anchored in its history. Its motto, *Fluctuat nec mergitur,*[6] seems to make it invincible and endow it with the touch of eternity so often sung by the poets. Despite the invasions, wars, and numerous transformations and expansions over the centuries, Paris has maintained its original structure. As a result, in the twenty-first century, the city is still topographically similar to the metropolis conceived by the Romans when they settled on the site in the first century.

Thus, between the north and south on the one hand and the east and west on the other, Paris is basically a "crossroads," an "encounter," between a country lane and a waterway. The north-south axis, which the Romans called the *cardo,* was the road that led from the Nordic countries all the way to Rome and, later, to Spain. Traders, conquerors, and other travelers—pilgrims on their way to or coming back from Santiago de Compostela—stopped there. The east-west axis, known as the *decumanus,* ran alongside the river. Generations of royal architects and gardeners were aware of this powerfully symbolic topography and set it off splendidly over the centuries to the greater glory of kings, emperors, and other leaders of France.

According to the Roman concept of city planning, the *cardo* was the axis of the city's social and economic life. It was at the intersection of *cardo* and *decumanus* that the forum was located. However, in Latin, *cardo* means pivot or central point, and the Romans also associated it with the hub of the heavenly wheel, the center of its orbital motion. In Paris, the three axes meet on the Île de la Cité, which is shaped like a boat on the river. It is there that the vertical axis and its transcendental dimension joins with the two horizontal axes, one earthbound, the other fluvial, to make of this spatial configuration a true conception of the world.

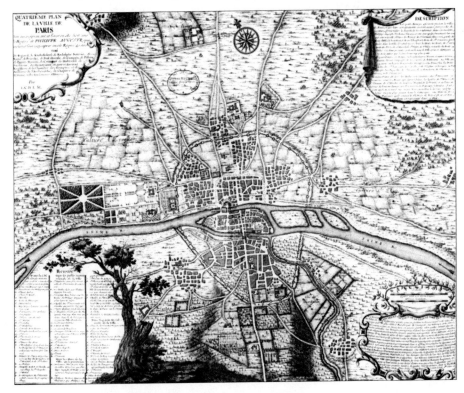

Fourth map of the City of Paris under the Reign of Philippe Auguste (1165-1223).

The walls that were built around the periphery of the city, which were in place from Gallo-Roman times to the nineteenth century, never altered its basic circular shape. It thus grew outward, forming a series of concentric rings over the centuries, always maintaining its original topography, which defined a space that was simultaneously temporal, spiritual, and cosmic. There were intertwined opposing or complementary elements, such as earth, water, air (the heavens), and fire, when one considers that the sun represents the king, and Leo, a fire sign, governs France, of which Paris is the heart. In other words, a Totality; hence the historic and symbolic significance of France's highly centralized structure, a model from which it is still struggling to free itself. Yet does one ever free oneself from one's "heart," until one is about to die?

These broad outlines of my city and its identity are already evidence that Paris is not merely a "major urban area" or a "large collection of houses arranged on streets," according to the dictionary definition of "city." No, Paris is not just a city! For myself, and for most Parisians and French people, it is a complex and intimate inner space within which one is deeply continually engaged in a sensual relationship to oneself, to others, and to the whole environment—whether one loves it or hates it, depending on one's mood or the color of the sky.

> Tears flow in my heart
> As rain falls on the town
> What languor is this
> That creeps into my heart?

wrote Verlaine, the "prince of poets."[7]

An intimate space; almost an intimate "being." A place that has come alive, as if by some uncanny magic, and takes on the qualities of a person, to serve as the container of our most secret emotions. A living being, one with virtues, flaws, ambiguities, and mysteries and one with shadows But most especially it is a being with light, a being that pulsates to the rhythm of time, its surface revealing what it is willing to show of its conscious life. Secretly hidden beneath it, lie all the depth and wealth of an unconscious with a long and eventful past, reaching back centuries and millennia. Henri IV called Paris "a country in itself"; Montaigne said it was "the glory of France and one of the world's most noble ornaments."[8] For Victor Hugo, author of *Les Misérables* and *Notre Dame de Paris*, "Paris rhymes with life."

Paris is a metropolis, certainly one of the world's great capitals, but it has a human dimension and from the beginning was built so that its inhabitants could live there harmoniously. Though they may work, they also have the right to do nothing. Enjoyment of the city is primordial for a Parisian, strolling the avenues with their view of the sky and the abundant light it sheds, enabling the trees to grow. Living the city, truly and simply. Paris's beautiful dimensions often remind me of Leonardo da Vinci's *Vitruvian Man*, whose proportions reflect those of the universe, and vice versa. In Paris, a royal capital from the beginning of the sixth century, man, the city, and the universe are all in these proportions.

The striking thing about Paris is that unlike other major cities, everything seems naturally designed to facilitate encounters and exchange. This is probably a legacy from the god Mercury, who was worshipped widely in the Gallo-Roman era. In many other cities, the river might have been perceived as an obstacle to expansion. But it is quite the contrary with Paris, which has always developed harmoniously on both banks. Over a distance of barely eight miles, almost forty bridges carry pedestrians and vehicles across the water. Whether it is made of stone and is several centuries old or whether it is made of wrought iron, concrete, or the most contemporary materials, even the most common of these bridges exudes a special charm as it spans the Seine.[9] Moreover, the sinuous curves the river makes as it meanders through Paris have always prompted comparisons to an amorous embrace. Countless poems, songs, and films have celebrated the love and the lovers to whom—as everyone knows—Paris has always belonged.

Paris attracts throngs of tourists from around the world, but this, too, is an old tradition. In the Middle Ages, it was already a cosmopolitan city, teeming with tradesmen and visitors. From the great north came fur merchants; from the south, tinsmiths rattled in with their wares. The city was bustling with foreigners; travelers were constantly passing through, meeting, and going on their way. Inns and taverns hosted everyone, where traders, aristocrats, scholars, pious pilgrims, and bandits and outlaws mingled. Rue Saint-Jacques, for example, was lined with convents and monasteries where pilgrims for Santiago de Compostela could take shelter. Several are still standing today, even though the Revolution destroyed almost all of them. To get some idea of the austere beauty of these buildings that ran along the *cardo* from north to south, simply gaze upon that masterpiece of Cistercian Gothic architecture, the Collège des Bernardins.[10]

"Woman," "the feminine," "elegance," "encounters," "exchanges," the "pleasure of life," "love," "sensuality," "space," "light," "spirituality" ... The essential personality of the city may not always be evident to the visitor, but these various expressions used about Paris reveal it to be a city that has depth, although it is also lively, heady with excitement and a myriad of subtle sensations. These at times are not overt—they can be rather introverted, we might say—and might initially be perceived as coldness by people accustomed to loud fanfare and noisy bonhomie. The warmth is there, nevertheless: gentle, vibrant, and sometimes even incredibly intense, for he or she who knows how to be receptive to it in the appropriate places.

For example, warmth suffuses the many open-air markets found in every neighborhood of the city, rich, fashionable, or poor. All year round, vendors loudly hawk their produce to housewives carrying baskets or pulling carts, filling them with fresh fruit and vegetables. Addressing the customers with terms of endearment like "my darling" or "my beautiful," "my little lady" and many more besides, accompanying the naughtier ones with a wink, they create an affectionate atmosphere of closeness and distance that has unwritten rules that everyone knows well. Likewise, the brasseries (some of which have been in business since the mid-seventeenth century[11]) and terraces are overflowing with people, even in winter. Depending on the neighborhood, you'll find shopkeepers, carpenters, students, scholars, and artists. The bistros are yet another phenomenon, truly a Parisian institution: regardless of the hour, day or night, they are serving up coffee, beer, or white wine by the glass ("*petit blanc*"). Customers lounge against the zinc counter, chatting with whoever is around: the waiters, the boss, and each other, offering their opinion on the news of the day and setting the world straight in an instant. Lastly, in a multitude of restaurants, from the simplest to the most elegant, Parisians enjoy getting together with friends and sharing interminable feasts that may last far into the night. Again, the conversation is lively with philosophical observations on politics, sports, the latest books, or the subtleties of Woody Allen movies.

For Paris is still haunted by the spirit of Mercury, who was also the god of eloquence and wit. This is a city that loves discourse about everything and nothing, an outlet for an extraversion of thinking that absolutely must be expressed,

Rue Mouffetard's open market

Photograph by François Berton

118

for better or worse. Parisians talk and speak to each other on practically any subject. The essential goal is to express ideas they firmly believe to be the most original in the world, steeped in intellect. Parisian thinking is the very quintessence of French thinking. Full of paradoxes, it loves debate, though it finds contradiction nearly unbearable. It takes pride in open-mindedness, unless a different opinion arises, in which case the person who dared express the idea is ruthlessly attacked. As a result, discussion, which is a favorite Parisian pastime, is constantly going on everywhere. It is often amusing to observe: even the cafe on the corner can feel like a lecture hall at the Sorbonne, with each of the patrons presenting and defending his or her thesis with conviction. Inhabitants of other cities may be irritated by this face of Parisians, a face that contributes to the notion that they are arrogant and pretentious. But the flow of words coursing through the city enlivens and stimulates intellectual life, and conversations sparkle with wit and originality.

Paris's broad perspectives, tree-lined boulevards, and flowering parks and gardens elegantly wed the soothing beauty of nature to its personality as a major city leading an intense intellectual life.

Since the sixteenth century, architects and gardeners have been studying ways to make this city a harmonious blend of urban and natural virtues. They demonstrated remarkable intuition in taking this path long before the latest neuroscientific findings showed that a city tends to have a disruptive effect on the brain, whereas nature can improve brain function.[12] Even if, as everywhere else, urbanization at times has ravaged the environment, unlike many other cities, Paris wisely chose to preserve nature at its core. Thus, Paris is probably the only world capital where it is possible for a person to stroll throughout the city without ever losing sight of some form of vegetation, such as brightly colored and elegantly planted flower beds in parks, squares, and gardens, connected by avenues lined with majestic and even exotic trees. Moreover, often the landscaping enhances a rich and varied architectural or cultural heritage: Roman ruins,[13] marvels of Gothic art,[14] and palaces and castles dating from the Middle Ages to the eighteenth century. And we must include the extraordinary harmony of the Haussmann buildings,[15] which are never more than six or seven stories high and feature rounded façades, curved wrought-iron balconies, and elaborate stone balustrades. The impression they make is one of the most charming features of a city glowing with feminine grace right down to the delicate ochre tones of its buildings' façades.

Why did so many painters, musicians, sculptors, writers, and poets come from such distant places to live in Paris? Modigliani, Stravinsky, Joyce, Max Ernst, Picasso, Henry James, Soutine, Gertrude Stein, Edith Wharton, Man

Louis-Philippe
Bridge,
Île de la Cité &
Notre-Dame
Cathedral.

*Photograph by
François Berton*

Ray, Hemingway, Fujita, Ezra Pound, U. Zürn, Chagall, Arp, and so many others ... What did they seek here? "I came to Paris because I was curious to see and know about the concept of 'clarté' and the light here, which results from the place and times," said painter A. R. Penck in 1981, just after he had escaped from East Germany.[16] Paris's charisma acts as a magnet for a person seeking clarity, whether it is outside, in the world and its surroundings, or inside, in himself, in the inner person. It is for one who is looking for a center, his or her own center, reflected in the image of Paris.

Artists have long been attracted by the great inspiration of Paris, a Muse who generously responds to their hopes by freeing and giving life to their creative expression: Impressionism, Surrealism, Dadaism, Nouvelle Vague, and others. But it is not just artists who have sought out the city. All those who search and search for themselves looking in the mirror of the Totality that Paris reflects are revealed to themselves in turn.

However, the symmetry, order, gentleness, and clarity all have a shadow. It is red. Red like the fire that burned the Templars alive early in the fourteenth century, like the blood that streamed through the streets of Paris on the day of the

Saint Barthélemy, when all the Protestants in the city were savagely murdered.[17] Red like the blood of all the heads guillotined during the darkest years of the Revolution,[18] despite its wish to make all men free and equal. Red like the blood of a people who rebelled against a tyrannical regime, like that of the thousands of workers shot point-blank, with no trial whatsoever, in May 1871.[19] Red like the anger of the students in May 1968 or that of the forgotten youths of the housing projects, no longer able to bear discrimination.[20] The shadowy face of Paris cannot be ignored. Its Dionysian madness matches its enchanting Eros; the terrifying moment when the wise maiden becomes a foolish one. An *anima* figure suddenly drained of life, dispensing only destruction and death.

Paris, with its tri-axial dimensions, its temporal, spiritual, and cosmic space, and its concentric structure, the heart of which originated in the Neolithic era, reflects the slow maturation process of a psyche that has been structured step by step, over the centuries. Yes, as Victor Hugo observed, Paris "is" life, a life that is also what Jung once described as "a story of the self-realization of the unconscious."[21]

Despite Paris's somber and sometimes even disturbing side, the visitor is bound to be impressed by the city's marvelous light. Victor Hugo (him again!) expresses my feelings about it well:

> I love these calm clear evening hours—these hours
> When sunset gilds the brows of ancient towers
> Shrouded in shrubbery,
> Or distant fog spreads out in fiery rows,
> Or countless rays strike archipelagos
> Of clouds in heaven's sea.[22]

Yes, I love these summer evenings that stretch on interminably until late, when night finally steals in. When the sun has completed its journey from east to west, lingering on the horizon to spread its light on the sumptuous perspective laid out by Le Nôtre over three centuries ago.[23] Starting at the Louvre, it goes through the gardens of the Tuileries and up the Champs Élysées, all the way to the Arc de Triomphe and then very far to the west, to the Arche de La Défense, behind which one can see hints of gradually darkening forests. It is the magical time of day when Paris glows with a light that is both warm and magnetic, a visual symphony conducted by the Master of the World. A brief and awe-inspiring instant of eternity, when the gilding on the domes and columns is echoed in the windows of the palaces, which blaze with a thousand lights that illuminate the already deep-indigo sky on the city's eastern edge. They reverberate in a chorus on the surface of the tranquil river, sparkling in response to the smile of the stars rising in the heavens. This cosmic symphony sets the entire city ablaze until the last ray of daylight finally vanishes. And that is when the Master of the World allows the Fairy of Electricity to wave her wand, and thousands of shining lamps brighten the Parisian night.

Resolutely turning my back on the sunset, I follow the banks of the Seine back to Notre-Dame and Île Saint-Louis for a twilight stroll. Everything is calm here, despite a throng of Parisian lovers who have tacitly agreed to meet here to taste the pleasures of the night, which will last until the morning light appears once again in the east. All I can hear is the lapping of the water and the light breeze rustling the leaves of the trees. Like an arabesque by Debussy.

Notes

1   According to Egyptologist G. Maspéro (1846–1916).
2   On this subject, see the film *Is Paris Burning?*
3   Historians say that von Choltitz, who had previously already burned down Sebastopol and Rotterdam, sensing that an Allied victory was imminent, was probably motivated to disobey the Führer's orders more by concerns about his own personal future than by any real love for Paris and French culture.
4   Unlike Warsaw, 85 percent of which was destroyed at the same moment, Paris was untouched.
5   I have a theory that von Choltitz, faced with Hitler's madness, which had reached a peak at that precise moment, underwent a psychological upheaval that caused him to experience a reversal of values, or enantiodromia. This enabled his *anima* (or unconscious feminine half), hitherto split off and inactive, to come back to life and begin exerting an influence that was beneficial in two respects: it saved him, by making him more human, and, more especially, it saved Paris.
6   "Pitched by waves, she does not sink."
7   French poet Paul Verlaine (1844–1896):

> *Il pleure dans mon cœur*
> *Comme il pleut sur la ville*
> *Quelle est cette langueur*
> *Qui pénètre mon coeur?*

In *The Anchor Anthology of French Poetry, from Nerval to Valéry in English Translation*, ed. Angel Flores (New York: Random House Inc., 2000), p. 92.
8   Michel de Montaigne, *Essais*, Livre III, §IX.
9   The Pont-Neuf was built in 1604, the Pont Marie in 1635, and the Pont-Royal in 1685.
10   Collège des Bernardins, 20 rue de Poissy, in the 5th *arrondissement*.
11   Like Le Procope, for example.
12   See the research report by Marc G. Berman, John Jonides, and Stephen Kaplan: "The Cognitive Benefits of Interacting with Nature," *Psychological Science* 19, no. 12 (2008): 1207–1212.

13 Thermes de Cluny, Arènes de Lutèce.

14 Notre-Dame (12th–13th c.), Sainte-Chapelle (13th c.), Cloître des Billettes (13th c.), Saint Germain l'Auxerrois (13th–14th c.), Saint-Eustache (16th c.).

15 In the mid-nineteenth century, Baron Haussmann, prefect of Paris, transformed and modernized the city.

16 A. R. Penck, born in 1939, left East Germany in 1980.

17 24 August 1572.

18 Particularly during the Terror, 1792–1794.

19 Rebellion against King Charles X in 1830, Louis Philippe in 1848, the Paris Commune's "bloody week" in May 1871.

20 In the fall of 2005, there were three weeks of rioting in the poorest neighborhoods just outside the city.

21 C. G. Jung, *Memories, Dreams, Reflections*, first sentence of the Prologue.

22 *J'aime les soirs sereins et beaux, j'aime les soirs*
    Soit qu'ils dorent le front des antiques manoirs
    Ensevelis dans les feuillages;
    Soit que la brume au loin s'allonge en bancs de feu;
    Soit que mille rayons se brisent dans un ciel bleu
    A des archipels de nuages.

Victor Hugo, "Soleils couchants," in *Selected Poems of Victor Hugo: A Bilingual Edition*, ed. A. M. Blackmore (Chicago: University of Chicago Press, 2001), p. 47.

23 Le Nôtre (1613–1700) was the principal gardener of King Louis XIV. He was responsible for the design and construction of the park of the Palace of Versailles as well as many other castles. His work represents the height of the French formal style: *jardin à la française.*

The One and Many Souls of New York City

BEVERLEY ZABRISKIE

The city seems to have a life of its own. If we cannot understand how this works, we are not likely to get very far with human society at large.
—LEWIS THOMAS[1]

The psyche is made up of processes whose energy springs from the equilibration of all kinds of opposites.
—C. G. JUNG[2]

You perceive differences only thru that which is a likeness to the differences in yourself.
—C. G. JUNG[3]

Soul on a Corner

At the corner of Fred Lebow Place and Museum Mile, 115 feet above sea level, the calls of seagulls and ducks blend with the traffic's hum and human buzz. The curved windows of the Guggenheim Museum reflect the white hawk on a branch and the oval reservoir in the park across the avenue. Weaving between the carts of kitsch hawkers, hot dog and falafel stands, and children's buggies and strollers, the art-hungry stream into the museum, joggers sprint into the park, and the rehabilitated workers from Ready, Willing & Able tend their trash baskets.

If seen as a freeze frame of hieroglyphs, like those in the nearby Metropolitan Museum, each figure and form would be perceived not only as itself but also in an interplay with its surround. To an ancient Egyptian eye, the hawk would signify the ba soul, a configuration of dynamic essence, moving between body and spirit, between the here and now of one lifetime and a beyond that exists only in imagination.

In the twenty-first century, this hawk is not a ba soul but a local mascot, a city's totem of negotiation and survival. Named Pale Male by the local populace, its perch is not on a desert's edge near the Nile Delta but on the East Side of a narrow island, an urban vertical center surrounded by flowing currents of rivers and ocean.

There is soul at this corner of Museum Mile and Fred Lebow Place. Better known as Fifth Avenue and East 89th Street, island and borough of Manhattan, city of New York, this corner's street signs epitomize the experiential bias that celebrates striving and achieving. Fred Lebow initiated the New York Marathon and founded the New York Road Runners Club.[4] The Mile of Museums is an urban tribute to the muses and witness to human creativity.

This is a magnet corner of a magnet city in a magnet country. At this intersection, everyone seems to arrive and depart with purpose. Consummate New Yorkers who could live nowhere else mix with the "glad to visit but wouldn't want to live here." Protected children from the neighborhood's private schools and privileged homes run among the uniformed men from Ready, Willing & Able. Once homeless, incarcerated, or addicted, these men belong to a hard, tough, and forgiving town, itself no stranger to the skids of despair and the resilience of recovery. The mix of residents, tourists, children, and the recovering who are ready, willing, and able epitomizes the self-sufficiency and interdependence essential for being in New York.

Soul in Your Face

Soul is liminal. It invites a reach beyond grasp and givens, it moves beyond knowns toward otherness. It hovers at thresholds and edges, at intersections, bridges, corners, shores, harbors; it rests in parentheses, pauses, and commas. It resides in all locales where differences and opposites meet: reality and fantasy, the known and not yet imagined, I and the other, you and me, me and myself.

Soul is receptive. Its relies on encounter, discourse, and response, is open to humor and surprise. With its capacity for reflection and relationship, soul generates, accepts change and being changed.

When asked to write of New York City, I intended to seek out soul in the hidden nooks and precious crannies of an otherwise brash and rushed metropolis. But like the city itself, the soul of New York is explicit, in your face, in your ears, and directly in front of you. In New York, one need not search for soul, as soul is always seeking and searching.

If soul is imagined as the effluence of interest and curiosity, as harmony from dissonance, as fluidity from friction and the smoothed after abrasions, soul thrives in the auras and accents of compromise. It arises and alights in places of many cultures, eras, stages, and seasons. It moves easily through a constantly becoming city that we continuously are coming to know.

Soul and History

The island of Manhattan is the sigh of a continent—a sliver of rock, a spit of land emerging from waters—only 14,478 acres across 22.7 square miles, 13.4 miles long and 2.3 miles wide at it broadest point.[5] As Manahatta, "island of many hills," it was an indigenous trading post. As New Amsterdam in the seventeenth century, it became "the island at the center of the world" that reoriented the globe.[6]

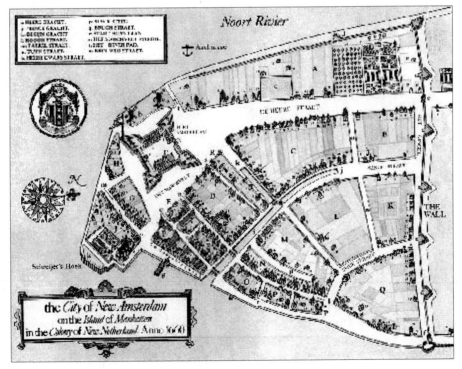

New Amsterdam, c. 1660.

Manhattan's threshold geography matches its edgy personality and psychology. It requires a physical crossing—across oceans, rivers, streams, marshes, bays, and creeks. Its promise has seduced many to cross great waters, brave edges, transgress boundaries, cover millions of miles, move through multiple time zones and time warps for a temporary refuge or a dream destination. It also demands a psychic reach toward the foreign and strange, requires an equilibrium amid tensions between replanted old societies and the cutting edges of new worlds. Its energy emerges from a chemistry of nature and culture, familiar and exotic, focused singularity and planetary connectedness.

Sailors' tales of New Amsterdam's deep harbors invited those thirsty for adventure and hungry for abundance. An outpost of Dutch enterprise and social philosophy, it was and is a liberal society with a fluid view of race, station, and religion. Once a British possession, New York became a hybrid compromise—English name and rule, Dutch mores and sensibility.

When the new world wished to rid itself of the old, New York became a locus of revolution and then the first capital of a young nation. The Bill of Rights was conceived and signed on the soil of lower Manhattan, its freedom-preserving tenets wedding the social philosophy of seventeenth-century Netherlands with the English notion of governance.

Contemporary Manhattan is a fantasy construct of desire and determination, autonomy and license. Its beckoning postcard image intimates both place and state of mind: the city as a realization, a telos, a goal. Manhattan is also a material center of global culture and commerce. Manhattan's grid, imposed in 1811 to flatten and discipline its hills and trails, is simple.[7] Yet its street names represent realms of action—Wall Street, Broadway, Madison Avenue, Christopher Street—capitalism, theater, advertising, gay liberation. The successes and failures on these thoroughfares send light or cast a shadow around the globe, for good and ill, with benefit and detriment.

Soul on the Circumference

Look at a map of Manhattan. Moving on its west rim from its original southern settlement, from south to north, the Hudson River is on the left, the city on the right. The West Side Drive starts at the Battery, near the site of the original European trading post and the World Trade Center, moving up the Hudson past Downtown, Midtown, and the Upper West Side to Manhattan's northern end, with the Bronx across the water to the north. Near the George Washington Bridge, the Hudson opens and widens at the Palisades, where 400 years ago

Hendrick Hudson sailed upstream into the continent. Turning right and east near Manhattan's north end and then south onto the island's east rim, first the Harlem River and then the East River separate Manhattan from the Bronx, Queens, and Brooklyn, which are reachable only through tunnels and over bridges. East Side Drive passes hospitals, universities, the United Nations, midtown, downtown, Wall Street's financial district, and returns to the Battery at the island's southern tip, where one can see the outlines of Staten Island off the coast. This trip around Manhattan island is short, but arrival may be long.

This global icon island is only one, and indeed the smallest, of New York City's five boroughs (from the Dutch *burcht* and the English *bury* or *burg*): Manhattan, Brooklyn, Queens, the Bronx, and Staten Island. The geography, variety, and diversity of the greater city's energies and quotidian realities are impossible to capture in a photograph or a chapter in a book.

Greater New York City is spread over 469 square miles, 305 of land and 164 of water, with 578 miles of coastline. Water not only surrounds the city but is part of it.[8] Now interconnected by a municipal government, a concentrated power grid, a subway, and an extensive water system, the five distinct and different boroughs became one city in 1898 to create an in-your-face and elusive, gritty and romantic, maddening and magical metropolis.[9]

"Above Manhattan," aerial image of New York.

Copyright Richard Wanderman, www.richards-notes.org.

129

In its shifting dynamics and ever-changing demographics, New York City is still a collective experiment. With 8.3 million city residents, it is the most populous region of the nation to which it belongs—and does not quite belong. New York, New York, " so nice they named it twice," refers to a city in a state. It also suggests the duality of a metropolis that is more international than American and yet, in its openness and fluidity, quintessentially of America.

New York is an old American settlement that is constantly newly settled. In 2010, 37 percent of New York's current residents were foreign born.[10] Some immigrants come on long detours, sending their wages to families left at home in advance of their own return. Others have followed kin from ancestral places, creating little old worlds and recolonizing neighborhoods with the esoteric dialects of the 140 languages spoken in the city. They come to rewrite individual and generational narratives and to become citizens who enter and generate a new order. (In the 2009 city elections, the minority vote outnumbered the white majority for the first time; 51 percent of the voters identified themselves as other than non-Hispanic whites.[11])

In New York, the first query between strangers, "Where are you from?" assumes that all New Yorkers, both native and foreign born, are in the city by choice. The second question is not "Who is your family?" or "Where do you live?" but "What do you do?" Both queries expose the concerns of this city's soul: quest and odyssey, taking action and creating context, engagement and aspiration.

Soul's Emergence

For the alchemists, soul arose when different elements and chemicals were mixed in a retort. In modern parlance, soul is in the emergent and the complex, arising when the meeting of two creates dimensions far beyond the sum of its parts. Cities are retorts for human chemistry and alchemy.

In *Emergence: The Connected Lives of Ants, Brains, Cities, and Software,* Steven Johnson describes "two kinds of complexity fundamental to the city, two experiences with very different implications for the individual trying to make sense of them." The first is "the more conventional sense of complexity as sensory overload, the city stretching the human nervous system to its very extremes, and in the process teaching it a new series of reflexes—and leading the way for a complementary series of aesthetic values, which develop out like a scab around the original wound." The second is "complexity as a self-organizing system: it describes the system of the city itself, and not its experiential reception by the city dweller. The city is complex because it overwhelms, but also because it has a coherent personality, a personality that self-organizes out of millions of individual decision, a global order built out of local interaction—a strange kind of order, a pattern in the streets."[12]

To discern the patterns of the city converging at the corner of Fifth Avenue and 89th Street takes a keen eye and a tolerance for movement coming from and moving toward all directions. To be part of the city, one must move out in many directions without knowing exactly what one will meet and find.

The New Yorkers at Fifth Avenue and 89th Street have strolled down the block or have come on ferries from Staten Island, taken the bridges from the Bronx, crossed Hudson River spans, arrived through tunnels from Queens, cycled across the East River from Brooklyn. The outlanders who have traveled here for a day of metropolitan sophistication, synchrony, or stridence would be among the 47 million annual tourists, 8.8 million from foreign countries.[13]

The crowd has arrived via one of 4,300 buses[14] or survived the fits and starts of one of the city's 13,000 licensed taxis.[15] Drivers from Haiti and Turkey, from the Punjab, Bengal, and Bangalore, feint for position with cabbies from Karachi and Islamabad who possibly never drove a car in their birth lands. Muslims, Hindus, and Sikhs, Russians and Georgians who would be archenemies in their native homes eat at the same diners, start and stop at the same garages, coexist in the same apartment houses.

Other commuters have emerged from one of 468 subway stops of the busiest 24-hour metropolitan transportation system in the world, its unceasing schedule making New York "the city that never sleeps." Knowing New York requires taking the subway, noting the trust, wariness, explicit distance, and implicit cooperation that keep an energy-efficient city on the move. Each day, 7 million folk, including a billionaire mayor, use its 842 miles of track for 5 million trips per month under and over city thoroughfares.[16]

In his study of behavior and complex systems, Johnson describes looking at an ant colony:

> I realize with a start that the dirt coating the plastic boxes is, in fact, thousands of harvester ants, crammed so tightly into their quarters that I had originally mistaken them for an undifferentiated mass. A second later, I can see that the whole simulated colony is wonderfully alive, the cluster of ants pulsing steadily with movement. The tubing and cramped conditions and surging crowds bring one thought immediately to mind: the New York subway system, rush hour.[17]

Jung and Paracelsus in the Subway

The subway exemplifies the New York that could be crushing to soul, but it also offers the blinking, instant, and subliminal contacts that evoke soul. At midnight, in the maze of underground walkways and rails, ladies in mink coats and men in tuxedos mingle with office cleaners who have just finished their night shifts. They share the movement, the bustle, the hustle, the sounds and the sights of an underground world.

The subway's Music Under New York program provides live performing art. The syncopations of Brooklyn rappers, Bronx hip-hoppers, and Harlem jazz trumpeters are in counterpoint with the windpipes from Peru and Bolivia, drums from Africa, and classical clarinet and flute. In city lore, the keen of ear hear the wheels on some subway routes sound chords from the beginning of "Somewhere," the Broadway ballad of the immigrant from the musical *West Side Story*: "There's a place for us / Somewhere a place for us."[18] In its 1957 Manhattan Romeo-and-Juliet story, Polish American Tony's romance with the newly arrived Puerto Rican Maria is thwarted by the ethnic turf wars of Manhattan's Hell's Kitchen neighborhood. (A half-century later, Puerto Ricans are one group among the various populations that constitute the city's 21 percent Hispanic population.[19])

The city's Arts for Transit program has funded permanent art installations reflecting the aboveground site and topography in subway stations throughout the system. *Under Bryant Park* by Samm Kunce, located near the New York Public Library at 42nd Street and Fifth Avenue, is one of the largest artworks. Tiles create a mosaic of rock outcroppings, tree roots, pipes, animal burrows, and literary quotations based on the idea of systems. The artist writes:

People travel the subway system, water and other utility services are delivered by pipes, and plants and trees that provide grace and softness against the city's sharper edges find their way to water and nutrients underground through a system of roots. In a similar way, literature is shared by systems of learning and lending, and many animals inhabit systems of burrows just as humans systematically divide portions of larger habitats aboveground.[20]

At the west end of the subway tunnel, a frieze of rock and plant forms offers these words: "Nature *must not* win the game, but she *cannot* lose," a quotation from Jung's essay on the medical alchemist, "Paracelsus as a Spiritual Phenomenon."[21]

"Under Bryant Park," Samm Kunce (2002).
Photograph by Alexandra Zabriskie

The rush in the underground alleys, at subway stops, and up the stairs to the street is for the nimble and the quick who leave subway, bus, and taxi to join the surge on the sidewalks of New York. To proceed, one learns to weave and feint, twist and turn, jostle and pause, huddle and forebear. Both body and soul muster to master the city's sidewalks, to reach the corner between the museum and the park.

Everyone is a New Yorker on the city's sidewalks, creating and adding to their patterns. As Jane Jacobs wrote, sidewalks are

the primary conduits for the flow of information between city residents. Neighbors learn from each other because they pass each other—and each other's stores and dwellings—on the sidewalk. Sidewalks allow relatively high bandwidth communication between total strangers, and they mix large numbers of individuals in random configurations.[22]

If sidewalk mastery increases the social intelligence and adaptation intrinsic to survival, here one must learn quickly. New Yorkers are the nation's fastest walkers[23] and the eighth fastest urban walkers in the world (Tokyoites are the fastest). Jacobs writes: "Sidewalks work because they permit local interactions to create global order."[24]

Soul on the A Train

The sidewalks to the north of the Guggenheim Museum belong to a specific New York neighborhood, Carnegie Hill, while its institutions represent the religious, ethnic, and cultural soul traditions of the world. At 90th Street, the Episcopal Church of the Heavenly Rest offers cots for earthly rest to some of the city's 120,000 homeless.[25] The former Andrew Carnegie Mansion, which gave its owner's name to the neighborhood, is now the Smithsonian's Cooper Hewitt Museum of Design; the Roman Catholic Convent of the Sacred Heart in 91st Street mansion is on the facing corner. The Jewish Museum on 93rd Street (there are more Jews in New York than in metropolitan Tel Aviv[26]) is only a few blocks south of Mount Sinai Hospital, a teaching and medical center. Close by, the mosque of the Islamic Cultural Center of New York is oriented toward Mecca. Further up Fifth Avenue, the New York Academy of Medicine on 103rd Street (where Jung presented in 1912) is next to the Museum of the City of New York, which displays the city's Native, Dutch, English, and American history, and across from the soul's retreat in Central Park's only formal garden, the six-acre Conservatory Garden.[27]

Central Park's north border touches on the old Dutch town of Haarlam. At the northeast corner of Central Park at 110th Street, Duke Ellington's statue stands by his piano in the middle of Duke Ellington Circle. Tito Puente Way cuts into East or Spanish Harlem, "El Barrio," an homage to the Latin soul of the Puerto Rican king of mambo (there are more Puerto Ricans in New York than in San Juan).[28] The Duke was the music laureate of West Harlem, a place where music mixed African soul with city jazz rhythms. When the Duke's orchestra played "You must take the A Train / To go to Sugar Hill way up in Harlem," he linked the hilly curves of northwest Harlem with the listening world. The A train then connected southeast Brooklyn with the northwest Bronx, passing under the East River, across Manhattan, through Harlem. Now its 31-mile route connects the Far Rockaways of Brooklyn's ocean edge, stops at JFK Airport in Queens, and goes under the East River across Manhattan to the Upper West Side, where a transfer to the #1 goes seven miles further into the Bronx. As another song jubilantly proclaims: "New York, New York, it's a wonderful town / The Bronx is up and the Battery down / The people ride in a hole in the ground / New York, New York, It's a wonderful town."

World Soul, New York Soul

Returning to our magnet corner, we walk south along Museum Mile, where street banners show images from neighborhood museums, including the intimate Neue Gallerie of Austrian and German Art and the grande dame of the Mile, the Metropolitan Museum of Art. The arts of the world are at work on the soul of this worldly city, making subliminal impressions on the mind's eyes even when intent is focused elsewhere.

When Jung first visited New York in 1909, he visited the Metropolitan's Egyptian and Cretan collections. He explored the Museum of Natural History on the park's western perimeter, where generations of city children have learned about flora and fauna, earth and sky. He walked and talked with Freud on the pathways and noticed the many children at play.

With 4.5 million visitors each year, the Metropolitan is the world's fifth most visited art collection.[29] Occupying four city blocks, the "Met" displays some of its 2 million pieces from 6,000 years of human culture. (Most of New York's 164 museums are not on Museum Mile. The Museum of Modern Art, the fifteenth most visited, is in Midtown Manhattan. The small jewel of the Rubin Museum of Art is downtown in Chelsea. The Rubin's exhibit of Jung's private illuminated journal, *The Red Book,* opened in October 2009, 100 years after Jung's first journey to America and New York.)

In the Met's north wing, beyond the mummies, the Temple of Dendur, transported from the Nile and dedicated to the Egyptian widow goddess Isis, faces the reservoir named for a revered American widow, Jacqueline Kennedy Onassis. Behind the Metropolitan Museum, one Egyptian obelisk stands on a rise in its own small court. One of a pair commissioned by a pharaoh 3,500 years ago for the Temple of the Rising Sun in Heliopolis, it was moved in 13 BCE by Augustus to Alexandria's Caesarium, Cleopatra's monument to Marc Antony. The obelisk was gifted by Egypt to the United States in the nineteenth century. (Its mate was sent to England and now stands on London's Victoria Embankment.) On this "Cleopatra's Needle," stone carvings of falcon and hawk invoke Isis's son Horus, the victorious spirit of the rising sun, and evoke images of the hawk-headed ba soul who accompanied the Egyptian throughout life and through death to an afterworld.

The tip of the obelisk is visible from the Metropolitan's rooftop sculpture garden, where Rodin's *Three Shades* watch over those who gaze at Midtown's skyline silhouettes to the south, the lower Harlem skyline to the north, and the landmark residences on east and west that frame Central Park. In the morning, the east-facing windows of West Side buildings, like a modern Stonehenge, reflect the rising sun back to the East Side. In the evening, East Side windows that face west reflect the setting sun to their West Side neighbors.

Central Park is soul's refuge in nature, Manhattan's landscape of cultured nature, a green rectangle between the rivers and the city grid. Its 843 acres of sculpted and natural landscape is 6 percent of Manhattan's total acreage, stretching 2.5 miles south to north from midtown's 59th Street to Harlem's 110th Street, its half-mile east-west expanse separating and connecting the east and west sides of the island from Fifth Avenue to Central Park West. Each year, 25 million human visitors walk its 58 miles of paths, sit on its 9,000 benches, find peace in its 7 designated quiet zones, and clamber in its 21 playgrounds. Meanwhile, 275 species of migratory birds rest on or around its 7 water bodies or perch on or under its more than 25,000 trees.[30] Romance and soul traverse Central Park, tended by the city and a citizen conservancy. Each day of the year, New Yorkers and international marathoners walk and run around the park's billion-gallon reservoir,[31] visit the skating rinks, the puppet theater, and the zoos.

Central Park is a playground for members of New York's favorite hawk family. A few years ago, the white-faced red-tailed hawk Pale Male and his mate Lola nested on a celebrity-occupied Fifth Avenue apartment building. When the couple was evicted by the management, irate New Yorkers protested, picketing the building for days, stopping traffic on Fifth Avenue. After the outcry, the birds were allowed to return. But Lola, preferring her West Side perch, refused to return to the East Side. Even birds take part in New York real estate sagas.

When the biological and professional heirs of Jung came to New York for the publication and exhibit of *The Red Book,* just as they emerged onto the Metropolitan Museum's roof deck, Pale Male, with bushy eyebrows reminiscent of C. G., landed on the aluminum branches of *Maelstrom,* a sculpture by Roxy Paine. We looked at it and he looked at us, then flew off to join his carved-in-stone cousin on the obelisk.

A few blocks south, twenty-first-century children clamber over the Alice in Wonderland statues and send toy boats across the sailing pool. In the carefully

Pale Male perched on "Maelstrom," a sculpture by Roxy Paine.

Photograph by Andreas Jung

tended Shakespeare garden around the open-air theater, the Bard's verses are written on placards planted amid the flowers mentioned in his plays. Familiar rhymes come to mind amid the statues of Poet's Walk. On the boating lake, the incongruity of a Venetian gondolier pushing his craft is silly and soulful at sunset.

Near the orchestra shell on Olmstead and Faux Way, the 72nd Street transverse named for the park's landscape designers, the global mix of sounds echo the streets of the world. Rap and Latin rhythms accompany skateboard performances, while Mozart and Bach are practiced in the open air by music students and musicians en route to rehearsal across the park at Lincoln Center.

Lincoln Center stands where the city's diagonal artery, Broadway, links uptown and midtown. The twelve art groups and schools of Lincoln Center are links between the muses and the metropolis. In the summertime, Lincoln Center's Plaza is the city's dance floor, where young lovers, old couples, and fathers and daughters swirl and dip to dance bands playing around the fountain.

While music emanates from Lincoln Center, it is heard throughout the city: in the little church just down the street, in Carnegie Hall just down the avenue, in the halls of smaller museums, in shells in parks and barges on the rivers, from the musicians on corners, in city parks and subway stations, and on the median of the city's signature street, Broadway.

Soul's Broad Way

In the rectangular city grid, Broadway is a thirteen-mile diagonal cutting through the island, Manhattan's only true north-south road; it was once an indigenous Wickquasgeck trail. From its northern tip, Broadway (from the Dutch *Brede Weg*) continues Route 9 of the Hudson Valley into the city, moving from the heights and palisades of the Upper West to the Lower East tip of the island. North of Lincoln Center, Broadway passes near the City University of New York and directly by Union Theological Seminary, Jewish Theological Seminary, Columbia University, Barnard College, and Fordham University.

South of Lincoln Center, Broadway makes an uncustomary round at Columbus Circle. It then becomes the Great White Way, the signifier of theatrical exuberance and dramatic fantasy, blazing into the neon spectacle of the theater district. Its name marks the core and circumference—if not the geography—of live theater and spectacle: Broadway, off-Broadway, off-off-Broadway.

If Manhattan has a belly, it is Times Square. Once the hard core of gritty and darker soul, Times Square is now a family destination with a wholesome patina on the old underbelly of a port city. Now a more fit tummy, its faux magic is epitomized by the broad red stairway of the theater ticket booth at its nexus. Two million huddle here on New Year's Eve to watch the crystal ball fall at midnight.

From Broadway and 42nd Street, a changing "crossroads of the world," the underground artery of the cross-town subway shuttle links the West Side's raucous Times Square to the East Side's Grand Central Terminal. The shuttle travels under the city's crown jewel, the New York Public Library, spread across two blocks of Fifth Avenue. What the museums are to visual arts, what concert and church halls are to music, the NYPL is to soul's expression in word and text. From its imposing headquarter, the NYPL has 89 branches with more than 20 million books and 30 million videos, maps, and other forms of media.[32] The forwards of many books acknowledge hours spent in the library's vaulted halls, guarded from intrusions by the massive stone lions at its entrance.

Directly east, Madison Avenue has given its moniker to the ad world of *Mad Men,* with its seductive promises of soul through the body's pleasures. In 1909, Jung, Freud, and Ferenczi stayed at the Manhattan Hotel, then on the corner of Madison Avenue and East 42nd Street.

Soul at the Center

One block east, at 89 E. 42nd Street and Park Avenue, there is another universe: the 48 acres and several levels of the city's solar plexus, Grand Central Terminal, built and rebuilt over cow pens and freight yards. The four-faced clock at the center of the grand hall is New York's central mandala. By any measure, New York is a city running in a race with time (if not always on time).

Each day, half a million visitors and 75,000 commuters[33] enter and exit the arched spaces, moving like flocks of birds in shifting, emerging patterns. But birds might be disoriented by the ceiling's version of a sky with reversed constellations. When this was mentioned to Grand Central's Vanderbilt investors, they declared—with typical New York humor and hubris—that indeed the artist had painted the sky as it looked to the eyes of God!

Symbol of the city, the terminal also belongs to the country. Since 09/11/2001, an immense American flag has hung from the ceiling. In those terrible autumn days, the crowds paused to search the faces of the missing in the photographs along the terminal's hall and entryways, as they did in the spontaneous shrines twenty-five blocks south in Union Square. During those aching days, altars of candles, notes, and photographs testified to the missing. Further south again, near the original Dutch settlement of New Amsterdam, heart-wrenching notes and images covered the fences of St. Paul's Chapel and Trinity Church, located on the edges of the smoking and gaping hole. The hole is still there—on lower Man-

139

hattan's soil, and in New Yorkers' hearts. Now midtown's Empire State Building is once again the tallest building in a proud city, a sad reminder of the death and devastation at the crumbled Twin Towers. An art-deco architectural tribute to the empire city in the Empire State, it can be seen from the streets of the city, the ocean, the rivers, from New Jersey across the Hudson, and by any who have ever seen King Kong capture the damsel in one of the great Gotham horror movies. The colors of the Empire State Building's façade often signify collective holidays and may also be hired to display favorite colors for personal celebrations.[34]

As Broadway goes to the southeast, it skirts Greenwich Village, Soho, and the Lower East Side, once a crowded settlement of Jewish immigrants. One local son, George Gershwin, combined the soulful lamentations of Jewish strains with African soul rhythms. Now the old tenements are occupied by a vibrant Chinatown, remnants of Little Italy, and the espresso bars that announce gentrification.

The edgy downtown neighborhoods between the East River and the Hudson are familiar locations of movies and TV shows. On the east, the Bowery has followed a typical New York cycle. Once the Dutch governor Peter Stuyvesant's thoroughfare, it declined into the risky street home of *Guys and Dolls,* "Bowery bums," and Salvation Army missionaries. Artists moved into industrial lofts, and now The New Museum, hotels, cafes have followed.

The old-town and new-hip flavor of the West Village is a mix of cozy, down-home, and "with it." Emanating from Greenwich Village's Christopher Street, the site of the Stone Wall Tavern and gay identity, confrontation, and liberation, an annual parade now celebrates gay pride in many cities on all the continents. The television program *Sex and the City,* the ever-hopeful and excessive Cinderella fairy tale of a consumerist New York era, fostered fantasies of fashionable urbanite neuroses. Meanwhile, from the concrete canyons of Wall Street to the south, the stock exchange's ups and downs, losses and gains impact the finances of the city, the state, the nations, and the planet.

Soul and Number

One cannot write of New York without reference to numbers. I have included a number of numbers. Numbers tell their own tales of a city's diminishment and a city's growth.

Beginning with the purchase price of 60 guilders that Peter Minuit paid in 1625 to the Lenape tribe, numbers remain central to the New York experience and enterprise, signifying not just quantity but the multiplied quality of its human waves, its restless strivings, its successes and failures. The city's interdependence with the nation and the world is expressed in numbers.

It is a mental strain to calculate the material enormity of New York. The city's centrality in American finance is reflected in the fact that in the first decade of the twenty-first century, New York City paid $11 billion more in taxes each year to the federal government and New York State than it receives from either.[35]

How does one imagine a city with an annual gross domestic product of $1.13 trillion? In absolute terms, there are only 14 *countries* in the world with bigger economies than that of New York City, which is second only to Tokyo in terms of wealth.[36] In 2008, New York's mayor, Michael Bloomberg, contributed $235 million to charity—more than any one individual in the nation.

If one were to visit a New York City restaurant once a day, it would take 46 years to sample the ethnic variety of the city's restaurants. And is there anyone who has visited all of the city's 164 museums?

Jung remarked that only through disturbances and "shocks do you become aware of having a soul."[37] Numbers reckon the shock of the never-to-be-accepted. On a routine business day, 17,000 people worked in the World Trade Center. Now Ground Zero is the name for the still-empty hole where nearly 3,000 victims from ninety different countries were killed when terrorists used planes to crash into the Twin Towers. On 09/11, the city's bravest helped evacuate 15,000 workers and visitors—often at the expense of their own lives.[38]

New York responded in grief—not anger, not the desire to retaliate, not the desire to go to war. This democratic and liberal city first felt horror at the World Trade Center tragedy and then a horror at its being used as an excuse for a war that was a travesty to its soul. New Yorkers felt the World Trade Center attack as a violence against multiculturalism. New York's soul did not contract. Jewish, Christian, Buddhist, Hindu, and Muslim New Yorkers came together to grieve in a new chapter of the city's history.

New York discovered it is a *polis* of citizens as well as immigrants and residents. New York's "If I can make it there, I'll make it anywhere" resilience permeated all five boroughs. Another reaction was reactive, a determination to overcome a depressive sorrow. The flight into the financial bubble that later burst, a fantasy of numbers, was in part, I believe, a manic reaction to its profound shock. For a time, the notion of unceasing progress died in New York's collective soul. As I write nearly a decade later, many complain of New York's insufficiencies in not rebuilding on the devastated land, but to me, the emptiness of zero suggests a soulful response to an assault that may not ever be assimilated.

In more somber emotional and financial times, the mood of the city is quieter, yet not resigned. The sense on the streets remains that life is change, that the city is change—both for better and for worse. Newcomers retain the faith that they have more hope here than elsewhere. Old-timers who have known the city's ups and downs know their own and the city's resilience.

During recessions, the mayor speaks of a city that is bent but will not break. And new signs of life emerge from the dust and ashes—artists show their work in empty retail storefronts; rents fall, beckoning actors, artists, and musicians to more affordable spaces. And in a city of four seasons, change is sure to be only weeks away.

The Souls of the Ancestors

A city's coherence is somehow imposed on a perpetual flux of people and structures. Like the standing wave in front of a rock in a fast moving stream, a city is a pattern in time.

—JOHN HOLLAND[39]

The editor's request to track family and personal histories with the city led me to historical research and personal remembrance across centuries and eras that are tied to the tides, times, and fortunes of New Amsterdam and New York as a destination or place of passage.

The Italian sailor Verrazzano brought his ship into Manahatta's waters in 1524. He did not stay. On 8 January 1609, a Dutch merchant company signed a contract to search for a western route to the Far East with an English navigator, Hendrick Hudson. When Hudson arrived in New York Bay in September 1609, he disembarked for trade with local tribes and claimed the island for the Dutch company. Having survived the quixotic tulip mania, when Dutch families bet and lost their fortunes buying the perfect tulip bulb, the Dutch were not in quest of a religious utopia for brethren of shared faith, a Puritan model of perfection far from sin. And they were not empowered by notions of transoceanic empire. Rather, they wanted mercantile markets.

The settlement at the island's south end received and absorbed men and women of many backgrounds and appetites, an open port for settlers, pirates, and invaders. It grew so quickly that the wall at its northern edge, Wall Street, was outdated before it was complete.

The Dutch formally founded New Amsterdam in 1624. In 1625, the first European, Sarah, was born there. In 1626, Peter Minuit purchased the island from the Lenni Lenape Indians. A Dutch report states: "They have purchased the Island Manhattes from the Indians for the value of 60 guilders; it is 11,000 morgens in size."[40]

In 1912, the *New York Times* published an interview with C. G. Jung, who said: "Your Puritans, the Huguenots, and all those to whom the idea of God was greater than anything else, learned to think so well that they left their own homes, and you are descendents of those people."[41] That is the story of my husband's family. Machtelt Van der Linde was born of Dutch settlers in 1661, was christened at its Dutch Reform Church, and was raised among the 1,500 in residence when New Amsterdam became New York and New Jersey in 1664. In 1677, 16-year-old Machtelt married the 38-year-old Albrecht Zaborowskij (1638–1711), a Huguenot who had left Catholic Prussia (now Poland) as a religious refugee for tolerant Amsterdam.

Albrecht sailed to the new continent on *d'Vos* (*The Fox*). He paid 42 guilders for transportation, with 3 extra guilders for a seacoat and a berth. He disembarked on 2 September 1662, at the foot of Wall Street.[42] Two years after Albrecht's landing, the English defeated the Dutch without a shot. The Dutch declaration of their rights under the British, the Articles of Capitulation, was later the template for the Bill of Rights, signed in 1791 on Wall Street. This document, which was attached to the Constitution of the United States, stated that the multicultural, multiracial settlers "here shall enjoy the liberty of their Consciences."[43]

Albrecht, who became an interpreter for the Algonquin tribes, was granted farmland in northern New Jersey, where he and Machtelt raised five sons, including Jacob, who lived with (or was kidnapped by) the Indians.

Ninety-nine years after their marriage, Albrecht and Machtelt's Zabriskie descendents were on both sides of the American Revolution. Peter Zabriskie was a delegate to the general congress of American colonies. The Battle of New York was the worst conflict known in the city up to that time. In family lore, after losing that battle, Washington retreated across the Hudson and spent at least one night in Peter Zabriskie's home in northern New Jersey. Other relatives were Royalists. John Jr., originally a colonial delegate, changed allegiance in 1776 to the English king. His home in North Hackensack, New Jersey, was confiscated and given to the revolutionary warrior, Baron von Steuben. Today it is the Steuben House.

Several generations later, my husband Philip Zabriskie's grandfather, George Zabriskie, founded a law firm at 49 Wall Street, near Albrecht's landing place. He described himself as a Republican, thus announcing his opposition to the graft of Tammany Hall, which the Democrats controlled. Like other Republicans, he argued against the construction of the New York subway on the grounds that it would run up a deficit.[44] (Despite his best efforts, the subway opened in 1904, and today the deficit of the Manhattan Transit Authority goes well beyond 1 billion dollars.) In 1906, George moved his family from West 48th Street to the south side of a filled-in swamp known as Gramercy Park. The seller donated the proceeds of the $55,000 sale to the Sons of the American Revolution, who used the money to restore Fraunces Tavern, a landmark from the Revolutionary War era. (A century later, 23 Gramercy Park South was on the market for $20 million.[45])

In 1912, George dedicated three stained-glass windows—of St. Constantine, The Cross, and St. Helena—in Calvary Church just off Gramercy Park in memory of his daughter, Helen, who had died at thirteen. That same year, Jung sailed into New York on 18 September to lecture at Fordham, New York Psychiatric Institute, Bellevue Hospital, and the New York Academy of Medicine. And in that year, 250 years after Albrecht's arrival, while the Zabriskies grieved at Gramercy Park and Jung lectured and gave newspaper interviews, my paternal grandfather Georgio DeLucia left a coastal Italian village in view of Mount Vesuvius and arrived in New York Harbor on a boat called *The Canada*. His name was on a list of "Aliens Retained for Inquiry" at Ellis Island. He had sailed back and forth between America and Italy three times before bringing his wife and three children to settle in upstate New York. One year later, my maternal grandmother left a village near Ovid's birthplace in the Abruzzi mountains east of Rome. In 1913, she transited through Ellis Island and the city for her journey to upstate New York. Despite their shared Italian heritage, my grandparents spoke different dialects, and my parents' wedding a quarter-century later was considered a mixed marriage.

A Lifetime and New York Time

Why does a field of wildflowers suddenly bloom in the spring? What does water turn to ice? Both systems undergo "phase transitions"—changing from one defined state to another at a critical juncture—in response to changing levels of energy flowing through them.

—STEVEN JOHNSON[46]

When I imagine my grandparents sailing into New York Harbor, I fantasize that their brave souls had special attachment to their port of entry, and this informed my own attachment to New York City.

On his first New York visit, Jung went to the Plaza Hotel, with its "columns and all the obligatory splendor." As he wrote Emma Jung: "Your knees go soft when you enter. Extreme worldliness on a grand scale in every way."[47] My knees also went soft when, at twelve years old, I first entered and (like the fictional Eloise) stayed at the Plaza Hotel. At that moment, New York became a dream destination. After several decades of living here, it remains my dream and reality.

New York is a different city for different life periods. The eras of my lifetime have coincided with the different phases of New York's socioeconomic history. My alma mater was near "the city," and every other Thursday, I occupied the box my college reserved at the old (now-demolished) Metropolitan Opera House. After graduation, I relished the New York single life of low and high culture until my marriage and a move to Zurich for study at the Jung Institute. The New York to which our young family returned in the 1970s was a challenging, impecunious, and dangerous city. After the race riots of the 60s, after the city's bankruptcy in the 70s, after the crack epidemic of the 90s, entire neighborhoods became off bounds and off limits. Schoolchildren were mugged. There were great swaths and neighborhoods where one would dare not go. Barack Obama also moved to New York, found it harsh, became a hermit, and claimed his intellect here.[48] He and we and the resilient city held on. Today, with the significant exception of the least privileged and most in need, the city is secure and safe, less abrasive and edgy, the population healthier and longer living than in any other area of the nation. Each of what Manhattan-centric New Yorkers call "the outer boroughs," has its own center of vibrant life and resilient character. If each borough were an independent city, Brooklyn, Queens, Manhattan, and the Bronx would each be one of the ten most populous cities in the country, while Staten Island hovers on the ocean horizon. The world comes to each of them, and each of them is its own world.

Soul's Poetry on the Bridge to Brooklyn

I too lived, Brooklyn of ample hills, was mine;
I too walk'd the streets of Manhattan Island, and bathed in the waters around it;
I too felt the curious abrupt questionings stir within me,
In the day, among crowds of people, sometimes they came upon me,
In my walks home late at night, or as I lay in my bed, they came upon me....

—WALT WHITMAN[49]

Each June, a New York institution, Poets' House, gathers its supporters to walk from the Manhattan's City Hall across the East River on the Brooklyn Bridge, one of the city's 2,000 bridges.[50] Poems are read at sections of the bridge and again at the Landing in Brooklyn, where lines of Walt Whitman's poetry are forged in the iron fence. The walkers from Manhattan are greeted by a Brooklyn official, as if they were visitors from a far-off land. Whitman scholar and poet Galway Kinnell recites "Crossing Brooklyn Ferry," from *Leaves of Grass,* Walt Whitman's ode to city, country, humanity, body, and soul. When I first made this crossing, the poet stood by the river, across from a Manhattan skyline dominated by the Twin Towers of the World Trade Center. Since 2001, the towers and all who died within have been absent presences in the downtown silhouette skyscrapers on the narrow island tip.

Brooklyn's population of 2.5 million covers 71 miles. If it was not incorporated into New York City, Brooklyn (for the Dutch Breuckelen) would be the fourth largest American city.[51] When the Brooklyn Dodgers, named for the residents' penchant for dodging trolley cars, hired the African American Jackie Robinson in 1947, they broke the color barrier in big-league American sports. Given the sports-minded American psyche, some trace a color line from Robinson to another barrier breaker, President Obama. Brooklyn still smarts from the soul wound it suffered fifty years ago when the Dodgers emigrated to Los Angeles. But Brooklyn continues to receive immigrants from everywhere. Jewish refugees in Bushwick, Poles in Greenpoint, Arab grocers on Atlantic Avenue, Orthodox and African American neighbors and neighborhoods manage to coexist, while Hasidim and Palestinians, Russians and Georgians suffer the subway together to reach the far edges of the borough.

In 1977, *Saturday Night Fever,* a film about young Brooklynites longing to make the river crossing to Manhattan, hit the tone of those times. Now when soul is young and restless or seeks to settle down, it heads to Brooklyn. Brooklyn is a destination for young refugees from Manhattan and the Midwest, seeking space for baby buggies and scooters. Brooklyn is the hot music scene, the hot dating scene, the young chef scene, the performing scene (at the Brooklyn Academy of Music's Next Wave Festival). For Egyptomaniacs who cannot make it to Cairo, the ancient goddesses in the vast collection of antiquities of the Brooklyn Museum serve as the ancestresses of the museum's new and unique Feminist Art Center.

Soul Disappears and Reappears in the Bronx

The Bronx is the only borough of New York connected to the North American mainland. The Bronx is the Phoenix of New York. It rises up and burns down and emerges again. With extreme fortunes, the Bronx has hosted indigenous camping grounds, Dutch farmland (owned by Jonas Bronck, whose name the borough bears), an English homestead, middle-class Irish neighborhoods, street corners for Italian grocers and wise guys, Hispanic barrios. It burned during the race riots of the 1970s and crumbled under the crack epidemic that destroyed lives, homes, and entire neighborhoods in the 1980s and the recession of the 1990s. It is still the borough with the highest rate of unemployment and lowest measure of health. But now, where Broadway crosses the bridge north into the South Bronx, it is a lively stretch of a human thoroughfare.

It is a borough of contrasts and unexpected elements. While associated with urban blocks, one-fifth, or 7,000 acres, of its 42 square miles is open space and parkland. Fordham University, the extraordinary oases of the Bronx Zoo, and the New York Botanical Garden are soul-nourishing for those in search of education, the animal kingdom, and cultivated nature. The immense opera sets for the Metropolitan Opera stage are stored and preserved in Bronx warehouses. The Bronx Bombers, better known as the New York Yankees, have their home plate in the shining oval of a new and controversial stadium, an expensive extravagance in times of dire economic stress.

The Bronx has chewed up the marginal and sheltered the neediest, including illegal immigrants and political refugees. The journalist Phil Zabriskie's narration of the arrival of a Nepali family, exiled from Bhutan to a refugee camp in India, describes their first journey from Kennedy Airport to their New World refuge, a tale reenacted every day.

They're speeding north on the Van Wyck Expressway, perk up when they cross the Whitestone Bridge and get their first skyline view. The "Welcome to the

Bronx" sign, the turns that lead to East Fordham Road, the glimpses of the Bronx Zoo and Fordham University mean nothing. The place itself is a mystery. They'd never even seen pictures.

The driver turns onto Decatur Avenue and pulls over short of 193rd Street. As the family piles out, a car alarm wails. Rap pumps out of a passing SUV.

At their first English class in Manhattan they meet "a Chinese Uighur woman wearing a headscarf, a woman from Chad with tribal tattoos on her face, a pale-skinned Kosovar woman, a bespectacled Senegalese man, and two Karen women from Burma, one with a Karen-English dictionary printed by missionaries in the 1950s. At the other table is a Nepali Bhutanese couple and two slight Burmese men, one wearing a cowboy hat and dark glasses, missing the tips of several fingers and part of his nose due to leprosy."

After some weeks, the family takes the big trip to the ethnically diverse Jackson Heights in the sister borough of Queens.

The first destination is the Merit Kebab Palace, which offers "Indian/Tibetan/Nepali/Bhutanese cuisine." Everyone orders *momos*, a staple Nepali dish they haven't had in the weeks since they left Asia. Hindi music drifts into the streets as they pass Bangladesh Plaza, Jaipur Emporium, and the Kashmir Grill. They walk past an Indonesian Pentecostal Church and the Jesus Love Mission Church (signs in Korean and Spanish) to the Satya Narayan Mandir Temple. The family goes home happy, finding in Queens what they hadn't found in the Bronx.[52]

Finding Soul in Queens

A city is a kind of pattern-amplifying machine: its neighborhoods are a way of measuring and expressing the repeated behavior of larger collectivities— capturing information about group behavior, and sharing that information with the group.

—STEVEN JOHNSON[53]

Brooklyn is King's County, and Queens is the Queen's County. With 2.3 million persons spread over its 109 square miles, Queens is the most ethnically diverse area in the country.[54] If not incorporated into New York, it would be the fifth largest city in the nation. My colleague, Donald Grasing, is a refugee from Manhattan's West Side (the old Hell's Kitchen neighborhood of West Side

Story, now gentrified as Clinton) who recently crossed the East River to live in the Queens neighborhood named after the Astors, Astoria. Donald writes of his newly adopted borough and town.

Astoria, in Northwest Queens, has deep working class roots. In the 1870's, Henry Steinway built a Victorian village for the workers in his piano factory, sawmill and foundry. Still, many shops are family-owned—although many of the younger generation become professionals and move to prosperous suburbs.

Astoria was and is again a vibrant film and television center. Kaufman Astoria Studios, where the Marx Brothers once cracked wise, succumbed as Hollywood thrived in the middle of the last century. Revived in the 1980s, it is now the country's fourth largest studio, with productions such as *The Cotton Club* and *Sesame Street*; Silvercup Studios, home to *Gangs of New York* and *Sex and the City*, and the American Museum of the Moving Image, on the site of the old Paramount Studio.

Astoria's current script is played out on smaller stages. A mecca for Greek restaurants, tavernas, and specialty shops, it is home to tens of thousands of Greeks, Cypriots, and Albanians. It is home to a large Italian-American community, and clusters of Czechs, Bangladeshis, Brazilians, Lebanese, Arabs and Indians. On Steinway Street you can peruse the city's largest selection of hookahs, in Little Egypt.

Lately, waves of young hipsters are moving into apartments that might have been occupied by second- and third-generation Greeks and Italians.

The mathematical magic of city life is optimized here. You see your neighbors, know the local merchants, and even though always rushing by—this is New York—you eventually have a rapport with the people different from the luxury-condo-and-supermarket routine.

Astoria's architecture adds to its success as a community. With few buildings higher than four stories, blocks of two-, three-, and four-family dwellings are intersected by busy avenues lined with cafes, ethnic food stores, and one-of-a-kind businesses. Surrounded by children and the old, a trip to the corner store includes an earful of wisdom or gossip, a version of Jane Jacobs' optimal amount of accident and chaos in city life, encouraging a lively, regular interface with neighbors, and a gradual progression to the many faces of the larger community—a contrast to the abrupt entry from a high apartment tower to the streets of Midtown Manhattan.

Queens has the right chemistry for interfacing with the "other," in increments one can handle. People watch each other, know each other, and they're on their way, but enriched with a sense of their own context. It's about assimilation, industriousness, cosmopolitan sensibility, curiosity, and identity that's rooted in family and ethnicity—or in quirky, web-inspired hipster sensibility—but willing to challenge itself. While much of the socializing is in living rooms with the accents of Athens, Cairo and Istanbul, big tables at the restaurants also invite the young Americans who get a sense of their own identity through the gaze of their more traditional neighbors.)

Astoria is about coming here and making it, a more humane New York than the past's brute confrontation of Ellis Island, ethnic ghettos or corporate trainees in a box of an apartment just across the East River on the far east side of Manhattan. The feeling is "we want to be here, give it our best, striving and savoring, dreaming." One summer evening, the Trade Fair supermarket on Ditmars Boulevard was unusually empty. The idle young cashiers in their headscarves were yearning to be out there, in the hazy heat. It was the Fourth of July.[55]

The Fifth Borough

I have never been around Staten Island, a suburban greenbelt, thrust between Manhattan and the sea. I have taken the free Staten Island ferry for its thrilling views of islands, boroughs, ocean, and Lady Liberty. Some of the 481,700 people who live on Staten Island's 58 square miles have never been to Manhattan.[56]

City ferries and buses connect the island to the other boroughs, but there is no subway there. The other New York boroughs vote as Democrats, but not Staten Island, the one Republican foothold in the city. New York City residents sometimes speak of seceding from New York State, but Staten Islanders speak of seceding from the city. Once I am finished with this essay, I will visit Staten Island.

Soul on a Frontier

From its founding as a commercial port, there have always been financial fiascos, investment manias, merchants, and pirates in New York. The metropolis can seem unattainably first world and despairingly third world at the same time. Great private wealth coexists with city deficits that are as large as the entire budget of some nations. Triumphs of matter for the ever-striving and ever-seeking

New York ego can bring loss of perspective, loss of soul, and loss of appetite, endangering cultural creativity and the city's eros.

New York is still a frontier, constantly building and demolishing, very raw as well as very done. New folk and flocks of birds move and migrate to and through New York season after season. New surges of populations enter year after year. Neighborhoods change from rich to poor, from poor to ethnic, from ethnic to arty, from arty to gentrified, from gentrified to gay, from gay to chic—and then the cycle begins again. With its changing flows of populations and fluid fortunes, the relentless, jerky, and graceful motion of the newly arrived and the strange, the unsleeping city startles, surprises, and shocks. It is never stagnant, nor can those who survive remain as they were. Soul constantly arrives and never leaves.

C. G. Jung evoked an image that captured this New World city filled with so many traditions and mores when he alluded to the "alchemistic melting pot." [57] New York demands jumping into the mix, mixing it up, being mixed up: in other words, entering, engaging, and experiencing life. This appeals to those in search: to be here is to arrive—and never arrive. New Yorkers most likely live longer because they are afraid to miss whatever is about to happen.

Soul thrives in process. Soul thrives in the constant mirroring festival of New York streets. It stimulates the brain's mirror neurons through interdependent interactions. It increases social intelligence, fosters adaptations. The city offers immense psychic space and mandates alternations of surrender and defiance, reciprocity and individualism, attending to oneself and mirroring what transpires with the many others.

In a 4,000 year old Egyptian text, possibly the soul's oldest manifesto, "The Dialogue of a World-Weary Man with His Ba," the hawk-headed soul asks a depressive man, "Are you alive at all?" In a back and forth, the soul urges the man to become at one with himself and his soul, to reenter life so that he may both live and die well. [58]

If I have a ba soul, it has alighted in New York. This is my miracle city, the place I have chosen to come, to live, to stay. An irrational mix of soul, body and spirit, New York, like any city, is a human experiment, miraculous in that it works at all, multiply miraculous in that so much potential is made real. Soul is amused. Soul smiles.

Notes

1   Lewis Thomas, *The Lives of A Cell: Notes of a Biology Watcher* (New York: Bantam, 1984), p. 133.

2   C. G. Jung, *The Collected Works of C. G. Jung*, vol. 8, *The Structure of the Psyche* (Princeton: Princeton University Press, 1970), p. 207.

3   C. G. Jung, *Visions: Notes of the Seminar Given in 1930–1934*, ed. Claire Douglas (Princeton: Princeton University Press, 1997), p. 1357.

4   ING, "History of the ING New York City Marathon," http://www.nycmarathon.org/about/history.htm.

5   New York City Web site, "NYC statistics," http://www.nycgo.com/?event=view.article&id=78912.

6   Russell Shorto, *The Island at the Center of the World: The Epic Story of Dutch Manhattan and the Forgotten Colony That Shaped America* (New York: Vintage, 2005).

7   Cornell University Library, "Remarks of the Commissioners Report for Laying Out Streets and Roads in the City of New York, Under the Act of April 3, 1807," http://www.library.cornell.edu/Reps/DOCS/nyc1811.htm.

8   Sam Roberts, "It's Still a Big City, Just Not Quite So Big," *New York Times*, 22 May 2008.

9   New York City Web site, "The 100 Year Anniversary of the Consolidation of the 5 Boroughs into New York City," http://www.nyc.gov/html/nyc100/html/classroom/hist_info/100aniv.html.

10 U.S. Census Bureau, "2006–2008 American Community Survey 3-Year Estimates," http://factfinder.census.gov/home/saff/main.html?_lang=en.

11 Sam Roberts, "Minority Voters Were a Majority in New York Election," *New York Times*, 26 December 2009.

12 Steven Johnson, *Emergence: The Connected Lives of Ants, Brains, Cities, and Software* (New York: Scribner, 2001), pp. 38–40.

13 NYC Board of Tourism, "NYC Statistics," http://www.nycgo.com/?event=view.article&id=78912.

14 "New York City Bus System," http://www.ny.com/transportation/buses/.

15 New York City Taxi and Limousine Commission, *Annual Report 2009*, p. 11, http://www.nyc.gov/html/tlc/downloads/pdf/tlc_annual_report_2009.pdf.

16 NYC Metropolitan Transportation Authority, "Subway and Bus Ridership Statistics 2008," http://mta.info/nyct/facts/ridership/index.htm.

17 Johnson, *Emergence*, p. 30.

18 Jim Dwyer, "Under Broadway, the Subway Hums Bernstein," *The New York Times*, 22 February 2009.

19 Roberts, "Minority Voters Were a Majority in New York Election."

20 Samm Kunce, quoted on the NYC Metropolitan Transportation Authority website, http://www.mta.info/mta/aft/permanentart/permart.html?agency=n&line=V&station=8&artist=1&img=3&xdev=720

21 C. W. Jung, "Paracelsus as a Spiritual Phenomenon," in *The Collected Works of C. G. Jung*, vol. 13, *Alchemical Studies*, ed. Herbert Read, Michael Fordham, Gerhard Adler, and William McGuire, trans. R. F. C. Hull (1918; repr., London: Routledge & Kegan Paul; Princeton: Princeton University Press, 1967).

22 Jane Jacobs, *The Death and Life of Great American Cities* (New York: Random House, 1961), p. 94.

23 Clive Thompson, "Why New Yorkers Last Longer," *New York Magazine*, 13 August 2007.

24 Jacobs, *The Death and Life of Great American Cities*, p. 96.

25 Coalition for the Homeless, "Basic Facts about New York City Homelessness," http://www.coalitionforthehomeless.org/pages/basic-facts.

26 Simple to Remember, "World Jewish Population," http://www.simpletoremember.com/vitals/world-jewish-population.htm#_Toc26172080.

27 Central Park Conservancy, "The Conservatory Garden," http://www.centralpark.com/pages/attractions/conservatory-garden.html.

28 785,000 Puerto Ricans live in New York City and 363,000 live in San Juan; U.S. Census Bureau, "Fact Finder," http://factfinder.census.gov.

29 Art News Blog, "The Most Popular Art Museums in the World," http://www.artnewsblog.com/2008/02/most-popular-art-museums-in-world.htm.

30 Central Park Conservancy, "About the Central Park Conservancy," http://www.central-parknyc.org/about/.

31 Central Park Conservancy, "Reservoir," http://www.centralparknyc.org/visit/things-to-see/reservoir/reservoir.html.

32 New York Public Library, "History of the New York Public Library," http://www.nypl.org/help/about-nypl/history.

33 Grand Central Terminal Web site, "Demographics," http://grandcentralterminal.com/info/demographics.cfm.

34 Empire State Building, "Lighting Schedule," http://www.esbnyc.com/tourism/tourism_lightingschedule.cfm.

35 Sewell Chan and Michael Cooper, "Bloomberg Says Spitzer's Budget Would 'Carve a Hole' in City's Budget," *The New York Times*, 6 February 2007.

36 Joshua Zumbrun, "World's Most Economically Powerful Cities," *Forbes Magazine*, 15 July 2008.

37 Jung, *Visions*, p. 1357.

38 Centers for Disease Control, "Preliminary Results from the World Trade Center Evacuation Study," http://www.cdc.gov/mmwr/preview/mmwrhtml/mm5335a3.htm.

39 John Holland, *Hidden Order: How Adaptation Builds Complexity* (New York: Basic Books, 1996), p. 1.

40 New Netherland Institute, "Peter Schaghen Letter," http://www.nnp.org/nnp/documents/schagen_main.html.

41 "America Facing Its Most Tragic Moment," *New York Times*, 29 September 1912.

42 George Olin Zabriskie, *The Zabriskie Family: A Three Hundred and One Year History of the Descendants of Albrecht Zaborowskij*, 2 vols. (Published by the author, 1963).

43 New Netherland Organization, "The History of New Netherland and the *Half Moon*: Articles of Capitulation," http://www.newnetherland.org/history.html#AoC.

44 "Opposition to the Subway," *New York Times*, 20 October 1897.

45 "Sale of 23 Gramercy Park Authorized," *New York Times*, 4 March 1906.

46 Johnson, *Emergence*, p. 11.

47 Deidre Bair, *Jung: A Biography* (Boston: Little, Brown, 2004), p. 162.

48 Barack Obama, *Dreams from My Father: A Story of Race and Inheritance* (New York: New York Times Books, 1995).

49 Walt Whitman, "Crossing Brooklyn Ferry," in *Leaves of Grass: The Original 1855 Edition* (Nashville, TN: American Renaissance, 2009).

50 New York City Department of Transportation, "Bridges Information," http://www.nyc.gov/html/dot/html/bridges/bridges.shtml.

51 U.S. Census Bureau, "Kings County, New York," http://factfinder.census.gov.

52 E-mail from Phil Zabriskie to author, 2009.

53 Johnson, *Emergence*, p. 40.
54 "Queens," http://www.nycgo.com/?event=view.article&id=76310.
55 E-mail from Donald Grasing to author, 2009.
56 U.S. Census Bureau, "Quick Facts: Richmond County," http://quickfacts.census.gov/qfd/states/36/36085.html.
57 Jung, *Visions*, p. 487.
58 Marie-Louise von Franz and Siegmund Hurwitz Jacobson, *Timeless Documents of the Soul: Studies in Jungian Thought* (Evanston, Ill.: Northwestern University Press, 1968).

8 The Soul of New Orleans: Archetypal Density & the Unconscious

CHARLOTTE M. MATHES

Beneath and emanating from all cities is the collective psychological archetype that Jung called "the city archetype." Jung saw the city as the symbolic image of the feminine aspect of the Self. Babylon—the chthonic, dark, secular version, is contrasted with Jerusalem—the heavenly, spiritual, divine version. These personifications of the city archetype are purely unconscious, as Jung stated. "Such things cannot be thought up, but must grow again from the forgotten depths if they are to express the deepest insights of consciousness and the loftiest intuitions of the spirit."[1]

Sharing in the city archetype, each metropolis exhibits a vast human richness, contrasts between the human light and dark, as well as a more or less lengthy existence, the substantial history of which suggests both permanence and the dangers that may undermine it. If all cities are such, one can reasonably say that New Orleans is more so. For its small size (pop. 500,000 before Hurricane Katrina devastated the city on August 29, 2005, and 300,000 after), it has an especially vivid and diverse human richness, and its long history continually manifests not only a greater aliveness but also shadows so dark that they prophesy complete destruction.

New Orleans is known throughout the world as a city with "soul." Because it is such a vivid example of the city archetype, no discussion of the many other subsidiary archetypal energies long conditioning New Orleans's particular soul will exhaust its nearly infinite variety and high color. Exploring a few of this city's special institutions, however, will help depict both its underlying multiplicity and the tone of its signature unity. Such a way into the city's unique soul will take us to the city's rituals of food, to its worship of the Muses, especially music and literature, to the ritual complex of the Mardi Gras, to its high-pitched religiosity, and to the particular shadow that may darken its future.

But before making an excursion into these institutional expressions of the city's soul, a few basic facts must be explored: New Orleans's geography, both actual and symbolic; its compressed manifestations of archetypal bipolarity; and its complexly rich cultural history.

Geography

{ FLOODING, SWAMPLAND, AND THE INNER LIFE }

The French needed a colony at the mouth of the Mississippi in order to control the interior of North America, but the river ended in a labyrinth of bayous and swamps. At a curve in the great river, Jean-Baptiste Le Moyne de Bienville found a rare piece of higher ground with a natural levee and claimed the Île d'Orléans for France in 1718. Geologists Kolb and Van Topik describe the site selected for the new French colony as "a land between earth and sea, belonging to neither and alternately claimed by both."

New Orleans is shaped like a bowl, surrounded on three sides by water, and 70% of it is below sea level. The archetypal struggle of man's attempt to tame and conquer his environment has been constant throughout New Orleans history. The fear of a great flood has haunted the city since its inception. In 1721, a hurricane destroyed the hundred hovels that had been constructed in a hot, wet land infested with mosquitoes, snakes, and alligators. Sauvé's Crevasse, a Mississippi River levee breach around River Ridge, left 12,000 people homeless in the great flood of 1849. During the 1927 flood, bankers influenced politicians to blast a crevasse in the levee of neighboring Plaquemines Parish, drowning thousands of homes in an unnecessary attempt to save the city. Due to destruction of barrier islands and coastal wetlands, New Orleans has now sunk to an average of six feet below sea level. Scientists had written many warnings about the city's contemporary vulnerability to a great storm. In 2001, it came as "Hurricane Katrina."[2]

Just as the city is vulnerable to flooding, so it seems that New Orleans consciousness is susceptible to flooding from the collective unconscious. Situated below sea level, the city infects its inhabitants with a dreamlike unconsciousness. Humidity and heat deter action and rationality. In individuals as in societies, having access to the collective unconscious enhances both creativity and madness. In New Orleans, a visitor can be drawn strongly into archetypal fields that make him feel seduced or even possessed by the all-pervading spirits. He is opened to dimensions of the sacred, encouraged to seek the occult, and brought closer to a conscious awareness of the shadow. Much of New Orleans' psyche resides in the transpersonal, that which is beyond rational experience. Voodoo, gris-gris, haunted houses, spirit-infected areas, and all manner of occult phenomena are at home here.

New Orleans is also a swampland. Dig down thirty feet and you will find clay, not bedrock. Psychologically, swampland is a metaphor for times of depression and suffering, being closer to death but also to rebirth. These are times when we look to the unconscious realm, to find answers in dreams, to see what the Self requires as opposed to the ego. Because New Orleans is largely unconscious, her collective ego, the center of consciousness, fails to thrive. Her acceptance of the status quo can provide an antidote to the Protestant excessive striving characteristic of other American cities, but her denial about realities such as poor schools, failing levees, poverty, and diminishing wetlands increases her vulnerability.

❡ CRESCENT CITY AND ARCHETYPAL FEMININITY ❧

Closely connected with her underwater character and unconsciousness is the shape of New Orleans and its suggestions of deep femininity. Spreading around the curving Mississippi, New Orleans is also the "Crescent City." Like the crescent of the moon, she is forever changing form, mysteriously promising an antidote to America's rush towards growth and competition. She shape-shifts as Southern Belle and Storyville prostitute, the Voodoo Woman of Bourbon Street, Marie Laveau and the Virgin Mary, Mahalia Jackson, Blanche Dubois, and the mythical Mardi Gras Queen. As the Terrible Mother, she is the devouring "Great Flood," and the bone-wreathed lady of the place of the skulls. As the Good Mother, she is Queen of Heaven, Our Lady of Prompt Succor, and Mater Dolorosa. She is the desired goddess praised in songs like "City of New Orleans," and the femme fatale in "The House of the Rising Sun" and "Basin Street Blues." Mostly denied is the Woman-New Orleans who was born from a greedy search for treasure and power, backbreaking slavery, oppression, cruelty, and war. Though she gave birth to jazz, celebration, and cuisine, the majority of her people still suffer in poverty and racial discrimination.

The Archetypal Bipolar Movements: Land, Sea, and Within

If a visitor stays long enough, he will begin to recognize how the psychic energy of the city plays on him in a bipolar movement of land and sea, abundance and deprivation, greed and generosity, suffering and ecstasy, Apollonian and Dionysian attitudes, and, as the names of two streets suggest, Piety and Desire. Though all cities display archetypes and all archetypes are inherently bipolar, in its small compass New Orleans manifests archetypal bipolarity in unusually intense ways. The complexity of the archetypal feminine frankly expresses itself in collective worship of the Madonna and in easy toleration of prostitution. Here *joie de vivre*, having no cares, and letting the good times roll meet the dark facts of a recent Mardi Gras day, when with the streets full of celebrating families, six people were shot. Here suffering and joy exist in near simultaneity—most typically in the jazz funeral, which starts with mourning and ends with celebration. Here alongside a Big Easy toleration of gays, transvestites, or Bohemian artists, one encounters the most rigid exclusion from "high society" of everyone not born into it. New Orleans accepts itself as both Sin City and cleaned up Tourist City. A lack of zoning puts both a mansion and funky old houses on the same street. People have a great interest in preservation of such places as the French Quarter with its iron balconies or the beautiful St. Louis Cathedral overlooking Jackson Square, yet they allow the most flagrant urban decay nearby. All such manifest bipolarities, rising to the archetypal level, create a tension in the psychological air that gives the city a special kind of energy. As one longtime resident, once an immigrant from a distant but rather typical American city, put it: "Many other cities are boring, but New Orleans is not boring."

Though some are discussed in detail later, seeing some of New Orleans's packed polarities gives one the full effect of how this city embodies oppositions. And though many are not unique, the number of such dichotomies and contradictions is greater per capita than in almost any other American city. Many of the polarities are also more hard-edged, more dramatized than in other places. Encounters with contradictions then become part of the daily air New Orleans citizens breathe. Their collective psychology is forced to become unusually intense, thick, full—often skeptical, ironic, and even bitter. Sooner or later, however, most citizens are forced to develop a psychological breadth not typical of Americans. Though the soul of New Orleans is often amused and angry, and habitually unsurprised, it inevitably becomes also accepting, and with acceptance comes maturity. Thereby, New Orleans acquires a certain roundness, an amplitude, of soul.

{ SOME NEW ORLEANS POLARITIES }

Geography claimed as land	Geography claimed by sea
Majestic Garden District	Wasted Lower Ninth Ward
Superdome 1975, symbol of architectural excellence	Katrina Superdome: symbol of shame
Tourism needed by city	Fears that tourism will affect authenticity
Love of neighbor	Fear of murder (having among the USA's highest homicide rates)
Southern Belle	Blanche Dubois, the fictional Southern Belle with a lurid past in Tennessee Williams's play *A Streetcar Named Desire*
Streets smelling of jasmine	Streets smelling of alcohol
New Orleans, birthplace of jazz	Jazz's flight to Chicago during segregation
Louis Armstrong, official American cultural ambassador	Louis Armstrong, forced out of the city by segregation
City built by slave labor	Blacks still suffer discrimination
Political corruption during White Power	Political Corruption during Black Power
Expensive, private preschools	Shameful public education system
Corruption in public schools deprives Black children	Schools run by corrupt Black leaders like William Jefferson
William Jefferson pretends to innocence	$90,000 cash found in his freezer
Family values	Senator David Vitter caught with Washington prostitute
Councilman Oliver Thomas, Katrina hero, respected by both Blacks and Whites	Councilman hero indicted on corruption charges
Policemen to protect	Vice squad indicted for corruption
Strong, friendly Black neighborhoods	Drug wars
Evangelicals' exclusivity	Large, widely-accepted gay community
Southern antebellum lifestyle	Faulknerian eccentricities in families
Jewish families make great philanthropic contributions to city	Jewish families excluded from elite Mardi Gras rituals
Uptown elitism	French Quarter funky lifestyle
Mardi Gras as party for all	Mardi Gras as restricted party for elite
Mardi Gras drains peoples' pockets	Mardi Gras brings money to the city
Praise of strong, matriarchal Black families	Refusal to raise minimum wage for Black working mothers
Local love of food	Local rampant obesity
Moviemaking brings revenue to city	Stars' purchasing houses hikes home prices
Strong local Catholic condemnation of homosexuality	Gays and pedophiles within the local priesthood
Local power elite's patriarchal society	Local devotion to the Virgin
Mother Church-Madonna	Storyville Madam-Whore
Vieux Carré called "French Quarter"	More Spanish influence than French
City as Jerusalem	City as Babylon

⁌ HISTORICAL LAYERS IN NEW ORLEANS'S COLLECTIVE SOUL ⁍

The soul of New Orleans is also enriched by its complex cultural history. One aspect of that complexity derives from the city's symbolic being. For New Orleans, as readers have already noticed, has its own mythology—many facets of it reflected in the polarities just described. In the early eighteenth century, the originally named Île d'Orléans was more image than reality. Early image-makers described the city as a "center of civilization in an oasis of wilderness." Though it became a haven for trappers and gold-seekers traveling down the Mississippi, it was not the cultural center of the New World that Europeans then imagined. Yet, today New Orleans's soul is partly sustained by this and the storied layers held in collective memory. [3]

Criminality and Corruption

In 1717, John Law and his investment company were given proprietary rights to Louisiana. He rounded up prostitutes, criminals, beggars, and orphans to people New Orleans. Law issued more paper notes than he could pay out in coins. When his shares crashed, he deceived his aristocratic European investors, establishing a local culture of criminality and poverty tolerated throughout New Orleans's history. [4]

French Gaiety and Luxury

New Orleans was named for Philippe, duc d'Orléans, who moved the French court from Versailles to Paris, where he became known for serving gourmet meals, creating France's reputation for haute cuisine. When he visited New Orleans in the late eighteenth century, fashionable Creoles (in this sense, "Creole" refers to native-born whites) turned out elaborate five- and six-course menus in his honor. That visit is cherished by locals as contributing to the city's psychic identity. [5]

Native Americans and the Fur Trade

Native Americans predated all European arrivals, and their strong cultural presence continued throughout the nineteenth century. Centered in New Orleans, an important fur-trading commerce covered a vast region. Descendants of early French traders built the first steamboats that plied the distant Missouri River.

Black African Slavery

Most of the slaves brought by the French came from the Senegambia region of West Africa. Having lived along African trade routes south of the Sahara, they were somewhat sophisticated and brought valuable skills. Slave ships also brought rice, which the Senegambians knew how to cultivate. Though enslaved, they practiced their African traditions and established community. The folkways of slave and free Blacks made a unique contribution to New Orleans's developing soul.

Spanish Rule and Slavery

From 1763 until 1800, New Orleans was under Spanish rule, which left one of its marks in the widely recognized wrought-iron architectural elements. The culture was transformed by the arrival of many new African slaves, particularly from the Congo. Under Spanish law, regulations governing African slaves were less harsh than they later became. Slaves could be freed by their masters, could own property, and could contract for their freedom. The practice of *plaçage* (a French word for a Spanish innovation) enabled free women of color to become contract concubines. White gentlemen fathered their children and often gave this second family a home and even slaves of their own.

The Social Elite: Cavalier and Yankee, Aristocracy and Calvinism

As plantations prospered along the Mississippi River, the Vieux Carré, the French Quarter of New Orleans, became the center of a socially elite "Winter Season," now corresponding to the Carnival period from January 6 to Ash Wednesday. Public balls, operas, and plays were regularly attended. After the Louisiana Purchase, Americans began to settle uptown outside the Vieux Carré, building elaborate Greek Revival homes in what became the Garden District. They brought with them their Protestant work ethic and Calvinistic morality. Creoles did not understand their aggressiveness, nor did they want to speak English, but the two cultures gradually began to intermingle.[6]

Commerce and Prosperity: Add Irish and Germans

By 1840, the city population was around 102,000—the fourth-largest city in the United States. New Orleans became noted for its cosmopolitan population and mixture of cultures. Riverboats, steamers, and ocean sailing vessels brought exciting wildness and adventure. Based on the slave trade, prosperity seemed boundless. Beginning a decade earlier, Irish immigrants arrived on empty cotton ships returning from Liverpool. Many died building the New Basin Canal.

In the 1840s and 1850s, Germans arrived by the thousands to become farmers, their immigration only stopping with the Civil War.[7]

The Abolishment of Slavery and Reconstruction

New Orleans was captured by the Union forces without battle. The repressive regime of Union General Benjamin F. Butler, who ruled New Orleans after Federal occupation, caused residents to hate him. Words written in 1899 by Henry J. Hearsey, editor of the New Orleans *Daily States*, show the bitterness and racism that prevailed among the white ruling class.

> We bulldozed the negroes; we killed the worst of them; we killed carpetbaggers; we patrolled the roads at midnight; we established in many localities a reign of terror. Why? Not to suppress or restrict the freedom of the ballot. The Republicans had the niggers, the Carpetbaggers, the federal army and navy united in an effort to crush the white people out of the state. We had only our undaunted hearts and fearless arms to defend our liberties, our property, our civilization, and we defeated our oppressors with such resources as God and nature had placed in our hands, and we redeemed our state.[8]

The determination of whites to impose segregation in Louisiana led to one of the most momentous decisions rendered by the United States Supreme Court. Plessey, an African American from New Orleans, lost his famous case against Ferguson. This ruling established the so-called "separate but equal" facilities that led to all-out segregation until the Court reversed itself in the case of Brown v. Board of Education in 1954. A period of violence and unrest continued until New Orleans schools were integrated. In 1960, state legislator Moon Landrieu cast the lone vote against measures to block school integration. With the help of black voters, he was elected to two terms as Mayor of New Orleans, ushering in a new era of political power for African Americans.

Four New Orleans Archetypal Institutions and their Psychological Meanings

{ BREAKING BREAD }

From earliest times, in such ways as careful preparation, rituals of celebration, and offering hospitality through sharing, humankind has shown reverence for food and eating. When breaking bread together, all peoples have ritually dedicated their food to the gods, connecting to divine power through the acts and ceremonies of eating. In many cultures, even today, breaking bread together is seen as forming inviolable bonds between individuals and groups.

The Breaking Bread archetype is fundamental to the New Orleans soul. Food—preparing it, sharing it, eating it, talking about it—is the quintessential element in New Orleans culture. Ask any displaced native what he misses most about his hometown, and he answers, "The food." Doubtless, someone in his family mastered the art of cooking jambalaya and seafood gumbo just to his liking. Or he remembers walking to a modest neighborhood restaurant that still covers the table with white cloths and serves really good daily specials of fried catfish, oyster patties, or smoked pork chops. Or he reminisces about the last Jazz and Heritage Festival and the dazzling food choices he had—like crawfish bread, pecan pie, catfish *meunière*, alligator pie, and Creole stuffed crab. Folks away from home miss the red beans and rice served in most homes and restaurants on Mondays, and the weekly crayfish boils throughout the Lenten season, or the po-boy Saturday afternoon lunch. (The po-boy is the creation of two inventive streetcar drivers: they covered long loaves of French bread with bits of meat dripping with gravy, and then served them to jobless men—the poor boys). Missing his native culture after he left New Orleans for Chicago, Louis Armstrong always signed his letters, "Red Beans and Ricely Yours."[9]

Over the centuries, New Orleans rituals of eating together have evolved to include banquets, feasts, and, most spectacularly, dining at fine restaurants offering food, hospitality, and entertainment to the public. Both the everyday fare of New Orleanians and the *haute cuisine* served in its internationally acclaimed restaurants are products of the city's dense cultural history, including layers of French, Cajun, Spanish, West Indian, and local Native American influence.

Originally the name Creole was given to people of French heritage born in New Orleans. Later, the term referred to mixed Spanish and French and to free

Beignets and
café au lait, a
New Orleans
tradition.

*Photograph by
Victoria Grant*

people of color with mixed heritage. From the French, Creole women adopted a meticulous care in preparing sauces, particularly the *roux*—dark gravy that remains the essential ingredient in Creole dishes today. Traditionally, Creole cuisine was an elegant affair with several courses that may have included Louisiana herbed rice, crayfish *étouffée*, shrimp Creole, crusty French bread, and a bread pudding dessert.[10]

When mid-eighteenth-century, French-speaking Acadians were exiled from Canada by British conquest, many settled along the bayous and marshes surrounding New Orleans. Called "Cajuns" (the word is a derivation of "Acadia"), they fished and harvested oysters, shrimp, and crayfish from the salty bayous and marshes surrounding the city. Their culinary creations were less formal than those of the Creoles, but equally delicious. Chefs like John Folse have made Cajun cooking famous throughout the world. Cajun and Creole styles often blend together to form much of what we think of as New Orleans cuisine.

Three internationally celebrated, family-owned restaurants demonstrate how food rises to mythological experience for New Orleans locals, who savor gourmet dishes within an atmosphere of traditional ritual. Established in 1840, Antoine's has a ceremonial aura. Many of the thematically decorated dining rooms, named after such old-line Mardi Gras Krewes as "Proteus," "Hermes," and "Rex," are adorned with photos of Carnival royalty and memorabilia including crowns and scepters from past celebrations. Using a special side door, elite clients enter the restaurant to the Mystery Room, where alcohol was served during Prohibition. On the wall, a picture titled *The Pursuit of Vanity* first appears to be a skull, but on closer examination becomes a lady at her dressing table. Like folk art from Mexico's Dia de los Muertos, it symbolizes New Orleanians' understanding that even in their elegant preoccupations, death lurks in the background.[11]

Most ordinary folk and tourists approach the restaurant through its main door, entering a vast dining room. While some local people prefer this space, I remember how incensed my friend became the year we were displaced from her usual "Escargot Room" by a group of businessmen. Though we were comfortably seated in the "Large Annex," and though the waiter served us the same fine wines, Oysters Rockefeller, and entrees, when exiled from her ritual space she could not be happy.

Where one sits is also important at Galatoire's, a classic Vieux Carré restaurant steeped in tradition, and home to many who can afford it. On Friday afternoons, the place is packed with regulars. Most know one another and enjoy the Galatoire tradition of table-hopping to greet their friends. To obtain a table, even the most important guests have to arrive very early and stand in a line that gradually snakes around the block. Galatoire's takes no reservations for first-floor dining, and few locals would accept a second-floor table. They want a familiar contained space, particularly for their Friday afternoon ritual. Once inside, locals drink their milk punch or Sazerac cocktail, and often order the same favorite foods and wine, week after week. They are on intimate terms with a special waiter who has served them for years and memorized just how they want any menu item prepared. Alcohol flows freely through the long afternoon.

On one grand occasion, friends and I lined up outside Galatoire's at 10 A.M. in order to secure a large first-floor table for celebrating a seventieth birthday. Later, an acquaintance's email read: "A photograph of you and Richard from your seventieth-birthday meal at Galatoire's is in *Garden and Gun*" (a recently-launched fashionable magazine). Another friend telephoned: "There's a picture of Richard and you in *Garden and Gun*." Baffled, I searched my brain: "Who is this Richard? No one invited any Richard." At last, I understood: "Yes, our waiter! Not me, *he* is the reason my photo's in the magazine, because *he* is a celebrity."

For years, the Garden District restaurant Commander's Palace, owned by the Brennan family, has been voted the most popular restaurant in the city. Under Ella Brennan's management, the restaurant trained chefs who are now independently famous, like Emeril Lagasse and Paul Prudhomme. Award-winning dishes rival excellent food anywhere, but what makes the place so popular is the generous reception and entertainment focused on each table by the owners, waiters, and jazz musicians. The Brennans have spun off many other excellent restaurants, but all the family—hardworking Irish-American fathers, mothers, cousins, aunts, and uncles—offer the genuine, unassuming hospitality that is part of New Orleans's archetypal treatment of food: "Where ya at? Yall come. De all aksd for you." As lines from the songs suggest, "Come on in an' pass a good time." New Orleans people feel that life is too short to have a bad meal, and that breaking bread is more than eating. To feel like a queen or king, to leave cares behind, and to be genuinely welcomed into community, "Ya have to break bread."

❧ THE MUSES ❧

Calliope—Muse of epic poetry. Clio—Muse of history. Erato—Muse of love poetry. Euterpe—Muse of music. Melpomene—Muse of tragedy. Polyhymnia—Muse of sacred poetry (spelled "Polymnia" in New Orleans). Terpsichore—Muse of dance. Thalia—Muse of comedy. Urania—Muse of astronomy.

The Muses, those Greek divinities of arts and science, inhabit New Orleans in many ways. There is a street named after each one. More important is their archetypal presence in ceremony, in their inspiration of creative people, in the city's reputation for giving home to them, and above all in the music that fills its past and present.

166

The overwhelming popularity of the Mardi Gras "Muses Parade" exemplifies the love locals have for creative play, and how, unknowingly, so many individuals live close to the Muses' influence throughout the year. Founded by prominent businesswomen, membership in the Krewe of Muses is open to all. But membership doesn't insure a woman's right to experience the thrill of riding in the parade on the Friday night before Mardi Gras. Few will ever secure a spot on the Muses' float and throw trinkets to the masses, for old members are rarely willing to give up their seats. To ride, the Muse must smile on you, as my two friends—both educated, mature women—would surely attest. They claim their "greatest desire" is to throw glass beads and flashing plastic shoes from a Muses float before they die. This aspiration has nothing to do with social climbing, but reflects a desire for thespian reenactment of the goddesses—becoming, in one magnificent experience, divinities for a night.

The ancient poet Hesiod describes the Muses as inspiring goddesses, and believes that those whom the Muses love are happiest. "For though a man has sorrow and grief in his soul, and the servant of the muse sings, at once he forgets his dark thought and remembers not his troubles. Such is the holy gift of the muses."[12] But was this the blessing developers had in mind when they named the Lower Garden District streets after these divinities? Between the Creoles' Vieux Carré and the elegant American Garden District, a faubourg (neighborhood) was designed in the early 1800s to accommodate new arrivals. Streets were named for each of the Nine. The elaborate plan for the development, never completed, included fountains, churches, markets, and even a coliseum. Though parts of the area are becoming gentrified, the Muses' streets now wind through some of the poorest areas of the city.

One of these streets is named for Melpomene, the Muse of tragedy. In mythology she is usually depicted with a tragic mask, the sword of Hercules, and the *cothurnus*, a kind of boot traditionally worn by tragic actors. It is she, more than other Muses, whose dark tones are heard in most of the distinguished literary works set in New Orleans. For when she sings here, Melpomene inevitably evokes its unique multicultural heritage and complex issues of gender, class, and race. From the 1800s to the present, varying historical views of these issues have been voiced by such writers as George Washington Cable, Lafcadio Hearn, Kate Chopin, William Faulkner, and Tennessee Williams.

The tragic Muse in Kate Chopin's *The Awakening*[13] creates a female protagonist who cannot reconcile the traditional Creole woman's role with her desire to be liberated and discover her own identity. Edna is forced to respond to the gender- and race-restrictive society in which she lives. Her personal voice and inner growth occur within an outer world of slave girls, mulattos, and quadroons. Returning to New Orleans from a trip to Grand Isle, she simply drops much of her usual work supervising servants. Her husband notices the new, unrepressed energy in her glances and gestures, observing that his wife has a "silly notion about the eternal rights of women." Edna attempts to throw off her old life by leaving her husband's house and having an affair. She declares she is no longer and never will be the possession of any man. Returning to Grand Isle, she swims out into the ocean, further out than any woman has gone, tragically taking her life.

In *Absalom! Absalom!*[14] William Faulkner uses various narrators to express their differing interpretations of the rise and fall of Thomas Sutpen. Central to the story is the question of race. When he learns she is of mixed race, Sutpen abandons his child and his wife Eulalia. When his daughter from a second marriage, Judith, wants to marry Charles Bon, Sutpen tells son Henry that Bon is actually his half brother, son of Eulalia. Henry refuses to believe his father and accompanies his friend Charles to New Orleans, where Henry learns that Charles has a *plaçage* relationship with a woman of color. Charles tries to convince Henry that his having had a child by an octoroon will not conflict with his plan to marry Judith. Much of the New Orleans visit is dominated by a near-mythic description of a quadroon ball.

In *A Streetcar Named Desire*,[15] Tennessee Williams positions New Orleans somewhere between the Old South of the Garden District, the elegant American sector with its Greek Revival mansions, and the New South of Faubourg Marigny, where white immigrants and blacks live side by side, and where visiting Blanche Dubois, dressed in white gloves and pearl necklace, is out of place. Hoping she has come to the wrong part of town, Blanche explains to her sister's neighbor, "They told me to take a streetcar named Desire, transfer to one called Cemeteries, and get off at Elysian Fields." These directions are symbolic of the mythological motifs that permeate the city.

While visiting her sister, Blanche continues to play the role of Southern Belle, but her brother-in-law Stanley finds out about her promiscuity, ruins her chance for marriage, and rapes her. New Orleans holds no solace for Blanche, because despite its exotic charm, it is a port city inhabited by immigrants like Stanley Kowalski.

Each year, locals remember the lasting contribution Williams has made to New Orleans in sustaining the archetypally exotic and romantic images of the city in *A Streetcar Named Desire*. The Tennessee Williams/New Orleans Literary Festival invokes the Muses' inspiration through reenactments of Williams's plays and fiction-writing contests. True to New Orleans's complexly rich psychological atmosphere, which can self-consciously combine such diverse tones as tragedy and comedy, celebration and cynicism, guests attending the opening gala arrive dressed like their favorite Tennessee Williams characters. In the closing ceremony, people compete by giving their best imitations of Stanley Kowalski's scream to Stella.

The setting for another festival, mixing both historical layers and psychological tones, is William Faulkner's French Quarter apartment, now home to Faulkner House Books on Pirates' Alley, across from St. Louis Cathedral. The Pirates' Alley Faulkner Society sponsors its annual World and Music Arts Festival, again featuring regional writers, workshops, and creative-writing contests. A New Orleans Literary Tour walks the French Quarter, highlighting places that have given inspiration not only to Faulkner and Williams, but also to such other writers as Walker Percy, Ann Rice, and John Kennedy Toole.

Toole committed suicide after completing *A Confederacy of Dunces*.[16] That book's slovenly Ignatius Reilly epitomizes the city's eccentric spirit. Searching for a job, he encounters characters typical of New Orleans subcultures: inept policemen, crazies, strip-club dancers, hot dog vendors, and flamboyant homosexuals. Like Tennessee Williams, Toole uses the setting of the Crescent City to celebrate the socially marginalized, those who not only survive but live with gusto in the face of the majority's disapproval.

Reveling in the eccentricities found in the works of their writers, most New Orleans natives like to imagine their French Quarter as home to a fluid multicultural mix that accepts everyone. Hoping to further support their views of a unique, multifarious culture blessed by the Muses, they proudly boast how their city is the birthplace of jazz. Though such boosters choose to ignore much of the dark past and present of which they are well aware, there is no doubt that New Orleans was the place where jazz began. Jazz and other forms of music are crucial parts of the city's collective psychological existence.

Jazz's distant origin can be found in Congo Square. Central to New Orleans collective memory and imagination, this is the archetypal place most closely linked with the origin of what is distinctly American in music—for it was here that African music became a component of jazz. During Spanish rule, slaves could celebrate on Sundays, and "Congo Square" was the established place for free people of color and slaves to practice their traditional music and dance. Then one could see, clustered in tribal groupings, as many as six hundred unsupervised slaves and free blacks dancing and singing in harmony.

Naked except for a sash, the men had adorned their arms and legs with animal tails, ribbons, bells, and shells. Women wore silk, muslin, or percale dresses.

They danced playing on their native drums, gourds, banjo-like instruments, and pipes made from reeds, as well as on such European instruments as the violin, tambourines, and triangles. Calling forth the spirits of their ancestors, they sang a "second line" to the melody, a kind of counterpoint that would later find its way into jazz.[17]

Years later, Storyville, a section of New Orleans that became a symbol of sin, fostered the growth of many musicians. This ambiguous ancestry is typical of New Orleans and, naturally, of the archetypal musical energy fields that permeate the city's psychological atmosphere. In 1897, thirty-eight blocks, south of the Basin Street train station, were designated by social reformers as a prostitution district. Brothels were busy all day, and musicians worked for tips, playing piano to entertain customers. Though jazz appeared elsewhere in the city, decades before Storyville, many believe it came of age there, and that Storyville remained its center until the district was shut down by the Navy in 1917.

In Storyville, Jelly Roll Morton was a "professor," the term used for piano players working in bordello parlors. Expected to play a variety of music to entertain whoever dropped in, Jelly Roll was an important transitional figure between ragtime and jazz styles. Jelly Roll's "Wolverine Blues" and "'Black Bottom Stump" popularized the Spanish Tinge, an Afro-Caribbean mixture of exotic rhythms. He was the first in a line of talented New Orleans piano players: Tut Washington, Professor Longhair, James Booker, Harry Connick, Jr., and Mac Rebennack. Sidney Bechet and Louis Armstrong were apprentices in short pants when Jelly Roll performed in Storyville. From a young age, Bechet played the cornet, later switching to the clarinet, but he is best remembered as master of the soprano saxophone. He said that music in New Orleans was as natural as the air. "The people were ready for it, like it was sun and rain. The music it was where you lived. It was like waking up in the morning and eating; it was your regular life."[18]

Like many Black jazz musicians after him, Jelly Roll Morton left New Orleans, becoming a wanderer who spread jazz throughout the western world. Louis Armstrong, the most influential jazz master of the twentieth century, became a model for all jazz musicians. A New Orleans Black forbidden to play before a white audience, he moved to Chicago during the Jazz Age that emerged after World War I. Ever idolized by young African-American musicians, he returned to New Orleans in 1949 to be King of Zulu, the African-American Mardi Gras Krewe. Satchmo mused, "I'm accepted all over the world, and when New Orleans accepts me, I'll be home."[19]

Music is
as natural
as the air.

*Photograph by
Victoria Grant*

In the late 1960s, New Orleans honored Satchmo by building Louis Armstrong Park on what was Congo Square, and erecting his statue there. Today, because of local crime and violence, Congo Square is locked and unused. But elsewhere, Preservation Hall, a home for New Orleans's multicultural musical roots, is nightly filled to capacity. People eagerly gather to hear such gospel hymns and popular tunes as "Basin Street Blues," "When the Saints Go Marching In," and "You Tell Me Your Dream," played by veteran musicians in their seventies and eighties. Younger musicians learn from those oldies, who say there is no way to master New Orleans jazz by listening to records.

Though the city may contain more traditional jazz fans per capita than any place in the world, modern jazz has also become very popular, particularly under the influence of the Marsalis family. Ellis Marsalis, a renowned educator, has imparted his extensive knowledge of jazz to his four sons: Bradford, saxophonist; Wynton, trumpet player; Delfeayo, trombone player; and Jason, drummer. Ellis can still be seen performing at Snug Harbor jazz bistro on Friday nights. As artistic director of Lincoln Center, Wynton believes that even when musicians leave, they always take New Orleans culture with them. Ellis's former student Harry Connick has worked with the oldest son, Bradford, to establish a musicians' community for those who lost homes during Katrina. Over seventy individual homes have been built, along with a 5.5-million-dollar center, named for Ellis Marsalis and designed to nurture and preserve New Orleans musical heritage.[20]

Despite its shadowed history, music is a collective psychological fact that helps keep many locals here despite harsh post-Katrina living conditions. Indeed, New Orleans music has been growing more vibrant than ever. Young musicians pay their respects to the patron saints of the city's music, but they are also making sounds that reject the post-Katrina plight. New Orleans rapper Lil Wayne, a 2009 Grammy winner who grew up in crime-ridden Hollygrove, sold a million copies of *Tha Carter III* the first week it was released. Dr. John, the stage name of pianist, singer, and songwriter Malcolm Rebennack, won the Best Contemporary Blues Album Grammy for *The City That Care Forgot*, a work Nancy Wilson in *USA Today* (August 3, 2008) calls "a rambunctious and furious post-Katrina polemic that addresses government indifference, vanishing wetlands, the diaspora, and his unwavering love for the Crescent City."

Every year, the last weekend in April and the first in May are devoted to the New Orleans Jazz and Heritage Festival. After Hurricane Katrina, the festival has been better than ever, since musicians worldwide have come to help the city. Local musicians who have left to live elsewhere always remember where they came from, and mostly want to return. Their longing and nostalgia is expressed in hundreds of songs written about New Orleans.

⟨ MARDI GRAS ⟩

The tradition of Mardi Gras came to American in 1699, when Iberville explored the Mississippi River and set up camp near the present New Orleans. He named the site Point du Mardi Gras on the day of the French Festival that marked the beginning of a forty-day Lenten season. Under the French government, banquets, balls, and parades were held during this Carnival season. The tradition continued when the Spanish arrived in 1766. Almost a hundred years later, an elite group of men from the finest families created the Mystic Krewe of Comus, a secretive men's group whose motto was, *Sic volo, sic iubeo*, "As I wish, I command." They presented a Torchlight Parade followed by a private tableau ball, with classical myths that became the model for organizations called Krewes, groups that presented a parade or a ball during Carnival.[21]

In the tableaus, pure love was purged of sensuality and lustfulness, and Dionysian passion mainly went underground. This Mardi Gras began as masculine revelry, true to Apollo, Greek god of fine art, music, poetry, and eloquence, and lord of the Pythian games. In 1872, civic leaders and businessmen invented Rex, a new Krewe with a King of Carnival whose name was known to the public. On Mardi Gras Day, Rex descended from Mount Olympus and rode through the city waving his scepter and blessing the people. New Orleans blue-bloods had lost the civil war, and because of slave emancipation they had seen their businesses fail. But in the ritualistic enactment of their royal kingdom, they created an insular fantasy.

After Reconstruction, the elite Carnival societies—Comus, Rex, Proteus, and Momus—came to dominate the social and power structure of New Orleans. Like the Olympian gods, their true nature remained invisible to the masses. Except for identifying King Rex each year, these old-line Krewes adhered to a strict code of secrecy, never revealing who was behind the mask. Only the debutante queens and their courts were featured in newspaper society columns. The women who had received special elaborate invitations to the ball sat together to watch the tableau, and waited until they were "called out" by a masked "nobleman." After their dance together, the secret partner bestowed a small gift, a "favor," to the lady. Then she returned to her seat and watched the masked Duke beckon other invitees to dance. This ritual remained standard procedure for all balls, even when civic leaders and businessmen introduced the Krewe of Rex and invented a King of Carnival. Archaic, exclusive, paternalistic, and patriarchal attitudes of New Orleans were reflected in the highly ritualized procedures of these events. It was largely an Apollonian world with strict adherence to form and social order. A certain privileged level of society was thereby able to lift itself to mythological heights, and avoid realities. The King and his Krewe brought good fortune to revelers on Mardi Gras Day, but their refusal to look at the city's root problems of racism and poverty would gradually keep New Orleans from the prosperity of other Gulf cities. Fittingly, the Greek god Apollo had an intrinsically dual nature: he could bring good fortune, but he could also inflict evil.[22]

In 1991, Councilwoman Dorothy Mae Taylor pushed legislation to require all Krewes parading on public streets to accept members regardless of race, gender, handicap, or sexual orientation. Krewe Momus responded pompously: "Momus, son of Night, God of Mockery and Ridicule, regretfully and respectfully informs his friends, supporters and his public that he will not parade on the streets of New Orleans on the Thursday evening before Shrove Tuesday, 1992, as he has customarily since 1872."[23]

Except for the Rex parade on Mardi Gras Day, the old-liners no longer roll, but they continue their tableau balls, teaching their young girls to be princesses, their boys to be pages, and their debutante daughters to aspire to be queen. The grand finale comes at midnight on Shrove Tuesday, with the traditional Meeting of the Courts of the Mistick Krewe of Comus and Rex. The royalty of both Krewes come together with Queens, Maids of Honor, Dukes, and King glittering with thousands of rhinestones and twinkling lights.

Dionysus wandered the world spreading his worship of grapes and revelry. His followers, the Bacchanals, exhibited a type of ecstasy and enthusiasm hitherto foreign to the Greeks. With his gift of wine, Dionysus offered devotees relief from the struggles of everyday life, but he was persecuted for introducing ecstatic religious rites. Insanity and violence came to those overcome by too much Dionysian influence. Because any archetype always has a bipolar nature, New Orleans Mardi Gras could not have sustained itself without some Dionysian energy being pumped into its celebrations.

Recognizing the need to revitalize Mardi Gras, a handful of local businessmen staged the first Krewe of Bacchus parade in 1969. The theme was "The Best Things in Life," and the procession was led by celebrity king Danny Kaye. The 15-float, 250-member ensemble took to the streets, showering thousands of spectators with over a million strings of beads and 300,000 "doubloons." The new parade was a smashing success. Now, with more than 1,350 members and 33 animated super-floats, the Krewe of Bacchus is revered as one of the most spectacular in Carnival history. With the birth of Bacchus, the Dionysian spirit invaded the old-line exclusivity. Dionysus, the disquieting god, forces his way into human hearts and disrupts the social order. Today, although the older Krewes like Momus still refuse to parade, new Krewes have evolved that require few social credentials and are open to all who can afford them. Instead of balls with tableaus and traditional "call out" dancing, their parades end with dining and dancing to big-name entertainment. No longer dominated by aristocratic authority, Mardi Gras is a celebration for people who live in New Orleans. Bands, drill teams, majorettes, and flambeau carriers practice the year round. Committees meet to choose the themes of their parade. Floats are designed by famous craftsmen like Blaine Kern, making artistic work big business. There are parties for Krewe members to view the floats, and shops for purchasing beads and throws. Many families spend large portions of discretionary income on costumes, Mardi Gras ball gowns, throws, and membership fees in order to participate in what is claimed to be "The Greatest Free Show on Earth." Each part of the parade has its special character, and onlookers know what kind of throws (beads, trinkets, and doubloons) to expect, and what kinds of themes will be portrayed (some parades are notably irreverent and satirical). They learn the parade route, fight the crowds, and stake out their place to view the most celebrated and spectacular elements, or they leisurely walk around the corner to watch the floats and marching bands from their neighborhood.[24]

During segregation, neighborhood Afro-American Social Aid and Pleasure Clubs were the first form of insurance for Black communities. After paying dues to their club, members could share their spiritual traditions in community and also receive financial aid for sickness and proper burial. Rituals combining Christian beliefs with Caribbean and African folkways are reenacted at Mardi Gras. A New Orleans newspaper, *Gambit*, in an article headlined "Nothin but the Bones" (January 26, 2008), describes how Bruce "Suppie" Barnes starts his Mardi Gras Day:

> He begins quietly in the darkened pre-dawn hours as he takes a solitary journey to the cemetery to commune with the dead. Kneeling before graves, he asks the spirits of the past to enter his body so that he can become their living vessel, joining his soul with theirs as he takes to the streets. Later, at sunrise, he emerges in full costume, calling out and waking up the Treme neighborhood with his group, "The Northside Skull and Bones Gang," which has followed the Carnival tradition for decades. They bring the dead spirits to the streets of New Orleans.

In 2009, the Afro-American Zulu Social Aid and Pleasure Club marks its hundredth year of Mardi Gras parading. Mocking the uptown blue-blood Krewes, the first paraders, dressed in raggedy pants, attended a king whose crown was a lard can and whose scepter, a banana stalk. By 1915 though, Zulus were creating their own floats. Initially given no distinctive place in the parade route, now they precede Rex. Zulus, with their blackened faces and grass skirts, profess to be a service club for everyone, but in truth, riding a Zulu float or attending their ball is quite prestigious. Of all the throws from any parade, the beautifully painted Zulu coconut handed down to a pleading reveler is the prize Fat Tuesday catch.[25]

The "Mardi Gras Indians" also have roots in Afro-American neighborhoods, but evolved separately from the social aid and pleasure clubs. They are masked as "Indians," both because they share a common experience of subjugation and because indigenous tribes once provided refuge to runaway slaves. With Choctaw, Seminole, and Chickasaw help, escaped slaves set up "Maroon" camps away from the city. As early as 1746, New Orleans slaves began to dress as Indians to celebrate Mardi Gras. They had bonded with the Indians, sharing their worship of ancestors, their love of ritual costumes, and their celebration of the seasons. After the Civil War, the Black Mardi Gras Indians organized into neighborhood gangs who wanted to protect their turf. In an exulting freedom beyond their limits, they were often overtaken by a destructive, dark Dionysian energy that resulted in stabbings and shootings on Mardi Gras Day.

By the 1960s, these violent showdowns had ceased, and the competition among gangs, now called tribes, shifted to a contest over who could produce the most elaborate costumes and who could best dance, sing, and engage in confrontational posturing. As they dance around, the Big Chief sings the call and neighbors chant responses that have no common meaning. The Afro-American community honors those who spend so much of their lives reclaiming old traditions. Today, people go to great lengths to spot the Mardi Gras Indians, who parade along no pre-planned route, and their fabulous popularity restores the sense of power they were forced to relinquish as slaves.[26]

❴ FOLK CATHOLICISM ❵

New Orleans is a city permeated by religion. Whether they are practicing Catholics or not, most New Orleanians are psychologically affected by Catholicism's customs and worldview. Here Catholicism was made unique from the start, by being influenced by the scandalous reputation of the city's namesake, Philippe, duc d' Orléans. His philosophical alignment with Voltaire had a lasting effect, for as late as 1917, bishops struggling to contain clashes between Irish Catholics and French Creoles complained that the Creoles' loose interpretation of Catholic church dogma and social mores still lingered.[27]

History tells that bishops and nuns had a rough time ministering to the prostitutes, criminals, beggars, and orphans whom John Law brought to people the colony. Ursuline nuns protected the first decent young women that arrived, sixteen girls given free passage and a small dowry trunk, the so-called "casket girls." Later, the nuns began educating Indians, colored, and the daughters of wealthy Creole families. These girls quickly blended their evangelical Catholic instruction with traditional belief systems, often combining Voodoo rituals with their love of Sainte Maria, the rosary, and Christian miracles.

Influenced by Europeans, Africans, or Native Americans, West Indians, and Latinos, here is a folk Catholicism that incorporates the worship of ancestors, altars, icons, archangels, and saints.

In both Voodoo and Catholicism, the saints are active in people's everyday lives. Legends of Marie Laveau, the nineteenth-century Voodoo Queen, abound. In flowing cotton dress and tignon, she joined hundreds of slaves and free people of color who danced in Congo Square to the beat of drums and tambourines. Singing "Calinda, boudoum, boudoum, boudoum," she invited the serpent to

Skeleton
Singers.

*Photograph by
Victoria Grant*

enter her body as she whirled into a climax of spirit possession. Because she became a procurer of quadroon and octoroon women for wealthy men, there are many stories about her knowledge of intimate secrets. All levels of society came to her for spiritual advice. She nursed hundreds of cholera victims with herbal remedies, and prayed with prisoners condemned to death. At her Voodoo services, she remembered the ancestors with food and wine, and placed amulets and medicine bags on her altars.[28]

Today, there are Voodooists practicing in New Orleans, the most educated and authentic one being Sallie Ann Glassman. Initiated as the Haitian Voodoo priestess "Mango," she consented to be interviewed and invited me into her modest shop on Piety Street. Though filled with healing herbs and syncretic Catholic/Voodoo icons, it's a place a tourist would have a difficulty finding. "It is certainly more possible to practice Vodou [Sallie prefers the Haitian spelling] in New Orleans than in other parts of the United States," she says.

> All types of Vodouists are protected here, and when our community has a public head-washing ceremony at Bayou St. John, the police are present to monitor. We charge no fees and there is no secrecy about our ceremonies performed each Saturday night at our Vodou temple. Our ceremonies work in terms of the Eternal, effecting real healings that take time to develop and take into account the well-being of the whole community, and the revelation of the spirit. Since Katrina, our community has grown to include people from all walks of life. Crime has reduced 65% in our neighborhood since we began our crime prevention ceremonies.

As I continue to talk to Sallie, a Jew schooled in the mystic Kabala who turned to Vodou in 1976, I begin to imagine her religion as helping effect a healing for New Orleans's polarities. She tells me that a "primary purpose of Vodou ritual ceremonies is the restoration of equilibrium." Each of the Lwa, the Vodou spirits or demigods, is representative of an archetypal force within God's nature. The life force is a holism of these diverse and particular Lwa. The religion is energic, and parallels aspects of quantum physics theories in that matter, nature, and humans are all understood as dynamic energy. These energies come into play in spiritual possession, a transcendental experience that restores balance. The Vodou devotee recognizes and accepts all these archetypal components. Sally says that "Vodou forms an integrated, holistic system, not of worship but of energy transformation. There is no judgment in Vodou; we dance within the archetypal waters. By honoring the spiritual content within all life, Vodou accomplishes the redemption, repair, and transformation of the world."

Old-timers, Creole, African-American, West Indian, Irish, Italian, and Sicilian find little contradiction in a wide range of religious folk traditions. St. Joseph, father of the Holy Family, is buried upside down in the garden of a home put up for sale. No one seems to know the origin of this ritual, but many believe it is a key factor in determining whether the house will sell. Other traditions are traced to a particular segment of the multicultured community.

Treasuring fava beans, one in your wallet and one in your pantry, will insure wealth. The ancient custom dates back to times of famine in Sicily, when fava beans were the only staple. Each March 19th, New Orleans Sicilians decorate church altars with handmade breads, cookies, and other sweets, in an elaborate display in thanks to St. Joseph for protecting them from famine. One of the most beautiful altars in the city is found at St. Joseph Catholic Church, established in 1844. Few people today have the knowledge to prepare an altar that adheres to the strict instructions of the tradition. In Sicily, the custom has all but died out, but in timeless New Orleans, this and many other antiquated rituals linger on. In an inexplicable mixture of New Orleans tradition, the Mardi Gras Indians have chosen the eve of March 19th to parade in their poverty-stricken neighborhoods. The Indians and their followers wield flashlights against darkness, illuminating their elaborate creations in beadwork, feathers, and plumes inspired by the ceremonial suits and headdresses of the Plains Indians of the nineteenth century. They take to the middle of the street as if it were the Mardi Gras date, dancing out into the night in search of rival Indian gangs and drawing their neighbors off their stoops and porches. This mixture of Sicilian Catholic worship and African tribal tradition is part of the cultural gumbo that is New Orleans.[29]

Most prominent in the roster of New Orleans saints is "St. Ant'ny," originally St. Anthony of Padua, Italy, who wrought many miracles for the Italian poor. St. Anthony was also known to slaves who had worshiped him in the Congo as a leader in the Christian antislavery movement. Keeping the vision of freedom alive, they sang "Salve Antoniana!" The response was "Mercy, mercy, St. Anthony," and today people in the streets still cry, "Mercy, Lord have mercy," to ward off misfortune. During hurricane season, churches distribute printed-card prayers asking for protection from storms. Prayers are made to Our Lady of Prompt Succor, sometimes just called "Our Lady," known for having saved the city from the British in the War of 1812.[30]

Catholic traditions are intertwined with New Orleanians' never-ending awareness of death. On All Saints Day, cars line up at the entrances to New Orleans cemeteries as families decorate the graves of loved ones. The above-ground cemeteries are often referred to as "cities of the dead." Because the water table is high, settlers found that coffins floated to the top after heavy rainstorms, so they built vaults above-ground to hold the dead. Bodies are placed on top of one another, making the vault reusable. The elaborate monuments tell fascinating stories and have become a major tourist attraction. St. Roch cemetery contains a chapel built in thanksgiving for deliverance from one of the frequent yellow fever epidemics of the nineteenth century. People leave mementos of cures attributed to St. Roch. The chapel is the most unusual in the city, with its hundreds of braces, crutches, and replicas of body parts that line the walls.

Catholics share their concern for the deceased with the Africans who bring their ancestor spirits to their ritual dances, and American Indians who enact a ritual similar to All Saints Day. Catholicism melds with African tradition in the unique jazz funeral. The funeral begins with a march by family, friends, and a jazz band playing slow dirge music like "The Old Rugged Cross" and "Just a Closer Walk with Thee." Once the ceremony has taken place, the march proceeds from the cemetery to a gathering place, and the solemn music is replaced by loud, upbeat music. Onlookers join in a dance/march, frequently raising their umbrellas and waving handkerchiefs, no longer needed for tears, above their heads. The celebration symbolizes the cutting of the soul from earthly ties and is the origin of the "second line" dance. The presence of an archetype is felt through its effects. The energetic component of an archetype creates a field that exerts its influence over time and space.[31]

What Lies Ahead

If psychic energy is a force driving the unfolding of events, then New Orleans's soul has aim and direction. Five years after Katrina, the worst natural disaster in United States history, an unprecedented volunteer response remains ever active. Help has come from the hearts of Americans. Through Habitat for Humanity, The Jimmy and Rosalyn Carter Work Project Gulf Coast, The Bush-Clinton Relief Fund, the Brad Pitt Make-It-Right Foundation, Women of the Storm, and hundreds of faith-based ministries, help continues to come.

A unique contribution comes from Vodou priestess Sallie Glassman, who with her husband Press Kabacoff, a prominent New Orleans developer, are creating a holistic healing center, a principal goal of which is to heal the racial and economic divisions exacerbated since Katrina. The project has already received four million dollars in private and public funding. The Healing Center will provide specialists to ameliorate stress, a street university for adult learning, a "Healing Café," and a cooperative grocery store.

What has been most amazing is the resilience of the storm victims themselves—they rebuild against all odds, pass a good time on a Sunday afternoon, play their music, and rave about their Mamas' *roux*. When musician Dr. John's album, *The City That Care Forgot*, won the 2009 Grammy award for Best Contemporary Blues, he told *USA Today* (August 3, 2008), "You have lovin' people here. People will feed you, clothe you, and put you up. Sharing is as much a part of the culture as music. And we're proud of our culture, as whacked as it may be."

Notes

1 Cited in Aniela Jaffé, "Symbolism in the Visual Arts," in *Man and his Symbols*, ed. C. G. Jung (New York: Doubleday, 1964), p. 243.

2 Douglas Brinkley, *The Great Deluge* (New York: Harper Collins, 2006), pp. 8-13.

3 Barbara Eckstein, *Sustaining New Orleans: Literature, Local Memory, and the Fate of a City* (New York: Routledge, 2005), p. 7.

4 Ned Sublette, *The World that Made New Orleans: From Spanish Silver to Congo Square* (Chicago: Lawrence Hill, 2008), pp. 48-54.

5 The Junior League of New Orleans, *The Plantation Cookbook* (New York: Doubleday, 1972), pp. 4-5.

6 *Ibid.*, pp. 6-7.

7 Sublette, *The World that Made New Orleans*, pp. 33, 252.

8 John Wilds, Charles L. Dufour, and Walter G. Cowan, *Louisiana Yesterday and Today* (Baton Rouge: Louisiana State University Press, 1996), p. 50.

9 Grace Lichtenstein and Laura Dankner, *Musical Gumbo: The Music of New Orleans* (New York: W. W. Norton, 1993), p. 49.

10 Lafcadio Hearn, *Lafcadio Hearn's Cookbook* (Gretna, LA: Pelican,1990), introduction.

11 Antoines Restaurant, "Dining Rooms," http://www.antoines.com/gallery.html.

12 Hesiod, *Theogony*, trans. H. G. Evelyn -White, http://www.theoi.com/Text/HesiodTheogony. html. Classified E Text, lines 95-103.

13 Kate Chopin, *The Awakening* (New York: Bantam Dell, 1981).

14 William Faulkner, *Absalom, Absalom!* (New York: Vintage Books International 1986).

15 Tennessee Williams, *A Streetcar Named Desire* (New York: New Directions, 1947).

16 John Kennedy Toole, *A Confederacy of Dunces* (Baton Rouge: Louisiana State University Press, 1980).

17 Sublette, *The World that Made New Orleans*, pp. 281-283.

18 Nancy Wilson, "Sidney Bechet, Soprano Sax," (NPR Music Download, July 18, 2007) http://www.npr.org/templates/story/story.php) storyId=11821859.

19 Lichtenstein and Dankner, *Musical Gumbo*, p. 57.

20 New Orleans Habitat Musicians Village (http://www.nolamusiciansvillage.org/).

21 Myron Tassin and Gaspar Stall, *Mardi Gras and Bacchus* (Gretna, LA: Pelican, 1984), p. 19.

22 *Ibid.*, pp. 24-34.
23 Reid Mitchell, *All on a Mardi Gras Day* (Cambridge: Harvard University Press, 1995), pp. 199-201.
24 Tassin and Stall, *Mardi Gras and Bacchus*, pp. 61-64.
25 *Ibid.*, pp. 45-53.
26 Mitchell, *All on a Mardi Gras Day*, pp. 113-120.
27 Sublette, *The World that Made New Orleans*, pp. 42-49.
28 Martha Ward, *Voodoo Queen* (Jackson: University Press of Mississippi, 2004), pp. 23-30.
29 Earl J. Higgins, *The Joy of Yat Catholicism* (Gretna, LA: Pelican, 2007), pp. 130-133.
30 *Ibid.*, p. 149.
31 *Ibid.*, p. 155.

9 Moscow is Like a Sweet Berry

Elena Pourtova

In my childhood, I perceived letters and some words in certain colors. The letter "M" was obviously red, and the word "Moscow" was crimson, reminding me of a sweet-tasting raspberry. The actual taste of raspberry was almost unknown to me then; rather, it was an image picked up from different songs, including the one called "Kalinka":[1]

Kalinka, kalinka moya, sladka yagoga malinka moya.

Kalinka is the red berry of the snowball tree; *malinka* means a little raspberry. So it means something like: "My little red berry, my sweet little raspberry." I firmly believed that Moscow was like a sweet berry.

I lived in Siberia. My parents told me about Moscow and their visit to Lenin's Mausoleum. We had some books about Moscow with pictures of the Kremlin and the Bolshoi Theater. But my notion of Moscow was formed not as much by such books as by the story about the chimes of the Kremlin clock.

Two boys came to Siberia with their mother on New Year's Eve to visit their father. Together, they listened to the broadcast of the chimes of the clock on the Kremlin Spassky Tower, announcing the arrival of the New Year. The boys knew that those chimes were heard all over the huge Soviet country—in cities, mountains, steppes, taiga, and at sea. Those chimes were really important, because not only did the people verify their time by the Kremlin clock, but also the course of their life. The episode about the family greeting the New Year was accompanied by the text known to all Soviet schoolchildren: "*Everyone understands in one's own way what happiness is. But to live honestly, work hard, love and protect this huge, happy land, called the Soviet country, is known to all.*"[2]

With the chimes of the Kremlin clock, everyone identified themselves with that huge, happy Soviet land. And everything depended on the course of Kremlin time. This is what Moscow, the center of the Motherland and patriotism, means.

At the age of six, I saw Moscow with my own eyes. My parents hired a taxi to take us, the children, to the places that we had seen only in pictures before. I hardly remember the places we passed, though the driver told us a lot along the way. In my consciousness, this gap is easily filled by scenes from the famous film *Three Poplars on Plyushchikha*.[3] Its heroine comes to Moscow from a god-forsaken village, and a taxi driver, going the long way to Plyushchikha Street, shows her the well-known places of Moscow. They flow before her eyes, producing the impression of being close to something great and significant.

I do remember the endless streams of people everywhere. At the GUM, the State Department Store on Red Square in Moscow, I had looked forward to seeing the miracles sold there, but I failed even to get to the display cases. I saw only people's backs, felt my Mom's strong hand holding me, and periodically heard her anxious voice saying the names of her three children, thus checking that they all were near her. It was Moscow, a very big city.

At present, I have been living in Moscow longer than anywhere else in my life, even longer than in my native Siberia, and I am trying to understand what this place nourishes my soul with.

I think here of Carl Jung's essay "Mind and Earth," describing how the early American settlers' past influenced the psyche of modern Americans. The modern Americans, it says, have become "European[s] with Negro behaviour and an Indian soul."[4] To describe their psyche, Jung uses the metaphor of a modern house with the solid foundation of the previous civilizations and cultures constantly affecting its inhabitants. Reflecting on Moscow, I also think that the unconscious forces accumulated by its inhabitants from generation to generation exert a strong influence on the life of the modern Muscovites, either natives or newcomers. But how does it happen?

"Individuation" of Moscow

Moscow, first mentioned in the annals in 1147, was a distant Russian fortress located on Borovitsky Hill at the outskirts of the princedom subordinate to Kiev. Finding this place attractive, Prince Yuri Dolgoruky killed the local prince, Kuchka, and became the landlord of Moscow. But the dynasty of the Moscow princes was founded by Prince Daniel Alexandrovich, who ruled from

1276 to 1303. It was he who began to gather the disunited Russian lands around Moscow.

In 1328, Ivan I Kalita[5] was granted the title of the Great Prince, bypassing the inheritance rules, owing to his cooperation with the Golden Horde (Mongols and Tatars). He continued to gather the lands around Moscow, and made the Kremlin the residence of the Great Prince and the Holy Hierarch. Moreover, the Russian Orthodox Church separated from Byzantine Constantinople. The unity of the secular and religious powers in Moscow was strengthened by Prince Dimitry Donskoy, ruling with the support of such outstanding figures of the Russian Orthodox Church as the Holy Hierarch Alexis and Saint Sergius of Radonezh. They blessed the Russian army before the Battle of Kulikovo, in which it gained the decisive victory over the Tatar hordes.

In 1365, Dimitry Donskoy built up the white-walled Kremlin. Later, Ivan III invited Italian masters to rebuild it, who replaced the white walls with the red brick ones. The reign of Ivan III (1462-1505) is especially significant. He overthrew the Mongol-Tatar yoke and acquired the title of "the Great Prince of All Russia." Moscow became the capital of Russia, which had previously been called Rus. Moscow lost its status as capital between 1712 and 1918, during which time St. Petersburg (later Petrograd) was the capital, but regained it during World War I. In 1923, Josef Stalin launched a grandiose reconstruction of Moscow that in many respects defines its modern appearance. Being the capital is the main feature of Moscow.

Moscow's development, its gradual integration, could be looked upon as a sort of "individuation." The gathering of Russian lands by Ivan I Kalita and his sons from private persons, monasteries, and small princedoms was the beginning, perhaps, of an "ego." In the view of many historians, the clear-cut hierarchic administrative structure of the khans of the Golden Horde helped the Moscow princes a great deal in holding their princedom together, preventing disintegration. The help received from the Golden Horde could be imaged as making use of the energy of the "shadow." Ivan Kalita often went to the Horde with gifts and was a welcome guest there. According to Klyuchevsky,[6] the Moscow princes acted with diplomacy and "restrained wisdom," and as a result, the Moscow Prince managed to get the title of the Great Prince and was given real authority, including tax collecting for the Golden Horde, that helped a great deal in gathering the Russian lands. The unification of secular and spiritual authorities, which resulted in the special mission of Moscow to be the "Third Rome" and serve as an embodiment of true belief and a stronghold of Orthodoxy in the world, brings in the notion of the "Self."

Moscow—Center of Projections

What is projected onto Moscow? Moscow is the ego and the persona of the state. To live in Moscow is to enjoy unique opportunities of the collective ego—to be successful; to have access to the exclusive resources of the capital in goods, culture, education, and trade; to use what is accessible to the elite; and to participate in something new and forward-looking and feel the pulse of the country.

But perhaps Moscow is more than the ego for Russia. It is often said that Moscow is the heart or soul of Russia, and to live in harmony with the soul means to enjoy life and be happy. Therefore, to live in Moscow is to live in the world of miracles where all hopes come true; to be happy, lucky, and have no problems.

The "magic" part of Moscow is embodied by *terems, terem* chambers, and small houses with the turrets decorated either with tiles made before the times of Peter the Great or tiles of modernist style. A *terem* is a house like a tower or such a room in the upper part of a house, an ancient Russian style of building. The *teremnoy* style was used in the building of Belarus and Riga railway stations, the Historical Museum, and the Tretiyakov Gallery. Some city constructions evoke strong associations with the images of Russian fairy tales.[7]

Moscow is expected to be an everlastingly festive city. A client of mine recalls that in her childhood Moscow seemed to be a place for a never-ending New Year celebration, with wonders and gifts. A heroine of *Eugenie Onegin* says:

> *"Let's go to Moscow, to the brides' fair!*
> *They say there are a lot of festive places there."*[8]

There are other sayings about this, such as:

To Moscow—clearly
  Not to feel weary

or

If to Moscow you've never been
  No beauty have you seen.

A modern writer, Alexei Tsvetkov Jr., describes Moscow using a saying of the 1920s as an epigraph: *Go to Moscow, damn, there you'll see a tram!*

And Moscow is waiting for us; her ruby constellation shines tempting and victorious. The air of Moscow will make all free and help overcome grief forever. Only there, people do not suffer from illnesses, do not quarrel, and are obedient to the invisible conductor's baton; they dance on squares where there is no shooting apart from Christmas crackers; they enjoy the five-wing rubies and check themselves by the most exact clock. Red flags. A peal of church bells. The main celebration, New Year, arrives again in winter. Muscovites sing and dance in a ring around proud, elegant fir-trees; New Year descends to them from the stars in a helicopter and gives out to everyone what he (or she) had, for twelve months, been praying for. New Year, called here the Old Man-Cold, pours out hundreds of unusual gifts from his shining bag into the outstretched hands of excited children, and plenty of snow on the fir-tree collars and minarets of the Kremlin. [9]

Another architectural image of Moscow that reflects the idea of dreams coming true is Stalin's Moscow, with its seven high-rise, palace-like buildings known as Seven Sisters. Five buildings hold different official organizations, but two are residential houses, showing that some outstanding personalities among the Soviet people deserve to live in a palace. [10]

Similarly, the Moscow Metro stations were constructed as underground palaces for ordinary people. Even nowadays, Moscow guests are amazed at the beauty of its stations, which look like museums of the first temples of the new Soviet religion. This is described in a poem by Vladimir Kirillov:

> I step on the escalator
> That takes me slowly down
> And I feel myself triumphant, later,
> In the marble comfort of the underground.
> And the marble gently smiles;
> There is no match for its colors,
> And the door slides open—
> Please, get in, the voice invites us.
> The nickel shines in the matte light
> Of the milky-white lamps and
> All is made from the best, right
> From the riches of my Motherland. [11]

Moscow as Hope

The image of Moscow as Hope was very inspiring for the builders of the new social order. It is fascinatingly shown in a painting by Yuri Pimenov, *New Moscow.*[12] Its impressionist style easily reproduces the sensation of morning washed by a rain. All elements in the picture, including the woman, the street receding into the distance, and the atmosphere of the morning air, create the sensation of something new, fresh, attractive, and connected with the future.

"New Moscow," by Yuriy Pimenov.

In Soviet cinematography, Moscow becomes not simply a background, but an independent figure defining the behavior of its heroes, in films such as *I Step Through Moscow*[13] and *Moscow Does Not Believe in Tears.*[14] The characters of these films are young people building the Metro or going to college; they live in the future and sincerely believe the best is ahead of them.

Summer rains or heavy showers, cleaning and renewing, serve as a special image of Moscow as Hope. The film *I Step Through Moscow* begins with this image. A girl is walking barefoot in the rain, holding her shoes in her hands; she is followed by a young man on a bicycle trying to hold an umbrella over her. Each time, the girl escapes his umbrella. It is clear that she is absolutely happy to be under this rain. In the film *Three Poplars on Plyushchikha*, a taxi driver with a passenger, a young, beautiful woman from the provinces, is forced to stop his car because the heavy rain has flooded the windshield. His radio is tuned to a song that his companion suddenly starts singing. Another such image is used in *Heat*,[15] a youth film about modern Moscow. Its characters, languid with Moscow's summer heat, find that the long-awaited rain changes their condition and the succession of events.

Moscow as Mandala and Buried Treasure

The ring structure of Moscow can be seen as embodying both the concentric structure of the ego and the mandala structure of the Self. Old maps of Moscow show the image of the city in its radial-ring structure. On the map of ancient Russia, Moscow is the center of the Russian plain, on the main trade artery—the Moscow River—between the White and Black seas.

Moscow at night.

Photograph by Alexey Kochemasov

Perhaps it is this concentric, mandala structure that causes too many expectations of Moscow. This idea is expressed in the school verse about Moscow:

> *Moscow... How sweet it sounds to the Russian heart!*
> *It's captured Russian hearts and minds!*
> *Because for them it means a lot!*[16]

Indeed, it means a lot, even too much.

The stories about "secret treasures" that are thought to be kept in Moscow in underground vaults also contribute to this idea. The "diggers"[17] found twelve levels and twenty-four sublevels in a city vault. Man-made labyrinths and tunnels appeared in Moscow during the reign of Ivan the Terrible, who is believed to have "dug up and down all Russia."[18] According to a legend, the network of tunnels was dug to connect princedoms.[19]

The Library of Ivan the Terrible, known as the Byzantine Library,[20] is the most legendary secret. Italian masters Aristotle Fioravanti and Antonio Solari, reconstructing the Kremlin, foresaw the need for vaults and crypts in the construction of Uspensky and Blagoveshchensky cathedrals for the reliable protection of the library. In 1601, the library disappeared, but historians assume that it is still kept in the Kremlin vaults.

It appears that the most sinister rulers of Russia, Ivan the Terrible and Joseph Stalin, had a special interest in the Moscow vaults. During the Stalin era, the public underground was built to serve as a bombproof shelter for the population. The special Metro lines, the so-called Metro-2, were also constructed to provide rapid transportation for official purposes. Metro-2 connects the Kremlin with strategically important points in Moscow as well as special military airfields, and makes it possible to leave the capital quickly in case of danger.

Furthermore, the government bunkers were built by Stalin. They were actively used during World War II. At present, two of them have been sold to private companies and are now open for visitors.[21]

Moscow and Russia

In the past, Russians were often called Muscovites, and Russia called Moskovia. This suggests that Moscow is the city representing Russia, reflecting all its features and what it means to be a Russian. However, it is also true that Moscow is often looked at as a separate state, and Muscovites a special nationality disliked by other Russians. People often say, "Russia begins behind the MKAD,"[22] emphasizing that Moscow is beyond comparison with any other city. Moreover, the capital and the state are set against each other.

I think such opposite points of view are connected with the vastness of Russia, so difficult to comprehend. A foreign colleague, an amateur mountaineer, once asked me how far from Moscow the nearest mountains were. "Not really far," I said. "The Urals and the Caucasus are only about a two-hour plane flight from here." His bewilderment showed me that my notions of far or not far were quite different from his.

One city could hardly embody all the properties of such a huge country, with so many expectations and projections set on the capital. Therefore, there is a lot of tension, mutual charm and then dissatisfaction, in the interaction of these two.

Moscow's aspects of unconsciousness are easily projected onto wider Russia. Projections of the shadow exist in the scornful, haughty attitude toward the provinces displayed in questions like, "Are you from the Urals?" The latter comes from a scene in a popular film,[23] whose heroine, fashionably dressed, is nevertheless fully ignorant of the modern fashion. Another Soviet film[24] tells us about a woman from faraway Siberia who comes to Moscow to see a man who, on a business trip, has had a short affair with her. Her stay in Moscow brings different reactions. Her former boyfriend is ashamed of her provinciality, expressed in her sincerity and frankness. His women friends make fun of her clothes, but not because of her lack of taste. They like her hat, and ask at what shop she bought it, but when they find she has made it herself, they lose all interest in it. However, the parents of the young man appreciate her as a true Russian woman, an excellent model from classical Russian literature.

Admiration for the "true" women and men from the provinces is also typical of Muscovites. It may well be related to anima-animus projections suggesting that the true Russian woman (or man) lives in the provinces. In the film *Three Poplars on Plyushchikha*, the Moscow taxi driver likes the woman from the provinces because she is quite different from Moscow women, and has some air of "a true Russian" that exists only outside Moscow.

The ideas about "something true" often have to do with the personal feeling that all really important things take place on the periphery. The Komsomol construction sites, the tending of the virgin soil, the work at an assigned place—all are places for displaying ego-heroism and feeling oneself to be true, original, and authentic. These are projections of the Self. The heroine-Muscovite in the film *I Step Through Moscow* gets acquainted with a friend of her admirer. The young man courting her is a builder of the Moscow Metro, quite a heroic work in those days. But she prefers the guy from Siberia, who personifies her dreams about "the true life"—self-realizing and being useful to the Motherland.

Unconscious aspects of the relations between the center and periphery are tinged not only by mutual charm but also, very often, by mutual hatred and envy. At the time of Brezhnev, Muscovites were disliked in the army—they were believed to be smart people always able to settle their problems at somebody else's expense. Muscovites disliked the visitors who were buying up goods that were in short supply. There were even the so-called "sausage trains" that brought people to Moscow for one day to buy food. Moscow did not like newcomers from the provinces[25] who took jobs, thus posing a threat to Muscovites. The periphery repaid in kind, believing that Moscow thrived at the expense of the regions that worked hard. During Perestroika and the development of capitalism, the Moscow expansion to the regions rich in resources also caused flashes of aggression. The people believed that "Muscovites bought up everything."

The tense relations between the provinces and the capital should be considered not only at the objective, external level but also at the subjective, internal one. This intense contradiction is deeply internalized by Moscow, and has become its unique characteristic. Whether you are a newcomer or a Muscovite by birth, you may easily identify yourself with both parts of Moscow, the capital and the provincial. Both parts coexist in Moscow, and each lives an independent life. How is it possible to distinguish these two parts?

The streets at the periphery of Moscow are named after the USSR cities.[26] The streets named after the southern cities are in the south of Moscow, the northern cities in the north, and so on. The streets in the center were often named after the churches located in those places.[27] Some of them received the names of the nearest cities to Moscow[28] because they led toward those cities.

The Ostanskinskaya Tower,[29] the Seven Sisters, and other monuments of Moscow emphasize its specificity. When you are near them, you feel yourself being truly *in* Moscow. At the same time, the feeling of belonging to Moscow substantially weakens if you are in the faceless "bedroom communities" at its outskirts. Moscow is everything that is in the center. *The Irony of Fate, or Enjoy Your Bath*,[30] a popular film, makes fun of the faceless architecture in the bedroom communities. On New Year's Eve, its hero, a Muscovite, gets so tipsy enjoying his bath that he accidentally boards a plane to Leningrad. When he gets off, still believing he is in Moscow, he goes home to his apartment at Third Builder's Street. He is confused by the same name of the street, the similar house, similar apartment, and even similar furniture. The bedroom communities are like Third Builder's Street in this film, looking absolutely alike in Moscow, Leningrad, or anywhere else.

What is the heart of Moscow, the Kremlin or Red Square? If it is two parts of the heart, then they are divided by the same logic. The Kremlin is mainly a closed and inaccessible part. You may visit it on certain days, moving around only within certain limits. Red Square, on the contrary, is open and accessible to everyone. One marks one's visit to the capital by going to Red Square. However, Moscow was not always the capital—it faced the question of "to be or not to be" the capital several times in its history.

St. Georgy and the Dragon, depicted on the coat of arms of Moscow, is a symbol of Moscow reflecting the two parts mentioned above. St. Georgy could personify the ego, and the dragon stand for archaic, unconscious provinciality. It is curious that the essence of Moscow reflects the symbol of a separation battle. The map of modern Moscow reminds one of a web, bringing another association connected with an image of the Archaic Mother, dragging away and sucking in.

Thus, being the capital and being provincial are coexisting characteristics of Moscow, as ego and shadow. And I assume that a change of identification or an internal transition from one part to the other is an important moment in the personal development for the people living here. This is always the next stage of individuation, whether the status of a Muscovite is acquired anew or its former significance is lost and a new problem arises.

Moscow as Mother

Perceiving Moscow as Mother is a starting point for individuation in this city. The motherly function of Moscow is to satisfy different needs. There is so much of everything in Moscow that everyone may find their own place.

> Moscow!
> What an enormous house!
> No strangers it turns away.
> The homeless in Russia are poor as a church mouse.
> We'll all come to you anyway.[31]

Another poet was also fond of Moscow:

> Moscow, Moscow! I love you as a son.
> And as a Russian—strongly, passionately, and tenderly.[32]

A chance to be adopted by this city is touchingly shown in the film *Found-ling*.[33] A girl gets lost in Moscow, and during her all-day-long wanderings in the city is taken to a kindergarten. Moreover, two neighbors in a communal apartment,[34] and then a married couple, are ready to adopt her. It seems that your presence or absence in Moscow will be noticed. And if you are lost, you will by all means be found and given help.

Muscovites describe their early attitudes to Moscow as if it were a loving mother or grandmother, or a maternal space giving limitless opportunities of growth and development. They also describe the Moscow yards or communal apartments, where children grew up in one place and were looked after by the adults together.

An important motherly quality of Moscow is feeding. Moscow with its taverns and restaurants is a place where everyone eats. Meal scenes are present in any novel, film, or canvass about Moscow life. For instance, the heroine's main scenes in *Moscow Does Not Believe in Tears* take place at a table.

The opposite role of Moscow—Stepmother—is more often experienced by newcomers. Here she is also a great and important mother, but the relations with her are not so straightforward. Some people describe their mutual relations with her as exhausting doses of narcotics. She is loved and hated at the same time. Dependence on her is captivating and humiliating.

Many people feel no mutuality in their relations with Moscow. A young woman arriving in Moscow sees Moscow as a fat merchant woman, or a vulgar noisy woman selling gingerbreads and *barankas*.[35] She feels herself as a poor scrofulous girl or a tramp who would not get even a cracker in this motley market. The merchant woman is absolutely indifferent to her sufferings. If the girl dies, nobody will notice—there are already too many of such poor souls! In the first years of his life in Moscow, a client of mine imagined it as a fat, lazy prostitute. He felt himself as an insignificant little man waiting his turn with this magnificent woman, but without any hope of getting her. He lacked the required sum to pay for her services. Therefore, he had nothing to do but to look at her beautiful body and deeply envy the others. In such stories, the ego dealing with Moscow is experienced as something poor and impotent, unable to share mutuality. And this experience becomes a powerful impulse stimulating the development of the new qualities of the ego. For example, a nurse from Leningrad, the main heroine in the film *Intergirl*,[36] is not as successful as her colleagues from the provinces. In one of their interchanges, they explain to her that homelessness is their energizing, motivating force.

This is exactly what happens in Moscow. The most competitive fields of activity (show business and politics) are occupied by newcomers. And in Soviet times, the capital was "impregnated" with the secretaries general of the Communist Party, coming mainly from distant provincial places. They were considered to be fresh blood for the capital.

The collision of the ego with Moscow and the opposition to it are experienced as a stage of maturing. At a certain time, Moscow ceases to be a symbiotic background for an individual and becomes a figure, a separate character that requires new relationship. The heroic deed of the ego, comparable to the battle of St. Georgy Pobedonosets, is developed as an act of crossing the border from the internal sensation of being peripheral in education, trade, and private life into the area of "centrality." Such migration inside this circle results in change of the ego-identity and the persona.

The most significant task of the ego in Moscow is to resolve the dwelling question. In this respect, Moscow reflects all Russia, where general homelessness and the loss of roots are the result of the revolutionary trauma. Alexander Pushkin wrote in the nineteenth century:

> There is nobody in Russia who would not have their own dwelling. A beggar, setting out on wandering in the world, leaves his log hut. This is non-existent in other countries. To have a cow anywhere in Europe is a sign of luxury; not to have a cow in our country is a sign of terrible poverty.[37]

At the beginning of the twentieth century, the majority of Russian townspeople lived in houses. Houses, rooms, places of settlement were precisely connected with social identity. And all this collapsed in 1917, due to reducing space per person in dwellings, introducing communal apartments, the number of refugees in the large cities, and the expropriation of apartments for organizations. Perhaps, "the apartment question, which has spoiled Muscovites" is most brilliantly depicted in *The Master and Margarita*.[38]

Compulsory registration introduced an additional barrier to finding a place in the sun in Moscow. You may live in Moscow without the registration, but you do not exist officially. You have no right to work, no access to health services, education, and so forth. Fake marriages or divorces for the sake of registration or receiving an apartment were typical solutions to dwelling questions.

In my therapeutic practice, I constantly hear my clients stressing the importance of the dwelling question. Personal reasons for this problem may vary, but it is always a question connected with development and individuation. For the majority, the need for possessing one's own apartment, and its difficulty, reflect separation problems. For newcomers, buying an apartment is a question of survival. For those who need a chance to separate from their parents or former spouse it is the only way to acquire their own separateness. For some, the apartment is a matter of sibling and Oedipal relations, in dividing the parental property and competing for parental love.

Furthermore, the apartment may be looked at as a matter of genealogical continuity, suggesting the apartments and summer residences of grandmothers or grandfathers, lonely aunties and high-ranking ancestors of Soviet times. There are the cases when it is impossible to keep the inheritance of a famous grandfather-scientist or a grandmother who married again, and after whose death everything was inherited by her second husband's family. Apartments become a symbol of what has been held or lost from the psychic inheritance of the ancestors.

The location and size of an apartment is a question of changing status and persona. In Moscow, to move from the faceless district to the prestigious one is a sign of success. When Muscovites living in the communal apartments in the center of Moscow were given separate apartments somewhere in Orekhovo,[39] it was perceived rather as a great loss than a solution of their dwelling question.

St. Georgy and the Dragon

For many Muscovites, the battle with the dragon is the defense of their territory against those who pose a threat, be it the waves of migrants from the villages after the revolution of 1917 or modern *gastarbeiters* (guest-workers) from Central Asia. In their genetic memory, Muscovites tend to treat them like Mongols and Tatars in the times of ancient Russia. A modern poet writes:

> We're tortured by the seed of hordes,
> The yoke of infidels presses us,
> But in our veins boils
> The sky of Slavs![40]

An image of the battle between St. Georgy Pobedonosets and the dragon (similar to the icon on the next page) played a key role in the life of my client who saw Moscow as a prostitute. After ten years of living in Moscow, he noticed the

"St. Georgy: Miracle of the Dragon," Icon of Novgorod, 14th century.

change in the internal image of his mutual relations with Moscow. He identified himself with St. Georgy, and Moscow became the dragon. The image of
St. Georgy[41] radiates a lot of energy. When my client went into churches, he was
always searching for this icon, to put a candle near it. Every time he passed the
stele with St. Georgy Pobedonosets killing the dragon on its top, he said with
a thrill: *"Hit him again, hit him again!"* Later, it became clear to him that he
experienced this battle as sex with that magnificent woman, Moscow. He had
varying feelings about that, from his fear that Moscow would absorb him and
make him a "background" of its life, to his belief that he had conquered Moscow. There were also happy moments in their mutual love.

This experience is in tune with what Leo Tolstoy wrote in *War and Peace*
about the difference in the perception of Moscow by Russians and by foreigners:
"Any Russian, looking at Moscow, feels that it is Mother; any foreigner, looking at it and not knowing its motherly value, should feel the womanly character
of this city, and Napoleon felt it." Again, a popular actor wrote in his memoirs
about his attempt to survive in Moscow:

> I had no place to live and was taking shelter with friends. At night, I used to go to
> Red Square and ask aloud: "Moscow, don't you really need me? Won't you really
> accept me, a Siberian, and allow me to live in your lanes?" Moscow is a woman
> and she needs tender words. Only she did not hear me at once ...[42]

Later, my client's feeling of being the conqueror disappeared. He understood
it one day when he came into a church and as usual was looking for the icon of St.
Georgy, but found something unexpected. In this church, St. Georgy Pobedonosets was depicted with two female saints rather than the dragon (see image, previous page).[43] The battle was over. The dragon turned into the woman-partner
for life. It was the beginning of a new stage in his relations with Moscow, most
likely matrimonial; their common child might appear.

This story about the transformation of the image of Moscow is very typical.
In other cases, Moscow as a market-woman turned into a woman serving in
church, serving a dose of narcotics to a spouse, serving the eternal New Year to
a close partner in business, etc. It is important that these relations changed into
deeper and more sharing ones. The feeling of the interchange with Moscow was
significant and productive for all parties.

The film *Moscow Does Not Believe in Tears* emphasizes this same transition, when after so much has been achieved in life, there appears a new space,
intimate and loving. The thing in its entirety—all parts of Moscow, capital and

periphery—become significant, not its separate parts or regions. So, we may well say, together with the heroine of this film, that *"after 40 years life is just beginning."*

Magnificent Woman—Moscow

Considering Moscow as a person, it should be noted that, in addition to motherly and other female images, Moscow is also shown as a widow when it lost its status as capital: "Sources of tears like a widow's poured from my eyes, cheerful images are silent on my walls....Since then and hitherto I have lost the pleasure of watching monks staying within my walls."[44] Thus, Moscow appears as a mother, a bride, a wife, and a widow. Moscow is certainly a woman.

Moscow's sex and characteristics are often described in contrast to St. Petersburg's. For example, in the view of Alexander Pushkin: "Moscow was as famous for brides as Vyazma for gingerbreads. ... Haughty Petersburg laughed from afar and did not interfere in the fancies of the old woman Moscow."[45] Nikolai Gogol perceived Moscow as

an old stay-at-home that bakes pancakes, looks from afar and listens to a story about events in the world without rising from the armchair; Petersburg is a smart fellow who never sits at home. ... Moscow is a female, Petersburg is a male. In Moscow, everything is brides; in Petersburg, everything is bridegrooms.[46]

Modern writers perceive Moscow in a similar way:

Moscow is of a female, feminine, and motherly nature. Moscow—the capital obviously sounds female to the Russian ear. A town *Petushki*[47] or, say, Petersburg, is quite a different matter. A phallic Peter the Cockerel is clearly heard in such names. The Petersburg project of Peter the Great was in fact an attempt to redirect Russia from the Motherly nature to the Fatherly one. Moscow, despite the efforts of the monk Philopheos[48] and Tsar Ivan, failed to become the Third Rome. A pope would have been necessary for this purpose; Moscow had, perhaps, only Roman moms.

... Moscow is not quite as a Mother and not quite as a woman. It is a symbiotic mother, i.e., a mother of very early infancy. And at such an early age, the image of mother is unreal. It is defined by infantile fantasies about a phallic mother, i.e., a mother possessing both motherly and fatherly attributes and functions. Such a mother possesses a phallus in infantile unconscious imagination. Similarly, Moscow has the phallic towers of the Kremlin sticking out of its body. And Moscow is an androgen. It is either a male-like woman or a female-like man or a woman possessing masculinity or a man possessing femininity.[49]

The phallic nature of the present Moscow is obvious. There is too much glamorous street advertising; large models of cars on the roads are in fashion; grandiosity of architecture overburdens Moscow. The construction gigantism began with erecting high-rise buildings under Stalin. In the meantime, more than four hundred churches and other valuable monuments of history and culture were torn down under the pretext of a prospective happy future. The deputy of the chief architect of Moscow, Alexander Zaslavsky, boasted in 1934: "In the field of construction, we shall surpass Bramante and Michelangelo taken together. The fewer historical buildings we have, the fewer problems are left to our descendants for reconstruction." Each political leader coming to power was tearing down the constructions of his predecessors to build new ones, more grandiose. And such a process continues, because the historical city center is under construction. It looks like a narcissistic desire to improve the appearance, connected with a rejection of the self and reality.

The exaggerated value of the persona, phallic features, and the "festive" style of Moscow life push everyday energy, including masculine efforts, into the shadow. The complement of the Moscow-merchant-woman is the man subordinate to her. Here are the words from the famous *Woes of Wits:*

> Of all the wife's attendants,
> The husband-servant or the husband-boy is the ideal
> That Moscow husbands should enjoy.[50]

The Moscow husbands in all films mentioned here are usual and ordinary people of unpretentious appearance. But they effect surprising transformations in the women they love, who acquire femininity and sexuality instead of power and superiority. The shadow energies, making Moscow whole, are masculine energies barely visible, daily efforts of people working hard like ants, introverted intuition and deep spirituality. The junction of these flows makes Moscow an unusually attractive, powerful funnel, a dynamic whirlpool that changes the fates of its dwellers and of Russia.

Now, Moscow is not only crimson in color and taste for me. I know other shades and tastes, but a sweet-tasting raspberry still remains dominant. This note of brightness and sweetness brings me near to those who are mad about Moscow, who cannot imagine their life outside it.

For many people, Moscow is simply the hub of the universe. Believing that *Moscow never sleeps*, the Moscow maniacal extraverts, for instance, sing in their so-called hymn:

> *If you've got here, there is no way back.*
> *Here people live today, not in tomorrow's track.*
> *If you also think the way we sing,*
> *You are ready for Moscow, you do not stink.*[51]

But the passion for Moscow may be also introverted. A popular poet devoted his song to Arbat, an old street in the center of Moscow.

> You flow as a river. What a strange name to hear!
> Asphalt is clear as water in a reef.
> Ah, Arbat, my Arbat, you're calling for me here.
> You are my pleasure as well as my grief.
> Your pedestrians – people not really great,
> Their heels are heard – all of them are hurried.
> Ah, Arbat, my Arbat, you're my faith.
> Under me your roadways are buried.
> It's impossible to be rid of the loving hand
> Of your many roads laid on sand.
> Ah, Arbat, my Arbat, you're my Motherland ,
> How difficult it is to reach your end.[52]

The feeling for the place in this poem is compared to a mission, a religion, and the fatherland. This passion is deeper and has more value because it is more mature, experienced, and spiritual. Such an attitude to the city is filled not with expectations but with past history having its own character as a result of conscious love, fidelity, and readiness to serve. When I plunge into this, the word "Moscow" appears to me in a new color—a golden one.

I am especially grateful to Susanne Short for her personal attention. I am also grateful to Maria Loseva for her help in preparing some of the material, as well as to my students and clients for the stories of their relations with the city.

Notes

1   A Russian song written by the composer Ivan Larionov in 1860.

2   Arkadi Gaidar (1904-1941), *Chuck and Gueck*, vol. 3 (Moscow: Detskaya Literatura, 1972), p. 66.

3   A 1967 Soviet film directed by Tatiana Lioznova.

4   C. G. Jung, "Mind and Earth," in *Collected Works*, vol. 10, *Civilization in Transition* (Princeton, NJ: Princeton University Press, 1978) § 103.

5   "Kalita" is his nickname, meaning "a purse or money bag."

6   Vasily Ocipovich Klyuchevsky (1841-1911), *The Course of Russian History*, vol. 2 (Moscow: Mysl, 1987), p. 14.

7   Among them are such buildings as Chistoprudny Boulevard 14, whose walls are decorated with carvings of fantastic animals; the French Embassy on Bolshaya Yakimanka in the Old Russian style; the Chinese tea house as a pagoda on Myasnitskaya Street; and Ivan Tsvetkov's house-casket on Prechistenka Quay.

8   Alexander Pushkin, *Eugenie Onegin*, in *Complete Works*, vol. 3 (Moscow: Pravda, 1954), p. 117.

9   Alexei Tsvetkov Jr., "Moscow" (1979), in *THE* (Moscow: Paley, 1997), p. 69.

10   The residential houses are on Kotelnicheskaya Embankment and Vostaniya Square. The five other buildings are Moscow State University on Vorobevy Mountains, the Ministry for Foreign Affairs on Smolensk Square, Hotel Ukraine on Kutuzov Prospect, the Railway Ministry on Sadovo-Spasskaya Street, and Hotel Leningrad on Kalancheskaya Street.

11   Vladimir Kirillov, in *Wonderful Moscow*, ed. O. Zhukova (Moscow: AST, 2007), p. 453.

12   A young woman at the wheel of an open car is portrayed in it. She is shown from the back because she is looking ahead at the road, and the perspective of one of the central streets, with government buildings, cars, and pedestrians, unfolds in front of her wind shield. This picture was created at the height of Stalinist repressions.

13   A 1964 Soviet film directed by Georgi Daneliya.

14   A 1979 Soviet film directed by Vladimir Menshov. The film won an Academy Award for Best Foreign Language Film in 1980. It was the first Oscar received in the Soviet Union.

15   A 2006 Russian film directed by Rezo Guiguineishvili.

16   Alexander Pushkin, *Eugenie Onegin*, p. 121.

17   "Diggers" are researchers of the underground caves. They began this activity in Moscow 20 years ago.

18   This is the opinion of Vadim Mikhailov, the founder of the Digger Movement in Moscow.

19   The existence of Neolithic caves and the Moscow Sea in the huge karst cavities facilitated digging vaults, tunnels, and labyrinths. According to Vadim Mikhailov, there are 12 levels and 24 sublevels in the Moscow underground space. Karst cavities filled with underground water, known as the Moscow Sea, occupy the eleventh level.

20   It was brought together with the dowry of the bride for Ivan III, Sofia Paleolog, the successor of the last Byzantine emperor and a famous personality all over Europe.

21   One of them is located near Taganka Square (Kotelnichesky Pereulok 11), at a depth of 60 meters with an area of 7,000 sq. meters. The other is located under the stadium of the All-Union Sports Complex in Izmailovo (Soviet Street, 80, building 1) and holds the branch of the Central Museum of the Armed Forces.

22   The Moscow Automobile Circular Road, defining the modern limits of Moscow.

23   *The Most Charming and Attractive*, a 1985 Soviet film directed by Gerald Bezhanov.

24   *Holiday at One's Own Expense*, a 1981 Soviet film directed by Viktor Titov.

25 Newcomers from the provinces got the scornful name *"limitchiki"* or *"limita"* because they were allowed to work in Moscow only in limited numbers.

26 Kirovogradskaya Street, Dnepropetrovskaya Street, etc.

27 Zachatievsky Pereulok, Kharotonievsky Pereulok, Zlatousky Pereulok, Yakovopostolsky Pereulok, etc. *Pereulok* is a Russian word for a lane.

28 Kaluzhskaya, Tverskaya, etc.

29 The main TV tower, visible from afar.

30 A 1975 Soviet film directed by Eldar Ryazanov.

31 Marina Tsvetaeva (1892-1941), *Works* (Moscow: Khudozhestvennaya Literatura, 1988), p. 63.

32 Michael Lermontov (1814-1841), *Sashka*, in *Complete Works*, vol. 2 (Leningrad: Nauka, 1980), p. 277.

33 A 1939 Soviet film directed by Tatiana Lukashevich.

34 A communal apartment is an apartment that is shared by several families, sometimes by more than ten.

35 Such an image strongly recalls the merchant women in Kustodiev's pictures, who are often depicted at a lavish table. Boris Kustodiev is a Russian artist (1878-1927). A *baranka* is a ring-shaped roll.

36 A 1989 Soviet film directed by Peter Todorovsky.

37 Alexander Pushkin, *A Trip from Petersburg to Moscow*, in *Complete Works*, vol. 5 (Moscow: Pravda, 1954), p. 169.

38 The satirical novel of Michel Bulgakov (1891-1940), a Russian novelist and playwright.

39 Orekhovo is a district at the outskirts of Moscow.

40 *The Sky of Slavs* by K. Kinchev, online at http://www.peoples.ru/art/music/rock/alisa/nebo_slavjan.shtml.

41 This name is equivalent to the Russian name Yuri, the name of the founder of Moscow, Yuri Dolgoruky, and the name of the present mayor, Yuri Luzhkov, who significantly renovated Moscow.

42 Alexander Pankratov-Chyorny, a well-known Russian actor.

43 Here, the icon is similar but differently presented: the dragon is tamed by the woman.

44 M.M. Shcherbatov, "Moscow Asks for Her Oblivion" (1860), in *Moscow in the Descriptions of the Eighteenth Century* (Moscow, 1997), p. 256.

45 Alexander Pushkin, *A Trip from Petersburg to Moscow*, in *Complete Works*, 1954, vol. 5, Moscow, Pravda, pp. 272-273.

46 Nikolai Gogol, *Petersburg Notes of 1836*, in *Complete Works*, vol. 7 (Moscow: Pravda, 1984), p. 164.

47 *Petushki* (Russian) means cockerels.

48 Monk Phylopheos of Pskov, at the beginning of the sixteenth century, put forward his idea of Moscow as the Third Rome.

49 N. A. Blagoveshchensky, *The Case of Venya E.*, Psychoanalytical Study of the Poem *Moscow–Petoskey*, in *Complete Works*, vol. 6 (Academy of Humanities, 2006), pp. 10-13.

50 Alexander Griboyedov (1795-1829), *Woes of Wits* (Moscow: Khudozhestvennaya Literatura, 1988), p. 129—from the brilliant verse comedy about Russia in the nineteenth century.

51 Timothy and GJ Smash, fashionable performers in Moscow's club life; *Moscow never sleeps* is the song's refrain.

52 Bulat Okujava, "The Song about Arbat," 1959, http://www.stihi-rus.ru/1/okud/30.htm.

10 Montreal: La Grande Dame

Thomas Kelly

{ SITE AND PSYCHE }

It never ceases to impress me how each city has its own special character and feel to it, palpable from the moment one arrives. What is it about a city that determines and defines the psychic energy it carries? As when we meet someone new, our initial impression is usually of whatever feature has the strongest impact. While all cities have points of resemblance, each has its own unique flavor and character, its particular "vibe." These vibes inform us not only about the present, but also about something of the city's past and of the events that have shaped it into what it has become today.

As an analytical psychologist, I am, of course, interested in and respectful of the individual nature of each person. Through Jung's notion of the individuation process—in my opinion one of his most profound contributions to the understanding of psyche and psychic process—Jung highlighted the profound specificity of each individual, and of the path each has to follow in life. I think the same can be said of a city—each city is unique and has become what it is today because of its location, climate, past history and, not least of all, its inhabitants. There is a definite relationship between land and psyche, but the city is also shaped by the people who live there, just as it has contributed to shaping the character and psyche of its people.

In this chapter, I would like to present a case report, not on an individual, but on Montreal, the city I have lived in for over twenty years. The fact that I am not a native of Montreal, that I have lived on three different continents and have travelled widely, allows me to have a kaleidoscopic perspective with which to view the city. In keeping with the usual format for a case report, I will begin by looking at the initial impressions one may have when arriving.

Initial Impressions and Background History

Whether one arrives from abroad or even from another part of Canada, it is immediately clear upon landing in Montreal that this place is somehow very different. Though still in North America, the traveller will hear French announcements along with English at the airport. If you are arriving from another country, the customs officers will likely greet you in French. Signs and advertisements will also be primarily in French. While there are shops with familiar names, such as GAP, West Coast, Roots, the Bay, the signs they display are all in French. English will also be heard, of course, but not nearly as frequently, and then often with a French accent. For people from other parts of Canada, this city can feel as foreign as it does to someone from another country. When you arrive in Montreal, you are in the French-speaking part of Canada, and the differences you will encounter go well beyond the language. People not only speak differently, they look different, dress differently, and carry themselves in a different manner.

An evening stroll in Old Montreal with a view of Jacques Cartier Bridge.

© Marie-Reine Mattera

206

On the journey from the airport to the city center, either by taxi or bus, the traveller will see many large, old brick warehouses as well as many church spires with green copper roofs. The warehouses stand mute and inactive today, silent reminders of the industrial past of this city and of a time when trade and industry defined Montreal as the business capital of Canada. The ubiquitous church spires recall the predominance and power of the Catholic Church and of its significant role in influencing the city and its psyche.

Upon arriving in the city center, the traveller will immediately sense the hustle and bustle of activity, with a cacophony of traffic, noise from cars and ambulances and people rushing about. If you have taken a taxi into the city, you will also have had the opportunity to notice that cars and pedestrians are in constant battle for the right of way on these busy urban streets and boulevards. Though it may seem chaotic at first glance, there is a code of behavior behind the wheel that drivers adhere to. Pedestrians in Montreal are renowned for not respecting traffic signs. If there is the slightest possibility of crossing a busy intersection, little heed is paid to whether the traffic light is green. One needs to understand that winters in Montreal can be rather challenging, and that pedestrians try to survive the bitter cold by crossing the intersections whenever an opportunity presents itself. This habit seems to be so deeply ingrained, however, that it hardly matters whether it is winter or summer—if there is a chance to cross at a busy street corner, there will be no hesitation.

Historical Roots of Montreal

The origins of the settlement of Montreal are intimately tied to the history of Canada itself. In 1534, Jacques Cartier discovered the New World after landing on the eastern shores of Québec in what is now called Gaspé. He immediately claimed this land in the name of the King, erecting a cross on the shore and calling it *La Nouvelle France*, New France. Returning a year later, he sailed down the mighty St. Lawrence River and established one small settlement in what is now known as Québec City, and a second, Ville Marie—now called Montreal.

The long and arduous journey over the turbulent waters of the Atlantic Ocean, a journey into the unknown, had led them to a world that was strange and unfamiliar, yet fascinating and full of promise and potential. Psychologically, we can only imagine the impact on the collective psyche of Cartier and his men, as well as on the collective psyche of the court of France and its citizens. The "New World" became the recipient of archetypal projections: this would be the Promised Land, with gold and riches beyond description—a huge acquisition that immediately expanded the power and influence of France and of the French court.

The search for a passage to India led Cartier and his men to call the colorful indigenous peoples—so very different in every aspect from the white settlers—Indians. From the very start, there was little respect for them; they were viewed at best as primitive, and at worst as savages. With little regard for their history, beliefs, or traditions, or for the fact that they were the first inhabitants of this "New World," the conquerors imposed themselves, their mores, and their beliefs in exchange for a few trinkets, blankets, and mirrors—items that carried a certain fascination for the indigenous population. In the early years of the colony, many settlers would come to respect the native peoples, because they had developed ways of surviving the harsh climatic conditions of this land. Survival depended on learning from them how to make it through the long, dark, and bitterly cold winter months.

If this history were recounted as a fairy tale, it would be of a protagonist caught in a power complex, needing to discover and respect what the other unknown and unfamiliar parts of his psyche have to offer. It would be the story of a character, the ego, ready to exploit the unconscious for its own self-centered purposes, and totally identified with its own power drive. The history of the first settlers is comparable to the fairy-tale motif: it is often those aspects most devalued by the ego that end up being essential for survival and for accomplishment of the task presented at the start of the tale.

In contrast to the Puritans who set out from England in search of religious freedom and who eventually set down roots in New England, the first settlers in New France were adventurers and explorers. Many had been convicted of crimes and sent to the new colony as a punishment. Some of the women were prostitutes or orphans, *les filles du roi*, who were sent overseas in an attempt to clean up the streets of France. Others were attracted by the adventure the New World provided and came willingly to these new settlements, intent on recreating what they had left behind, and on profiting, in as many ways as possible, from the vast expanse of undeveloped land and what it offered. Farming was essential for the survival of the two small settlements, and the fur trade (furs were sent back to France) provided much-needed funds for the economy.

Because the early settlers wanted to re-create the conditions they had left behind, members of French Catholic religious communities were also sent to provide for the spiritual needs of the settlers and to convert the "pagan" indigenous population of New France. Catholicism provided a container for the hardships encountered from the very beginning by the early settlers, and its institutions became an imposing presence in the small colony, with a powerful influence on its history. Later on, as we will see, these Catholic institutions played a pivotal role in maintaining and preserving the French identity of the inhabitants of the small colony.

While religion was clearly important, it was not—in contrast with New England—the primary reason for the settlers coming to the New World. Trade, not religion, was the colony's original and primary purpose. The difference between the settlers of New France and the Puritans of New England is significant, and has consequences that still reverberate in the psyche of the people today. The optimism of these early settlers and their colorful backgrounds account, at least in part, for a certain quality of presence, a *joie de vivre*, a sensuality and creativity that is still palpable throughout the province of Québec, but especially in its largest city, Montreal.

In a major battle fought on the Plaines of Abraham in Québec City in 1759, British troops defeated the French forces and became the dominant power, not only in these two small settlements but in the entire New World. Rather suddenly, *la Nouvelle France* became British North America. The defeat of the French imposed a change of government, of language, and of allegiance to a new country. For the French Canadian settlers, the defeat was a bitter blow, a collective traumatic experience that still reverberates vividly today in the depths of the collective psyche of the inhabitants of the province, and that still powerfully influences the political landscape. Suddenly, the French were the minority, their language and customs threatened with extinction and their religion subject to the whims of the conquering forces. They now became subjects of the British crown, no longer colonizers, but colonized. Humiliated in defeat, their dreams of making this vast country part of France shattered, the proud French Canadians were at the mercy of the British, who imposed British law, British currency, and the English language.

The Catholic clergy, in an attempt to preserve French language and culture, negotiated with the conquering British and managed to extract from them an agreement to allow the Catholic Church to continue to function under British rule, and for French schools and hospitals to remain open under the auspices of the Catholic religious orders. The clergy encouraged French-Canadian settlers to move into rural areas, away from the larger settlements and later cities, in order to minimize contact with the British. By limiting the possibility of contact, they hoped they could prevent assimilation into the dominant group.

While these measures did in many ways succeed, they also had some other important consequences that, in turn, contributed significantly to perpetuating the feeling of being conquered and colonized. The French-Canadian settlers who followed the advice of the Catholic clergy became financially disadvantaged. Working the land in a country with such a harsh climate made life very difficult. The English became the merchants and businessmen of the new colony, and benefitted from the riches the New World had to offer. What the early French settlers had envisaged and dreamed of as their own was now becoming a reality for the conquering English. In order to preserve their language and culture the French were, for all intents and purposes, virtually excluded from the financial growth and development of the new colony. As a colonized people, especially if they didn't speak English, they were denied financial success and any possibility of advancement in the business world. Occupational choices were limited to farming, teaching, or joining a religious community; the English, on the other hand, were merchants, bankers, professionals, politicians, and the ruling class.

The inherent injustice and inequality in this system led to unexpressed anger, resentment, and hatred that, combined with the shame of having become a colonized people, grew in the collective psyche of the French-Canadian population. The trauma of defeat and the humiliations subsequently imposed festered like a raw wound.

The untenable tension finally erupted in what is now referred to as the Rebellion of 1837. A group of French-Canadian rebels, *les Patriots*, provoked an offensive against the British forces. In three towns outside of Montreal, army barracks were attacked and burned and government officials routed. The British response was swift and without mercy: a number of the rebels were imprisoned and eventually executed. The rebellion, though short-lived, nevertheless made it clear that the status quo could not persist forever. It marked the beginning of a demand for respect for French-Canadian language and culture on par with those of the English language, and although not successful then, this demand became more vocal and insistent in the next century. The rebels' cause would not die, nor would it be silenced by the heavy-handed military response of the British forces, and today the traditional public holiday in May dedicated to mark the Queen's birthday is also used in Québec to commemorate *les Patriots* of the 1837 Rebellion.

Echoes of 1837 could be heard in what eventually came to be known as the Quiet Revolution. In the global upheaval and new *zeitgeist* of the 1960s, radical change also started to take root in the province of Québec, and especially Montreal. In his 1968 book, *The White Niggers of America*, Pierre Vallières chronicled the history of the French-Canadian settlers and decried the social injustice and inequities they suffered.[1] The Catholic religion, which heretofore

210

had been considered the protector of the French language and culture, was now attacked for having collaborated with the English establishment to maintain power and control over the French populace, and for having perpetuated existing inequalities and exploitation by English entrepreneurs. The clergy were accused of abusing the power vested in them. Pierre Vallières became the leader of a separatist movement called, Le Front de Libération du Québec, and his book was a call to arms against exploitation and oppression.

An interesting anecdote recounted by Mario Jacoby, well-known Jungian analyst from Zurich, gives a flavor of the power of the Catholic Church and the clergy before the Quiet Revolution. Before becoming an analyst, Dr. Jacoby was a violinist and member of an orchestra in Zurich. In the early 1950s, the orchestra was invited to give a North American tour, to include a performance in Chicoutimi, a small rural town north of Québec City. Dr. Jacoby recalls how surprised he was that the performance could not begin until the local bishop, the last person to enter the hall, had taken his place. At the end of the performance, no one dared to applaud before the bishop had first shown his approval and appreciation and begun the applause. The clergy ruled like royalty over subjects, and wielded tremendous political power.

The Quiet Revolution opened the floodgates to change. The protective container the Catholic Church had provided was now felt to be too confining and restrictive. A powerful revolutionary cry for equality and recognition erupted among French Canadians and replaced the old attitude of passive acquiescence. As the sole French enclave on the North American continent, the threat of being overwhelmed and absorbed by the dominant English culture, be it from the other parts of Canada or the United States, made it evident to French Canadians that they had to take command of their collective destiny by asserting the right to language, religion, and culture.

In a relatively short period of time, the political landscape of the province changed significantly. By the 1980s, the Catholic Church was ousted from control over education and health services; the authority for these services now handed over to the provincial government and its ruling separatist party, *le Partie Québécois*. In addition, a law mandating French as the official language of government and business was decisively passed .

The shock waves from these measures were felt throughout Canada. Prior to the Quiet Revolution, Montreal had been the financial capital of the country. In the late 1970s, with the election to power of a separatist party in the province of Québec, the financial institutions gradually moved their head offices from Montreal to Toronto. In addition, many of the English-speaking Quebecers, uncertain of their future and uneasy with the radical changes taking place around them, left the province for other parts of English-speaking Canada. Montreal, La Grande Dame of Canadian cities, was beginning to lose some of its glamour and appeal for many English-speaking Canadians. For French Canadians, however, La Grande Dame was simply going through a much needed change.

In the past, it was possible to live and work in Montreal without any knowledge of French; today that is virtually impossible. To live in the province of Québec and in its largest city, Montreal, it is essential to speak French. The French Canadians are very proud of their language—which, from the perspective of European French, is considered a dialect. Ironically, the French-Canadian "dialect" has been studied and shown to be closer to French as it was spoken four hundred years ago than to current-day European French, because the isolation of the French Canadians until relatively recently seems to have preserved certain aspects of the language.

French Canadians are open and welcoming of immigrants, and encourage immigration to their province. Immigrants, however, are expected to learn French. To ensure that this happens, immigrants are offered French courses free of charge and are encouraged to integrate into the French culture as much as possible. It is expected that children of immigrants will attend French school.

French-Canadian culture today is alive and vibrant, especially in Montreal. Music, theatre, dance, literature, the cinema, and the culinary arts thrive. French-Canadian singers are known at home and abroad. Céline Dion, the world-renowned diva, is perhaps the best example. Theatre thrives everywhere in the province, especially in Montreal, as does the film industry. Some of the creative Québécois celebrities are known well beyond the boundaries of the province—for example, Robert Lepage, the innovative theatre director, and Yannik Nézet-Séguin, the young but acclaimed orchestra conductor.

With this history and background in mind, let us now turn our attention to how these historical events have helped shape the psyche of this city, in an attempt to understand Montreal today.

Cultural Complexes

The foregoing brief history of French Canada provides a striking example of what Thomas Singer and Samuel Kimbles refer to as a "cultural complex." In addition to personal complexes, they suggest, "another level of complexes exists within the psyche of the group (and within the individual at the group level of their psyche). We call these group complexes, 'cultural complexes,' and they, too, can be defined as an emotionally charged aggregate of ideas and images that cluster around an archetypal core."[2] They go on to say that "mostly these group complexes have to do with trauma, discrimination, feelings of oppression and inferiority at the hands of another offending group—although the 'offending groups' can just as frequently feel discriminated against and unfairly treated."[3]

The notion of a cultural complex rests on that of a cultural unconscious, a concept elucidated by Dr. Joseph Henderson, and which he defined as:

> … an area of historical memory that lies between the collective unconscious and the manifest pattern of the culture. It may include both these modalities, conscious and unconscious, for it has some kind of identity arising from the archetypes of the collective unconscious, which assists in the formation of myth and ritual and also promotes the process of development in individuals.[4]

Kimbles points out that "Dr. Henderson's reference to an area of historical memory points to a kind of living continuity between past and present at the level of the group unconscious."[5]

We can suppose that the defeat of the French forces by the British troops on the Plains of Abraham in 1759 represented a major collective trauma to the psyche of the French-Canadian settlers, resulting in the formation of a cultural complex at the level of the collective cultural unconscious. Furthermore, this cultural complex became engrained and strengthened as a result of the "build-up over centuries of repetitive traumatic experiences"[6] as a colonized people at the hands of the dominant and domineering English power structure. We can also see how this cultural complex provided "a kind of group skin,"[7] that on the positive side, allowed for the containment of the French-Canadian settlers and their cultural identity, but, in its shadow aspect, maintained and perpetuated the feeling tone of an oppressed people, thus limiting and constricting their sense of identity and of potential. The Quiet Revolution of the early 1960s led to a shattering of the constraints imposed by this group skin, and to an affirmation of the right to exist as a people with a language and culture different from but equally valuable to that of the dominant language and culture surrounding them. Psychologically, this can be understood as a very significant step in the individuation of the French-Canadian group psyche that liberated them from the shackles of the constraining aspects of the cultural complex.

The changes that have occurred in French-speaking Canada since the Quiet Revolution are quite impressive. French is now recognized as the official language of the province and is protected by law. The use of French in schools and government is closely monitored to ensure that it does not lose ground to the ever-present threat of English. All signs and advertisements must be predominantly in French, and the English text cannot be more than one-quarter the size of the French. Tensions between the English and French populations still exist, but the quality of that tension is vastly different from what it was before the Quiet Revolution. The tension is no longer one of the colonizer overpowering the colonized; rather, the tension is now on a more equal basis, one that is the source of much creativity as both sides struggle to recognize and appreciate their differences and work on how to coexist for the benefit and growth of both groups. This tension contributes to a vibrant energy that is palpable in Montreal, the container of the vast majority of the English population. James Hillman, who was in Montreal in 1987 to give a series of lectures at l'Université du Québec à Montréal, summed it up well in an off-handed comment he made at the time: "Isn't it wonderful to live in a city that has an irresolvable conflict." Hillman's insightful comment pinpoints clearly how the creativity and *joie de vivre* of this city are directly connected to the tension that Montreal has learned to carry and contain over the years. Rather than co-existing as "Two Solitudes"—the title of a book by Hugh MacLennan, published in 1945, that describes the seemingly unbridgeable gulf in understanding between the English and the French in Canada at the time,[8] the two very different and separate *Weltanschauungen*—there is now a more dynamic relationship based on equality and mutual respect.

IDENTIFIABLE COMPLEXES

Following our metaphorical "case report" on Montreal, it is interesting to consider the various quarters of this fair city as reflections of its composite complexes. The Old Port, the oldest section, houses buildings from the time of the French settlement, thus bearing witness to Montreal's historical roots. The architecture is clearly old European—gray stone buildings lining the narrow

City Hall, a majestic architectural gem recalling the French heritage of Montreal.

© 1998, 2008, Hans Boldt & Sylvana Grisonich-Boldt

streets, with high ceilings and exposed beams. Many are former warehouses, and have been transformed into chic art galleries, restaurants, or nightclubs. A good number have also been gentrified and turned into condominiums.

The Old Port offers *divertissements* of all kinds. Artists, clowns, and street performers vie for your time and attention (and, of course, generosity), and there are bicycles for rent. In summer, it is possible to take a boat excursion and, if you fancy, have a dinner cruise on the St. Laurence. In winter, an outdoor skating rink, cross-country skiing, ice sculpting, and other activities for the family all contribute to making the season not only bearable, but enjoyable.

The city hall or Hôtel de Ville—in my opinion the most elegant and beautiful building in Montreal—reflects well the city's grand past. Its architecture recalls its French roots, while its grandeur bespeaks the power and influence that Montreal exerted at one time. This distinguished old building is most befitting to "La Grande Dame," a name often used to describe Montreal that reflects the capacity of this city to contain tension and difference in a distinctly feminine manner. The sensuality of its people— their charm, warmth, and feeling-related attitude—all mirror Montreal's profoundly feminine character.

At the center of the city stands Mount Royal, crowned with a huge metal cross that is lit at night. This cross is meant as a reminder of the one that Cartier was said to have erected when he arrived on the shores of the St. Lawrence and claimed the land in the name of the King of France. From the belvedere at the top of Mount Royal, there is an imposing panoramic view of the city, and there are church spires visible in every direction: Notre Dame Cathedral, St. Joseph's Oratory, and Mary Queen of the World Church, whose central altar is a replica of that of St. Peter's in Rome.

Notre Dame Cathedral, with its richly decorated interior, provides perhaps the best architectural example of the Catholic Church's former dominance, while the rich, blue *fleur-de-lys* pattern on the walls—national symbol for Québec—and the flower on its flag reflect profound French roots. But all these spires inform the visitor of the central role the Catholic Church played in the history of Montreal and especially of its French-Canadian people. Many today stand like relics of the past, recalling a very different era. Some are no longer used as places of prayer and worship because there are not enough people to maintain them; others have been sold to land developers and transformed into expensive and highly sought-after condominiums.

Notre Dame Basilica: its grandeur and beauty remind us of the deep roots of the Catholic Church in the history of Montreal.

Le photographe masqué

The pivotal role of religion in the history of this city and province raises the question of where the religious function of the collective psyche now finds expression. In part, we can say that some of this psychic energy has been channelled into the creative energy of the arts. At the same time, the rapid transformation of French-Canadian society into a consumer society belies the unmet spiritual needs that the Catholic Church attempted to respond to and fulfill in the past. While, as a collective, French Canadians are enjoying the relative freedom of not being controlled by any outer religious structure, I believe that it will eventually be essential to find new avenues for their spiritual needs. Because the Catholic Church has lost favor in the collective does not mean that spiritual needs are any less present. On the contrary, they may, in fact, be even more prevalent and even more pressing.

Just north, the financial district stands in sharp contrast to the Old Port. This sector of the city houses the banks, the stock market, numerous businesses and multinational corporations, as well as slick, modern five-star hotels. In contrast to the old part of town, the financial sector reflects the twentieth and twenty-first centuries. Skyscrapers vie with each other for architectural prominence, reaching to ever new heights in an attempt to dominate the Montreal skyline. These modern buildings have replaced the church spires of the past and, for many, business has become the new religion, but they also mirror the profound changes that have taken place in Montreal since the Quiet Revolution. Here, businesses are owned and operated by French Canadians, and business is conducted in French. Companies with an international reputation, such as the French Canadian firm Bombardier, experts in aviation and other forms of transportation, are based here. La Caisse de Dépot, a financial institution, ranks among the largest in the world. No longer is business solely the domain of the English. French Canadians have shown they are capable of stepping up to the plate, taking their place and holding their own in local and global markets.

Yet the divide between the two founding groups still exists, and is given expression in a number of ways. Montreal is home to four universities, two English and two French. The downtown area is a shopper's paradise, where English and French together share the pleasures that any consumer society has to offer. There are also, however, sectors of the city where the shops use predominantly one or the other. Boutiques and shops on Laurier Street, for example, are clearly French, while those on Greene Avenue service a more exclusively English population. The same holds true for restaurants and night-life. While *joie de vivre* is present everywhere in Montreal, and restaurants cater to tastes and budgets covering a wide spectrum, St. Denis Street's Latin sector in the east is predominantly French, and Crescent Street, in the west, predominantly English. East-end Montreal has traditionally been considered French, while the west end has been English, with St. Laurent Street as the dividing line. Interestingly, on St. Laurent Street one finds restaurants and nightclubs that cater to both groups, where both mingle in harmony and with great pleasure. St. Laurent Street, also referred to as "the Main," stands as a symbol of the point of union of the former "Two Solitudes" that have now learned—and are still learning—how to be together, to the benefit of both. Along St. Laurent Street, the two formerly polarized groups are united to form something new and different that transcends the polarities and opens up exciting possibilities for the future, contributing to the vibrancy of the city and to the richness it has to offer its citizens and its visitors.

Though I have focused on the French and English groups in this chapter, it is important to note that Montreal is a multicultural, multi-ethnic city. In the early part of the twentieth century, Montreal welcomed and became home to large immigrant groups from Eastern Europe, including a large Jewish population who set down roots and contributed to its rich tapestry. Montreal is home to the largest Hassidic community in North America, after New York. In the past twenty years, many immigrants from Asia, Africa, and other parts of the world have been welcomed and encouraged to integrate into French-Canadian society. Montreal is greatly enriched by the presence of these immigrants and their different cultures.

Montreal's Typology

From the point of view of typology, Montreal is clearly a feeling-type city. People here are open, curious, and tolerant. They exude warmth and acceptance in a simple and personable manner. Having suffered under the yoke of the harsh, judgmental, and controlling attitude of the Catholic Church, there is now a respect for and acceptance of difference that is quite exceptional. People who settle in Montreal from abroad are always impressed by how easily they are accepted and integrated into the lives of the people they meet or work with.

Montreal is a sensuous city and its inhabitants a sensuous people. In local lore, this is attributed to the Latin roots of the French-Canadian population. People, especially women, are attentive to what they wear and how they present themselves. Eating is not considered just a basic requirement of life in this city— it is nothing short of a passion, if not an obsession. People are interested in the latest restaurants, young and innovative chefs, and daring new recipes; they are also very proud of their traditional dishes and regional specialties. Exploring the world of wines and finding the right one to accompany a dish is a national sport. In contrast to the other parts of Canada, where consumption of spirits exceeds that of wine, in Québec wine is the beverage of choice and is usually present at every meal. Music—be it classical, jazz, funk, or modern—is readily available at the numerous nightclubs throughout the city. Place des Arts has a wonderful concert hall and theatre where local artists can see their productions come to life.

All of this contributes to the *joie de vivre* of this city—mentioned so often in this chapter. While we can consider this *joie de vivre* as carrying a compensatory Dionysian aspect in reaction to the dire and restrictive norms imposed by the Catholic Church, I think this is but one aspect of the explanation. The *joie de vivre* that you will discover in Montreal is very much a part of the soul of this city, and is rooted, I believe, in something that the earliest settlers arrived here with and left as a legacy—a joy in the freedom and potential that the expansive New World represented. This deeply soulful quality survived the traumatic experience of defeat and humiliation, and is very much alive and present in Montreal. La Grande Dame is always ready to extend her hospitality!

Notes

1   Pierre Vallières, *White Niggers of America: The Precocious Autobiography of a Québec Terrorist* (Toronto: McClelland and Steward, 1971).

2   Joseph Cambray and Linda Carter, eds., *Analytical Psychology: Contemporary Perspectives in Jungian Analysis* (London: Brunner Routledge, 2004), p.176.

3   *Ibid.*, p. 178.

4   Cited in *ibid.*, p. 182.

5   *Ibid.*, p. 183.

6   *Ibid.*, p. 186.

7   *Ibid.*, p. 184.

8   Hugh MacLennan, *Two Solitudes* (New York: Duell, Sloan and Pearce, 1945).

11 Mexico City: Longing for Quetzalcóatl

Jacqueline Gerson

I live in Mexico City, a sprawling, overcrowded, haphazard, yet somehow endearing metropolis. Like most other *Chilangos*,[1] I have to admit that the city has lost its soul and sits in quiet desperation, cocooned in nostalgia, waiting for the appearance of a Messianic figure who will deliver it from its physical misery, redeem it from its soulless state, and restore it to its former glory. This realization was driven home to me rather forcefully one evening, as I inched through the city's traffic-choked streets on my way to a concert. The experience evoked some thoughts and associations that I would like to explore in greater depth in the following reflections.

———

Recently, I had the opportunity of attending a concert featuring the music of the Italian composer Ennio Morricone at the National Auditorium. As a composer, Morricone is best known for his numerous film scores, and that night he was slated to conduct the music he wrote for the movie *The Mission* (1986). I love the music that accompanies good movies, and the magnificent score that Morricone wrote for this film is among my favorites. So it was a rare treat for me to be able to witness him conduct this particular composition. Besides, he was 80 years old, and this was probably the last time he would be visiting Mexico City. It was an event that I could not possibly miss, and I took every precaution to make sure that that would not happen.

The National Auditorium is an elegant building, located beside Chapultepec Park on Mexico City's grandest and most important avenue, Paseo de la

Reforma. Under normal traffic conditions, it is no more than a ten-minute drive from where I live. Nevertheless, I wasn't taking any chances. I decided to leave home an hour and a half before the concert was scheduled to begin, determined to arrive on time and not miss a single moment of this once-in-a-lifetime event.

Mexico City traffic.

Photograph by Jacqueline Gerson Cwilich

Driving in Mexico City is as unpredictable as it is perilous. There was a time, not too long ago, when it was possible to get around this city with a fair amount of certainty that you would reach your destination safely and in a reasonable amount of time. You could plan your trip to avoid peak traffic flows by factoring in paydays (once every two weeks), weekend revelers, crowds rushing to or from work (twice a day), the weather, the size of the road, the part of town you would be driving through, and so on. For security reasons, you never drove alone if you could help it, or late at night, or in the poorer parts of the city (especially if you were driving a new or expensive car). But now, even these measures are futile. Staggering under the weight of its sheer size and the accelerating growth of its population, the city has become all but immobilized.

With a population of nearly 22 million living in the Greater Metropolitan Area,[2] Mexico City is the second largest metropolitan area in the world. Nearly one-fifth of the country's inhabitants are crammed within its borders, giving the area a population density of over 10,000 people per square kilometer, well beyond that of New York City, London, and Tokyo-Yokohama. A thick blanket of yellow-gray smog smothers the city, choking out the life and numbing the soul of its residents. The individual becomes just another face in the crowd, a blurred speck in the fabric of the city's life, uncared-for, concerned more with merely surviving than with living a soul-nourishing life.

My strategy for getting to the concert on time was to leave home early and give myself plenty of time to get to the theater. What I had not factored in was that hundreds of other concert-goers were counting on the same strategy. The Reforma was hopelessly clogged, and in my impatience, I decided to get off it and reach the theater by means of side streets. But other Morricone fans had beaten me to it, and I found myself in an impossible traffic jam in a narrow side street, which now resembled a crowded parking lot. After being stuck in the same block for twenty minutes, I began to entertain the fantasy of abandoning the car and walking to the theater. At the rate the traffic was moving, I could easily have reached the theater on foot before the cars got there, except for the fact that I did not relish the prospect of walking through the yellow-gray haze that is Mexico City air.

Mexico City is one of the most polluted cities in the world. Located in a geographical basin, the city is almost entirely surrounded by mountains, which serve to trap in the exhaust fumes from the 4 million vehicles that ply the streets of the metropolitan area. The air is so thick with pollutants that it is oppressively difficult to breath. The acrid air stings the eyes, causing them to water and blink reflexively to ease the pain. The nose reacts similarly, either drying out completely or emitting a watery discharge tinged with blood. The skin turns dry and chapped, like cardboard, taking on the form of an odd kind of armor against the city's assault on the body. Here, indeed, is one manifestation of the city's shadow. It is as if the city is striking back at humanity for years of abuse, neglect, self-interest, corruption, politicking, mismanagement, and incompetence.

There was a time when the snow-capped mountains surrounding the Valley of Mexico could be seen quite clearly from the city. Today they are all but invisible through the soupy smog. Carlos Fuentes[3] titled his first novel, in which Mexico City is the main character, *Where the Air Is Clear*.[4] The title was ironic in its own metaphorical way when the book was first published in 1958, but it takes on a new ironic significance in a quite literal sense in 2009. In a television interview on the occasion of his 80th birthday, Fuentes was asked if he would give the book the same title if he were writing it today. I noticed his bitter smile and detected an edge in his voice as he replied that he certainly would not.

Fuentes's surrealistic novel has an undercurrent of nostalgia, of deep insatiable longing, like so many other novels by Mexican writers. One thinks of Elena Poniatowska's *Querido Diego, te abraza Quiela*,[5] a series of twelve fictional letters purportedly written by the Russian painter Angelina Beloff from Paris to her lover Diego Rivera after he abandoned her and returned to Mexico following a ten-year romance. In one of these letters, Angelina writes, "I look at the gray sky and imagine your fiercely blue sky, the one you described to me."[6] And again, "You have forgotten me there in that Mexico of yours that I wanted so much to get to know. The Atlantic is between us—here the sky is gray and there in your country it is always blue ..."[7] And still later, recalling their time together, she writes: "I noticed that you had *le mal du pays*[8]—you turned your eyes to the pale sun and remembered another. Deep down inside, you wanted to leave."[9]

This *mal du pays*, this homesickness, this deep longing for something missing haunts every resident of Mexico City, whether living away from the city or right in the city itself, even if he or she is too young to have ever seen firsthand the "clear air" of Fuentes and the "fiercely blue skies" of Rivera. These cultural "artifacts" of the past are part of our collective memory as a city, but of course, our collective memory goes back even farther in time to the days when the city went by the name of Tenochtitlán and was populated by the Aztecs. The valley was beautiful then, pristine and unspoiled. Tenochtitlán sat on an island in the middle of Lake Texcoco, the largest of five interconnected lakes. The city was crisscrossed by a network of canals, along which people could move freely in their canoes and access any of the city's twenty districts. Unlike its modern counterpart, Tenochtitlán was well-organized and well-maintained, the center of a vibrant, thriving culture. The descriptions of Tenochtitlán by the Europeans who first saw this New World marvel[10] are enough to fill any modern-day *Chilango* with envy and nostalgia—and a bit of faded pride.

Our collective memories of Mexico City's glorious past inspire yearnings that the city is no longer able to satisfy, robbed as it is not only of its visual clarity by the toxic fallout of progress, but also of the inner clearness of vision that constitutes its soul. Bereft of self-awareness, the city is functionally blind: it cannot see beyond the end of its own nose.

———

I had to abandon the idea of abandoning the car and walking to the concert—not just because I could not face the prospect of battling the foul smog, but also because there was simply nowhere to park my car. I was surrounded by an ocean of cars on all sides, bumper to bumper, shoulder to shoulder. As I looked out over this "ocean," I felt a sudden surge of panic as all my points of reference began to slip away. My sense of distance, of time, of speed, of spatial relations, of the layout of the city streets—all lost their meaning. This was the city of my birth, and I could no longer recognize it, and I was no longer even remotely at home in it. I felt completely impotent, like all the other drivers around me, who sat impatiently at their steering wheels, honking futilely in helpless desperation, abandoned, it would seem, even by the gods. On the brink of tears, I wondered: How did we let this happen? How did it come to this? How did we manage to lose our city? How did we allow ourselves to become so paralyzed?

———

Paralysis is a basic paradigm of life in Mexico City. Wherever you go, there is a sense of immobility, of things having come to a standstill, of life having frozen in time. Movement of any sort is severely restricted. What the residents of other cities take for granted is considered a privilege in Mexico City, and when we are able to move, no matter how small that movement is, we are appropriately grateful. This physical paralysis is partly due to the sheer size of the city and the density of its population, but there is an inner paralysis as well that prevents people from inner movement, from taking any action to bring about change, from climbing the social ladder, from aiming for a better, more fulfilling life. Instead, there is a sense of resignation, an unquestioning acceptance of our fate, an utter numbness of soul.

Movement is vital to life—some would say a fundamental human right. The constitutions of some countries even guarantee their citizens freedom of movement, but in Mexico City this freedom exists only in theory. The practical reality is that the city's inhabitants feel trapped, imprisoned in a cage of immobility. The centrality of movement and the deep-seated yearning for it that is felt in Mexico City has its roots in the ancient myth of Quetzalcóatl, a Mesoamerican deity traditionally depicted as the Plumed Serpent, for it is with him that movement in the cosmos originated. The Mexican historian Enrique Florescano notes that "[a]ccording to the oldest cosmogonies, Quetzalcóatl was born when there was neither light nor movement nor life in the world, and he established a fundamental order in the cosmos."[11] Florescano goes on to describe Quetzalcóatl's transcendental role along the coast of the Gulf of Mexico, where he was known as Ehécatl, the god of the wind. Florescano cites the Mixtec codices, in which Ehécatl is portrayed as the vital breath, present at the time when darkness and chaos ruled; it is he who first infuses movement throughout the cosmos by blowing his life-giving breath into it. In the Mayan tradition, he appears as Hun Nal Ye, the First Father, and also as the Corn God, who travels to the underworld, gathers corn seeds from a cave there, and brings them back for human sustenance. In the cosmogony of this tradition, it is the First Father who orders the universe, creates human beings, and sets the world in motion.[12]

Quetzalcóatl as the generator of movement and the one who brings light and order out of darkness and chaos is often seen as an apt archetypal figure for 21st-century Mexico City, a city paradoxically stuck in the dark quagmire of its progress. It is also, perhaps, appropriate that Quetzalcóatl was worshipped in ancient Mexico as the god of urban centers. According to David Carrasco, he was the "patron of the urban structure as a living and vital form," "the symbol of the authority of the urban form and structure itself."[13] But Quetzalcóatl, too, has a dark side, a shadow. He is the god/leader who abandons his people. The story, a long and complex one, is simplified here to its bare essentials.

In the Toltec tradition, Quetzalcóatl is depicted not only as a god, but also as a cultural hero and the supreme priest of the city of Tula, highly revered and greatly loved. The Toltecs attributed all their cultural achievements—the invention of agriculture, the calendar, writing, astronomy, astrology, medicine, dream interpretation, silversmithing—to Quetzalcóatl, the bringer of civilization, a sort of New-World Prometheus. In addition, Quetzalcóatl is presented as the embodiment of all the archetypal qualities of priestly virtue and is celebrated for his chastity and celibacy. In some of the Toltec texts, the god Quetzalcóatl becomes fused with a priest-king of the same name, the legendary king of Tula, who reigns over a peaceful and prosperous kingdom. However, into this idyllic setting, a note of discord is introduced. Quetzalcóatl's longtime rival, the god Tezcatlipoca, who, in Jungian terms, might be seen as his shadow, plots his downfall by arranging to get Quetzalcóatl drunk. In his drunken state, Quetzalcóatl sends for his sister, Queen Quetzalpetatl, and has sexual intercourse with her, in violation of his priestly vows. He wakes up the next morning "mortified and crying, filled with grief and anguish, when he realize[s] that his misdeeds [are] already common knowledge. With nobody to comfort him, he crie[s] before [the divine order]."[14] At the same time, Tezcatlipoca brings down a series of disasters upon the people of Tula: plagues, droughts, frost, starvation, war, and other unimaginable horrors. He breaks the established order. Disgraced before his people and unable to do anything to save them from the ravages wreaked by Tezcatlipoca, Quetzalcóatl has no choice but to abdicate his throne, flee from the city, and retreat into self-imposed exile. He undertakes a journey of atonement, heading for the Red Earth, promising to return from the East, redeem his people, and restore the kingdom.

> When he arrived at the shore, he constructed a vessel made out of snakes, and once it was formed, he sat in it and used it as a boat. ... When he reached the other end of the immense sea ... he started a bonfire and threw himself into it. ... When the fire stopped burning, his heart went up to the sky. There it became a star, and that star is [both] the Morning Star and the Evening Star. Before that [however] he descended to the Region of Death, and after seven days, he was raised, transformed into a star.[15]

"Quetzalcóatl,"
by Erika
Fainsilber
Gerson

227

The abandonment by Quetzalcóatl and the prophecy of his return are deeply etched in the consciousness of the residents of Mexico City today, as it was in the minds of their ancestors. Then, as now, the people projected their innermost needs for security, order, certainty, and a sense of well-being onto a heroic redeemer figure. It was precisely this sort of projection onto the mythic messianic figure of Quetzalcóatl, aided by nostalgia for the glory of the past, that primed the Aztecs for the arrival of the Spanish conqueror Hernán Cortés and the Conquest of Mexico in 1519. Their readiness for Quetzalcoatl´s return was only enhanced by a series of "bad omens," which reportedly occurred just prior to the arrival of the Spaniards—there were signs in the sky and on land that terrified the people. These terrifying signs and omens included the appearance of a comet with an enormous blazing tail that was visible by night for a whole year; a fire that seemingly broke out spontaneously in a temple and burned it to the ground; a bolt of lightning that struck another temple; a tidal wave that devastated the city; a ghostly female voice wailing in the night, "My children, we must flee far away from this city!"; the appearance of monstrous two-headed humans in the city streets; a whirlwind that appeared repeatedly for a whole year; and so on.[16] Writing around 1585, in *Historia de Tlaxcala*, Diego Muñoz Camargo, a *mestizo*[17] born of a Spanish father and a native mother, recorded the reaction of the locals to these traumatic events as follows:

> To the natives, these marvels augured their death and ruin, signifying that the end of the world was coming and that other peoples would be created to inhabit the earth. They were so frightened and grief-stricken that they could form no judgment about these things, so new and strange and never before seen or reported.[18]

It isn't any wonder, then, that when Cortés arrived in Mexico, the Aztecs welcomed him as a savior, as Quetzalcóatl returning in triumph to deliver them from the evil that had befallen them and restore the lost kingdom. According to Miguel León-Portilla, it was the only way that they could fit the arrival of the Spaniards into the framework of their belief system and especially their cosmology.[19] In making sense of the presence of strangers in their midst, they had nothing to fall back on except the ancient myth of Quetzalcóatl.[20] León-Portilla quotes a contemporary eyewitness account of the Aztec king Moctezuma's reception of Cortés, taking from the 16th-century *Florentine Codex*, written partly in Spanish and partly in Náhuatl, the language spoken by the Aztecs:

The year 13-Rabbit now approached its end. And when it was about to end, they [the strangers] appeared, they were seen again. The report of their coming was brought to Motecuhzoma [i.e., Moctezuma], who immediately sent out messengers. It was as if he thought the new arrival was our prince Quetzalcoatl.

This is what he felt in his heart: *He has appeared! He has come back! He will come here, to the place of his throne and canopy, for that is what he promised when he departed!*

Motecuhzoma sent five messengers to greet the strangers and to bring them gifts.[21]

Moctezuma lavished Cortés with tribute, including gold, precious stones, and ornaments of various kinds, as well as clothing befitting his status as Quetzalcóatl. The contemporary account says: "These were many kinds of adornments that were known as 'divine adornments.' They were placed in the possession of the messengers to be taken as gifts of welcome along with many other objects, such as a golden snail shell and a golden diadem."[22] The account goes on to describe in minute detail how Cortés was dressed up by Moctezuma's men in this divine-royal regalia so that he could assume his role as the now-returned Quetzalcóatl, the long-awaited deliverer, in the proper manner.

So blinded were the natives by their projections and the traumas they had experienced in the preceding years that they could not see Cortés for who he really was. Even their leader, Moctezuma, was taken in by the delusion and abdicated his throne with surprising willingness in favor of Cortés. Contemporary accounts indicate that Moctezuma was as traumatized as his people—perhaps even more so. In the *Florentine Codex*, Moctezuma is portrayed as having been precipitated into a deep personal crisis: "'Moctezuma enjoyed no sleep, no food, not one [person] spoke more to him. Whatsoever he did, it was as if he were in torment. Oftentimes it was as if he sighed, became weak, felt weak.'"[23] He soliloquizes: "'What will now befall us? Who indeed standeth ...? Alas, until now, I. In great torment is my heart, as if it was washed in chili water it indeed burneth, it smarteth. Where in truth [may we go] O our lord?'"[24] It is clear from these lines that Moctezuma was experiencing "depression and [a] feeling of powerlessness"[25] in the face of this new challenge, which appears to have completely overwhelmed him.

Moctezuma's experience closely parallels that of the priest-king Quetzalcóatl when he went through his own personal crisis. It will be recalled that after the disgrace of his drunken debauchery, Quetzalcóatl is isolated (as Moctezuma is) and questions his legitimacy as the leader of his people (as Moctezuma does), and he eventually abdicates his throne and abandons his people (as Moctezuma does). It is, therefore, something of an irony that the Aztecs identified Cortés with Quetzalcóatl, when it was in fact Moctezuma who most closely resembled the mythic hero-god, while Cortés played the role of Quetzalcóatl's arch-rival, Tezcatlipoca, by bringing calamity and darkness upon Tenochtitlán.

Moctezuma's experience also displays close parallels to the experience of the present-day residents of Mexico City. His depression, his feelings of powerlessness, the internal conflict that gradually paralyzed him,[26] his eventual abdication of his position—all of these have their counterparts in the paralyzed helplessness and resignation of his 21st-century posterity. Even more broadly, the experience of the citizens of ancient Tenochtitlán, traumatized by the apocalyptic signs and omens that presaged the advent of Cortés, finds resonances in the trauma of today's inhabitants of Mexico City, attacked by the acrid air, immobilized by the sheer mass of people trying to get around the city, and abandoned to their sufferings by their leaders. Like Moctezuma and the Aztecs, we are overwhelmed by the collapse of the civic, social, and mythological order, and like them, we look for the coming of a deliverer, a savior who will rescue us from our urgent plight.

———

An eternity dragged by as I sat immobilized in my car on my way to the concert, waiting for the traffic to move. Then suddenly it came to me, like a slender ray of light in the thickening darkness: I was going to make it! I *would* be at the concert that night and I *would* hear the music I loved, conducted by its composer—and I *would* get there on time. I did not know how to account for this unexpected feeling of absolute certainty. Perhaps it was inspired by the plot of the movie for which that music was composed. In *The Mission*, Jesuit missionaries in 18th-century South America refuse to abandon their outpost in what is now Brazil, when Spain signs a treaty with Portugal surrendering the land on which the mission is built to the Portuguese, and the Vatican decides to shut down the mission to appease the Portuguese. Perhaps I was inspired by the movie not to give up hope. Whatever the inspiration, I realized that I had to forget about my destination for the time being and concentrate solely on keeping moving, even if it was only a few inches at a time. As long as I was moving, there was hope, and every inch would bring me that much closer to the theater. This realization was almost redeeming: my worry about missing the performance vanished as if by magic. I did, in fact, arrive at the theater in time, and I enjoyed the experience of a lifetime, one that I will not soon forget.

———

Times of crisis tend to constellate certain archetypes. This was the unique insight of C.G. Jung. He wrote:

> If there is a question of a general incompatibility or an otherwise injurious condition productive of neuroses in relatively large number of individuals, then we must assume the presence of constellated archetypes. Since neuroses are in most cases not just private concerns, but social phenomena, we must assume that archetypes are constellated in these cases too. The archetype corresponding to the situation is activated, and as a result those explosive and dangerous forces hidden in the archetype come into action, frequently with unpredictable consequences.[27]

Mexico City has had a long history of crises and traumas, and over the centuries it has developed a collective neurosis that indicates, as Jung would see it, the constellation of some particular archetype. In our case, this archetype might be called the Quetzalcóatl archetype, which is itself a manifestation of the broader Savior archetype (also known as the Redeemer or Messiah archetype). For the Mexicans of the 16th century, helpless and vulnerable under the invasive force of the Spanish conquistadors, the constellation of the Quetzalcóatl archetype was inevitable. But the Savior archetype was unable to deliver on its promise. Cortés turned out to be a disappointment rather than a savior, and Quetzalcóatl began to take on the aspect of the God Who Never Returns. The longing for his ever awaited reappearance became rooted in the Mexican psyche and shaped the subsequent history of our country.

Tenochtitlán became a Spanish colony, and for the next three hundred years was pervaded, from a psychological point of view, by the archetype of the God Who Never Returns. Quetzalcóatl became the focal point of a desperate longing. His simulated reappearance as Cortés had been a complete disaster, constellating what the Jungian analyst Luigi Zoja in his essay, "Trauma and Abuse: The Development of a Cultural Complex in the History of Latin America," has called the experience of betrayal by the gods.[28] Repeatedly, Mexicans have felt betrayed by "the gods," and repeatedly, they have gone back to longing for their return. In every new round of elections, the people vote as if expecting that from it will emerge a new First Father, who will restore order and civilized life and forge a coherent cultural identity. We keep falling back into the same destructive projection as our Aztec forebears. Over and over again, their psychic drama has been replayed throughout our history.

During the colonial period, the subjugated indigenous peoples looked to the Creoles[29] as their potential savior. The Creoles had been pushing hard for equal rights with the Spaniards, and the natives clung to the hope that they could ride on the coattails of their slightly more powerful compatriots. However, just as Cortés had used the non-Aztec tribes to fight against the Aztecs and then oppressed them when the victory was won, so the Creoles used the natives in the Mexican War of Independence (1810-1821) and then abandoned them to their own devices. The same pattern of misplaced hope and betrayed trust has been repeated with every new turn of the political tide. The French, the Americans, the Institutional Revolutionary Party (PRI) (which was formed at the time of the Mexican Revolution and managed to hold on to power for 71 years), and recently the National Action Party (PAN)—each in turn has been invested with the archetypal role of the Great Deliverer, and each in turn has failed to deliver. Each of these would-be saviors has been dressed up imaginally in the ceremonial robes and "divine adornments" of Quetzalcóatl, as Cortés was dressed up literally by Moctezuma, and each, in turn, has been found to be naked, like the vain emperor in Hans Christian Andersen's fairy tale. Paradoxically, the revelation of their nakedness has only intensified our longing for Quetzalcóatl's return.

It seems to me that the real problem with Mexico City is that it has misunderstood the Savior archetype. Or rather, it has focused on only one aspect of the archetype—that is, the "rescuing" aspect—to the exclusion all others. The archetypal Savior is not a Conquering Hero (like Cortés) who *leads* the way to peace, order, security, and enlightenment. Rather, he is the one who *shows* the way through his own struggle with himself and his eventual victory over his own inner demons. Typically, he goes through a "long dark night of the soul," a personal crisis, a *nekyia* (a symbolic descent into the underworld, or a "night sea journey" as Jung called it[30]), he tackles his neurosis head on, he comes to terms with his own frailties, he embraces his shadow, and he emerges victorious through a process of self-redemption and self-renewal. By virtue of his own struggle and overcoming, he serves as an example to others of the means of achieving self-acceptance, taking responsibility for one's actions, and returning to the original state of wholeness. He often sacrifices himself symbolically on behalf of others and is reborn or resurrected to return with renewed vigor. It is in this sense that he is a liberator or deliverer.

If we examine the Quetzalcóatl myth closely, we see that it has all the hallmarks of this classic Savior archetype. The priest-king Quetzalcóatl experiences a downfall, recognizes his fault, and repents. He goes through a personal crisis, a long dark night of the soul (much as Moctezuma did when confronted with the figure of Cortés). He undertakes a journey across the sea on a raft of snakes. He sacrifices himself by building a fire and throwing himself into it. In this symbolic death, he descends to the underworld where he remains for seven days. From the ashes of his pyre, he is resurrected or reborn, and rises into the sky as the Morning Star and the Evening Star. These aspects of the myth are rarely considered in the Mexican reframing of it. In our abandonment trauma, we tend to fixate only on the promise of his return. But even in this, we are misguided, for we take the prophecy, as the Aztecs appear to have done, far too literally. If we understand the story symbolically, the return of Quetzalcóatl is an internal rather than an external experience. Only when we go beyond the literal is it possible for us to discover that Quetzalcóatl does come back in the inner light of the Morning Star and the Evening Star to illuminate and re-establish order in our inner darkness.

This insight was at the core of the "revelation" that came to me on my way to the concert, as I sat paralyzed in my car on that congested side street waiting for the traffic to move. The true meaning of Quetzalcóatl's return is the return of a "Quetzalcóatl consciousness." This means that every inhabitant of the city will take responsibility for his or her actions, as Quetzalcóatl did for his, for in a very real sense, we, as citizens of this city, are all complicit in its downfall, each having contributed our share to its degradation by what we have done individually, as well as what we have left undone. Only then will the city, hopefully, seek to atone for its own failings by plunging into the symbolic fire and rising purified and renewed from the ashes.

There is far too much blame going around in Mexico City today. From venerating our leaders, as we did in the days of Moctezuma, we have come to despise them, greet their public statements with cynicism, hold them responsible for the deplorable conditions we are forced to live under, and curse them for the rapidly deteriorating quality of life in our city. I am reminded of what the Israeli writer Amos Oz said about conditions in his own country:

Naturally I have every respect for the brave child who shouts that the emperor is naked when the crowd is cheering Long live the emperor. But the situation today is that the crowd is yelling that the emperor is naked and maybe for that reason the child ought to find something new to shout, or else he should say what he has to say without shouting.[31]

Rural citizens flock to the city hoping for a better life.
Photograph by Juan Rulfo

My experience on the way to the concert made me feel like screaming. I felt utterly abandoned, and truly missed the old Mexican order, in which one was able to move about freely. I was mourning deeply the loss of Quetzalcóatl. But it was just then that my idea emerged, *I will move centimeter by centimeter,* and that I knew was the way to arrive at my destination.

Paradoxically, this experience helped me to find something new to shout about, or perhaps to say without shouting. What I found myself saying was that the emperor's nakedness is my nakedness and the nakedness of every citizen of Mexico City. We are all naked, all pretending to be clothed. Like the emperor in the fairy tale, we are really deceiving and betraying ourselves, just as Quetzalcóatl betrayed himself by violating his priestly code of conduct. But like Quetzalcóatl, we can atone for this betrayal through personal and individual soul searching, self-sacrifice, and inner renewal.

My drive to the theater in the gathering twilight to attend a concert that would be a once-in-a-lifetime experience can be seen as an allegory for the city's journey to wholeness and self-renewal. Just as my trip started out well-planned, with plenty of time allowed for delays and plenty of optimism that I would reach my destination in time, so Mexico City started out well-organized and prosperous, with a bright future ahead of it. However, along the way, complications set in. I became impatient and got off the main track, lured by the possibility of better conditions on the side streets, and ended up in a worse traffic jam, virtually paralyzed and completely disoriented in time and space. Likewise, the city got sidetracked by external circumstances such as invasions, wars, and natural disasters, and was lured from its original path by the enticements of progress. The result has been a degradation in its physical condition and a corresponding eclipse of its soul. That is the state in which Mexico City finds itself today. But just as I was able to reorient myself and focus on movement, and finally reached my destination, so, I hope, the city will be able to reorient itself and finally achieve the renewal and rejuvenation it seeks. Just as the movement of my car, miniscule though it was, influenced the movement of the cars around me, and their movement in turn influenced the cars around them, until the movement spread through the whole throng of cars, so the movement of each citizen of this city towards the city's overall goal will bring about the movement of other citizens and they in turn will spread the movement along. And we will eventually overcome our collective neurosis one individual neurosis at a time.

I believe Quetzalcóatl did return to Mexico City in the twilight traffic on that ordinary yet memorable evening. He did not come with great fanfare, dressed in his kingly attire and adorned with the trappings of his priestly office. He did not even return in the form of the Evening Star in the darkening sky. He came quietly, unobtrusively, in the metaphorical form of a little ray of light that seemed to penetrate my mind. And he can come to each citizen of Mexico City as he came to me, if only we will recognize his presence and let him in.

As I drove home that evening after the concert, my thoughts turned to Angelina Beloff and Diego Rivera and the "fiercely blue" Mexican skies of a now-distant past. I thought of Carlos Fuentes and the transparency of the "clear air" of *his* Mexico City. And I thought once again of my little ray of light. Perhaps we will never be able to reclaim our once-blue skies and our once-clear air. But at least we can reclaim the city's lost soul though the redemptive power of the myth of Quetzalcóatl. The secret lies not in longing for Quetzalcóatl to return, but rather in realizing that he does return if we only let him in. As a Jungian analyst working with the people of Mexico City, I have come to realize that the Mexican yearning for Quetzalcóatl cannot be satisfied by an external savior-figure. It can be satisfied only by recognizing that within each of us is a divine spark that provides us with the capacity to embody the Quetzalcóatl archetype ourselves, to be our own savior and thus save our city as well. Just as surely as I overcame the paralysis of Mexico City traffic that evening, so surely will this city be transformed when Quetzalcóatl is allowed to come home to each of its citizens individually.

Notes

1   *Chilango* is the term used colloquially by residents of Mexico City to designate themselves. Originally a derogatory term, it was used to refer to those *mestizos* (people of mixed Spanish and indigenous descent) who regarded themselves as being superior because of their Spanish blood. Over time, however, it came to be embraced with considerable pride by the people of the capital and is today accepted by the Mexican Academy of Language as a term meaning "belonging or pertaining to Mexico City" and referring particularly to the people of the city. There are two other (slightly more formal) terms for Mexico City residents: *Defeños* (derived from D.F., *Distrito Federal*) and *Capitalino*.
2   According to 2009 estimates.
3   Carlos Fuentes is a Mexican by birth and currently a part-time resident of Mexico City. He is widely considered to be Mexico's leading novelist and critic, and *Where the Air Is Clear* is held by many to be his masterpiece.
4   This is the title of the English translation of the novel, which was published in 1960. The original Spanish title is *La región más transparente* (The Most Transparent Region).
5   Elena Poniatowska, *Querido Diego, te abraza Quiela* (Mexico City: Biblioteca Era, 1978). Translated into English as *Dear Diego* (Pantheon Books, 1986) by Katherine Silver.
6   *Ibid.*, p. 18. (All quotations from the novel are my modification of Silver's translation. The page numbers refer to the Spanish edition).
7   *Ibid.*, p. 26.
8   "Homesickness." The original French phrase suggests deep longing for one's country.
9   Poniatowska, p. 62.
10   See, for example, *Historia verdadera de la conquista de la Neuva España* (*The True History of the Conquest of New Spain*) by Bernal Díaz del Castillo (1492-1585). Translated into English as *The Conquest of New Spain* by J. M. Cohen (1963).
11   Enrique Florescano, "Quetzalcóatl: A Myth Made out of Myths," in *Mitos Mexicanos*, ed., Enrique Florescano (Mexico City: Taurus, 2001), p. 145 (all translation by the author).
12   *Ibid.*
13   David Carrasco, *Quetzalcoatl and the Irony of Empire: Myths and Prophecies in the Aztec Tradition* (Chicago, IL: University of Chicago Press, 1982), p. 8.
14   Miguel León-Portilla and Earl Shorris, eds., *Antigua y neuva palabra* (Old and New Word) (Mexico City: Aguilar, 2004), p. 246 (my translation).
15   *Ibid.*, pp. 251-252 (my translation).
16   Miguel León-Portilla, ed., *Visión de los vencidos* (*Viewpoint of the Vanquished*) (Mexico City: Fondo de Cultural Economica, 2003 [1959]), pp. 3-12. An English translation of this book was published (a few years after the original came out) under a different title. The English edition used here is: Miguel Leon-Portilla, ed., *The Broken Spears: The Aztec Account of the Conquest*

of Mexico, trans. Lysander Kemp, expanded and updated ed. (Boston, MA: Beacon Press, 1992 [1962]). All subsequent references to this text will be to this English edition.

17 A Mexican of mixed descent, usually Spanish and native.

18 León-Portilla, p. 11.

19 *Ibid.*, p. 20.

20 Carrasco, p. 195.

21 León-Portilla, pp. 22-23.

22 *Ibid.*, p. 24.

23 Quoted in Carrasco, p. 196.

24 *Ibid.*

25 *Ibid.*

26 Luigi Zoja, "Trauma and Abuse: The Development of a Cultural Complex in the History of Latin America," in *Violence in History, Culture, and the Psyche: Essays* (New Orleans, LA: Spring Journal Books, 2008), p. 39.

27 C.G. Jung, "The Concept of the Collective Unconscious," *The Collected Works of C.G. Jung*, ed. Herbert Read, *et al.*, trans. R. F. C. Hull, vol. 9i (Princeton, NJ: Princeton University Press, 1971 [1936]), § 98 (hereafter abbreviated to *CW*, followed by volume number and paragraph number).

28 Zoja, p. 39. This idea is developed further in Jacqueline Gerson, "Kidnapping: Latin American Terror," in *Terror, Violence, and the Impulse to Destroy*, ed. John Beebe (Einsiedeln, Switzerland: Daimon Verlag, 2003).

29 This term is used in Mexico to refer to Mexicans of pure Spanish descent who were born in the New World.

30 "The night sea journey is a kind of *descensus ad inferos*—a descent into Hades and a journey to the land of ghosts somewhere beyond this world, beyond consciousness, hence an immersion in the unconscious."—C.G. Jung, "The Psychology of the Transference," *CW* 16, § 455.

31 Amos Oz, *The Same Sea*, trans. Nicholas de Lange (Orlando, FL: Harcourt, 2001), p. 144.

12 Angels and Idols: Los Angeles, A City of Contrasts

NANCY FURLOTTI

We Are an Enigma

Los Angeles is a city to love and to hate—it is almost cool to hate L.A. these days, especially if you are a new transplant from the East Coast. These transplants that have come in droves over the years, criticizing Los Angeles while clogging the highways and suburban neighborhoods, have turned *my* L.A. into a city difficult to like. I think all Angelenos feel this way, and have done so since the city's founding. We have other transplants, from the Hispanic countries to the south and from across the Pacific, who are happy to be here and create their own communities within the larger city. As a matter of fact, Latinos are now the largest ethnic group in Los Angeles, as they were at its founding. There are about four million of us Angelenos, making L.A. the second largest U.S. metropolis and the forty-fifth largest city in the world. We cover close to 500 square miles of land. If you include all of L.A. County, which is easy to do because we are one big sprawl, we have about 10 million people speaking 224 different languages, and covering 4060 square miles. That makes us the most populous county in the U.S. Our economy ranks sixteenth in the world! That is bigger than the entire economy of Russia, and illustrates the enormity of our place.[1]

How do you get your mind around a place this big? Frequently, one's first experience of Los Angeles is a bird's-eye view from an airplane. When I fly over the city on a trip in or out, I am always amazed by its expansiveness. L.A. is organized into blocks, making up a grid of streets and neighborhoods that seems to go on forever. At night, yellow, green, and red lights sparkle across the flat basin surrounded by mountains on one side and the Pacific coastline on the other. Parks and trees are scattered across the terrain, but are not enough to soften its urban landscape. By day, the sky is usually a hazy, orange-tinged blanket that covers the basin. Clear blue sky is only visible after a rainstorm, usually in the fall or spring; on such days you can see from the ocean to the snow-peaked mountains surrounding the city.

Los Angeles has an active outdoor life, and on these frequent warm, clear days one cannot stay inside for long. We Angelenos are health conscious, and on a warm day the beaches are the place to cool down. You will find us jogging, biking, rollerblading, or walking from Pacific Palisades to Palos Verdes along the beach bike path, passing through the crazy street life of vendors, musicians, dancers, and weight lifters along the famous "muscle beach" in Venice. If you are lucky, you will see dolphins surfing the waves or swimming in pods up and down the coast. Whale watching and sailing take you out to sea, and if you don't stop you can make it all the way to Catalina—twenty-six miles away. Hikers with their dogs climb the many trails and fire roads in the foothills of the mountains. For those who stay closer to home, we have our gardens to tend and our trees to enjoy. We live in a natural habitat filled with animals: coyotes, raccoons, possums, mountain lions, and deer, to name a few. People here love their pets, too. The flat, open spaces make L.A. a happy environment for dogs and cats.

When people talk about the working side of L.A., they usually speak about "The Industry," the movie industry, as if that were all that goes on here. Actually, it accounts for only 8% of our economy—international trade, tourism, technology, and manufacturing account for the rest.[2] Yet its voice, the loudest, seems to get all the attention. The Industry provides endless idols to worship in the form of movie stars and singers. Our successful sports teams do, too. The Lakers, Kings, Dodgers, and Angels provide many of our glorious sports icons, whom our youth aspire to emulate. Idols or angels? That is a matter of viewpoint. We know where our idols are, but what and where are these angels after whom our city was named? For me, they are a metaphor for the hope and creative inspiration that are encouraged here. They are the city's muses, which draw people and inspire innovation. They are full of possibility, and they rule the city's psychological space. These angels, though, can easily turn into false idols where hope and inspiration are sacrificed on the altar of depression and despair. This shift from the highs of anticipation to the lows of reality points to a city of extremes. What we *feel*, in an experiential way, about L.A. are its contrasts. On the one side, our city of angels is full of bright lights, like our famous sunlight and the flashy movie stars with the beautiful clothes and eternal juvenescence. But the other side is the dark depression of our pollution, our traffic, our earthquakes, our flooding, our fires, and our super-gangs.

Growing Up

Those of us who have grown up here have witnessed L.A.'s growing pains as well as our own. We had the pleasure of living here in its childhood—a young, fresh city on the outskirts of the country. For me, that was in the 1950s. We love this city and would not think of moving anywhere else. Angelenos know a deeper layer that is calm and quiet and forever hopeful. We have our circles of friends and our secret routes to avoid traffic. We understand the city and respect its pulse. Over the years, we have seen it change dramatically, as if it were growing up! If I were to place L.A. in a stage of human development, I would say the sharp contrasts and moods we witness here recall that particular and peculiarly self-possessed stage called adolescence.[3] It is a period of exploration and self-discovery, where life is new and ever changing, with all the future possibilities to look forward to and fantasize about. This typifies the lust for potential in L.A. that draws people here. They come with their dreams; some are fulfilled, but many are not. The adolescent attitude reflects the popular superficial experience of our city—what many visitors find off-putting and alienating, or delightful and seductive. The seductive draw has always been here, but its nature has changed from youthful delight to a more frenzied attraction.

My experience begins with memories of that youthful L.A., of riding my bike everywhere—down Wilshire Blvd. from Beverly Hills to the Santa Monica beaches, past open fields and small friendly shopping areas interspersed with homes. There was no threat of danger; there was not a lot of traffic. Life was free and open, and the weather was perfect. The exception was in late August and September, when the thermometer would reach into the high 90s and 100s and the smog be unbearable. At these times we would not go outside, because it hurt to breathe. Implementing tough emission standards years ago has enabled us to reduce pollution to comfortable levels, yet recently the population increase is pushing the limits of our ability to control smog. We now need even tougher regulations. Yet they had been put on hold by the Bush administration, in collaboration with some Midwestern states that objected to the way Los Angeles pushes the envelope on regulations to control air pollution and other environmental issues. With the recent change in Washington, we finally have the go-ahead to raise our environmental standards.

Air quality is best on the Westside and, of course, worst on the Eastside, away from the ocean where lower-income folks live. This is the way of cities, and ours is no different, but because of its horizontal layout the separation is greater. L.A. is split into distinct areas, and you never have to travel through a dangerous or lower-income area if you do not want to. Segregation is profound here, unlike other cities where many classes reside next to each other. Here in L.A., one can remain oblivious to the struggles of others. That is certainly one of the darker angels that sit above our city. I remember with great fondness our black housekeeper, Beulah May, who took the bus a few days a week from the West Adams area, near the University of Southern California, to clean, cook, and take care of us four kids. In those days, I never quite knew where she lived or what her life was like. I just knew that she carried a large and very sharp razor blade in her purse as protection against assault, which I later learned was a constant threat on the buses heading into her part of the city. This memory typifies the contrast inherent in Los Angeles—in my world, I am able to maintain my fantasy of a beautiful life with potential, and in hers, she struggles to survive. These two ends of the spectrum rarely meet except in the movies, unless you venture out to explore the large variety of neighborhoods on your own, which I have done for years. My first date with my husband was a visit to the Watts Towers, a famous example of junkyard design. For dinner afterwards, we went to Mr. Jim's Beef, whose slogan was, "You don't need no teeth to eat my beef." That evening thirty-five years ago proved to be very successful! From youth to adolescence, L.A. and I grew up, although my rate of change was faster than the city's.

Influences from Below

L.A. is shaped by an interesting pantheon of *gods* (using the Greek gods as a template) that play their archetypal roles in predictable ways to influence us psychologically. Typical of this city of contrasts, we experience two sides of Aphrodite, the goddess of love. The heavenly side represents a spiritual love of body and soul, while the common side is the goddess of physical love. Aphrodite rules beauty, pleasure, performers, and remains perpetually youthful. She can be vain, ill-tempered, and easily offended. Both her light and dark sides are felt in L.A. Aphrodite is present in the seduction that beckons one to move here for success, recognition, and fortune. Shows put on in her honor are the Oscars, Emmys, and other award ceremonies. On these occasions, her beauty and vitality, along with her self-focused glance, are in full view. In contrast to this resplendent experience of life is her dark side, felt after her life-giving gaze falls away and one is left alone with unfulfilled dreams. This is the experience of many who move to L.A. only to find disillusionment rather than glory.

Aphrodite inspires the desire for relationship by creating attraction. Unfortunately, though, she is not interested in forging long-term or significant connections. That job is left up to her son, Eros, who fosters the caring element in relationships. He is an elusive god in this city, while his mother is busy setting hearts and passions ablaze, leaving the victims burnt out and alone. How frequently I hear from patients that they cannot meet anyone in L.A., and many turn to internet dating. Because of the huge pool to search through, these lonely hearts hold out for the *perfect match*, therefore finding no one. This adolescent attitude of looking for perfection severely limits the singles set of all ages. They seek an angel or idol on which to project perfection and desire, without realizing that they are really longing to connect to a hidden part of themselves. This can be found by turning their view inward to explore their own nature. In the process, they may discover the inner other, which refers to a man's feminine and to a woman's masculine nature. This process of self-discovery requires that they introvert from the city's extraversion and explore the multifaceted contrasts within. It is a journey to recover soul. Many reject this journey out of fear of finding only ordinary human qualities, rather than the angels and idols they so admire. For so many, their yearning remains unsatisfied.

Another charming god who resides in our fair city is Dionysus, the god of wine and ecstasy. He is the perpetually youthful, androgynous god who brings new life to worn-out attitudes and seduces the feminine part of our personality into a deep experience of our inner nature. The lucky ones are those who succeed in discovering and expressing their true natures—they are the ones who stay close to the ground of their being. The unlucky remain as husks of their former dreams—these unfortunates have lost their souls and given up their search. Both Aphrodite and Dionysus lurk in the shadows of L.A.'s exciting club and gym scene, where the lure of being close to the angels and idols can be exhilarating, yet dangerous for the soul. The focus is so extraverted and superficial that it is difficult to have a deep conversation; life revolves round The Industry's latest developments and what the stars are doing. My daughter, who is a costumer in the city, explained to me that the stars are now being used as billboards to sell clothing lines and jewelry. The hollow idols of this city that carry the projections of heroes and gods have now become reduced to billboards and agents of advertising. Another apt description came from a patient of mine who described L.A. as being like fool's gold. So many long to find the real gold of meaning, deep relationship, and soul, but instead are left with a worthless mirage.

Another powerful one of our ruling gods is Poseidon, the great earth shaker, who lies quietly under the soil of our city, ready to destroy us at any moment. He sets off earthquakes and floods, perhaps as a way of getting our attention, to radically shift our attitudes and lives. But we rarely heed him, or any other limiter for that matter. Saturn, the grand limiter, lives only in the shadows here, but exerts a powerful influence nonetheless, with his stern, heavy, punishing nature. Along with the rest of California, we have overspent our means and have one of the worst debt ratings of any state in the nation with a D-plus rating. Saturn sits over us.

These gods or archetypal patterns serve a collective as well as personal function. There may be other patterns that influence L.A, but these are the ones that stand out to me. As they rule L.A., they may also rule other cities, as well. As Angelenos, it is our task to understand and make peace with them. They can offer up passion and creativity, or depression and sterility. One must always approach a god with respect, not a frivolous adolescent attitude, and that is also true for the archetypal energy represented by the gods who inhabit our city.[4] Otherwise, when approached with a frivolous adolescent attitude, they can do great harm. I remember as a child being terrified of Poseidon, and even though I did not know him by name, I knew the power he exerted on every psyche in the city. I was so frightened by the thought of California falling into the Pacific Ocean that I always had a life preserver under my bed. In reality, a life preserver is used to keep us bobbing on the water's surface until help arrives. Metaphorically, it serves as a defense against going into spiritual depths. What we forget is that help comes from our own relationship to the depths of our being, not from some outside rescuer. We would be better off going down willingly, rather than remaining on the surface waiting for someone else to save us. In our city, the life preserver is much sought after, because the deep is so feared. It represents the underworld—the place of death, depression, chaos, and the dark unknown—but we must remember that it is also the source of creative potential and transformation. With no connection to the underworld, soul is forever lost to the unknown realm. Depression acts as the messenger that steps beyond our free will and drags us down. With the citywide tendency to avoid introversion, it is not surprising that traces of antidepressants have been found in L.A.'s water supply, presumably as the digestive residue of all those here who take them, according to a report released by the Metropolitan Water District of Southern California.[5]

The soul of Los Angeles has been depressed for years in its struggle to find its identity. In 1928, L.A. had the highest suicide rate in the nation. Soullessness in the way the city functions is reflected in a lack of soul among its inhabitants. Here, there is no agora, no city center with foot traffic and cafes where we can walk to and from work, greet familiar faces, or stop for a coffee. We drive everywhere, mostly alone, or as a last resort ride the bus or limited metro.[6] The experience of meandering is not something that comes naturally to this city. The adolescent we are is striving to find an identity, and too often the place for that striving is the mall, which now seems the communal watering hole. We have huge malls, beautiful open-air malls, gigantic enclosed malls, small strip centers, and malls that look like replicas of European streets. We go there to shop, to eat, to see movies, to be with other people, to feel a part of a community. This serves as worship of Aphrodite's dark side. The mall, much like the nightclub and gym, is another room in her temple. There she draws us to connect only fleetingly, not deeply. We part dissatisfied, to resume our singular lives. The biggest malls of all are our amusement parks. There we can escape into entertaining fantasy and briefly forget ourselves and all life's troubles.

Tracing Roots

How did Los Angeles become this city of contrasts? Geographically, we are the end of the road, the last stop on the train crossing the U.S. We reside on the edge of the Pacific Ocean, ready either to fall off or to thrive as the launching point to the Pacific Rim. "Go west, young man, go west!" is a call that generations of Americans have answered, and they ended up in L.A. with dreams of gold, silver, oil, cars, rockets, aerospace, Disneyland, and Hollywood. Fantasy and creativity thrive here and have merged into multibillion-dollar businesses. The past, in the form of history and culture, is present, but resides at a deeper unconscious level, mostly carried in the soil and scars of L.A.'s experience. This ancient voice seeps up from the collective layer into the newly transplanted inhabitant slowly. But, this is not as easy a voice to find as it is in other cities. Many come to L.A. and cannot quite find it; they only see the city superficially. It is too big, too glitzy, too ugly. Yet, what a mistake. What you see is really only the skin of a giant hiding beneath, much like an archetypal pattern ready to manifest, with a potent life force that carries the past and looks to the future. Within it are hidden jewels that the long-term inhabitants are privileged to see. These are the pockets of future potential, the flashes of genius in the adolescent youth, the stability and strength inherent in the personality. These jewels glitter more frequently as L.A. matures from its awkward and many times off-putting adolescence into the grand adult city she is becoming.

To understand us, it is helpful to start with the past that explains who we are and what has gone into forming our identity. The name *Los Angeles* is Spanish for *the angels*. In 1769, Father Juan Crespi led the first European land expedition through California and came upon a beautiful river, and named the land around it "Our Lady of the Angels of the Porcuiuncula," for the tiny chapel in Assisi given to St. Francis. *Porcuiuncula* means "very small parcel of land." In 1781, forty-four Mexican farmers were escorted to this site to settle what they called "The Town of Our Lady the Queen of the Angels." Before that, the area was home to the Chumash and later the Tongva tribe, sometimes called the Gabrielinos, who settled here about two thousand years ago. The mountains surrounding the Los Angeles basin are named the San Gabriel Mountains after this tribe. Juan Cabrillo stopped at present-day San Pedro in 1542 and was greeted by the Tongvan Indians. Seeing smoke from the inversion layer, he named our Santa Monica Bay, "The Bay of Smoke." This foreshadowed a constant environmental problem—smog—that would contribute to Los Angeles's identity. Other environmental challenges were the earthquakes and repeated river flooding that plagued the growing city. From then on, our basin was owned by Spain until title shifted to Mexico, at which time its inhabitants were called *Californios.*[7]

The first Americans arrived in 1826 and were ordered to leave by the *Californios*. That was only the beginning of a steady flow of immigrations from the east. The second largest ethnic group in 1835 was the French. California Governor Pio Pico expressed his concern about the Los Angeles of 1846 when he stated, "We find ourselves threatened by hordes of Yankee immigrants who have already begun to flock into our country and whose progress we cannot arrest."[8] (We now frequently hear this same complaint about the hordes of Latinos flooding our city, just as we still complain about the transplants from the East Coast!) That same year, the United States declared war on Mexico, and two years later the *Californios* capitulated to the Americans. California was ceded over to the United States. Los Angeles was incorporated as a city in 1850, but not without conflict between the Yankees and Latinos. By 1870, Yankees outnumbered Latinos and Indians for the first time. This proportion has changed recently. Latinos are now again the largest ethnic group in Southern California and continue to give L.A. its unmistakable Latino character. Immigrants continue pouring across the border in search of work and eventual legalization and, in fact, our economy would collapse without them. We are once again *Alta California.*[9]

The Los
Angeles Basin.
*Photograph
by the author*

In 1870, Los Angeles County was the nation's number one wine-producing county. It then became the nation's number one orange-producing area and the automotive capital of the world. Later still, the aviation, movie, and aerospace industries flourished. "The Industry" was originally located in Hollywood, which was founded by the prohibitionist Harvey Wilcox. It is ironic that his repressed Dionysian side found a suitable future container when The Industry flourished with glamour and debauchery. This is but one example of how those archetypal figures who influence us from the depths are not far away. They are revealed in the actions and behaviors of people as well as businesses, and even cities, states, and countries.[10]

What of our geological history? The Los Angeles basin was created when the San Andreas fault began to move, and in the process created the San Gabriel, Santa Monica, and Santa Ana mountains, which surround a large basin on three sides—the shoreline is on the fourth. Giant saber-toothed tigers, mastodons, mammoths, and other now-extinct animals roamed the area, many of whom were trapped in what is now known as the La Brea Tar Pits, actually located at the George Page Museum. From the remains of the large prehistoric animals, Los Angeles received the gift of a vast reserve of oil. Oil wells spotted the landscape from 1892 on, looking very much like resurrected dinosaurs, and are still seen within the city and along our coast.

Water represents the source of life and is key to this city. L.A. is an arid basin with no water source of its own except for the meager L.A. River, which could still flood at certain times of year. To contain its flooding and meandering, it was cemented into a channel that remains largely abandoned and forgotten. Just recently, portions of the river are being beautified and used as parkways. This reflects a more mature and soulful attitude towards nature, which I hope to see continue. In 1904, a handful of men with foresight, including the famous William Mulholland, depicted in the movie *China Town*, set out to buy land in the Owens Valley to supply our ever-growing thirst. Water from the Colorado River was diverted down to the city via the Los Angeles aqueduct, allowing the arid basin to blossom into a garden oasis with perennial flowers and green lawns. The geography and the availability of water encouraged the city to grow into an ever-widening sprawl, with one neighborhood giving way to the next. This expansion created a horizontal landscape of low-rise homes and businesses with the occasional clump of high-rise office buildings like Century City. This may be about to change, now that we are reaching full capacity and are experiencing increasingly severe droughts. Our leaders are actually beginning to think about solutions to our potential water shortage, besides asking us to conserve. One viable solution is to reuse processed water waste. Isn't this a maturing moment for the land of plenty where everything is easily thrown away and replaced? [11]

Growing Pains

The geography of the Los Angeles basin has been a key factor in how the city developed, and it contributed to the independent attitude that is so prevalent in Los Angeles. This attitude is what we are running up against as we run out of space. We prefer our own cars to public transportation, and our own house and garden to an apartment with a park down the road. We are those immigrants who ventured farthest west and those citizens who demand privacy. You could call us the final adventurers—who welcome the unknown and the new, but keep to ourselves at the same time. I have lived in the same house for thirty years and

Olvera Street.
Photograph by the author

barely know my neighbors; this is not uncommon. We drive our cars alone, to and from our single-family homes, with no place to congregate and meet for a chat. The city expanded horizontally from the original *pueblo*, Olvera Street, and became so large that neighborhoods with separate identities emerged. Most people remain within their neighborhood, where they shop, work, attend schools, and socialize. They rarely venture out except for special occasions.

Heavy traffic makes travel increasingly difficult, resulting in even more isolation from the rest of the city. It seems that our unflagging desire for privacy, convenience, and independence is turning back on us to create a monster. Traffic is the *bête noire* of our existence here. We talk about the traffic, not the weather. It is bad with no hope of getting better. At one time, we had a decent public transportation system—"the red car"—that was shut down by the early automotive and tire companies. It is virtually impossible now to use public transportation from one part of the city to another without wasting hours. Our population has increased exponentially, while our public transportation has only grown slightly. One learns the secret routes and goes out at non-rush hours. We sit in our cars alone and move around in an impersonal way, longing for contact and connection, but have a hard time finding it. This is certainly one of the darker influences on our collective identity.

As Los Angeles grew, one neighborhood after another sprouted up around a cultural similarity. The overall city can be seen as a vast society in which distinct neighborhoods support the social/relational matrix of the group. People tend to remain within their zone, and infrequently venture out to explore the surrounding diversity. This, of course, leads to a lack of overall cohesiveness. It is easy to remain in one's seemingly safe world and project danger onto the unknown other, a natural albeit unhealthy function of human nature. An early example of this was burned into my memory. I grew up in an area above Inglewood that is called View Park. It overlooks the city and mountains from the south, and was a lovely place to live. By my second-grade year, black families began moving into the neighborhood. My mother insisted we move out. We moved to another all-white neighborhood down the peninsula called Palos Verdes and, the following year, to Westwood. View Park remains a lovely neighborhood predominantly inhabited by well-educated, professional blacks, and Westwood remains mostly white (except for the diversity at UCLA). They are very distinct and separate places, the residents of each finding no reason to venture into the other. The good news is that each one has its own special character, but the bad news is that residents are isolated from both the problems and successes of the other.

This fact was made glaringly clear during the Watts riots in 1965, ignited by a confrontation between a white policeman and a black man. It was summer, and stiflingly hot. The black community was ready to explode from lack of opportunity and the desperation of poverty. The rest of the city was shocked when it actually did. This explosion was repeated during the Rodney King incident in 1991, after he was stopped for a traffic violation and beaten by white policemen. Riots broke out in violence, but it was despair that was being expressed. The neighborhood reaction was to send out a flare of warning and frustration for the lack of hope that pervades those pockets of L.A.—a cry for help—which has not yet been answered. Instead, these ghettos are plagued by gangs, black and Latino, who kill each other frequently. These gang wars are rarely reported in the news. I recently heard a news report of a shooting only because the gang gunfight had stopped traffic at a busy intersection. If violence spreads to other neighborhoods or takes the life of an innocent bystander, it will be reported. Otherwise it remains the dirty secret of that neighborhood. How sad is that! We remain in our safe neighborhoods with locked doors and alarm systems, keeping our gaze on the angels we think we are, leaving our unacknowledged devils to roam the undesirable landscapes of our city. We are *not* proud to be the home of the two fastest-growing and most powerful gangs in the world, the MS-13 and the Mara 18, which sprang up in the neighborhoods around our very own McArthur Park, and are deeply connected to Central America and our own prison system. The gang members are not just kids longing for a community and selling dope, but sophisticated criminals. Years of portraying and idealizing the gangster sociopath, with all his aggressive, bloody violence, on the silver screen has finally brought him to life. Frankenstein is born and is with us in a very real and dangerous form. These are the darkest of the dark idols—the angels that descended into dark imagination and were transformed into devils.[12]

This brings us back to the contrasts we live with in L.A. Here, there is a multiplicity of colors and differences. We have ghettos: black, and now latino. We have Koreatown, Chinatown, Little Tokyo, Little Ethiopia, and other neighborhoods of many other ethnicities. We have communities of those who are artsy, avant-garde, old guard, nouveau riche, gay, and young professionals. That adds greatly to the richness of our culture, but the isolation and lack of fluid movement from one neighborhood group to another are clearly negative. This is where the angels, representing our aspirations, need to touch down into the reality of our coexistence.[13]

The city in its youth was a joy—the open fields, low population and traffic, a feeling of safety. This was the city I remember in the 1950s and early '60s. Its adolescence has been brutal, but there is a scent of further change. We may be growing up out of necessity. L.A. has reached the end of its ability to grow horizontally; we have used up all available land; our water rights are being diminished by other needy communities, like Las Vegas. Many commuters can no longer afford to pay the high gas prices, and environmental impact can no longer be ignored. I say, let the dark sides of Aphrodite and Dionysus go to Las Vegas to play, while we encourage their positive sides to remain here to help us. Then we can grow into an adulthood imbued with beauty and creativity. Our leaders are having to rethink the way our city functions and are beginning to see the value of mixed-use development, which is more vertical than horizontal: shops with condos or apartments above. The original downtown city center is undergoing a remarkable renewal, and there is a push to improve the public transportation system and add bike lanes. Responsible verticality means not only going up, but also down. It means taking responsibility for the effects of the city. It is the journey down that is lacking in L.A.—the journey into the inner depths of one's being to connect with what is true and meaningful in life. A change in our attitude and the way we envision our city may well encourage a similar change in how we view our personal topography.

Is There Culture beyond "The Industry"?

The arts are a means to express feeling and soul. The voice of the city finds its way into the arts. L.A. has had a long and interesting historical connection to the arts. During World War II, many foreign composers, writers, musicians, and actors immigrated to our city and formed an exile community. We welcomed Otto Klemperer, Heinrich and Thomas Mann, Bertolt Brecht, Lion Feuchtwanger, Arthur Rubinstein, Arnold Schoenberg, Igor Stravinsky, Sergey Rachmaninoff, George Balanchine, Marlene Dietrich, and others. L.A. became the center of the musical world starting in the late '40s.[14] What is available culturally in this city now continues to be extensive and remarkable—from our exceptional Opera Company and Philharmonic Orchestra to our studio musicians and museums. My favorite is the Getty Villa in Malibu, which contains a stunning collection of classical art pieces, and offers outdoor theater and music in the summer. Its big brother, the Getty Museum, has a valuable collection of manuscripts and photographs, and the building and view are not to be missed.

There are numerous opportunities for our philanthropically minded to fund the improvement of our cultural landmarks. One such project is the Walt Disney Concert Hall, the home of the L.A. Philharmonic Orchestra. The structure itself represents a coming together of the two sides of life in Los Angeles: the fantasy world of imagination and frivolity joins the adult world of classical music. It seems that Mickey Mouse is finally growing up. The architect who designed the fantastic, postmodern or post-structuralist building was our very own Frank Gehry. The exterior offers a fresh, organic feeling, as if a flower were opening up, exposing the lushness of nature. The interior is reminiscent of the Spanish architect Antonio Gaudí's curvilinear designs, and makes one feel enclosed by a living organism. There are two distinct areas inside Disney Hall. The first is the large concert hall itself, which is beautiful and uplifting in its warm natural woods. The second area consists of narrow hallways that ring the concert hall, with no adequate place to congregate to discuss the beautiful music. The seats in the hall are crowded, and in some seating areas you literally feel as if you were hanging off a cliff. This design may be a case of function following form, but it accurately reflects the current feeling and soul of our city. The building is fresh, creative, glimmering, and sexy, but without a central order—much like our L.A., and very much like an adolescent with no distinct identity. Just as the Los Angeles County Museum of Art has had a number of facelifts, this structure may, too. In fact, the shiny exterior has already been toned down to reduce the painful heat reflected into the building across the street. Nevertheless, the beauty of the sound orchestrated by Esa-Pekka Salonen and now Gustavo Doudemel transports one to the realm of the angels and immediately one forgives any discomfort encountered in the building itself.

Frank Gehry's own house.

Photograph by the author

Frank Gehry's own house is a perfect example of the chaotic form, which is archetypally L.A. I was told a story by a friend of his about how his house evolved. According to the story, his neighbors parked their trucks on their lawns and campers in their driveways, with no concern for the aesthetics of the neighborhood. This gave Mr. Gehry the idea of altering his simple traditional house to fit in with the look of the neighborhood. To achieve this, he began to add odd structures and elements to its exterior. The result is an interesting junkyard design, although I am not sure he would call it that. It gives off a psychological quality that one recognizes in the adolescent who deconstructs all that is old in search for his or her own unique identity. Here, Mr. Gehry found his own voice.

We've Got Soul!

Where is the substance and soul of our young city? Where is the feeling, the continuity, the community? Soul is the *muse* who smiles back at us from the depth of our being, individually and collectively. She reflects the quality that personifies feeling, connection, and purpose. Soul is found in a quiet turning inward and introspection, and in the care one offers to one's own true nature and to friendship. She is felt in the concern and interest we show our environment and in our striving to change it to better reflect who we are becoming. In L.A., soul reveals herself in small ways: in groups of friends who attend churches, temples, schools, and institutes; in the book and music stores, and libraries that encourage thoughtfulness; in the discussions after a movie, or an opera performance, or a Lakers' game. She joins us at a small dinner party of close or new friends. Nature reveals its soul on a hike in the foothills overlooking the L.A. basin, a bike ride down the coast, or a quiet beach walk at dusk to watch the dolphins frolic. We are transported to her realm when we are able to see the entire coastline and the snowcapped mountains at once. She reveals herself when a driver in rush hour traffic takes the time to let you in, or when a clerk returns the $100 bill you thought was only $10. Soul is seen in the smile we all can give to a stranger, in knowing that L.A. has the second *smallest* carbon footprint per capita of all the cities in the U.S., and the fact that we have all changed our habits to make that possible. Many find this fact incredible with all our smog and traffic. We are not coal burners, and our near-perfect weather certainly helps.[15]

L.A. is a city full of surprises and should not to be underestimated as it moves quickly into a place of global importance: culturally, environmentally, and as a world trade center. This multifaceted metropolis can be as impersonal or as warm and mature as the face that is turned towards it. As a city of contrasts, L.A. is a place of sweet flowers with sharp thorns, home to our angels and idols. Our city's soul is found in our deep, rich ground of diversity, offering an ever-present potential for renewal, like the roses that bloom over and over all year long. We, Angelenos, all contribute to the matrix of that soul. While not all hear her whispers, many do; and for them, her gift of inspiration is rewarding.

Notes

1   *Los Angeles Almanac* (n.d.), retrieved February 18, 2008, from http://www.laalmanac.com; U.S. Census Bureau (n.d.), *Los Angeles (city), California*, retrieved July 12, 2008, from http://quickfacts.census.gov/qfd/states/06/0644000.html, and U. S. Census Bureau (n.d.), *Los Angeles(county), California* (n.d.), retrieved July 12, 2008, from Wikipedia: http://wikipedia.org/wiki/Los_Angeles,_California.

2   U.S. Census Bureau (n.d.), *Los Angeles County, California*, retrieved July 12, 2008, from http://quickfacts.census.gov/qfd/states/06/06037.html.

3   Lauren Greenfield, *Fast Forward: Growing up in the Shadow of Hollywood* (New York: Knopf, 1997).

4   James Hillman, *City & Soul* (Putnam, CT: Spring, 2006), and James Hillman, *The Dream and the Underworld* (New York: Harper & Row, 1979).

5   Metropolitan Water District of Southern California, January 30, 2006

6   Christopher Goffard, "Isolated in our cars, but suffering together," *Los Angeles Times*, June 8, 2008; Mary Lynn Kittelson, ed., *The Soul of Popular Culture: Looking at Contemporary Heros, Myths and Monsters* (Chicago: Open Court, 1998).

7   *Los Angeles Almanac* (n.d.), retrieved February 18, 2008, from http://www.laalmanac.com.

8   J. Michael Walker, *All the Saints of the City of the Angels* (Berkeley: Heyday, 2008), p. viii.

9   *Los Angeles Almanac* (n.d.), retrieved February 18, 2008, from http://www.laalmanac.com, and *L.A. County Online* (n.d.), retrieved February 18, 2008, from http://lacounty.gov/arts_culture.htm.

10 *Ibid.*

11 Delores McKinney, "The magic ingredient ... Water," *Brentwood News*, May 2008, p. 6.

12 Rocky Delgado. "Going global to fight gangs," *Los Angeles Times*, August 18, 2008; Richard Winton, Susanhah Rosenblatt, and Andrew Blankstein, "Gang mayhem cripples big area," *Los Angeles Times*, February 22, 2008; Scott Gold, "A New Look in East L.A.," *Los Angeles Times*, May 16, 2008.

13 Matthew Garrahan, "Diverse City Looks Beyond Challenges," *Financial Times Special Report*, Los Angeles (October 28, 2008); and Steve Harvey, *The Best of: Only in L.A.* (Los Angeles: Los Angeles Times Syndicate, 1996).

14 Tripod (n.d.), *Los Angeles*, retrieved February 18, 2008, from http://members.tripod.com/noemigarcia/lapaint/immigration.htm.

15 Ron Scherer, "How Does your City's Carbon Footprint Stack Up?" *The Christian Science Monitor* (May 29, 2008), retrieved October 5, 2009, from http://features.csmonitor.com/environment/2008/05/29/how-does-your-city's-carbon-footprint-stack-up/.

13

London Palimpsest: South, East, North, and West

Christopher Hauke

Soul as Surface

❮ THE COLOR RED ❯

Cities are living beings. Like all living things they may thrive and enjoy the fullest of lives, after which they decay and die. With some cities that might be the end, leaving nothing but traces to be unearthed centuries later. With other cities, despite the appearance of death, something continues; while the matter disintegrates, the *soul* of such cities persists. London is like this. For thousands of years the River Thames has wound its course through a valley where human settlements both grew and thrived and contracted and died. In a similar way, the soul of London is a thread that ensures, despite the devastation of plagues, bombings, or fires, that London will always be reborn.

But what does it mean to speak of the soul of London? When seeking the soul of a great city, the experience of the city as surface is often where we start, even if it is far from where we end. The surface appearance that impacts on our senses—whether it is visual, aural, or felt kinesthetically on our skin—is not trivial; it reaches us directly, not only as a reminder of where we are but also of what we imagine and what we expect. What we first *see* of London may be structures like the Houses of Parliament and Big Ben, Buckingham Palace, Tower Bridge, St. Paul's Cathedral—iconic architecture joined these days by the Gherkin, Canary Wharf, the Millennium Bridge, and the Tate Modern. We *hear* the voice of London in the Cockney[1] dialect with its rhythms, abbreviations, and rhyming-slang codes.[2] While London's fog is largely a thing of the past, mostly due to the ban on emissions from coal fires, we still *feel* the coolness of its gray, rainy days.

We may see more gray in the stone of great buildings or marble white where they are scrubbed clean, but above all, we see the persistence of one color: London's color is red. From red-brick Victorian terraces to the red post-boxes, from the red London bus to the uniforms of soldiers at Buckingham Palace, the city is splashed with red. The cabs of the nineteenth century were red, all the London Underground trains were once red, and most of the public phone boxes still are. "Red" was once the Cockney slang for gold, and long before communism, the red flag was invented in 1768 by London river-workers "as a token of radical discontent."[3] (In the sections on North London and East London below I will be mentioning how London was an important home to both Marx and Lenin and how in every century, violence and rebellion has left London's streets bloodied red.)

Red crosses were painted on the doors of victims of the plague in 1665, and the next year, 1666, the sky was red with the Great Fire of London—"a fire which, as John Locke noted, created 'Sunbeams of a strange red dim light' which covered the whole of the city."[4] Later I write of how the Great Fire resulted in the rebuilding of the City along specific mystical and rational lines and thus consolidated London as the financial center of the world.[5] In London, the color red not only announces where you are, it is the color of danger and emergency, of blood and of fire, of destruction and emergence. Against the gray-stone or red-brick solidity of the architecture and the layout of the streets, the gray crowds of business suits and the color of the Thames, London is splashed with red. Not only horizontally across the surface of the city we witness in the present, but vertically, down through all its layers—historically, ethnically, and emotionally— London is streaked with red. It is the color of death and of birth; it is the color of change and continuing.

❧ ACROSS AND DOWN: EXPLORING THE LONDON PALIMPSEST ❧

There is a way of exploring a city that follows the spirit of the aimless wanderer and spectator, the *flaneur*, that has led to the idea of psychogeography.[6] This chapter has arisen on the one hand from going downward through historical layers in library research (a vertical exploration) and through (re-)wandering London's streets (a horizontal journey). Exploring in this way, I simply let myself be led by whatever grabbed my attention: architecture, inscriptions, signs, statues, the names of and layout of the streets, and people and their languages, activities, clothing, customs, and institutions as they were enacted all around me.

In walking between places both iconic and unknown, listening, looking at (and sometimes photographing) what caught my eye, I was driven by an urge to vertically connect the layers beneath the surface and to realize the palimpsest that is London. But simultaneously, the other dimension was always involved. I was conscious of the real-time present experience of amplifying and connecting places in the horizontal plane, an inner linkage between who I had been when certain places featured in my life and what new connections I was making in the present. And doing all this from a subjective position of emotional resonance rather than one that is more rationally or historically objective. So in my exploration of the soul of London I have found that in addition to our sensory experience of the surface, it is also our own history and the knowledge that we both bring and rediscover as we discover the presence of the past both exposed and disguised through our present perception of the city.

But there is something else to be said. It is one thing to approach the soul of a city as strangers arriving for the first time or coming back again after many visits to a city that is not our own and not our permanent home. Another way to experience the soul of a city is one that arises from living a life in the city: being born, owning a home, loving, working, and raising children there. In this way the soul of the individual and the soul of the city create a dialogue. Just as an individual personality becomes shaped by the environment of this or that city, the city itself becomes more psychological through the experience of the indigenous individual. The life of a city and life in that city can speak to each other. This way, the individual not only knows about and carries characteristics of the city, but equally, the city may also be known, and even *know itself,* through the soul of the individuals that inhabit it, through their own self-knowledge and their psychology. A dialogue arises between person and place that affects both. The unconscious and conscious psyche does not respect the boundary of individual mentalities. Psyche is in the world and, as James Hillman has said, in the way the world displays itself,[7] and in our cities we are closer than ever to experiencing the flow between personal and collective human experience, whether we are conscious of it or not.

I have an advantage in that I am a Londoner. I, my sons, my father and mother, and my maternal grandparents were all born in London—Tooting, Lewisham, Pimlico, and Streatham, to be exact. In 1919, my paternal grandfather, Theodore Hauke from Brno (now in the Czech Republic but then in Moravia) and my grandmother from Nottingham met at the Hotel Russell in Russell Square

WC I, married, and set up house, first in Pimlico, SW I, then Willesden, NW 2, and finally in Balham, SW 17. I was born at 99 Nightingale Lane, Tooting, SW 12. Between the ages of two and nineteen, I lived thirty miles north of London. I returned to attend college in Anna Pavlova's old house[9] on North End Road near Hampstead Heath and have lived in North and South London for the last thirty-seven years.[10] My position as a Londoner is not the only place from which to describe the soul of this city, but it is the only one I can offer. It will be biased, selective, and enthusiastic in a very idiosyncratic way. It will be a view derived from my personal experience of life in London over forty years and from everything historical and cultural that fires my imagination.

SOUTH

❦ THE VIEW FROM GREENWICH ❧

For seven years during the 1990s, my consulting room was a small space at the top of one of the Georgian blocks in the center of Greenwich on the southern bank of the Thames. Greenwich has a bustling village atmosphere these days,[11] the tourist population now enhanced by the University of Greenwich and its students from around the world. The university has taken over the magnificent buildings that were once the Old Royal Naval College. First designed as the Royal Hospital for Seamen by Christopher Wren and Nicholas Hawksmoor in 1696, the buildings have an elegant frontage on the bank of the river with a gap designed to give uninterrupted views of the Thames from the Queen's House in Greenwich Royal Park. The Royal Hospital was finished in 1705, and Nelson lay in state in its great Painted Hall in January 1806. It closed in 1869, and the Royal Naval College took over the site from 1873 until 1998.

Command of the seas was a major factor in the success of British imperialism and the establishment of a British Empire that lasted until the end of World War II. The port of London has been the point of departure and arrival for British exploration and exploitation of the rest of the world since Roman times. In Shakespeare's day, one visitor was reported to have remarked that "London is not said to be in England, but rather England to be in London."[12] Until the closing of the docks in the 1970s, London was the world's premier port for international shipping,[13] and although it is far from the cartographical center of Britain—that would be further north—London has long been the historical and spiritual as well as the economic and governing center of Britain.

The icon of global centrality granted to London—and Greenwich—is the convention of Greenwich Mean Time, which established London as the chronological center for world time (and global distances). A world system of standard time based on Greenwich Mean Time was developed at the Prime Meridian Conference in Washington, D.C., in 1882 and accepted worldwide by 1904.[14] When I looked toward the Thames out of my tiny office window four floors above the street in Greenwich, two more icons of London's status—both based around trade and time—came into view. First I would see the masts and rigging of the *Cutty Sark*, a tea clipper standing in dry dock as a tourist attraction in the center of Greenwich.[15] When it imported its desirable cargo for the East Indian Company, it was the fastest sea transport in the world. When the docks closed down, the economic spirit of the locality was injected with speculative cash and grants resulting in the rise of London's highest office blocks, which were swiftly occupied by the big names in finance, including CitiBank, HSBC, and Credit Suisse. Beyond the *Cutty Sark* on the north side of the Thames in Docklands stands the Canary Wharf Tower, at 244 meters the tallest building in Britain. From my window I could gaze upon these two icons of modern capitalism almost superimposed upon each other. The connection was more than symbolic—they were articulated to each other on a traceable timeline of economic and entrepreneurial growth. Far from the past being buried beneath its streets, London past and London present are sometimes side by side, in front of each other in the here and now.

❲ YOUNG LONDON ❳

Before I moved to London, it was only thirty minutes away by train and much of my teens were spent on its streets and in its markets such as Camden Lock, Portobello Road, Kensington Market, and, on Sundays, Brick Lane. Soon, as a musician, I was playing the pub rock circuit (alongside bands like The Jam, The Police, and The Clash) at the Hope and Anchor Islington, the Rock Garden, Dingwalls, the Nashville, and the Marquee. Now my sons in their late teens play their own gigs in New Cross and Camden, north and south of the River.

The mods and hippies linked with the London music explosion of the 60s and 70s were not the first to make London a city of the young, however. London's culture of youth goes back hundreds of years with the apprentices of the London Guilds system. The Guild names remain a living presence in our London lives today. In addition to my analytic practice, I am a senior lecturer at Goldsmiths, a college of the University of London with over 3,000 students in New Cross, SE14.[16]

Just down the road, my sons attended the local high school Haberdashers Aske's Hatcham College, where they were taught by two men called Mr. Skinner, and over the years we have all played rugby against boys from Merchant Taylors School. Those names—Goldsmiths, Haberdashers, Skinners, and Merchant Taylors—refer to just four of the twelve trades still actively linked to these educational institutions and names that are now part of our modern lives. These four comprise a third of the Guilds and Livery Companies of the City of London, which are the earliest business and training communities and the key to the city's growth and wealth. Listed numerically they are:

1. Mercers
2. Grocers
3. Clothworkers
4. Fishmongers
5. Goldsmiths
6. Skinners
7. Merchant Taylors
8. Haberdashers
9. Salters
10. Iron Workers
11. Vintners
12. Drapers[17]

Not only did these Guilds form the core of the City of London and make it an economic hub of the world from the sixteenth century on, but they provided a particular local effect that is resonant today. They attracted an immigration of young men and women from the rest of England—a badly needed increase with mortality high and birth rates low. There was a time late in the reign of Elizabeth I when a sixth of Englishmen lived in London. Life expectancy in the late 1500s was 20–25 years, or 30–35 if you were rich. The draw of the guilds helped create a city of the young with a youthful male population—mainly apprentices to trades.[18] For better or worse, these gangs of young men have reemerged over the centuries, replaying their themes, although the role of apprentice is now all but gone. In their heyday, the apprentices were known for the trouble they caused in taverns and their riotous, ungoverned football tournaments—precursors to the contemporary mayhem and violence between fans of London football teams such as Chelsea, Arsenal, Tottenham Hotspur, or West Ham and their loutish behavior in pubs of the West End and all over London. The London youths' persecution of foreigners on May 1st—Evil May Day—in 1517 set the pace for racist marches such as Moseley's rallies in the 1930s and the British National Party in the 1970s. The aggressive young London male, setting the tone for all of England, has persisted in film characters such as Michael Caine's Harry Palmer and Bob Hoskins's Harold Shand in *The Long Good Friday* and real villains such as the Kray twins in the East End and the Richardson brothers south of the river.[19]

In 1976—ten years after the Rolling Stones championed the original antisocial image of bad-boy musicians[20]—the British punk rock scene burst aggressively upon London in the behavior and language of Johnny Rotten. Given a name that could have come from *The Beggar's Opera* in the eighteenth century, it is as if he was press-ganged into the Sex Pistols, a motley crew put together by Malcolm McLaren in a punk fashion shop called Boy in the Kings Road, Chelsea. With the snarling Sid Vicious and self-confessed guitar thief Paul Cook, they were that decade's London bad boys. In fact, they were part of a much longer line of fictional criminal heroes such as Dickens's Artful Dodger and John Gay's MacHeath[21] and factual villains such as Jack the Ripper and reached back to rebels such as Jack Cade and Wat Tyler, who 600 years earlier had led groups of revolting young men in the Peasant's Revolt and the uprising against Henry VI.

Even the more politically motivated gatherings had their loutish side. Just over 200 years ago the Gordon Riots (1780) "offered an opportunity for semi-articulated discontented malice to have its few nights of destroying, looting, burning, beating. The poor could show what they thought of the rich ... The drunken British oaf could show what he thought of the foreigners ... The Gordon Riots were more in the order of a primal scream."[22] The anti-Vietnam protests in Grosvenor Square in 1968, the Brixton Riots, and the Poll Tax protests in Trafalgar Square that contributed to the downfall of Prime Minister Margaret Thatcher are more recent—perhaps more fruitful—examples of young, rioting London.

EAST

It is such links between the past and the present and between the individual and the collective culture of the city that provide one of London's abiding qualities. The layering of the past and present is contained not only in the architecture, the street names, and the use of buildings, but it is also in the pattern of populations, their immigrations and departures, their activities from place to place and group to group, and the ebb and flow of all these as interests wax and wane, money comes and goes, and people live and die.

Recently the City became a new strand in my London life. I had been filming a documentary about an artist, Ray Bowler, in Cornwall on the themes of money and the loss of the "feminine" in our lives.[23] This led to us filming Ray as he paid a visit to the European Bank of Reconstruction and Development in the heart of the City of London. Together with Dave Williams, an archeologist friend, we met on a cold April day at the George Inn opposite my office on Borough High Street.[24] This pub was for many centuries one of the major coaching inns between London and the port of Dover and is the only one now left with its large courtyard and galleries like an Elizabethan theatre.[25] From there we stepped out toward the City, filming our conversations on money and spirit as we bought pies in Borough Market, ate them leaning against the walls of Southwark Cathedral, then walked across London Bridge, stopping next at The Monument on the north side. Two hundred and two feet (62m) tall, Christopher Wren's monument to the Great Fire of London of 1666 is the tallest isolated stone column in the world and stands exactly 202 feet from where the Great Fire started in a baker's shop in Pudding Lane. Various conspiracy theories claim the fire was started deliberately so that the city could be reconstructed on mystical Masonic lines for the benefit of the financiers' control of the system. It is indeed remarkable how the City sprang into importance and success (after being such a ramshackle mediaeval mess) once it was redesigned after the Great Fire, its mixture of secular towers and church spires celebrating, then as now, the winking agreement between God and Mammon.

Walking up Bishopsgate, the only coffee house we happened to pass was Costa Coffee, but back in the seventeenth and eighteenth centuries the coffee houses in the alleys between Cornhill and Lombard streets were home to the beginnings of financial trading as we know it. The origin of the London Stock Exchange seems to have been in Jonathan's Coffee House in Change Alley in 1698, when the first recorded trading in marketable stocks took place. In 1720, the same coffee house was at the center of the first major stock market crash: that of the South Sea Company.

As soon as we turned into Broadgate Square, we recognized the striking visual element that had first drawn us to the European Bank of Reconstruction and Development. Reclining a full ten meters in front of the bank is a huge, dark bronze statue of Venus—voluptuous in her metallic, heavy naked beauty.[26] The bank had long been well known for decorating its premises with expensive art. Such ostentatious purchases seemed at odds with the bank's *raison d'être* to provide funding for the reconstruction and development of poor communities. The sublimely feminine image of Venus outside the bank's own doors suggests an

The Pie Man's stall in Borough Market.

Photograph by the author

unconscious connection between pure finance and the deeper human needs of all communities. It says something about London and the City too. It's not just about money. It is what the money is about. This is what London is about.

❦ THE LONDON STONE ❦

As in many cities, we are used to finding statues of the great and the good that help us keep track of those who made London over the last 700 years. As with the Broadgate Venus, many of these also celebrate the wealthy donors who made their erection possible. Behind all this, however, there are hidden sites that stem from more ancient times. These sites and monuments have, by contrast, been vital to the "ordinary people" and form part of the ongoing, sacred interweaving of population and place from ancient London to the present day. The sites are often linked to the ancient concept of identity between the health of the king and the health of the land and its people. This idea is widespread, appearing in the legends of Parsifal and the Fisher King in Europe and implied in the "sickness" of the city-state in Sophocles' *Oedipus Rex*. The mound on Ludgate Hill where

St. Paul's Cathedral is built, Tower Hill, and Whitfield's Mount (the only round barrow left on Blackheath) are all "places of free speech, and this usually means it was a place of ancient sanctity."[27]

On Hampstead Heath, the Bronze Age mound now called Parliament Hill may well have had a stone circle on its summit. It was once called Llandin, and a corruption of this is thought to be one source of the name London.[28] The present Houses of Parliament are in the Palace of Westminster,[29] right by Westminster Abbey on a site known as Tothill on Thorney Island,[30] where another stone circle is thought to have been located. The post-Roman Christianization of London and Britain has masked the ancient sacred sites that once linked the ruler to a divine order, but they remain embedded deep in the earth and in the psyche of London.

Some are still just about visible. Obscured behind a grating in the wall of the Overseas Chinese Banking Corporation opposite Cannon Street station is the London Stone, perhaps the most ancient and historically revered stone monument in London. This fragment is all that remains of a huge menhir, the rest of which probably lies buried under Cannon Street. In 1598, John Stow reported "standing in Walbrook, on the south side of this High Street ... a great stone called London Stone, fixed in the ground very deep, fastened with bars of iron." Reduced now to the size of a television, the original stone may have been over eight feet tall; it is over 3,000 years old and is oolite limestone from Dorset. Some say it is the geomantic center of the city of London and has long been associated with the preservation and well-being of the capital, while others have regarded it as merely a Roman *milliaria* for measuring distance. It has been suggested the London stone was once part of a stone circle on top of Ludgate Hill where St. Paul's now stands.[31]

The Lonenstane or Londenstane was a landmark that was referred to on maps from as early as 1198, and the association of the London Stone with conferring legitimacy and power reemerged with the first mayor of London (appointed 1189–1193), who resided near the stone and hence was known as Henry Fitz-Ailwin de Londonestone. The stone became the traditional place to swear oaths or make a position known to the authorities—a famous case being that of John Mortimer (a.k.a. Jack Cade), who rebelled against Henry VI, leading over 30,000 followers up from Kent. He stopped at the London Stone and struck it with his sword, as Shakespeare dramatically chronicles.[32]

Queen Elizabeth I's occult advisor, Dr. John Dee, who lived close by and believed in the powers of the London Stone, is known to have removed a sample for use in his alchemical experiments. By 1671, what remained of the London stone was commandeered for the more ignominious function of ritually smashing substandard spectacles upon its hard surface. In 1742, the London Stone was moved from the road and was embedded in the wall of St. Swithun's Church until that was bombed in 1941. The stone was undamaged at the time, but the previous thousands of years had already diminished it in scale if not in importance for the soul of London.

❧ KING LUD, DIANA, AND APOLLO ❧

Up until Elizabethan times, London was assumed to have been founded by Brutus the Trojan, grandson of Aeneas, who fled his homeland and eventually landed on the shores of Britain at Totnes, after dreaming the goddess Diana told him "to seek a land beyond Gaul in the country of the setting sun."[33]

Because King Lud, a descendant of Brutus, lived in the city around 73 BCE, it became known as Caer-Ludd (Lud's Town). He is buried at Ludgate, and the statues of Lud and his two sons that once stood on the mediaeval Ludgate were brought to the porch of St. Dunstan-in-the-West on Fleet Street when Ludgate was demolished in 1760. Holinshed's *Chronicles* relate how King Lud

> himself caused buildings to be made between London Stone and Ludgate, and builded for himself not far from the said gate a fair palace, which is the Bishop of London's palace beside (St.) Paul's at this day, as some think ... He also built a fairer temple near to this said palace, which temple (as some take it) was after turned into a church, and at this day called Paul's.[34]

On the summit of Ludgate Hill, where St. Paul's now stands, excavations revealed that the Romans had a temple to Apollo. But the legend goes that this was built upon the site of a far earlier temple to Diana erected by Brutus in 1240 BCE. The historian Camden, writing in 1600, notes as evidence for this how

> the neighbouring buildings are called in the church records *Camera Dianae,* and in the reign of Edward 1st were dug up in the churchyard ... an incredible number of ox heads ... the remains of heathen sacrifices: and it is well known to the learned that Taurobolia were celebrated in honour of Diana.[35]

Chesca Potter writes of the persistence of another ancient practice, suggesting the grip such rituals have had on the London psyche:

Diana was Artemis, the sister of Apollo. Although originally an ancient solar woodland Goddess, Artemis ceded her solar aspect to Apollo, becoming a lunar Goddess of the Hunt. This may perhaps account for the rededication of the site to St Paul, who was renowned for his vehement suppression of the cult of Artemis at Ephesus ... However the survival of a peculiar pagan ceremony called the "Blowing of the Stag" which continued to be enacted until recently suggests that earlier associations with Artemis had not been forgotten. The head of a stag was brought into the church by clergymen and laid on the altar, and at this point huntsmen from the forests surrounding London blew their horns at the four quarters. This was followed by great feasting and celebrations.[36]

Much more recently, on 29 July 1981, St. Paul's was the chosen religious site for the marriage of the British heir to the throne, Prince Charles, to his bride, Diana Spencer, Princess of Wales.[37] Just over sixteen years later, Diana was dead, hunted down in Paris by paparazzi on motorbikes, the tale goes. Her funeral was held in Westminster Abbey. St. Paul's Cathedral was also known as the East Minster, the eastern counterpart to Westminster Abbey, previously noted as an ancient sacred site. The fifteenth-century monk and historian John Flete, referring to the partial return to paganism in the fifth century, wrote, "Then were restored the whole abominations ... London worships Diana, and the suburbs of Thorney offer incense to Apollo."[38] And Paul Devereux suggests that "if Flete's inference is correct, we can look upon Westminster as marking a pre-Christian solar (Apollo) site, and St Paul's as commemorating a lunar (Diana) location."[39] It might seem a mere coincidence of name, but the connection between this and modern events is uncanny.

NORTH

¶ CROSSING THE RIVER:
THE LINES THROUGH LONDON ⊅

Just across the river from St. Paul's Cathedral, my present consulting room is on Borough High Street, about 400 meters from London Bridge, which for hundreds of years was the sole crossing over the Thames.[40] The River Thames appears to be the one line that clearly divides North and South London down the middle, but even that is not reliable. At Greenwich, for example, the river makes a dramatic loop south then quickly heads back north. This means that when you are looking straight across from Greenwich to the other bank, instead of looking north, as would be true elsewhere in London, at one point you are looking west and at another point east.

There is no convenient grid system to most of the streets of London, but an aerial view of the City as it was rebuilt after the Great Fire of 1666 shows how the planners rationalized many streets along straight lines. Christopher Wren and his associates turned first to the Jewish Kabbalah and its Tree of Life and the Old Testament Book of Numbers to determine distances and proportions in the City. Two thousand cubits (about two-thirds of a mile) formed a key length, being

> the distance from Jerusalem to the Mount of Olives and the furthest a Jew is allowed to travel on the Sabbath ... It was a distance London's ancient builders had already set for the western boundary of the city, Temple Bar, which is 2,000 cubits from the western end of St. Paul's, and for the eastern boundary of the city, St Dunstan's in the East, which is 2,000 cubits from the eastern end of the cathedral ... Wren's team positioned the apex of their Kabbalah-inspired London a further 2,000 cubits to the east, beyond the Tower of London, on the site of an ancient well ... which was believed to possess healing powers and which stood on the sacred territory east of the city the Romans had left vacant."[41]

Since the 1920s, researchers inspired by Alfred Watkins's[42] study of ley lines[43] have found straight lines of connection from many of the religious buildings to ancient sites of Central London and the City. One runs from the London Stone and links the mounds at the Tower of London, St. Paul's Cathedral on Ludgate Hill, and St. Martin's Ludgate. Another ley line runs through St. Dunstan's Stepney and the Temple Church,[44] ending at St. Clement Danes. Whatever one thinks about the significance of ley lines, it is curious how after fires, bombings, and demolition, new buildings and institutions in London arise on the sites of the old, despite the utilitarian changes enforced on the infrastructure. Something draws Londoners' interests, emotional attachments, and needs back to the same sites time and again. London builds upon its dead, not just refusing to forget them but actively honoring them in ever-new forms.[45]

{ THE FLOW OF PEOPLE }

There is another line that forms an invisible arc, a crescent curving northwest from Stepney and Bethnal Green in the East End, up through the streets of

North London, West to Finchley, and onward to the edge of the countryside in Edgware and High Barnet. This route marks the progression of successive waves of immigrants who entered London up the Thames, established businesses in the East End, went on to improved housing in North London, and consolidated their lives after one or two generations in expensive homes in the northern suburbs of Finchley and Hampstead Gardens.

In the sixteenth century, displaced Protestants from northern Europe, the Huguenots, arrived, followed by several waves of Jewish immigrants also fleeing persecution. More recently, Asians from Kenya, Uganda, and Bangladesh; Vietnamese; Somalis; Bosnians; Serbs; and many others have followed. It is immigrant enterprise that ran the food and garment markets of Brick Lane and Middlesex Street in the East End, foreigners, alternately welcomed and abused, who have brought their food and customs to perfume and color otherwise gray streets of London for the last 500 years.

A rare example of one of the Protestant churches built by the Huguenots on the corner of Brick Lane and Fournier Street was converted into a synagogue in the nineteenth century, and in the twentieth it became a mosque. As a place of worship it is probably unique in having continuously served three contrasting religions in one and the same building. It still has the original Huguenot sundial on the wall inscribed with the motto *umbra sumus*—"We are shadows." It conveys a sense of both standing out and being ignored—a motto for many an immigrant who arrived on London's streets.

In the 1950s, first in Notting Hill, West London, then in Brixton in the south, generations of workers who had immigrated from the islands of the West Indies brought new varieties of foods, cuisine, accents, and music to the drab Victorian terraces. Further west, Southall, adjacent to Heathrow airport, has become the stopping place for newer waves of Asian immigration.

London, especially in the North and East End boroughs, is a city that has been energized by sustaining tensions and contradictions—between the immigrant and the indigenous people, between the rich and the poor, and between the owners and the laboring classes. I have already mentioned London's protests and marches against taxation, war, policing, or racism, but—to top it all—London can also be regarded as the birthplace of revolutionary communism and hence the communist state. It is extraordinary to contemplate how in 1903, London, the center of world capitalism, was host to the Second Congress of the Russian Social Democratic Party. It was organized by Lenin, and as the meeting resulted in the separation of the Bolsheviks and the Mensheviks it could be said that Bolshevism was founded in the Tottenham Court Road.[46] The founder of communism, Karl Marx, lived with his wife and six children in a tiny property in Soho among the poorest of the poor and wrote *Das Kapital* sitting hour after hour in the reading room of the British Library in Bloomsbury. One daughter, Eleanor, bought a house in Jews Walk, Sydenham SE23—a mile or so from where I now write—which in 2008 was honored with a blue plaque commemorating her residence. Karl Marx's *Communist Manifesto* may have urged workers to revolt with a cry of "all you have to lose is your chains," but nowadays the center of London has very few homes for such workers and no space for factories. Most of the workforce cannot afford to live within twenty miles of the center, and after commuting in on their crowded trains, they service the retail, financial, and tourism "industries" that now generate London's wealth.

A wet day in Soho.

Photograph by the author

271

WEST

{ CITY SYNCHRONICITIES IN THE WEST END }

Karl Marx is buried in the cemetery in Highgate, one of the highest points in North London. Many years before, around 1350, it was on Highgate Hill that Richard Whittington heard the bells of Bow Church telling him to turn and walk back down into the City to fulfill his destiny as the Lord Mayor of London, a role he occupied three times. Had he walked a little further to the west, he would have arrived in what is now Trafalgar Square and still wouldn't have left the countryside; the church on the east side of Trafalgar Square was named St. Martin-in-the-Fields for that reason. This was the edge of town as far as the City of London went in the 1300s, but as the city expanded, the area developed to form what we now know as the West End of London. In the northern hemisphere, prevailing winds blow from the West, moving stale, smoky, polluted air to the eastern side of cities. Consequently, as industry grew, the West End became a more desirable place to live. Nowadays, Trafalgar Square, or more strictly the Charing Cross monument in the station forecourt a hundred yards away, is regarded as the center of London.

London's West End is synonymous with entertainment, theatres, music, and media companies. I received my first Actors' Equity contract[47] and was cast in my first play in the Arts Theatre, Great Newport Street, on the same stage where Samuel Beckett's *Waiting for Godot* had its English premiere in 1955.[48] A few years later, in 1979, I worked nearby playing bass in *Elvis The Musical* at the Astoria Theatre at the top of Charing Cross Road.

Two years before I joined the show, in August 1977, the month that Elvis Presley died, I was laid up at home, recovering from a two-week hospital stay after a motorcycle accident.[49] I had been driving back from Fulham and had banged my head after slipping on a wet road near Lambeth Bridge. I was wearing a helmet and felt OK so I rode on. I recall getting as far as the top of Trafalgar Square heading north, with the National Portrait Gallery on my left and the statue of a famous woman on my right. This was the last I remembered before heading up Charing Cross Road. Next thing I knew I was waking up on the road over a mile further north with blood pouring from my face and a policeman asking me my name before I lost consciousness again. It seems that ten minutes after Trafalgar Square, I lost consciousness (maybe through delayed concussion) on the Hampstead Road above Euston and hit the back of a van that was stopped at the lights.

National
Portrait
Gallery.

*Photograph
by the author*

I had always thought the statue by the National Portrait Gallery (the last thing I remembered before the crash) was that of Marie Curie, the heroic scientist who developed radiotherapy treatment for cancer. The statue is, in fact, a monument to Edith Cavell, a World War I heroine. There is no Marie Curie statue or monument there, but my mother had died of cancer almost one year to the day before I had my crash. For the next three years my memory went uncorrected—and its source uninterpreted—until someone made the correction and the connection for me. All monuments, like the one to Nelson on his column in Trafalgar Square and the one to Edith Cavell (and somewhere, I expect, one to Marie Curie) act as remembrance; it seems to me now that my motorbike crash was my own monument to my mother, my remembrance for her death.

Working in the West End as a theatre musician, playing the same show night after night, soon lost its glamour. Rising late in the day, we would have brunch when others had tea, roll into the theatre, go to work, and really wake up once the show was over. Our nights often consisted of drinking and listening to music in the late-night clubs and restaurants that stayed open for us and reserved places for theatre workers and their friends. Our favorite haunt was in St. Giles High Street, one of an odd tangle of streets tucked away behind Charing Cross Road, which forms one side of a triangle bounded by Shaftesbury Avenue and New Oxford Street on the other two sides. So it did not surprise me to find out that St. Giles Parish had been one of the most notorious dives in London for hundreds of years. Known for drinking and vagrancy, this is the neighborhood depicted in William Hogarth's horrific scenes of the poor in *Gin Lane*. Nell Gwynne lived here at age fourteen before she became a famous courtesan, and in 1664, St. Giles was where the plague started. Not surprising really, when you consider St. Giles was the intercessionary saint for beggars and cripples and, as the patron saint of lepers, gave his name to this site for a chapel and hospital for lepers "among the fields and marshes, their contagion kept apart from the city." [50]

The area focused on St. Giles-in-the-Fields was a gateway to the City, hovering between town and country with taverns and hostels for the travelers. When proclamations in 1585 ejected all foreigners from the City, they settled in this parish on the boundary, where they were soon joined by other vagrants and the generally impoverished. "It functioned, then, as both an entrance and an exit; it greeted arrivals and harboured those who had been expelled from the city." [51] At St. Giles Circus, above where the Northern and Central lines of the London Underground cross, there was a gallows at the crossroads of Tottenham Court Road and New Oxford Street, and when that was moved and the condemned were taken to "Tyburn Tree" (what is now Marble Arch at the far end of

Oxford Street), the prisoners still stopped for a final ale at the Resurrection Gate of St. Giles-in-the-Fields. The parish was "celebrated or condemned, according to taste, for the number of taverns and the incidences of drunkenness."[52] Where the Dominion Theatre now stands, the Horseshoe Brewery exploded a vat in 1818, releasing 10,000 gallons of beer, flooding the streets and cellars and drowning eight people.

My bass-playing years are over, but I have continued to meet friends for drinks in the area. We tend toward Norman's (a.k.a. the Coach and Horses but always referred to by the name of its famous landlord) on Greek Street or the French House in Soho, where they will only serve half-pints and charge pre-decimal currency prices (like the Kings Head in Islington did). But I am just as happy in the Cambridge or the Marquis of Granby or the Porcupine back in Great Newport Street, where I began.

Further West through London are South Kensington and Gloucester Road, where I first landed in London in 1972 before heading north to my first bedsit in Crouch End. I remember these localities for the evenings singing in a restaurant before walking five miles home when I was twenty or the Natural History Museum and the Science Museum when I was forty, where my young sons would scamper about looking at dinosaurs and occasionally sharing activities with the children of a famous TV personality, another tired dad on a Sunday morning, minding his brood from a corner.

London and Britain have always looked west to the Americas. The daughter of Henry VIII, the "virgin queen" Elizabeth I, founded the state of Virginia with her money and her name, and as a ten-year-old boy I vividly remember meeting my first American on a boat on the Thames heading upstream to Hampton Court Palace on a school trip. She was from Maine. Beyond Hampton Court and Richmond Royal Park is Heathrow Airport—its runways looking like a pentangle from the air and built beside a Neolithic track or *cursus* as if the site has always been marked as a western portal for the metropolis. Before air flight was common, in 1912, my Czech grandfather Theodor Hauke arrived in London by rail from Vienna on the same Trans-European Express where he worked as a wine waiter. After several visits to the city he had decided to stay. I often wonder how life would have been if he had carried on west, if he had touched down not in London but had decided to sail on and had arrived at Ellis Island, New York. Had that happened, I would have been living in—and writing about—another city entirely. But I was born in this palimpsest of a city: the living, reborn, changing soul of the city that is London.

Notes

1   Although the Cockney and his accent has been more celebrated and appreciated since the fame of its actor-speakers such as Michael Caine and Bob Hoskins (or even Dick Van Dyke's effort in the film *Mary Poppins*), it had previously been lampooned for hundreds of years. Peter Ackroyd writes that "'cockney' is generally supposed to derive from the medieval term 'cokenay' or cock's egg; in other words an unnatural object or freak of nature." Peter Ackroyd, *London: The Biography* (London: Vintage, 2001), p. 163. This insult arose due to the city/countryside clash in years when the majority of the British population were tough, knowledgeable agricultural people for whom the townsman was an inferior fool who knew nothing of countryside ways. Since the success of London, of course, this situation has reversed and the country folk are regarded as the unsophisticated ones.

2   Rhyming slang was an innovation by dock workers to prevent managers and owners from understanding their communications about nefarious activities even if they were overheard.

3   Ackroyd, *London: The Biography*, p. 217.

4   *Ibid.*, p. 218.

5   A word about capitalization: "the City" when capitalized refers to the City of London, the one-square-mile borough that was the original city. "The Borough" refers to one of London's boroughs, located just across the river from the City, starting at the southern end of London Bridge.

6   A good place to start finding out about this is Merlin Coverley, *Psychogeography* (Harpenden: Pocket Essentials, 2006).

7   James Hillman commentary in the film *Carl Jung: Wisdom of the Dream*, dir. Stephen Segaller, 1989.

8   The London postcodes have become strongly associated with the quality of the areas they refer to and are significant in assessing crime and insurance statistics. Despite carrying such imaginative meanings for the population, they arose prosaically out of a mainly alphabetical listing of the boroughs in each compass direction. In South East London, for example, the postcode for The Borough is SE1, for Brockley SE4, for Camberwell SE5, for Catford SE6, and so on.

9   This housed the New College of Speech and Drama. Exiled from Central London after the World War II, this was once the drama department of the Royal Academy of Music in Marylebone, where my father studied music, and is now part of Middlesex University.

10 Apart from a weird year spent in Brighton, Sussex, and Mystic, Connecticut, in 1981 and 1982. I have bought and sold four homes in London and now live in the fifth. I have spent ten years of higher education and professional training in London. As a youngster I worked in its hospitals, publishing houses, pubs, and shops. I have held my practice as a Jungian analyst in consulting rooms in Greenwich, SE10, and in the Borough, London Bridge, SE1.

11 It receives the second most tourist visits after the Tower of London.

12 Ackroyd, *London: The Biography*, p. 106.

13 Until the high labor costs maintained by dockers' unions forced it to shift to the container ports of Holland, thus returning first place to Britain's longtime rivals in imperialism and trade, the Dutch.

14 Not only did I have my office a mere 500 meters from the zero degree meridian, but for the first year of my training analysis, my analyst lived in Greenwich and I would have to step back and forth across the meridian line five days a week.

15 At least it was, until last year, when a heater left on by one of those restoring the ship caused it to catch fire and it burned down to little more than a shell, now sadly screened by "sail-shaped" white plastic—to indicate its "shipness," I suppose.

16   And famous for its artistic alumni such as Damian Hirst and Bridget Riley, musicians in the groups Blur and Dire Straits, respectively, and social scientist Richard Hoggart.

17   There used to be much vying between the Skinners and Merchant Taylors guilds for their place in the list, hence giving rise to the phrase "to be at sixes and sevens," which refers to confusion or indecision over an issue.

18   There is an excellent description of the conditions of the apprentice in Elizabethan times in *The Lodger: Shakespeare on Silver Street* by Charles Nicholl (Penguin: London, 2008).

19   *The Long Good Friday*, dir. John Mackenzie, 1980.

20   Mick Jagger and Keith Richard both came from Dartford, just outside London. They met again on a train when attending London colleges. All their early gigs were in West and Central London.

21   The notorious lovable thief of Gay's *The Beggar's Opera*, written in 1728—and the inspiration for the song "Mack the Knife" and Bertolt Brecht's *The Threepenny Opera*.

22   A. N. Wilson, *London: A Short History* (London: Phoenix, 2005), p. 59. Such riots were typically a class protest and one against unjust or severe punishment, as shown by the attack on house of the unpopular Lord Mansfield, the Lord Chief Justice who presided over sessions in which 29 were sentenced to branding, 448 were transported, and 102 were hanged. *Ibid.*

23   The documentary is called *Green Ray* (a title less about the color of dollars and more a pun on the title of Eric Rohmer's *Le rayon vert*) and was publicly screened at festivals and the conference of the International Association of Jungian Studies in Greenwich, London, in July 2006.

24   David Williams has written interesting papers on the link between the development of consciousness in our forebears and their ancient monuments, such as Stonehenge. See D. Williams "Stonehenge and Arthurian Myth," *Harvest Journal for Jungian Studies* 48, no. 2 (2002): 81–105.

25   The rebuilt and relocated simulacra of Shakespeare's Globe Theatre is a stone's throw away on the bank of the Thames in the Borough.

26   The statue is by Fernando Botero.

27   Chesca Potter in John Matthews and Chesca Potter, eds., *The Aquarian Guide to Legendary London* (Wellingborough: Aquarian Press, 1990), p. 227.

28   *Ibid.*, p. 108.

29   With its famous clock tower called Big Ben after the huge bell that famously chimes London's time on the BBC radio.

30   *Tot* means "sacred mound" and "was recorded in a late Saxon charter as existing on Thorney Island, a gravel spur separated from the Thames shoreline by two streams of the River Tyburn. … The earliest crossing of the Thames was probably located there." Matthews and Potter, *The Aquarian Guide to Legendary London*, p. 108. Tothill Street SW1 runs down to Westminster Abbey today.

31   Reported on the BBC site under "The London Stone"; www.bbc.co.uk/dna/h2g2/A791101.

32   Cade's lines as found in William Shakespeare's *The Second Part of Henry VI*, ed. Michael Hattaway (Cambridge: Cambridge University Press, 1991) act 4, scene 6.

33   Matthews and Potter, *The Aquarian Guide to Legendary London*, p. 87.

34   Holinshed in *ibid.*, p. 93.

35   *Ibid.*, p. 109. The *taurobolium* was an ancient sacrifice in which the priest who was lying in a pit under the sacrificial table pierced with holes was drenched with the blood of a slain bull to symbolize the restoration of Mother Earth. It is thought the pagan nobility held on to the ritual in their attempts to resist the growing Christianization of the Roman Empire.

36   *Ibid.*, pp. 200–201.

37   For a reminder of the otherworldly pomp and splendor of this event and a sense of its resacralizing of the monarchy, check out BBC footage of the event on the "On This Day" page of the network's website: http://news.bbc.co.uk/player/nol/newsid_6530000/newsid_6530300/6530393.stm?bw=bb&mp=wm&news=1&ms3=6&ms_javascript=true&bbcws=2.

38   Quoted from Charles Knight in *Old England* (London: Sangster, 1860) in Matthews and Potter, *The Aquarian Guide to Legendary London*, p. 109.

39   *Ibid.*, p. 109 (published seven years before Diana's funeral).

40   The Roman version in wood was finished around 80 CE, replaced by a ferry when the Romans departed. A more lasting wooden bridge was built in the ninth century but was torn down by the Danes in 1014. The first stone bridge was begun in Henry II's reign in 1176, paid for by a tax on wool and finished thirty-three years later. This was twenty feet wide and nine hundred feet long and had twenty arches; it lasted 600 years. In 1212, a fire broke out at both ends in the houses that were built on the bridge that trapped and killed some 3,000 people. By the fifteenth century, buildings lined the whole length and reached across, touching at places, thus making the bridge a tunnel as well. London Bridge escaped the Great Fire of 1666 due to a break in its buildings at the northern end; the break itself was caused by an earlier fire in 1633. In 1722 the congestion was so bad that a legally enforced "drive on the left" was instituted for the first time ever on the bridge. In 1763 all the houses were removed, and in 1831 the first new bridge in 600 years was opened 180 feet to the west of the old one. By the 1960s this bridge was no longer able to cope with traffic, and it was sold in 1970 to Robert McCulloch of Arizona for $2,460,000—the largest antique ever sold, according to the *Guinness Book of Records*. The present London Bridge (which leads across to my office) was opened by Elizabeth II in 1973 and is the only hollow bridge over the Thames with pavements that are heated during cold spells to prevent icing. The existence of this river crossing made Borough on the southern bank and the City on the northern bank the first settlement and the center of what developed as London.

41   Ed Glinert, *East End Chronicles: Three Hundred Years of Mystery and Mayhem* (London: Penguin, 2006), pp. 11–12.

42   Alfred Watkins, *The Old Straight Track* (1925; repr., London: Garnestone Press, 1970).

43   Paul Devereux and Ian Thomson, *The Ley Hunter's Companion* (Thames and Hudson: London, 1979).

44   The Temple was founded by the Knights Templar and was dedicated in 1185 by the patriarch of the Church of the Holy Sepulcher in Jerusalem, upon which the London Temple church was modeled with its round nave and other dimensional correspondences.

45   London could be said to have an equivalent to the grid system of city planning (albeit of a virtual kind) in the map of the London Underground designed by Harry Beck. With its stations named after London localities and streets, the inexperienced visitor may be forgiven for thinking this plan of the underground railway corresponds to arrangements above ground. However, in this case the map is certainly not the territory. What it *is* is a triumph of graphic design that helpfully relates train lines to stopping points, but it is misleading when it comes to London's geographical layout and distances. The underground railway system itself also imposes a logic on the layout of London that has little to do with the geographic relation between the boroughs and can only serve half of London due to the weak gravel subsoil that prevents the expansion of the Underground.

46   Ackroyd, *London: The Biography*, p. 142.

47   This was the 1970s and, like the dockers' union, Equity Actors union was a closed shop and membership depended on that elusive first contract!

48   My play was the less enduring work *The Lion and Unicorn Rumpus*. It went on to tour London playgrounds all summer.

49   University College Hospital, in Gower Street, a center of excellence to whose staff I owe a great deal.

50   Ackroyd, *London: The Biography*, p. 131.

51   *Ibid.*, p. 132.

52   *Ibid.*

14 Jerusalem: Human Ground, Archetypal Spirit

EREL SHALIT

Unlike Rome, not all roads lead to Jerusalem, and those that do may all too easily lead the visitor astray in a labyrinth of divinity and madness. In the course of history, when Rome became the center of power, sanctity, and glory, Jerusalem sank into spiritual ruin and peripheral oblivion.[1] Thus, even those modern roads that bring you smoothly to the city may force the pilgrim to pass "through thorny hedges ... "[2] of his or her mind.

One may conveniently approach Jerusalem from the west, ascending the modern highway, which climbs eastward through the Judean Hills—like a Western mind moving toward the Orient.[3] By approaching Jerusalem driving on the comfortable asphalt that smoothly covers the ground and softens the bumps, one may arrive only to find a noisy and neglected city, tired by too much spirit and worn out by too much poverty. Slowly winding upward through the hills, parallel to the highway, runs the dusty old donkey path, burdened by archetypal history. Arriving this way, one may find the sparks of illumination that shine from within the dry stones, as well as the strife and conflict that cut through the rocks of Jerusalem.

Alternatively, one may proceed toward Jerusalem on the Route of the Patriarchs, from the desert in the east. This is the path on which the ancient Hebrews arrived, as they crossed the river into the land of Canaan, thus gaining their name and reputation as *Hebrews*, which means "those that came from across the river."

One may capture Jerusalem by drawing the sword against evil spells, as did King David from the Jebusites three millennia ago, or enter the city humbly on a donkey, like Jesus did and any future Messiah is supposed to do as well, or like the Caliph Omar majestically riding on a white camel. In whatever way one arrives, the visitor must be ready to overcome the obstacles of Earthly Jerusalem, which far from always mirrors her heavenly sister's image of completeness and redemption.

"Crouched among its hills,"[4] Jerusalem is immersed with mythological, religious, and symbolic significance. Yet, scarce in natural resources, the surrounding land is cultivated rather than fertile by nature, and the so-called Jerusalem stone, the pale limestone that characterizes many of the city houses, nearly cracks and shatters by carrying the burden of Heavenly Jerusalem. In its often shabby garb, terrestrial Jerusalem seems to want to shake off its celestial glory, releasing itself from the task of being "the gateway to heaven."[5] At other times, when the light from above is reflected in her harsh stones, Jerusalem seems to embrace the presence of the Shekhinah, the earthly dwelling of the divine.[6] Especially at dawn and at dusk, the reflection of the light may bring that which is below and that which is above, earth and heaven, reality and imagination, into play with each other—marble-like clouds weighing heavily above, and stones that radiate light.

Jerusalem wavers between the spirit that takes her to be God's joyous garden, the fountain of the awakening love and beauty of the Shulamite, the bride of Wise King Solomon, builder of the Temple,[7] and her godforsaken body, poor and neglected, a shameful and condemned whore, as she is described in Ezekiel.[8]

Significant Dates in the History of Jerusalem

Jerusalem dates back to the fourth millennium BCE. It became a permanently settled Canaanite city in the nineteenth century BCE, mentioned in the Egyptian Execration Texts as *Rushlamem*.[9] The Bible first mentions Jerusalem in Genesis 14:18-20, when Melchizedek, "king of Shalem," greeted and blessed Abram upon his arrival. According to the biblical narrative, it was a small, fortified Jebusite city for about two centuries until captured and made capital by King David in the tenth century BCE, after he had ruled for seven years in Hebron. He brought the Ark of the Covenant, holding the stone tablets with the engraved Ten Commandments, to Jerusalem. The Ark was later placed in the Holy of Holies in the Temple built by his son, King Solomon. The Babylonian King Nebuchadnezzar, who with his one hand built the Hanging Gardens of Babylon, destroyed Jerusalem with his other, and deported much of the population in 586 BCE. However, a few decades later, King Cyrus the Great allowed the

Jews to return and to rebuild the Temple. The Second Temple was completed in 516 BCE, and later enlarged by Herod in the first century BCE.

The Hellenistic period began with Alexander the Great's conquest of Jerusalem in 332 BCE. Following the Maccabean revolt, the Jews recaptured Jerusalem and restored the Temple in 164 BCE. However, a century later, General Pompey captured the city. The Romans would reign until the beginning of the Byzantine period, 324 CE.

Jesus, born ca. 6/5 BCE, towards the end of the great and cruel King Herod's reign, was crucified at the hill of Golgotha, then outside the ancient walls, probably in 30 CE. The Church of the Holy Sepulchre, inside the present walls surrounding the old city, was built by Emperor Constantine early in the fourth century, likely at the site of crucifixion.

The Second Temple was destroyed, presumably on the same day as the destruction of the first Temple, on the ninth of the Hebrew month Av, late summer 70 CE, which for the observant Jew is a day of fasting and mourning the destruction of Jerusalem. Yet Talmudic legend raises the idea of transformation, suggesting that the day of destruction signifies the birth of the Messiah. After defeating the revolt of Bar Kokhba in 135 CE, the Roman Emperor Hadrian renamed the destroyed city Aelia Capitolina. He prohibited the Jews from entering, and on the ruins of the former temple he built one to the worship of Jupiter.

The Byzantine period lasted from the beginning of the fourth to the middle of the seventh century, followed by the Muslim period. The al-Aqsa—i.e., "the furthest"—Mosque was built at the Temple Mount during the Umayyad period, early eighth century.

The Crusaders ruled from 1099, barring non-Christians from the city, which then was captured by Saladin in 1187. Following the Mameluk period, Jerusalem and the Holy Land were conquered by the Ottoman Empire in the early sixteenth century. Sultan Suleiman I, alternatively called the Magnificent and the Lawgiver, rebuilt the city walls, which had been razed three centuries earlier.

Jerusalem remained desolate for centuries. The Zurich-born Dominican Friar Felix Fabri, who visited the Holy Land late in the fifteenth century, wrote of Jerusalem's destroyed buildings, abandoned by its inhabitants. At the same time, Obadiah of Bertinoro, the intellectual leader of the Jewish community in Jerusalem, described the city as poor and largely desolate. While at the end of the Second Temple period the population of Jerusalem reached 100,000, it had been reduced to less than nine thousand in 1800. Only in the mid-1800s did the city wake up from its slumber, beginning to recover and grow again.

Jerusalem between Fact and Fiction,
Imagination and Forgery

In the second half of the nineteenth century, the first houses and neighborhoods were built outside the old city walls, and Jerusalem could start its metropolitan growth—today reaching a population of three quarters of a million of all denominations. One of the first houses built outside the old city walls has become known as The Ticho House, named after the artist Anna Ticho (1894-1980) and her ophthalmologist husband, who moved into the house in the early twentieth century. Squeezed between the old and bustling Jaffa Road, with its mixture of shops, restaurants, and marketplace, hooting buses and crisscrossing pedestrians, and the ultra-Orthodox Meah Shearim ("hundred gates"[10]) quarter creeping up from behind, the graceful house, with its garden of olive trees and pines, seems to hide away. It seems as if the house does not want to fully reveal itself, comfortable in its seclusion, trying to remain untouched by the surrounding noise and distractions of everyday, set apart in its deep and not so holy secrets ...[11]

... such as the antiquity dealer Moses Wilhelm Shapira (1830-1884), who lived in the house a century and a half ago, at a time when the renewed interest in the Holy Land began to breathe life into its archaeological artifacts. The discovery of the Moabite Stone (Mesha Stele), followed by clay figurines, vessels, and coins that somehow turned up in Shapira's well-respected antiquities shop, gave rise to the new scientific field of *Moabitica*. He attempted to sell "the earliest text of Deuteronomy ever found" to the British Museum at the price of a million pounds. Shapira "ended his life with a bullet to the head"[12] in Rotterdam, shortly after the text was disclosed as forgery, probably fabricated by his associate Salim al-Kari.

Yet, the Shapira parchment fragments bear some resemblance to the Dead Sea Scrolls; it seems as if, seventy years before their discovery, the dubious forger had in his mind conjured up the caves at Qumran ...

Religious imagination and archaeological evidence, history, tale, and legend, mix and merge like Uqbar and Qumran[13] in the enigmas of Jerusalem.

In 1948, Jerusalem was divided between Israel, which made West Jerusalem its capital, and Jordan, which annexed East Jerusalem. It was reunited in 1967, when Israel gained disputed control over Eastern Jerusalem as well as the Old City with the Temple Mount and the Dome of the Rock. A future of ongoing friction remains boiling under the ruins and glory of Jerusalem's very center, which happens also to be the very cradle of Western religious story, myth, and symbolism. The yearning for monotheistic hegemony—be it Jewish, Christian, or Muslim—casts a shadow of conflict that continuously disrupts the city and the world. The world's yearning for peace seems here to be constantly threatened, sacrificed like biblical Isaac, had he not been saved by the angel and the ram on top of Mount Moria, the Temple Mount, the innermost heart of the city.

Children playing.

Photograph by Yoram Bouzaglo

Jerusalem of Many Names

According to legend, Jerusalem has seventy names or more. In the Bible she is called City of Joy, Praise, Justice, and Righteousness; she is called Beautiful, Comely, and Beloved.[14] As the object of divine desire and dwelling, she is given names such as *Hephzibah*, i.e., "I Delight in Her," and *Ohalibah*, "My Tent Is in Her."[15] Jerusalem is the "Light of the World"—but infamous and filled with confusion, she is also called "Burdensome Stone," "Oppressing City," "A

Cup of Poison," and "City of Bloodshed."[16] Jerusalem is the Holy City (Heb. *I'r haKodesh*), which today is the name most commonly used in Arabic (*Al-Quds*).[17]

Poets have wandered the streets of Jerusalem, sung her praise and given her names. They have felt both the beating of her heart and the bleeding of her soul and her inhabitants—Jew, Christian, and Muslim. Drunk on her spirit, the poet's soul has been filled both with blissful light and the dark pain of Jerusalem: "Jerusalem stone is the only stone that can feel pain. It has a network of nerves."[18] Thus, the poets have called her names such as *early evening purple* (*argaman ha'arbayim*) and *awesome beauty, a wall of dreams* and *well of salvation, the sealed book* and *a bird of stone, holy fire, city and mother* (metropolis), *den of jackals* and *cup of ruins*.

The meaning of the name Jerusalem has been variously interpreted. Most commonly it has been understood as *I'r Shalem*, the city of Shalem, city of peace and wholeness, or as a combination of the Hebrew words *Jerusha* and *Shalem*, meaning legacy or heritage of peace. Often it is considered as a combination of the name that Abraham gave the place after the near-sacrifice (or binding, *akedah*) of Isaac, (*Adonai*)-*Yireh*, "the Lord sees,"[19] with *Shalem*, which can also be understood as "complete awe of God." The Septuagint and the Vulgate transliterate the name as Hierusalem, thus combining *Hieros*, the holy, with *Shalem*.

The plenitude of names, such as Gateway to Heaven,[20] reflects the extent to which Jerusalem is pregnant with archetypal imagery and projections of wholeness and proximity to divinity, often in tense contrast to the torment and conflicts it has suffered through history. Thus, some visitors to the city turn away in dismay at her neglected garb, while others become possessed by archetypal numinosity, sucked in by the myth- and religion-soaked ground they tread.

Shalem and Shahar

Originally Jerusalem was the City of Shalem (*I'r Shalem*), after its mythological founder Shalem, the Canaanite god of creation, completeness, and the setting sun.

However, while peace and wholeness have become the insignia of Heavenly Jerusalem, the darker side of Jerusalem is already there in its archetypal origin; in Canaanite mythology, the twin brother of Shalem was Shahar, the Morning Star. Shahar (as in *Shaharit*, the Jewish morning prayers), or in his Christian denomination, Lucifer, announces the arrival of light and consciousness. He brings the light that emerges from the shades of the dark, the light of consciousness that attempts to overthrow the rule of the gods, but due to hubris falls from heaven.[21]

Shahar and Shalem were the sons of the *hieros gamos*, the holy marriage between the sun-god El and Ashera, goddess of the grove and the sacred tree. In the Bible, she is treated with fear and disrespect; she must not be worshipped, but is to be cut down or burned, to be buried in the repressed shadow of the One God.[22] They were born out of the goddess's bottomless cavity, and, it says, "in the kiss ... and the embrace ... she bore Shahar and Shalem, the Dawn and the Evening."[23] While every evening Shalem announces the completion of the day and the death of the sun, Shahar pronounces the sun's rebirth in the morning.

Stones and Light

Jerusalem is a city of stones and of light, which sometimes reflect each other in majestic divinity. The *idea* of light is mirrored in stony *matter*, and the rough stones are illuminated by the light of red and gold. Sometimes it seems the light of divinity is trapped in the stony vessels; when the all too bright light struggles to release itself from its earthly imprisonment, the ground seems to tremble, casting dark shadows of blind violence and visionary hatred.

Jerusalem is stones, and it is the tombstones of the dead that surround the living city. There are cemeteries on Mount Herzl and on the Mount of Olives, at Sanhedria and Givat Shaul, as well as Muslim, Christian, and the Templar cemeteries. The shadow of the dead and the past crawls down the hills toward the living city, which spreads out from and around its heart at the Temple Mount.

And Jerusalem is light. Sometimes too much light. Yehuda Amichai laments, "All these stones, all this sadness, all this light."[24] Perhaps the weary sadness and tears of the stones ensure that most visitors to Jerusalem aren't carried away, floating in the air like dreamers in a Chagall painting, by the numinosity that like scattered glass twinkles between the ruins and the gates of the Old City.

Yet, often at nighttime, some do hear the voices of the saints and the prophets. The labyrinth of narrow streets—walked by Jesus and the money changers, by the prophets and the thieves, where the commercial *souk* districts and the places of worship compete like the religious objects and other paraphernalia on the vendor's shelf—seems to be a fertile womb both for divine blessing and elevated madness. As told in an ancient legend, "it was unnecessary for the brides of Jerusalem to perfume themselves, for the fragrance of the incense burnt in the Holy Temple would spread out, infusing the air with the odor of frankincense and perfuming the women as well."[25]

Often near the Western or "Wailing" Wall, in the nocturnal light of the moon, reflected in the stones of the wall, where centuries of tears squeeze together in the cracks, you might find a Moses or King David, a Messiah or the devil, John the Baptist, Jesus, or Virgin Mary in a lunar spectacle of reincarnated biblical figures. Just as ordinary people and many visitors speak to the Divine by means of handwritten notes inserted in the cracks in the Wall, to some the cracks become the mouth through which the voice of God speaks in unmediated communication with their souls. In the so-called Jerusalem Syndrome,[26] time has been set aside and the personal merges with the archetypal. This is when, as Jung writes, "something interior can seem to be exterior, and ... something exterior can appear to be interior," as he had become aware of from his Ravenna experience.[27]

Swedish author and Nobel laureate Selma Lagerlöf visited the city in 1900. In her novel *Jerusalem*, she writes that not everyone can live there, for

Jerusalem of
Stones — The
Western Wall.

*Photograph
by Yoram
Bouzaglo*

The Holy city depresses and weighs upon them, or else they go out of their minds—ay, it can even kill them outright ... one fancies one hears the noise of battle, one sees great armies advancing to attack the walls of the city, one sees Kings approaching in their war-chariots.[28]

The author Nikolai Gogol, having burned the two first versions of *Dead Souls*, believed a pilgrimage to Jerusalem would redeem his soul and relieve him from depression and writer's block. He was shocked by the noise and confusion in the Basilica of the Holy Sepulchre, discouraged by the scenery and the environs. "Not only were my prayers unable to rise up to heaven, I could not even tear them loose from my breast," he wrote in despair to Tolstoy.[29]

When Herman Melville visited Jerusalem a decade later in 1857, his harsh impression was of "stones to right and stones to left ... stony tombs; stony hills & stony hearts." He noticed dryly that there was "Too little to see and too much dust."[30]

287

The scenery had not changed much when Mark Twain visited the city another decade later. While he found it difficult to comprehend, he was actually "in the illustrious old city where Solomon dwelt, where Abraham held converse with the Deity, and where walls still stand that witnessed the spectacle of the Crucifixion"; what he found was an abundance of "Rags, wretchedness, poverty and dirt ... lepers, cripples, the blind and the idiotic." Mark Twain could not but observe "the numbers of maimed, malformed and diseased humanity that throng the holy places and obstruct the gates," concluding that Jerusalem is mournful and dreary, a place where he "would not desire to live." [31]

While Jerusalem has grown fifty times since a town of barely fourteen thousand at the time of Mark Twain's visit in 1867, poverty and neglect are seemingly a necessary concomitant to the religious fervor and spiritual quest that permeate the city, its dwellers and visitors.

Archetypal Image of Center and Wholeness

In Judeo-Christian tradition, Jerusalem is a central image of peace and wholeness, a symbol of unity, justice, and future redemption. [32] For Jews, the yearning for Jerusalem is expressed in the Psalms (137:1-6), "By the rivers of Babylon, there we sat down, we also wept, when we remembered Zion (Jerusalem)." The ancient Jewish prayer, "Next year in Jerusalem," entails a spiritual request for redemption no less than a physical quest for return.

In Revelation 21, John describes Heavenly Jerusalem: "I saw the holy city, new Jerusalem, coming down out of heaven from God, prepared as a bride adorned for her husband ... 'Behold, the dwelling place of God is with man.'" Jerusalem is then described as "having the glory of God, its radiance like a most rare jewel, like a jasper, clear as crystal ... the city was pure gold, clear as glass." Thus, Jerusalem is a prominent symbol of the Self as God-image, as an image of the seat of divinity in the soul of man.

In reference to Jerusalem as "the centre of the earth" Jung considers it to be a symbol of the Self. [33] However, as the heavenly bride and as "the goal of our longing for redemption," he emphasizes Jerusalem as an archetypal image of the mother. [34]

Likewise, God's feminine aspect, the *Shekhinah*, which means "dwelling," implies God's manifestation in the world. The Temple in Jerusalem represents the dwelling of the divine presence, and with its destruction, the legend tells us, the Shekhinah was forced into exile. This would indicate not only a split between the masculine and the feminine aspects of the God-image, but also that the sense of wholeness and completion is absent from the material dimension of the world. In the individual psyche, this reflects a condition of a split between ego and Self, an incapacitating separation from one's soul and inner sources, as expressed in Psalms (137:4-5): "How shall we sing the Lord's song in a foreign land? If I forget thee, O Jerusalem, let my right hand forget her cunning."

Judaism ascribes central events, such as the binding or sacrifice of Isaac (the *akedah*), to the Temple Mount at the center of Jerusalem. An ancient belief has it that Jerusalem is the navel of the universe, and here Adam, the first man, was supposed to have been born out of the dust, the earth, *adamah*.[35] Here, as well, the first capital crime was supposed to have taken place when Cain committed fratricide. Successive religions have claimed that the creation of the world began at the Foundation Stone of the Temple Mount, where the Muslim Dome of the Rock now stands. Legend says that this is the stone that God threw into the abyss, from which the world originated with Jerusalem at its center. The Kabalistic *Book of Splendor* (*Sefer HaZohar*) says, "groups of angels and cherubim hover above the Foundation Stone, and ... from there all the world is blessed."[36]

From the Foundation Stone, in Hebrew *Even haShetyiyah*, which also means "the stone from which you drink," the water of life[37] supposedly springs forth. Hidden beneath the stone is the source of all the rivers, springs, and fountains from which the world drinks. This well of imagination is sometimes called The Well of Souls. Here, according to ancient folklore, the voices of the dead who come to pray may sometimes be heard along with the sounds of the rivers of paradise. The well, says Eric Neumann,[38] is the gate to "the domain of the earth mother," to the wisdom from below. And beneath the well of souls is a passage leading into the bowels of the earth, where the Ark of the Covenant supposedly was hidden at the time of the destruction of the first Temple.

Between Man and God

In Christianity, the pivotal events taking place in Jerusalem are Jesus casting out the money changers and the pigeon sellers from the Temple, and the Passion story, with the crucifixion at its center. Jesus confronts the darker side of man, which has taken its seat in the house of prayer, and the corruption that has taken predominance over the spirit. Just as Jesus challenged conventional authority in Jerusalem, the process of individuation often requires a betrayal of collective loyalties.[39] The ensuing Passion story, with the crucifixion, burial, and resurrection of Jesus, entails the grand transition of *Yeshua*, Jesus of Nazareth, to *Christ*, the Anointed, the Messiah. In modern psychology, we translate this "once and for all event" into a story of human development in which the human ego "is nailed to the mandala-cross representing the Self."[40] As a psychological process, the crucifixion reflects the ego's transformation into Self.

Muhammad's night journey on his flying horse *al-Buraq*, which had the face of a woman, the body of a horse, and the tail of a peacock, is described in the seventeenth Sura of the Quran as taking place from the Holy Mosque in Mecca to "the farthest mosque" (*al-masjid al-Aqsa*). While al-Aqsa has been understood metaphorically, it is sometimes considered to be in recognition of Islam's roots in Judaism that al-Aqsa received its earthly location and was built at the Temple Mount in Jerusalem. According to legend, Muhammad tied the horse to the Western Wall of the Temple Mount, from where he ascended to the seventh heaven, together with the angel Gabriel. On his way, he met the guardians of heaven, the prophets of other religions—Adam, Jesus, St. John, Joseph, Moses, and Abraham—who accompanied him on his way, accepting him as their master. As Muhammad ascended to heaven, he left his footprint on the Foundation Stone, and upon his return, he brought the instruction for the daily prayers.

Muhammad's ascension and return from heaven took place on a ladder made up of the prophets that preceded him, thus serving as an axis between earth and heaven, between human and divine—similar to Jacob's dream of the ladder, the foot of which was in Beth-El (house of God), while its top, according to rabbinical folklore, reached the gates of heaven from Jerusalem.

It is at the Temple Mount that the stone tablets of the law that Moses brought down from Mount Sinai were kept inside the Holy of Holies. And it is here that the remarkable, awe-inspiring drama of the sacrifice of Isaac took place. This is the eternal and perhaps irresolvable conflict between Submission to the Father, whether as divine command or social dictate, and Devotion to the Future and the promise of one's offspring. Abraham (which means "father is sanctified") *nearly* sacrificed Isaac, but Isaac (which means "he laughed") was not *actually* sacrificed. The eleventh-century Rabbi Yona Ibn Yanach wrote that God only demanded a symbolic sacrifice, and Rabbi Yosef Ibn Caspi (early fourteenth century) claimed that Abraham's imagination had led him astray, making him believe that he had been commanded to sacrifice his son. The Hebrew term *Akedat Yitzhak*, "the Binding of Isaac," indicates the dramatic cultural transition from *actual deed* to *internalized faith*, from the worship of stone-hard gods to ideational images. In place of Isaac the ram was sacrificed to God, and Isaac was given to life. The sacrifice need not be literal. The centrality of this remarkable transitional event is reflected in tradition, which assumes that the sacrifice of the horned ram instead of Isaac took place on Mount Moriah, i.e., the Temple Mount, on Rosh Hashanah, the Jewish New Year. Thus, the ram's horn (the *shofar*) resounds from the synagogues at New Year and the Day of Atonement, as celebration and judgment call forth the chilly winds of autumn. They seem to announce the closing of the gates, as Jerusalem withdraws into herself, hibernating through winter, with an occasional day of complete standstill, as snow turns the city from gold to white.

Within the constricted geographical area of Jerusalem we have three mighty images of ascent, transition, and transformation, wherein the footprints on the stony ground, the *petroglyphs*, are transformed into sacred imprints, the *hieroglyphs* of spirit and creed. The archetypal weight of three theistic Gods may be too much for an area the size of less than one square kilometer, one third of a square mile; again and again Heavenly Harmony turns into Earthly Strife.

Self, Shadow, and Everyday Life

While Jerusalem is a symbol of wholeness, and man has tried to provide a dwelling for divinity in its innermost kernel, shadows lurk in every corner, as hinted in its archetypal origin.

The shadow aspects of the psychological myths pertaining to Jerusalem are evident in actual locations in this city, so full of places where religious events with great psychological implications have taken place. The tears at the Western Wall reflect the close proximity of shadow with Self; how close are not pain, agony, loss, and destruction to wholeness, and ascent to the fall from heaven?[41] Along *Via Dolorosa*, The Road of Agony, the elongated shadow stretches out as a gateway to the Self. When a new dispensation rises from the old, conflict is an inevitable outcome. One shadowy medieval offspring is the legend of Ahasver, the Wandering Jew. In the story, we are told that when Christ "was going to his Martyrdom," along the sorrowful way, "a Jew drove Him along wickedly: 'Go, go thou tempter' ... Christ answered him: 'I go and you will await me till I come again,'" forcing him to wander through the centuries.

The old city is divided into four quarters—Christian, Armenian, Jewish, and Muslim—making up a center of quaternity. Seven of the gates in the surrounding wall are open, including The Dung Gate. Significantly, the eighth one, The Golden Gate or The Gate of Eternal Life, through which the future Messiah is supposed to enter, has been sealed for twelve centuries.[42] Since human life may always be in need of redemption, it should preferably remain closed till the end of time; in the words of Kafka, "The Messiah will come only when he is no longer necessary."[43] Eight open gates would perhaps indicate an all too complete and infinite sense of union between heaven and earth.

The old city is encircled by hills and valleys, tombs and gardens. To the north lies Mount Scopus, "the place from which the city first became visible," as Josephus tells us (*Wars* V:2). Here Cestius Gallus, the Roman commander, set up his camp at the beginning of the Roman attack in 66 CE. Today it is the site of the Hebrew University.

To the east rises Mount of Olives with its many tombs in which the buried await resurrection at the nearby Valley of Jehoshaphat on the Day of Judgment. And here, at Gethsemane, the Garden of the Oil Press, an olive grove on the slopes of the mountain near the Beautiful Gate, Jesus awaited his betrayal by the kiss of Judas.[44] At the southwestern slopes of the hill was the original City of David, today's Silwan or Kfar Shiloah. Here was the outlet of the Gihon Spring, the main water source for ancient Jerusalem. Gihon is mentioned in Genesis 2:13 as one of the four rivers flowing out from the Garden of Eden. While Gihon "springs forth" (as its name in Hebrew means) in Jerusalem, neither biblical account nor the history of the present seem to hint that the Garden of Eden can be found in the vicinity of Jerusalem.

Farther south lies Armon haNatziv, so named after the mansion of the British high commissioner. This was the location of the country house of Caiaphas, the High Priest, where Judas Iscariot concluded the bargain to betray his Master. Ever since, the place bears its ill-famed name, The Hill of Evil Counsel.

Not far away from the Hill of Evil Counsel lies Gehenna, or "The Valley of Hell." Today you find the Jerusalem cinematheque at the slopes of the valley— by all accounts a good place for horror movies.

The Valley of Hell was once the site of a fire altar called *Tophet*, inferno. Children were burned here as sacrifice to the Ammonite god Melech or Moloch, the king-god, as mentioned in 2 Kings 23:10: "And he defiled the Tophet, which is in the valley of the son of Hinnom, that no man might make his son or his daughter to pass through the fire to Molech."

Eventually, the shrine was abandoned and became a dumping ground for criminals and outcasts, whose corpses were burned in the constantly burning fire, creating the smells and fires of hell. It was here, in the Valley of Hell, that the prophet Jeremiah stood before a crowd of priests and citizens, denouncing their pagan practices. He smashed an earthenware pot and cried out, "Thus says the Lord of hosts: So will I break this people and this city as one breaks a potter's vessel, so it can never be mended."[45] And in the Potter's Field at the southern part of the valley lies Akeldama, the Field of Blood, where Judas supposedly either hanged himself (Matthew 27:7) or died when he fell and his intestines burst forth (Acts 1:19).

Holy events and unholy deeds, redemption and betrayal, prophecy and destruction surround the Temple Mount and the inner quaternity of Jerusalem like a dragon's fire. Perhaps ordinary everyday life can only come about outside the dragon or the serpent that encircles the inner quarters. E'mek Rephaim, the biblical Valley of the Ghosts, was initially settled in the nineteenth century by German Templars.[46] Today, coffeehouses have replaced the fields of the ancient farmers and the Philistine army encampments along the southern exit route from the city. Southeast, at the suburb of Talpiot, one may still be reminded of the rivalry between two neighbors, well-known history professor Joseph Klausner (author Amos Oz's great-uncle) and the writer S. Y. Agnon. The former divided the world into the forces of light and darkness, quite naturally seeing himself as a proponent of the former, while Agnon crafted the foolish Professor Bachlam in his story "Shira," on the character of Klausner. Even after their death, they seem to tease each other, as Agnon's cube-like fortress resides uncomfortably at what is now 16 Klausner Street.

To the east, the palace of the American Colony stands as an oasis in the middle of controversy. Originally settled by Christian Americans, many of Swedish descent, searching for peace in their souls in the latter part of the nineteenth century, Baron Ustinov (grandfather of Sir Peter) turned it into a hotel a few years later. In spite of having suffered damage in the cross fire of military battles and political conflict, it remains an island of tranquility.

And to the north, people will go to the market at Mahane Yehuda, as if all that people have on their mind is the price of tomatoes, wild oregano, and toasted sesame seeds. For a brief moment, the everyday struggle to bring home food and basic necessities replaces the questions of war and peace, and the battle between Yahweh and Allah.

In the more comfortable western quarter of Talbiyeh stands the imposing home of the Israel Psychoanalytic Society, founded in 1933 by Max Eitington, a member of the secret ring, Freud's inner circle of seven. The shadow of the psychoanalytic institute has been intriguingly described, with considerable inside information, by Batya Gur in her detective story *The Saturday Morning Murder: A Psychoanalytic Case.*

In the opposite direction, at the eastern outskirts of the city, the security fence set up by Israel to prevent terrorists from entering is in fact a wall. While

The Mahane Yehuda Market.

Photograph by Yoram Bouzaglo

it has prevented the easy access of terrorists who previously had caused havoc among the Jerusalem population, during a few years killing or wounding one out of every two hundred Jerusalemites, it also severely hampers the free movement of innocent non-Israeli Palestinians.

And legend tells us that at the southern outskirts of Jerusalem, towards the desert, the scapegoat was released once a year at the imaginary cliff of Azazel, to carry away the people's sins into the habitat of the evil demons, into the wilderness where the source of the sins can be found.

Shadow and Self

Jerusalem reflects prominent aspects of Self and individuation symbolism: wholeness and unity of opposites, transformation from human to divine, or, psychologically, from ego to Self, and the ladder or axis between ego and Self.

However, as an image of Self and wholeness, it entails as well a powerful shadow of hell and evil, of conflict, loss, and mourning. Jerusalem reflects the interdependence between material and spiritual, human and divine, and between shadow and Self. This may be reflected in the following dream:

> I am looking for a wounded man that I am supposed to treat. I inquire with a clerk at the post office. The clerk tells me I can get help in Jerusalem. I am surprised when the clerk says it will only cost thirty-six (I don't know of what). I thought it would cost a thousand. "But," says the clerk, "I have to go and look, myself." As I wake up I notice the double connotation of "to look, myself"—"*by myself*" and "for my *self.*"[47]

This man is called to treat his wounded shadow. The humble clerk directs him to heal the shadow by coming to himself, to his inner wholeness, as symbolized by Jerusalem. The price is not high, but it is significant: thirty-six (*lamed vav*) righteous men who, according to legend, are present at all times in the world, humble and unknown to others as well as to themselves. Tradition has it that at least thirty-six *tzaddikim*, righteous, need to be present in the world to receive the Shekhinah, the Divine Presence in the world. Unknown, and unknown to themselves, they may be anywhere, they may reside in the soul of anyone, and one of them may appear, perhaps, in the manifestation of my worst enemy.

The dream makes a point of the tedious and lonely task of uniting the opposites of *shadow* and *wholeness*, through man's search for him or her self, by oneself. The shadow has a place in Jerusalem—that is, within the idea of peace and wholeness. However, the means of getting there are humble (thirty-six) rather than grandiose and absolute (a thousand).

Jerusalem seems to turn around the axis of Shalem and Shahar, of heavenly wholeness and fallen humanness, in a sometimes desperate effort to hold the tension between the opposites of divine and profane, good and evil, East and West, faith and conviction—circling around the not always holy triangle of the monotheistic religions and their alternate mutual embrace and fundamentalist exclusion.

The poet of Jerusalem, Yehuda Amichai, says it his way:

> I and Jerusalem are like a blind man and a cripple.
> She sees for me
> out to the Dead Sea, to the End of Days,
> And I hoist her up on my shoulders
> and walk blind in my darkness underneath.[48]

A Talmudic legend tells us that there were twenty-four dream interpreters in Jerusalem. If you brought the same dream to all of them, you would receive twenty-four different interpretations. For some reluctant visitors to the land of dreams, this may indicate the utter nonsense that babbles through the dream, while for others it may mean that there are at least twenty-four aspects to the dream, and our limited capability enables us to grasp but a fragment. And there may be thirty-six faces to righteousness. Likewise, the seventy-two or more names of Jerusalem indicate that we have to approach it and tread its ground with far more complexity than the split between its transcendent, archetypal image of wholeness, and its earthly ground of conflict, suggests.

Notes

1   Cf. Martin Goodman, *Rome and Jerusalem: The Clash of Ancient Civilizations* (New York: Vintage, 2008), for the history of the two cities and the civilizations they represent.

2   Zev Vilnay, *Legends of Jerusalem* (Philadelphia: Jewish Publication Society, 1973), p. 304.

3   It is by facing the orient, the east where the sun rises, that we find our way, i.e., orientate ourselves.

4   Yehuda Amichai, *Poems of Jerusalem and Love Poems* (New York: Sheep Meadow, 1992), p. 49.

5   "And Jacob awoke from his sleep, and he said, Surely the Lord is in this place; and I knew it not. And he was afraid, and said, How awesome is this place! This is no other but the house of God, and this is the gate of heaven" (Genesis 28:17). Rabbinic folklore (*midrash*) says that while the foot of Jacob's ladder was in Bet El, the top, which reached the gates of heaven, was in Jerusalem.

6   "And they shall call Jerusalem the Dwelling Place"; "At that time they shall call Jerusalem the throne of the Lord" (respective translations of Jeremiah 3:17).

7   Isaiah 51:3; Song of Songs, e.g. 7:1. The eleventh-century Rabbi Ibn Ezra interprets the Shulamite here to represent Jerusalem.

8   Ezekiel 16.

9   Menashe Har-El, *Golden Jerusalem* (Jerusalem: Gefen, 2004), p. 22.

10 Genesis 26:12, "Then Isaac sowed in that land, and reaped in the same year an hundredfold (*meah shearim*); and the Lord blessed him."

11 "Secret" is from Latin *secretus*, set apart. The Hebrew word for holy, *kadosh*, also means to set apart.

12 Irit Salmon, in *Truly Fake: Moses Wilhelm Shapira, Master Forger*, ed. Anna Barber (Jerusalem: Israel Museum, 2000), p. 8. Furthermore, Shapira's daughter, Myriam Perrault-Shapira (Jerusalem 1869-Neuilly-sur-Seine 1958), who became an author in France under the name of Myriam Harry, describes the house in which she grew up in *La Petite Fille de Jerusalem*.

13 While the authenticity of the scrolls discovered in 1947 in the caves at Qumran, close to the northwestern shores of the Dead Sea, has been proven, Uqbar and the civilization of Tlön is a fascinating fictional story written by Jorge Luis Borges in 1941 (*Labyrinths* [Harmondsworth: Penguin, 1970], pp. 27-43).

14   Jeremiah 49:25; Isaiah 1:21, 26; Song of Songs 6:4; Psalms 84:2.

15   Isaiah 62:4: "You shall be called Hephzibah"; Ezekiel 23:4: "Thus were their names: ... and Jerusalem Ohalibah."

16   Isaiah 60:3: "the nations shall come to your light ... "; Zechariah 12:3: "I will make Jerusalem a burdensome stone ... "; Isaiah 24:10; Ezekiel 22:2, 5; Zechariah 12:2; Zephaniah 3:1.

17   Isaiah 52:1.

18   Yehuda Amichai, *Poems of Jerusalem and Love Poems*, p. 51.

19   Genesis 22:1-14.

20   Gen. 28:17.

21   Isaiah 14:12-15: How are you fallen from heaven, O Shahar, son of the morning! How are you cut down to the ground ... For you have said in your heart, I will ascend to heaven, I will ascend to heaven, I will exalt my throne above the stars of God; ... I will ascend above the heights of the clouds; I will be like the most High. Yet you shall be brought down to hell, to the sides of the pit.

22   E.g., Judges 6:25, 26; cf. Erel Shalit, *Enemy, Cripple, Beggar: Shadows in the Hero's Path* (Hanford, CA: Fisher King Press, 2008), p. 21.

23   *New Larousse Encyclopedia of Mythology*, Introduction by Robert Graves (Twickenham, Middlesex: Hamlyn, 1968), p. 80.

24   Yehuda Amichai, *Poems of Jerusalem and Love Poems*, p. 81.

25   Vilnay, *Legends of Jerusalem*, p. 135.

26   The Jerusalem Syndrome closely resembles the Stendahl Syndrome, which affects some art-loving visitors to Florence, in whom artistic masterpieces may evoke psychotic reactions.

27   Carl Gustav Jung, *Memories, Dreams, Reflections* (New York: Vintage, 1965), p. 318. This bewilderment as regards interior and exterior is described in *Memories, Dreams, Reflections*, where Jung tells us about his fascination with the tomb of Galla Placidia in Ravenna. The empress Galla Placidia, a cultivated woman who lived with a barbarian prince, was, says Jung, "a suitable embodiment for my anima." When he went back to her tomb in Ravenna the second time, in the early nineteen thirties, he once more "fell into a strange mood" and "was deeply stirred" (p. 314). From Galla Placidia he went to the Baptistery of the Orthodox, where he was struck by "the mild blue light that filled the room." Jung tells us that "the wonder of this light without any visible source did not trouble me. I was somewhat amazed because, in place of the windows I remembered having seen on my first visit, there were now four great mosaic frescoes of incredible beauty which, it seemed, I had entirely forgotten." When back home, he asked his friend C. A. Meier to bring him pictures of the mosaics he had so vividly seen, only to find out that they did not exist. "This experience in Ravenna is among the most curious in my life. It can scarcely be explained," says Jung (p. 316), who seemed to wonder if he *projected* his anima, his soul, onto Galla Placidia, if he breathed life into her, or if he *introjected* her soul through the stone of her tomb and the light of the place.

28   Selma Lagerlöf, quoted from *Jerusalem: The Holy City in Literature*, ed. Miron Grindea (London: Kahn & Averill, 1981), pp. 195-196.

29   Henri Troyat, *Divided Soul: The Life of Gogol* (New York: Doubleday, 1973), p. 333.

30   Amos Elon, *Jerusalem: City of Mirrors* (London: Flamingo, 1996), p. 11.

31   Mark Twain, *The Innocents Abroad* (New York: Modern Library, 2003), p. 418.

32   Cf. Psalm 122:1-9; Revelation 21.

33   Carl Gustav Jung, *The Collected Works of C. G. Jung*, 20 vols. (Princeton: Princeton University Press, 1953-1979) (hereafter CW), 9/i, § 256.

34   Rev. 21:9; Jung, CW 5, § 318; CW 9/i, § 156; CW 11, § 612.

35   The Hebrew word *dam* means blood, *adam* is man (not only Adam the first man), and *adamah* is earth.

36 Vilnay, *Legends of Jerusalem*, p. 15. Cherubim are winged angels with human faces and animal traits, often depicted as a child with wings.

37 The Torah, the Jewish scripture, is often called the Water of Life.

38 Erich Neumann, *The Great Mother* (London: Routledge & Kegan Paul, 1963), p. 48.

39 Edward Edinger, *The Christian Archetype* (Toronto: Inner City Books, 1987), p. 83; Shalit, *Enemy Cripple, Beggar*, pp. 125ff.

40 Edinger, *The Christian Archetype*, p. 98.

41 Cf. Isaiah 14:12-15, note 21 above.

42 In fact, it was initially closed already at the end of the First Temple period (cf. Ezekiel 44:1: "the outer gate of the sanctuary, which faces the east, and it was closed"). In the New Testament it is called The Beautiful Gate (Acts 3:2).

43 Franz Kafka, *The Blue Octavo Notebooks* (Cambridge: Exact Change, 1991), p. 28.

44 For further discussion of this and some of the places mentioned here, from the perspective of analytical psychology, see Shalit, *Enemy, Cripple, Beggar*, pp. 125-151.

45 Jeremiah 19:11.

46 This Lutheran community, founded in 1861, was called "German Temple," because the founders intended to "bring God's people together, each person as a living spiritual building block in the temple of God in the Holy Land." They established communities in Jerusalem, Haifa, and a few smaller places, and were expelled by the British during and following World War II.

47 Erel Shalit, *The Hero and His Shadow: Psychopolitical Aspects of Myth and Reality in Israel*, new rev. ed. (Lanham, MA: University Press of America, 2004), p. 34.

48 Amichai, *Poems of Jerusalem and Love Poems*, p. 55.

15 Cape Town: Mother Nature, Mother City

PAUL ASHTON

Table Mountain

In the southern sky is a constellation called Mensa. It is the only constellation named after a geographical feature, Table Mountain. Although the constellation is too faint to be used for celestial navigation, its physical counterpart is used as a point of reference by countless Cape Townians. We orient ourselves by the mountain. Is it on our left or our right? Are we moving away from it or toward it? What does it look like from where we are? About fifty years ago one of my math teachers used the changing appearance of the mountain when viewed from different areas as a metaphor for the different philosophical viewpoints that arise from different points of origin, different suppositions. It all depends on where you stand.

Table Mountain on the other side of the City and Table Bay Harbour.

Standing in the City Bowl the center of Cape Town city, and gazing up at Table Mountain's India Face, Africa Crag, or Venster Buttress, with the square building of the upper cable station a couple of pixels higher than its flat surrounds, one sees that the outline rapidly descends on one's right to the *nek* (literally "pass") between Table Mountain and the serene, Sphinx-like Lion's Head. To the left the mountain curves round and descends sharply to another *nek,* from which a gentle looking slope ascends to the Major and Minor Peaks of Devil's Peak. (An extraordinary experience awaits the intrepid person who ascends the Minor Peak from this slope: one's overall view has so far been hidden, both by the massif of Table Mountain behind and the proximity of the rising earth in front; but then, on passing through a narrow gap in the rocks of the summit, one's view suddenly encompasses the curve of Table Bay opening into the Atlantic Ocean on the left, the wrinkled sweep of protected sea in False Bay—guarded by Cape Hangklip and Cape Point—on the right, the still, blue mountains of the Hottentots Holland range 30km away, and Africa itself behind. And in the flat space between all these features sprawl the signs of developing humanity.)

When viewed from the southern suburbs, buttresses, separated by deep ravines, slowly increase in height from left to right, and the mass ends in the jutting triangle that is Devil's Peak. Beneath the vertical cliffs the vegetation is lush, part indigenous forest that has survived, and part pine plantations. And some of it is the famous Kirstenbosch National Botanical Garden, home to hundreds of indigenous plant species as well as a variety of birds and small mammals. Below a certain level, the suburbs begin. At the high end are large plots with lush gardens and big houses, and as the distance from the mountain increases, the plots contract and the houses shrink.

Cecil John Rhodes

The fact that urban sprawl has not edged its way up the flanks of Table Mountain is due in large part to the farsightedness of a man not usually known for his moral sensibility. Cecil John Rhodes, who had been sent to the Cape because of ill health before he was twenty, made huge amounts of money during his short life (he died at age forty-two). He bought large tracts of land on the edges of the mountain and bequeathed that land to the nation. A memorial to Rhodes stands just above the University of Cape Town. Four pairs of bronze lions flank massive granite steps, and a bust of Rhodes squats under bronze lettering that spells out a few ambiguous lines written by Rudyard Kipling: "The immense and brooding spirit still shall quicken and control / Living he was the land, and dead his soul shall be her soul." Those words could have been written to describe another character from the Cape, this time a mythological one (if one can have myths dating from the sixteenth century.) Adamastor, conceived by the Portuguese poet Camões, was a titan whose affection for Thetis, a sea nymph, was not returned. He threatened her, she tricked him, and he ended up underneath the mountains of the Cape Peninsula, forever teased by the sea, reminded of what he could never have, jealously guarding the unknown ocean to the east of the Cape of Storms.

One of the companies that Rhodes was part of was the Rhodesian Ancient Ruins Ltd., which took over concessions from the British South Africa Company to "exploit" all ancient ruins south of the Zambezi. Exploit they did—with no questions asked! This is one of the reasons that the origins of the extraordinary ruins of the Great Zimbabwe civilization are still shrouded in mystery.

As these two contrasting examples of one man's actions attest, virtue and depravity, love and betrayal, arrogance and avarice, wealth and poverty, beauty and ugliness, nobility and suffering, creativity and entropy are all inextricably entwined in the history of Cape Town.

A Story, a Song, and Some Slaves

On the slopes of Devil's Peak, originally called Wind Berg (Windy Mountain), are two batteries called the King's Blockhouse and the Queen's Blockhouse. They were placed there because of the outlook that takes in both the harbor in Table Bay and a possible boat landing site at Muizenberg in False Bay. The batteries were never fired in defense, but they do offer imposing views. Beauty and power in one.

When the prevailing summer wind, the southeaster, blows strongly, Table Mountain is often covered by a blanket of cloud, called by locals "the table-cloth." Story has it that a retired trickster (some say a pirate) named Captain van Hunks was challenged to a smoking duel by the Devil. The prize was inordinate wealth, but if van Hunks lost, his soul would be taken by the Devil. Allegedly, van Hunks refused the wager because he already had more money than he could ever use—but he accepted the Devil's challenge just for fun. They took up their positions (comfortable ones, I would guess) on Windy Mountain, then smoked up a storm until the mountain was covered from end to end with whirling smoke. Van Hunks became increasingly cheerful, and the Devil became increasingly green until he finally admitted defeat. Despite having won, the Devil took van

Hunks. But the two return every so often, because the Devil is such a bad loser and van Hunks loves winning, and they resume their contest on the slopes of what we now call Devil's Peak.[1]

That story was about inflation and tricksterishness, but a well-known Cape song suggests both deflation and a sort of wishfulness. Usually sung in Afrikaans, the song originated among the Cape Malay people, who came from Malaysia and Indonesia as slaves in the seventeenth and eighteenth centuries.

The song is called *"Daar kom die Alibama"* ("There Comes the Alabama"). The *Alabama* was a Confederate war ship during the American Civil War; her task was to raid and sink Union merchant ships. A three-master that also had a powerful steam engine, she was capable of moving at about 13 knots. The combination of steam and sail made her extremely maneuverable, and during her brief career she sank more than seventy vessels owned by Union companies, costing the Union millions of dollars. What is remarkable is that the *Alabama* was a ship that supported slavery, and yet the victims of slavery were clearly so excited by her arrival in Cape Town's Table Bay that they made up this song about her, in a banjo-supported style "typical" of the slave descendants. The usual Afrikaans version is as follows:

Daar kom die Alibama,
Die Alibama kom oor die see
Daar kom die Alibama,
Die Alibama kom oor die see.
Nooi nooi die rietkooi nooi,
Die rietkooi is gemaak
Die rietkooi is vir my gemaak,
Om daar op te slaap

There are numerous repetitions, but this is the gist. It can be translated:

There comes the Alabama,
The Alabama comes over the sea,
There comes the Alabama,
The Alabama comes over the sea.
Girl, girl,[2] the reed bed, girl,
The reed bed it is made,
The reed bed it is made for me
For me to sleep upon.

Why they composed it is puzzling; perhaps it was a case of "identification with the aggressor," or perhaps they misidentified with the American South's apparent struggle for freedom. But it again demonstrates the entwined contrasts of Cape Town.

Some of the Malay families converted to Christianity, but most retained their original Islamic faith, even though the Dutch authorities prohibited them from building mosques. The area in which the Cape Malays lived was later called Die Bo-Kaap (literally "the above-Cape"), which somehow survived the apartheid era while a large "coloured" suburb on the other side of town, called District 6, was destroyed and its inhabitants forcibly removed. Today, the Malay quarter is a special part of older Cape Town, huddled around mosques that were built only after the English took over the Cape Colony. Its own definitive Malay flavor is now under a different sort of threat, as "yuppies" are prepared to pay high prices to live in such a picturesque area so close to the city center.

While these human machinations take place, the sphinx (Lion's Head), from her plinth adjacent to Table Mountain, looks inscrutably out to sea as she has done since time began. And the brew bubbles in the cauldron of the City Bowl within the emotionless curves of Nature—the mountains behind and on each side, and the sweep of the South Atlantic Ocean in front.

The image I want to convey is of a complex, even lumpy concoction, in which good and evil, consciousness and blindness, nobility and meanness all add their flavors. In this sense, Cape Town is like the Great Mother, as Erich Neumann so well described her: she is neither wholeheartedly evil nor sweetly benevolent, but a mixture of both. And she lies always in the manifest and dispassionate arms of Mother Nature herself.

More Stories

Another of the Cape Stories is of a witch-like figure called Antjie Somers, reputed to walk around with a sack on her back into which she stuffs naughty children. One version of the origin of this evil figure involved a successful fisherman, Andries Somers, a handsome and resourceful young man who was set upon by an envious group of peers. When the brawl was over, one of them lay dead. To avoid risking the hangman's noose, Andries fled, wearing a shawl round his head and a dress of his sister's, and carrying his few belongings in a basket.

Over the mountains he went, finally finding work and accommodation on a farm. He worked his way up from farm laborer to foreman, until he once more evoked gossip when his co-workers, again envious of him, found the dress and scarf he had hidden. Thereafter he was tormented by the taunts of his neighbors, who gave him the woman's nickname, Antjie. To avoid further trouble, Andries again fled, never to be seen again. But stories filtered down of how an old woman with a sack on her back, a scarf on her head, and a knife in her hand threatened to kidnap children, particularly those who were not being good.[3]

Another story concerns Sheik Yusuf, a holy man. At first an honorable soldier from Makassar in Malaysia, he gave himself up to the Dutch—whom he had been fighting—on the promise of a pardon. The Dutch, however, betrayed his trust, feeling that he was too dangerous an adversary to be set free, and sent him into exile in the Cape. On the long sea voyage, the ship ran out of water and those aboard became desperate from thirst. Legend has it that Sheik Yusuf dipped his foot (I would guess his left foot) into the sea, and the water around the ship became fresh and potable.

During his long life of exile, Sheik Yusuf remained a respected figure who, among other things, sheltered runaway slaves. After his death he was entombed in what is known as a *kramat*, or shrine, and the area where he lived in the Cape is now named Macassar. There is a circle of *kramats* around Cape Town, fulfilling an old prophecy, and it is now possible to visit these holy places whether or not one is Muslim. The *kramats* honor the ancestors of the religion, the holy men of the past. For the most part, the pattern of *kramats* is like a subterranean energy stream or the chakras of a body: their presence is felt but their specific whereabouts remain unknown to the uninitiated. When one stands barefoot in one of these holy places, one experiences a sense of awe that a people could remain true to their faith, withstanding the sort of depredations they had to endure and the attempts, both active and passive, to assimilate them.

During the apartheid regime, when the people of District 6 were forcibly moved to other areas and their homes demolished, all places of worship—churches, mosques, or temples—were left standing. I find this an extraordinary expression of sensitivity, or maybe it was sentimentality, or superstition, or perhaps all three. After all, as mentioned above, the Dutch, in the time of the Dutch East India Company, had forbidden the Malays to build mosques, and one of the theories about what motivated the early Portuguese explorers who first "discovered" the Cape was not so much commerce as a sort of holy expansionism, designed to outflank Islam.[4] Yet here is officialdom, deaf to the cries of the people but sensitive to the idea of the sacred—even of what is sacred to the other.

The Peoples of the Cape: Mythology to Reality

Malvern van Wyk Smith compiled and edited an anthology of poetry entitled *Shades of Adamastor*. Before the title page, he quotes Abioseh Nicol:

> You are not a country, Africa
> You are a concept,
> Fashioned in our minds, each to each,
> To hide our separate fears,
> To dream our separate dreams.[5]

This could also be about Cape Town.

Van Wyk Smith's book was published in 1988, to coincide with the fifth centenary celebrations of the first-known rounding of the Cape of Storms, by Bartolomeu Dias in 1488. The next and more famous doubling of the Cape was by another Portuguese fleet in 1497, under the command of Vasco da Gama. (The rather seedy suburb of Vasco is named after him, as is the up-market Marina da Gama, but the grandiose plans of connecting the marina with the sea so that yachts could sail directly into the bay never materialized.) Although Dias's voyage opened up the possibility of finding a sea route to the Indies, it was da Gama who succeeded in this expressed aim. But he did lose a ship, and a few hundred men to scurvy, in the process.

Smith writes of the Cape as being "the white man's paradise," and contrasts this imaginal "paradise of expectation" with the concrete "tempestuous headland of the seafarer's experience."[6] This connects with the way that Africa and its indigenous people seemed to evoke two distinct and opposing images for the early European explorers: the noble savage living in a heavenly Golden Age, and the malevolent brute surfacing from the hellish "heart of darkness."[7] The double nature of the Cape is reflected in the very names that it bears. Cabo Tormentoso (The Cape of Storms) was the name Dias gave it because of his experience there, but King John II of Portugal, who had not been there, insisted that it should be changed to Cabo de Boa Esperanza (Cape of Good Hope) to reflect the hope that the sea route to India could henceforward become a reality.

The sixteenth-century Portuguese poet Luíz Vaz de Camões wrote a long poem about da Gama's voyage called *The Lusiads*. In this, as mentioned above, he invents a new Titan called Adamastor, a personification of "that mighty Cape, occult and grand, / Stormy by nature, and 'Of Storms' by name."[8] Of immense size and power, Adamastor threatens, with "storms and hurricanes too hard to bear,"[9] those who intrude upon his domain now and in the future, prophesying their "wrecking and catastrophe." Twelve years after first rounding the Cape, Dias drowned when his ship sank during a storm in the South Atlantic.

Adamastor appears to sailors in the freak waves off the Cape Coast.

The idea of Adamastor has fueled the imagination of a large number of South African poets. Van Wyk Smith describes him as being "mighty but miserable," and he stands against the reverential Portuguese invaders as Bacchus stood against the status quo. One interpretation of this parallel, as Camões sees it, is that the Dionysian—with its illogicality and loss of control—is the bitter enemy of the Apollonian logical-scientific systems of the West, and can well be symbolized by the indigenous peoples. More concretely, the intentions of men seem deliberately thwarted by the dangers of the Cape Coast, where winds sweeping up from the Roaring Forties and strong currents that often flow counter to the wind combine to create huge waves. These so-called freak or rogue waves are capable of damaging even modern steel vessels. Thus primitive, dangerous, and unknown nature rises up against the "civilizing" influence.

Perhaps Adamastor stands against hubris, too, for another Dutch story from the Cape concerns an impatient Dutch sea captain who broke the custom of not sailing on Easter Day. Mocking the church and God, he set sail into what soon became a storm. Neither captain and crew nor his ship were ever seen again, but rumor has it that they were made to sail through storms for the rest of eternity.

Every now and again the ship, now called *The Flying Dutchman,* is seen flying before a storm with all sails set, just above the water. The ship glows red, blue fire sparks from the eyes of the crew, and a black bird circles the mast. One can imagine Cape sailors crossing themselves to ward off such chthonic magic.

The first people who inhabited the area of Cape Town are thought to have been a branch of the *San.* Known to have inhabited caves and rock shelters at least 2,000 years ago, these were the Strandlopers, literally the "beach walkers" (an important part of whose diet was the delicious Cape rock lobster). It is likely that these were the people da Gama encountered. One of the famous and then-notorious Strandlopers was a woman whose Christian name became Eva. She pleased the colonialist establishment by getting baptized and marrying a Dutch settler, Pieter van Meerhof, but then displeased them by enjoying alcohol and the amorous attentions of men. She ended her lonely life in Cape Town at age thirty-two, cut off from her origins through her conversion to Christianity and marriage to a Dutchman, widowed when he was murdered in Madagascar, and abandoned by her erstwhile friends when she sought solace in alcohol and "depravity." She had gone to live on Robben Island as its sole female inhabitant when van Meerhof was transferred there as superintendent of the convicts, and she was exiled from the island some years after her husband's death.

The *San*—sometimes called "little people" or "bushmen," but whose name actually means the "real people"—were conveniently thought by the colonizers to be less than human, and were systematically exterminated, in part because, as hunter-gatherers, it was easy to accuse them of being thieves. The Khoi, called Hottentots by the settlers, were cattle herders and required land for their livelihood; they were tricked and betrayed by the colonizers, and many died from smallpox infection. Cape Town—in fact, the world—is blessed to have had the linguist Dr. W. H. I. Bleek, who, with his sister-in-law Lucy Lloyd, collected an enormous amount of material about the San by interviewing "bushman" prisoners held at the Breakwater Prison and writing down the stories they told. Their work, now called the Bleek and Lloyd Collection, is in the archives of the University of Cape Town, although Bleek and Lloyd published two collections, one of Khoi and one of San folklore.[10] Subsequently, Bleek's daughter, Dorothea, who had continued his work, published a selection of stories for the general reader, and many other stories have been put into poetic form by A. Markowitz, Stephen Watson, and Antjie Krog, among others.

One of the well-known San stories is ostensibly about how the hare got a split lip, but it is actually a much more serious story about man's fear of death. One day Moon, an early San deity, instructed an insect (or tortoise) to take a message to man. The message was that "in the same way that I periodically die and yet come alive again so will man die and yet be reborn." Moon wanted man to realize that death was merely a stage of life. The insect (tortoise) set off and soon met hare, who asked "Where are you going?" "I am going to tell man that the moon has said 'as I die and yet come alive again, so will you die and come alive again.'" Hare boasted that he could run faster than any other animal and should take the message to man. Insect (tortoise) agreed, and hare bounded away, hopping, skipping, and repeating the message to himself. But attention not being his strong point, he soon forgot most of it. Coming to man, he told him: "Moon says that when you die, unlike Moon you will never rise again." He then returned to Moon and repeated what he had told man. In anger, Moon punched hare in the face, splitting his upper lip—forevermore a sign of the harm he had done to man.

An important mythological figure of the Khoi/San cosmology is Mantis, a trickster who, like the Winnebago trickster Paul Radin wrote about,[11] regularly breaks the established mores of his society and thus frequently gets into trouble and must be rescued by one of his family. Like the Winnebago trickster, his function seems to be twofold: he makes the clear boundaries between what is acceptable in that society and what is not, and he lays the groundwork for change to occur. One could say that he aids the development of consciousness. In addition, Mantis has shamanistic qualities. The South African Association of Jungian Analysts (SAAJA) publishes a twice-yearly journal named after him, and the SAAJA logo consists of four mantis heads in a circle, facing inward. Invoking the power of the dark and the not-yet-known, the logo developed for the seventeenth IAAP congress in Cape Town had a dancing shaman as its central image.

The Mother City

Cape Town has been called "the Mother City." Now, the first image usually conjured up when we speak of *Mother* is a good, nurturing mother; we expect of a mother that she should look after, feed, nourish, and love her children. But Neumann[12] has shattered our blind optimism by clearly showing that the Great Mother archetype has the potential for both good and evil, and undergoes an eventual differentiation into the Good Mother and the Terrible Mother.

And this is so for our Mother City, too. Cape Town was formally founded by the Dutch East India Company in about 1652, when Jan van Riebeck was sent to establish a settlement and tasked with building a fort, improving the anchorage, and arranging food supplies for the shipping; it was settled as a way-station on the long route from Europe to the East Indies. Company gardens were established to grow fresh vegetables for the ships, and cattle were bartered from the indigenous people and later raised for the supply of beef, as well. (This was a century before there was a clear link between scurvy and the lack of fresh fruit, meat, and vegetables.) So Cape Town was founded to have a "Good Mother" function. And yet from the very beginning, that function was made possible only through causing suffering to others. I refer particularly to the slaves who were brought from Malaysia, but also those who were imprisoned under the "white man's law" and used as laborers to help build the harbor and the castle. Many years later, prisoners of war, particularly from Italy, built mountain passes and reservoirs, stone upon stone. The results are exquisite testaments to the builders themselves, but also painful reminders of men in exile and bondage. (And all the time, Adamastor lies sleeping.) The reservoirs really are lovely. They are, in fact, small dams, built by the hands of stonemasons. Each stone in the dam wall is dressed and fitted to make it something beautiful, like an Italian cathedral, a monument to the sky and the mountain. As so often in Cape Town, opposites, like the beauty and the pain palpable in those walls, exist close together.

The water in the reservoirs is translucent although dark brown with a slightly reddish hue—like a rich brew of tea—stained by tannins from the surrounding plants. And yet the rocks, bared in summer when the water level is low, are a dazzling white, like the linen of a proud housewife. The variegated flora surrounding the dams looks magnificent, as though it must be growing on rich earth, but in reality the sandstone soils of the mountain are impoverished and phosphate poor, and the general environment is extreme with regard to temperature fluctuations, wind, and rain or drought.

The psychoanalyst Bion has written about "the container contained," and this makes me think of how Cape Town is contained between the mountain and the sea. Walking along the Sea Point promenade during a northwesterly gale, with the waves crashing and spewing behind and above the breakwater, one can experience the mighty chaos of the ocean while feeling the security of solid earth beneath one's feet. Being contained allows one to become conscious of what is otherwise too frightening to know about. Likewise, looking up at Table Mountain from the "bowl" during a southeasterly gale one is filled with awe as the thick cloud covering boils downward in silent clamor, while on the street one feels the wind in sudden gusts, powerful reminders that the Titan is abroad. Although it streams in descent, the cloud never reaches the bottom but turns in on itself, mirroring the emotional state of a schizoid individual who seems placid from a distance, calmly introverted, but seethes with discomfort once his defenses have been breached. Like that individual, from a distance, from across the bay, the cloud looks calm, a tablecloth laid for a feast. A feast for the gods, perhaps.

Simon van der Stel, estranged from his wife, who stayed in Europe, came to the Cape in 1679 as a commander in the Dutch East India Company. When the Cape became a colony in 1691, he became its first governor and had a beautiful residence built in what became known as the Cape Dutch style. This building, Groot Constantia, has been beautifully restored and maintained. It was the center of a farm and vineyards that still produce exceptional wine.

From early on, the Cape has been a wine-producing area and, like so much of what is embedded in its past, this has both noble and infamous aspects. On the noble side, one could mention the quality of the wines and the search for improvements that have led to interesting cultivars and blends, as well as the way the vineyards, oases of fertility, have been wrested from the impoverished soils. In addition, especially with regard to the older estates, the architecture—both of the homes and the cellars—blends beautifully with the mountains that seem to be a feature of most wine-growing areas. But there is also the infamy of the *dop* (or *tot*) system, whereby the laborers were paid some of their wages in wine—often a very young wine called *vaal-japie*, literally, "grey or drab simpleton" because of its cloudy appearance and powerful effect. This system saved the farmer hard cash, but rendered the workers slaves to alcohol and caused untold suffering among the families of the victims.

Simon van de Stel was himself the child of a Dutch man and a freed Indian slave woman. It is fascinating, given South Africa's obsession with race, that a half-caste man who would have been classified as "coloured" or *bruin* (literally "brown") by the apartheid machinery was the first governor of the Cape. (And this was more than three centuries before Barack Obama became president of the United States!)

One of the names given to Cape Town is "Gateway to Africa." Although it is located on the southernmost tip of the continent, it is not quite truly *Africa* to some of its populace. But neither is it any other place. Its inhabitants of European descent might articulate that they were away from "home" (as exiles perhaps), even though they had never been where "home" was and had lived all their lives in Cape Town. The white English-speaking inhabitants of Cape Town are predominantly of European extraction, and they keep contact with their histories through organizations such as the Alliance Française, the Portuguese and Italian clubs, and the Greek society. Those whose families originally came from England do not have their own society or club, but groups of Scots, Irish, and

Welsh keep old traditions alive. All these groups, including the "English," have at least a part of themselves "looking back." They look back toward the history and the geography of the places where they feel they have come from and where they will always partly belong, which gives them a feeling of security engendered by that which is "known." Of course, it may also prevent them from coming to terms with what is as yet unknown in the other cultures that surround them.

And what of the other racial groups that have their homes in Cape Town? The "first" people are here no more, although small pockets of San or Khoi do exist in Botswana, Namibia, and the Kalahari area of the Northern Cape. But in Cape Town, they are usually found only in museums or in the middle pages of newspapers when some issue arises, existing mostly as the presence of an absence. The Cape Malays have made an identity for themselves that is based on religion—Islam—more than on geography or language. In this sense, they have been truly acculturated and do not yearn for their country of origin. They speak Afrikaans or English or a picturesque mixture of the two, and some of the recipes and foodstuffs that they brought have entered common language—*bobotie, sosatie, breyani, brinjal,* to name a few. The Afrikaners, most of whom originally came from Holland, but some of whom came from France via Holland, have traditionally been farmers, and deeply connected with the land. Their language has its roots in Dutch but has been influenced by English, French, German, Malay, and Black African languages, and their culture has been strongly affected by the Calvinistic Dutch Reformed Church. I doubt that the average Afrikaner has a difficulty with identity. He or she is South African.

The history of Black indigenous peoples in Cape Town is another fraught area. In the early years of the Cape Colony, there were no indigenous Bantu people around Cape Town. The Bantu groups were busy with their migrations southward through what are now the northern and eastern parts of South Africa, Swaziland, Basutoland, and Zululand. Slaves were brought in from Madagascar on the east coast of Africa and from the "bulge" on the west coast. For some reason these populations died from disease at a much higher rate than the Malaysian slaves, and they did not form lasting communities.

There were early treaties with the Xhosa nation who lived to the east of Cape Town. These set the Great Fish River and the Kei River as boundaries between the Cape and Xhosa territories. After the great debacle of 1856, when the Xhosa slaughtered their own cattle after a young girl's vision prophesied that the white invaders would then leave the country, hunger forced people to seek work in the Cape. In the mid-twentieth century, the Nationalist government brought in legislation requiring Black people to carry passes so that the government could enforce its Group Areas Act and Job Reservation Act. This meant that only migrant laborers could enter Cape Town, and only without spouses. So for them, too, "home" was not Cape Town; it was the Transkei. Since the release of Mandela and other political prisoners in 1990, there has been a tremendous influx of Black people, mainly Xhosa-speaking, into the Cape environs, trying to find the "promised land" that will secure them food, shelter, and meaningful employment. Many of these individuals have been dislocated from their extended families, culture, and traditions, and it is likely that for them, too, psychological home is not yet Cape Town, but where the heart is and where the forefathers came from.

Nature and Beauty

Cape Town is beautiful, and part of its beauty is because it is so close to nature. But Cape Town also demonstrates a beauty that is apart from nature. Following Hillman, one could call this latter "man-made" rather than "God-given" beauty.[13] It is manifest in some of the architecture, in some of the older "stately homes" and places like the University of Cape Town, in its imposing setting on the slopes of Table Mountain. For me, the word "congruent" best describes what I find beautiful in the city, so that even a shopping mall that is unashamedly a shopping mall can have that descriptor. Even some township "informal settlements" carry such a congruence, and are expressions of the indomitable spirit of those who live there. (A glossy "coffee-table book" called *Shack Chic* presented photographs of the interiors of some of the makeshift dwellings in these informal settlements. The realization that they were "nice inside" came as a surprise to those who did not have to live there, and was perhaps extended to the unknown people who did.)

Part of the reason that nature is so important and even helpful to our city is that it tends to make relative, even to dwarf what could otherwise be construed as ugly. Anything man has yet produced otherwise might, in the absence of the massive Table Mountain, seem unsightly! Instead, it becomes just something that *is*; it does not fill the whole screen of our consciousness because it is so small in comparison with the mountain. This even applies to something as massive as the stadium built in Green Point for the Soccer World Cup of 2010. Although colossal by man's standards, it is as nothing when compared to what Mother Nature can produce. Hillman suggests that the natural is not necessarily beautiful and the beautiful not necessarily natural, but I take issue with that. I cannot think of anything that I have seen in nature that does not have a particular allure that transcends any notion of it being not-beautiful.

In the fabricated world, which is a world of rules, an Apollonian world, beauty is by definition based on order, fit, coherence, and meaning. None of these criteria are relevant to Nature, and it seems to me that we would find more beauty in the world if we could dispense with the sort of criteria mentioned above and see things simply as they are. That would be "soul beauty"—the beauty of the individual soul—as opposed to "spirit beauty," which implies that things "ought" to fit in certain ways. To achieve the former, one must become more grounded, more oneself; to achieve the latter, one must discover the rules and play by them.

With Cape Town, it is the city's connection with Nature that enhances her beauty and gives rise to the meditative way that Cape Townians engage with her. The citizens of Cape Town are often accused, by those from farther north in South Africa, of being insular and asocial. We are like that, probably because we have a tendency to look inward, to the natural universe within, rather than outward to man's creations. Paradoxically, being truly aware of the universe without ("God's grandeur," as Gerard Manly Hopkins called it) helps us connect inwardly.

And the Shadow

Of course, Cape Town also has what Hillman refers to as "the back ward."[14] Can we see the gods there, as he suggests we should? Do we see the gods there? Out of the island of seals, Robben Island, came one god in the form of Madiba, Nelson Mandela. For many in South Africa, he went to Robben Island as a terrorist, and for millions in South Africa and the world, he left it as a saint—carrying the hopes of the globe, that solid mandala, on his Atlantic shoulders. Was he transformed or were we the people transformed? I think we all were; and I think it was made possible, at least in part, through the directed energy of the Truth and Reconciliation Commission, which encouraged us to know the "back ward" in ourselves. And the knowing of *that* meant that we could withdraw, even for a little while, the projections that allow us to treat others inhumanely.

It also seems to me that Cape Town's great disparities involving the rich and the poor, the educated and the uneducated, the conscious and the unconscious, the honest and the dishonest, make it difficult to remain naïve or innocent. These disparities are so obvious that one would have to be blind or very well defended not to be aware of them. This means that it is difficult to remain what William James called "once born," or optimistic. [15] One soon becomes a "twice-born" pessimist, or what some would call a realist. But in psychological terms this means becoming aware of "what is" rather than "what one would like it to be." This is a differentiated position that is not inflated in itself and does not permit inflation (positive or negative) of others. And again it is made more possible for us because of the way nature surrounds us, tolerating all things in her non-judgmental way.

The Freedom to Play 2010.

Photograph by Frances Ashton

Cape Town stands on the brink of the unknown other world, symbolized by the ocean all around the peninsula on which she stands, and by the great bulk of Africa, the Dark Continent, to the north, from which she is separated by a series of mountain ranges. In geological time, the area was once an island, and some of it, the Cape Flats, was under water. And the water level in the ocean would have to rise less than ten meters for it to happen again. Then Adamastor would be entirely surrounded by sea, separated from the "interior" of Africa by a strait, a truncated version of the Straits of Magellan just north of Cape Horn.

Thinking about Cape Town as an island, I am reminded of the ideas of Jung and Neumann, especially as articulated by Edward Edinger.[16] They understood that the developing ego, the individual "I," separates out from the previously undifferentiated oneness of the psyche as a whole like an island from the surrounding ocean. For "undifferentiated oneness" one could read "as yet unknown," and that is what Africa is for many of us: the Great Dark Continent into which we can project both paradise and the infernal. And Cape Town is like purgatory in that it keeps in awareness—however intermittent—the discomfort of knowing that both extremes, heaven and hell, exist in oneself. What makes the difficult process of differentiation possible for us in this Mother City is her deep conscious connection with the natural world; always she is held in the dispassionate arms of Mother Nature. For Nature herself, there is nothing ever new, and yet to our awareness she continually provides something more.

Notes

1   P. W. Grobbelaar and K. Harries, *Famous South African Folk Tales*, trans. L Whitwell (Cape Town: Human and Rousseau, 1985), pp. 32ff.

2   The word *nooi* has the double meaning of "maiden" or "sweetheart" as well as "mistress" or "madam."

3   Grobbelaar and Harries, *Famous South African Folk Tales*, p. 197ff.

4   M. van Wyk Smith, comp., *Shades of Adamastor: Africa and the Portuguese Connection: An Anthology of Poetry* (Grahamstown: Institute for the Study of English in Africa, Rhodes University, 1988).

5   Abioseh Nicol, "The Meaning of Africa," in Smith, *Shades of Adamastor*, p. v.

6   Smith, "Introduction," in *Shades of Adamastor*, p. 10 and p. 12, respectively.

7   Joseph Conrad, *Heart of Darkness* (1922; repr., Middlesex: Penguin Books, 1973).

8   Luis Vaz de Camões, *The Lusiads*, in Smith, *Shades of Adamastor*, p. 54.

9   *Ibid.*, p. 52.

10 Wilhelm Bleek and Lucy Lloyd, *Specimens of Bushman Folklore* (London: G. Allen, 1911), about the San; Wilhelm Bleek and Lucy Lloyd, *Reynard the Fox in South Africa; or Hottentot Fables and Tales*, chiefly translated from original manuscripts in the library of His Excellency Sir George Grey (London: Trübner & Co., 1864), about the Khoi.

11 Paul Radin, *The Trickster: A Study in American Indian Mythology* (London: William Clowes and Sons, 1956).

12 Erich Neumann, *The Great Mother: An Analysis of the Archetype* (Princeton, NJ: Princeton University Press, 1963).

13 James Hillman, "Natural Beauty without Nature [1995]," in Hillman, *City and Soul* (Putnam, VT: Spring Publications, 2006), pp. 155ff.

14 James Hillman, "On Culture and Chronic Disorder [1981]," in Hillman, *City and Soul*, pp. 134ff.

15 William James, *The Varieties of Religious Experience* (London: The Fontana Library, 1960).

16 See Edward Edinger, *Ego and Archetype: Individuation and the Religious Function of the Psyche* (Boston & London: Shambhala, 1992).

16 Cairo: The Mother of the World

ANTONIO KARIM LANFRANCHI

❴ INTRODUCTION ❵

At the beginning of this journey back to Cairo in April 2009, I ask myself: After a twenty-five-year stretch of living in Italy, what will the city of Cairo bring about in me? I feel excited, pleased, but also confused, yet committed to the task. What if, after having become a father and a medical doctor, I discover something from the *"other side"* in those territories of inner Cairo that are vivid in my dreams? I was born in Cairo of an Egyptian mother and an Italian father, and grew up there; received an Italian education; then left in 1984, at the age of seventeen. But Cairo has always been alive in my heart, constantly returning in my dreams.

I am trying to recall memories and associations as if they were impressions of a *flaneur* in time and space (see Luigi Zoja's discussion of the *flaneur* elsewhere in this book), contemplating flashes of memory that inhabit the man I am today, willing to find and explore an inner dimension. So I say to myself: "Stop! Take—*steal*—that moment of absolute time. Stay there willingly and reflectively."

When I first arrived in Milan, I felt I was somehow required to lose part of my soul, and I had already lost my position in the soul of my own city, Cairo. The Egyptian in me was lost in Milan, forgotten. Once, as a young man, I cried when leaving New York City at the end of a vacation; I had never been there before, and as I left, I was already longing for the unknown yet unexpectedly familiar home I had found there. I was looking for my inner Cairo.

When I recently went back to Cairo, I felt what others, too, have felt: that the city was changing; and what it was changing into disturbed me. I felt estranged from what seemed a harder, more impatient, less tolerant city of endless ugly new buildings, a place far removed from the Cairo of my childhood. So I asked myself whether this "loss of soul" reflected a real change or a subjective perception of loss due to my geographical, albeit not emotional, distance. I felt Cairo was abandoning me.

This is why I was impressed when I read a poem written in 1911 by the great Greek poet, Constantine Cavafy, who spent his life in Alexandria. In "The God Abandons Antony,"[1] Cavafy conveys the instant when Mark Antony stands at an imaginative crossroads between Ptolemaic Egypt and the Roman Empire, more specifically, in Alexandria. Antony hears the "exquisite music, voices" of an "invisible procession." He has been abandoned by his god, Bacchus. His luck has failed him, his plans have backfired, and Octavian is about to enter the city in triumph. Antony is princely and dignified; he is a military hero "long prepared, and graced with courage," and he is about to take his own life. Then, in a brilliant shift of characterization, the city itself—which is etched within him— makes its own voice heard. It is Antony who must depart, and it is also Antony who must "say goodbye to her, the Alexandria that is leaving," the imaginative receptacle of his own self.

Cavafy evokes the relationship between a man's self and the soul of his city, unveiling how the soul of a town can manifest itself in a deeply personal individuating process: "the exquisite music, voices" he hears through the window, in this crucial moment of his life, are how the god actually speaks to Antony's heart, where the inner figures of the city have become essentially real. By rising to this higher listening, he overcomes the reductive deception of literalism, "his final delectation" being the ultimate encounter with his human limitedness and the deep emotion of the god's speaking to him through the sounds of the city. Only then, holding the tension, he can say goodbye to her, to the Alexandria he is losing. This is where I took my cue and stopped questioning myself, because I understood I could listen to today's Cairo with deep emotion and say goodbye to the Cairo I was losing.

Cairo, My Hometown

Al Qahira is the Arabic name for Cairo, a feminine word signifying "The Victorious." It is an immense metropolis of the third world. A proliferation of cities in *the city*. A densely populated, multifaceted society of human beings, beyond any reasonable understanding. But still it is the repository of the memory and soul of old, even ancient, Cairo. We should be careful, respectful when we walk in the city; the soil we tread upon is made of ruins, and of those who once were there in other days—their "footfalls echo in the memory."[2] Ancient cities have a depth under the sky.

Man's reshaping adds layers that go from inside to outside, from heart to skin; under your feet and in your heart are the springs and ruins of your own memory. *Natura naturans*: houses are the representation man makes of his own soul within the context of nature—that was my heartfelt perception, as an adolescent, of the beautiful buildings of Zamalek, the rich quarter where I grew up, but also an island in the middle of the Nile, a fortunate and envied microcosm in the dense immensity of greater Cairo.

Seen from on board the plane, Cairo is the interminable extension of a smog-producing, indefinitely expanding organism with a Moloch[3] anima. The immense pollution of Cairo is a cloud suffocating the city, participating in the destruction of the planet, consuming its resources, unsustainable. But the soul of the city is well reflected by my instantaneous sense of belonging. On leaving the plane, it is in the smell of the air, its warmth, the changes I recognize in familiar places, the feeling tone of the people that does resonate with my own, the love I feel for the mere fact of being here, the trepidation and joy when approaching the Nile, great image of life and its ever-flowing richness.

The contrast between life and death and their constant association are immediately felt in this city. Contrasts coexist, in my memory of Cairo, with an intensity uncommon to other places, opposing richness to poverty, beauty to ugliness, dogmatism to tolerance, submission to participation. I therefore propose to guide the reader through the lights and shadows of Cairo's soul, which so strikingly manifest themselves in the outer life of this metropolis.

From atop the Cairo Tower in Zamalek, an ugly construction erected by Nasser in the '50s, you can hear the endless, unnerving background sound so typical of a modern metropolis, made by millions of circulating vehicles. I would call it "the Roar of the Machine."

Cairo's participation in this machine is peculiar, though; it differs from some silent cities of the North in the continuous use of claxons by its drivers, somehow humanized, continuously interrupted by recognizable human modalities of horn-hooting—expressions of impatience, rage, timid intimations to cautiousness, salutations ... The human mass fragments itself into the innumerable individual realities, each not wishing to collaborate in the making of this monotonous tone, but doing so unconsciously. The dark background sound never stops, however, even at night. Here, we all miss silence, whereas in those neat cities of the North, we miss noises.

{ OVERPOPULATION⁴ }

I remember as a child going to visit my maid's home. She lived in extreme poverty. Many of the families in her neighborhood consisted of more than ten members, but due to the lack of space, they had to sleep in shifts, and there could be no such thing as private, individual space. I imagine that the relationship to the flow of time may be strongly conditioned by such an intense contraction of private space and by the constant presence of others.

I remember I felt these people's soulfulness always present in their struggle for survival. The incredible ways they find to answer to their soul's needs have been wonderfully described by Nagib Mahfouz and Albert Cossery—the latter a French-speaking Egyptian writer, about whom Henry Miller wrote: "No living writer that I know of describes more poignantly and implacably the lives of the vast submerged multitude of mankind."⁵

Parking a car has become virtually impossible in down-town Cairo. Moving from one part of the city to the other by car is a hostile, highly stressful misadventure. Living in the chaos of contemporary, hugely crowded Cairo has become a daily struggle, threatening physical well-being and psychological balance.⁶

The rich ones are trying to flee away. Nearly one million people now live in satellite towns and gated communities isolated from Cairo city. New corporations, IT industry, financial industries have all moved out ... a lot of what makes a big city 'work' is being shipped out to suburbs.

An Egyptian professor at AUC (American University in Cairo), Mona Abaza, said in an interview with ABC Radio National:

You might be astonished but my students have never known anything about downtown, have never even gone downtown because they live in the 6th of October or in Rehab, one of those (satellite) cities (made of villas and highly costly meadows in the desert); for me this is in a way very astonishing because it is as if the memory is being erased; I mean: is the American suburbia being replicated in Egypt?[7]

Today, even the American University has moved to one of the new quarters. These districts are built as luxurious residential areas for the rich, in reaction to a legitimate need for air and beauty.

⟨ BEAUTY ⟩

There is a huge modern-day risk of confounding beauty and the possibility of creative idleness (the Roman concept of *otium*) with luxury and the ready availability of commodities. Luxury (in pathology: *luxum*, a Latin word indicating dislocation) cannot feed the souls of men, but attracts them. Money "can't buy beauty" (nor love![8]). By believing that it can, I forget the unique disposition of the heart that opens my soul's senses and actively resonates, blossoms, whenever beauty speaks to me. This kind of experience is unforgettable. It is a function of man's heart as the organ of aesthetic perception. Beauty, if one has the "heart" to appreciate it, is inexhaustible, universal, and eternal. However, as Cossery says: "So much beauty in the world, so few eyes to see it."[9]

The prevalence, on a global scale, of pragmatic and materialist values is part of a collective psychic process that has privileged functionality over contemplation, efficiency over reflection, hyperactivity over melancholy, simplification over complexity, comfort over beauty. This phenomenon has been substantially integrated, and sometimes forcefully introjected, by most countries, including Egypt. It is active on a global scale. *Techne*'s rational regulation of reality and its need to control life to an end has overwhelmed *Psyche*, and has hidden our soul's thirst for transcendence and beauty behind a veil of rationality. The tokens of rational knowledge and security often replace bliss in our existence. Have we lost the sense of awe, which is inherent to life itself, which *is* ourselves? The angel of beauty is within; he is not free like man, he is inscribed in a unique choice, made once and forever—that of breaking the limits of existence (from Latin: *ex-stare*, to stay without) in order to open out existence to life[10] and death. If our gaze is only without, we may not take the risk of living fully, and we may lose beauty as reference for building our houses, our world, and ourselves. The relegation of beauty to museums and to the private domain in general has emptied the square. Beauty has deserted the city and has moved inside the palace.[11]

Man may most easily express his hunger for beauty and transcendence in indirect ways, especially if these needs remain unconscious. All sorts of surrogates or substitutes, such as electronic entertainment and consumerism, fill the void. Worldwide, including in Egypt, television is the commonest form of compensation for the absence of beauty and transcendence. The passive or limbo nature of this compensation does not bring growth or transformation, just deeper malaise and alienation in the absence of truly creative alternatives. This may be one reason that people in Cairo are returning to the mosque or church[12] with a moralistic fervor. In others, the same need may deviate towards a shadowy world of perversions, addictions, or crime. Often moralism and perversion coexist. Like many others, I have been struck by the moral degeneration of rich Arabs who travel from the most religious Gulf nations to visit the belly dancing clubs along the Pyramid road.

The City approaches the Pyramid.

Photograph by Cristina Guarneri

The government, with its "neoliberal" attitude, has not guided the planning of Cairo's expansion in the last few decades. Governmental civil servants consider it a lost battle, and are perceived as dysfunctional, authoritarian intruders by the population. Entire new districts have been built directly by the people, and recognized—if ever—only *after* their actual development, when they connect to the electrical and gas supply. Streets can often be so narrow as to prevent the passage of an ambulance or a normal car. The sewage system is often not even hooked up. And yet, incredibly, all the houses—even those of the very poor—carry parabolic television antennas on their roofs. The expansion of the city has almost reached the pyramids in Giza: more than ten miles of desert filled in by unplanned housing in less than two decades!

Today's new totalitarian anesthesia, television—this new dictatorship of ugliness, with its suppression of human feeling through uniform language, the degradation of beauty, the rhetoric of patriotism, the averaging ignorance, the veil of religiosity, and a continuously hungry eye on the market—reaches out even for the poorest, in the most wretched homes of Cairo.

The diffuse and profound poverty that affects millions of people who are still hardly meeting the most basic needs, and certainly not the need to be known and recognized. In this context of extreme poverty, *the possibility of self-reflection and growth does not exist. But the longing for love and imagination survives*—it may be degraded, but is reaffirmed below the level of consciousness. For instance, the kitsch of everyday objects makes endless reference to the eternal beauty of Cairo's past through color, image, decoration, dress—just walk in the market places of old Cairo and you will see it everywhere.

As Max Rodenbeck, correspondent for *The Economist*, writes in his excellent book on Cairo:

Cairo is, after all, the place that endowed the world with the myth of the phoenix. It was to ancient Heliopolis, the oldest of Cairo's many avatars, that the bird of fabulous plumage was said to return every 500 years, to settle on the burning altar at the great Temple of the Sun and then to rise again from its own ashes. [13]

A poor building in one of the new areas near the pyramids. *Photograph by Paolo Manacorda*
"Deeper understanding of the needs of the human soul is needed, observing how phenomena actualize in the physical world when basic soul needs are denied." [13]

❧ A NECESSARY DIGRESSION ABOUT ISLAM IN MODERN EGYPT ❧

An anecdote relates the story of the building of the Cairo Tower, a six-hundred-foot column in concrete mesh: It is said that Gamal Abdel Nasser diverted a three million dollar cash bribe to this frivolous construction as a slap in the face to Yankee meddling. The monument's form has been interpreted by many as Nasser's "giving the finger" to the CIA. [15]

Elements of Nasser's immature psychology mirrored the collective psyche of Cairo in its belief that Israel could be overpowered. Before the Six-Day War of 1967, Nasser had bragged about Egypt's power to destroy the state of Israel, and then appeared to have tears in his eyes during his television speech after Egypt's humiliating defeat by the Israeli army. As Nasser acknowledged defeat, reflecting the people's despair, he paradoxically diverted their attention from the loss of the war to the possibility of losing their leader when he announced that he was stepping down from the presidency. A mass demonstration demanded his return. The mobs ran out in the streets: their sun was setting, their light was dying! Most revolutions have built into them a yearning for a return to a primeval Golden Age. The archetypal need for the sun and light of the Pharaoh, still alive in Egyptians, manifested itself as a wish to return to the glory of earlier times and to preserve the leader as god. This phenomenon may be related to the docility with which the people of Egypt have always submitted to hierarchy in leadership. The president of the moment identifies with his role and undergoes a process of psychic inflation fuelled by the people's wish for a strong leader.[16]

⟨ THE ECONOMICS OF UGLINESS ⟩

The "economics of ugliness" have reigned in this part of the world since the Egyptian Revolution of 1952, which began on July 23 when a group of young army officers calling themselves "The Free Officers Movement" staged a military *coup d'état*. Initially led by General Muhammad Naguib, the real power behind the *coup* was Nasser. It had been preceded on January 26 with what was to be remembered as the "Black Saturday," as rioters attacking foreign businesses, and targeting British interests—airline offices, hotels, cinemas, bars, and department stores—in particular. Foreign observers who witnessed the burning of Cairo said it looked less like an unruly mob and more like a well-planned and disciplined action.

Cairo has become almost an organism of concrete, thanks to the huge demographic expansion and to the work of Arab contractors. This began in the 1970s, when the *infitah* ("open doors") policy under Sadat brought about economic and commercial growth. (The Ministry of Reconstruction was placed in the hands of Osman Ahmad Osman, who was also the owner of a gigantic multinational Arab enterprise.) During these years, many Egyptians had fled to Saudi Arabia for economic opportunity, and then started moving back and forth, introducing what some have called "Petro-Islam,"[17] i.e., a form of rigid orthodoxy based on Wahhabism.[18]

The Islamic veil has returned. It had virtually vanished in the 1960s, when the glimpse of a new worldview—promoted by Nasser—made the acceptance of a modern perspective possible. The crushing failure of Nasser's vision of pan-Arab political autonomy and self-determination gave way to a wave of Islamic puritanism. The number of veiled women in the streets of Cairo has progressively increased since then, and nowadays has become prevalent among Muslim Cairene women and all over Egypt and the Islamic world.

The repression of beauty as a central phenomenon of our time has triumphed in Cairo as elsewhere. Along with it has come another exquisitely modern phenomenon: the return of millions to orthodox Islam. Quite naturally, the average Egyptian gave full consent to the rich and pious outlook of the gulf emigrants, while condemning the immorality of the Western model of modernization.

As accurately described by Wolfgang Giegerich,

> an equivalent development of a self-sublation[19] and rising above itself did not take place in the Islamic world, where continued work upon a critical reflection of its own religion, tradition, social reality has not been undertaken. It has not dissolved the naive, unbroken unity with itself, its *participation mystique* with its own religion. The critical fight with, indeed against itself and its own orthodoxy has not taken place. Islam has not attempted to within itself distance itself from itself so as to be able to see itself as if from outside.[20]

I recall conversations about God that I have had with friends who belong to non-Westernized Egypt. What they constantly reaffirm is the utterly undeniable presence of the Only and Almighty. Atheism is not even conceivable in their minds. Nietzsche's declaration of "God's death" is an utterly immoral concept. Differentiation between temporal and spiritual domains is not yet psychologically possible. Although Anwar Sadat posed as a religious president, he became a Nobel Laureate for his efforts on the Camp David peace accord with Israel (1978), after which he often repeated the admonishment: "No religion in politics and no politics in religion."[21] He was assassinated in 1981 by an Islamic fundamentalist group from within the ranks of his own army!

Modernity—and its accompanying individual, existential anguish—is perceived as a great non-entity, of no importance in Cairo. To the Egyptian mind, the Western attitude is a threat to one's sense of a unified perception of reality and the existence of a spiritual dimension. For Westerners, it is important to remember the grave risk that non-Westerners face in losing a spiritual perspective as a consequence of moving too abruptly from a traditional to a modern outlook. Rapid transition has proven very threatening to the soul of Cairo; a process that took centuries in the West has been condensed and imported from the outside. The West has brought its *angst* and its functionalistic constriction of the soul.

Thus, to know Cairo's soul, one should live in one of the poor districts. I, the half-Italian half-Egyptian, who grew up with Zamalek's elite, with a European education, ought to be living in one of the poor neighborhoods such as Shubra, Imbaba, Sayyeda Zeinab, or Bulaq. The sense of obligation to the poor in me points to the great fractures within Cairene society, not only between rich and poor, but also between Nubians and Egyptians, Muslims and Christians, Khawagas[22] and Egyptians, colonialists and exploited, the government and the people, lay and religious, veiled and unveiled. In the most personal sense, all of this reflects the split between "me-the-half-Italian," raised in privileged Egypt, and Mohamed Atta, the suicidal young man who came from overpopulated Abdeen and led the terrorist attack against the Twin Towers in New York. The split was in Atta as well, although fed with lack of capacity or will toward integration.

In Search of Cairo's Anima

{ AN ARCHETYPAL EXCURSION INTO THE CAIRENE PSYCHE }

In my images of Cairo—who knows what are memories and what are dreams, what is personal and what is collective unconscious?—violent Egyptian black men and my own children are associated with the crocodile god of ancient Egypt, Sobek. The chthonic nature of the crocodile—long identified with the Nile itself—points to a primitive, reptilian form of instinctual life. Sobek may arouse the call of the "wildness within,"[23] which summons the man who is capable of rising to heroic stature to overcome his own lethargy, the regressive drive that might prevent him from becoming himself. The danger of being sucked by this drive into the realm of the fierce and terrible mother both challenges a man to overcome his childish dependence, and can fuel his fear of women and of his own feminine side. Men in the grips of this fear may rely on a severe, inner authority—that of the patriarchal father—who demands an unrealistic perfectionism. If the strict inner father does not take hold, a man must learn to withstand the devil of self-doubt, the temptation to take the easiest way, and carry the weight of ambivalence in enduring his adventure in the world.

Such a man might have to descend, like Osiris,[24] to the depths (of the unconscious)—the world of the dead where the experience of symbolic death might bring about transformation. Horus as child is known as Harpokrates, "the infant Horus," and was portrayed as a baby being suckled by Isis (an analogy with Mary). In later times, he was affiliated with the newborn sun. Harpokrates is pictured as a child sucking his thumb and standing on crocodiles while holding scorpions in one hand and snakes in the other hand. As Harmakhis, "Horus in the Horizon," he personified the rising sun, as a symbol of resurrection or eternal life. The Great Sphinx at the Giza Plateau is an example of this Horus. The begetting of Horus by Osiris after death is a symbol of the regeneration of life from death.[25] Horus will talk to his father and grant him full return, thereafter completing the cycle of rebirth. The myth states that a higher state of consciousness can be achieved and a new relation to the cosmos established.

A fragment from a bas-relief at Philae depicts Osiris in the character of Menu (the "god of the uplifted arm") and Harpokrates as they sit in the disk of the moon; below is the crocodile-god Sobek, bearing the mummy of the god on his back; to the left stands Isis. The process of transfiguration and rebirth into a higher consciousness is here clearly represented. I was moved when I saw this fragment for the first time, for I was until then completely unaware of the link between my own images and ancient Egyptian archetypes.

This story shows how images from ancient Egyptian mythology were lying below the surface in my own psyche, and arose to meet my soul's demand for a fuller life. And as the archetypal level of the psyche helped me to locate my ancient Egyptian roots, the memory of my great-grandmother gave me yet more solid, personal ground on which to base my Cairene identity. I have always felt that my great-grandmother incarnated a "genius" of the family in her capacity both to question deeply and to plant firmly the seeds of new meaning through her creative activities. Huda Sharawi displayed great wit and a fierce determination of spirit in her quest for women's liberation in Egypt in the first half of the twentieth century, her political and social activism leading her to become an eminent personality in the growing movement. She became an ardent proponent of reform in the country and in the region, and was the first woman in modern times to publicly shed the veil. She is one of the few women whose name is borne by one of Cairo's central streets.

My great-grandmother's courageous gesture of removing the veil symbolically set free the feminine potential that had been oppressed for centuries in Egypt and much of the Middle East. Born into an extremely wealthy family in 1878, she might therefore have led a leisurely, albeit frustrating, life, but she adamantly refused to do so. Despite a premature marriage to her senior cousin and tutor, she managed to break out of wedlock and acquire a solid education.

She loved classical music and became an accomplished pianist. She wrote poetry in French and Arabic, and was the author of many articles, which were published in magazines that she had founded. Her mentor, the French wife of an Egyptian Prime Minister, Eugenie Lebrun-Roushdi, helped her become widely read in the literature of the world. Eventually, Huda returned to her husband, by whom she had two children. She joined forces with him on the political scene, where he played a prominent role as the treasurer of the Wafd Party (the Party of the Delegation). He became one of the three members of a famous delegation to meet England's Lord Wingate in 1919, to advocate the liberation of Egypt from the British Protectorate. When the leaders of the party were arrested and sent into exile, she organized a peaceful protest of women, who marched through the streets of Cairo to the British embassy. In 1923, a year after her husband's death, she began to participate in the conferences of the International Alliance for Women's Suffrage (IAWS). In fact, it was on the occasion of her return from the first IAWS conference that she attended that she made her most daring political statement: As she was disembarking in the port of Alexandria, she removed her veil in a spectacular gesture. She was immediately followed in her action by all the women in attendance.

Huda Sharawi was in her early forties when she set up the Egyptian chapter of the IAWS, called the Egyptian Feminist Union. Many Egyptian ladies and several princesses from the royal family became members and helped her collect funds. She became friends with the members of the Bureau of the International Alliance, who convinced her to join them as a member. She became one of the Alliance's vice presidents, and remained in this position to the end of her life

Huda Sharawi, veiled ...

in 1947. She spent long years in the service of both organizations, advocating for education and health in Egypt. She helped build regular schools, vocational schools, and hospitals. She founded magazines in French as well as Arabic in which women's agendas were promoted. She offered prizes to Egyptian artists and worked hand in hand with the suffragettes of the Alliance. She held a weekly salon in her famous mansion ("La Maison de l'Égyptienne") where she entertained some of the greatest political and intellectual personalities of her time.

As Iman Hamam states in an article from the English weekly published by Egypt's main newspaper, *Al Ahram* (*The Pyramids*):

> Sharawi threw herself into nationalist politics only to discover that these left women more or less where they had started, the nationalists not being keen to open up male political monopoly to female competition. Once the nationalist struggle had achieved its immediate aims, women's concerns and grievances were left untouched and still lying on the table—and this, it might be added, is where some of them at least remain today.[26]

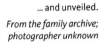

... and unveiled.

*From the family archive;
photographer unknown*

Women in this movement, Beth Baron writes,

relied on maternal authority and appealed to morality precisely because they had few options for making themselves heard. In spite of two decades of attempting to break into the political system, they had not yet obtained the right to vote, to run for parliament, or to hold office. Writing remained one of their few political weapons.[27]

My great-grand mother's legacy makes me think again of Egyptian myth. In *De Iside et Osiride*, Plutarch recounts:

The queen sent for her [Isis]... , and ... made her nurse to one of her sons. ... Isis fed the child by giving it her finger to suck instead of the breast; she likewise put him every night into the fire in order to consume his mortal part. ... Thus continued she to do so for some time, till the queen, who stood watching her, observing the child to be all in a flame, cried out, and thereby deprived him of that immortality which would otherwise have been conferred upon him.[28]

This suggests the paradoxical idea that good is concealed in evil. The wisdom of Isis includes both the light and the dark aspects of the mother, which are needed for the strengthening of life through (the psychological experience of) death. She thus expresses the wholeness of the psyche, which derives from the co-existence of opposites. Patriarchal societies, especially after the advent of monotheism, have given unilateral consideration to the light aspects of the feminine, thereby exalting maternal unconditional love and virginal innocence. By hiding or denying other aspects, such as feminine physicality, the need for independence, and the rejecting aspects of the mother, they have repressed them and pushed them into the dark alleys of the unconscious. These natural elements may suddenly resurface with a frightening aura. With this in mind, the "removal of the veil" is a self-explanatory symbol.

Is it in the richness of Ancient Egypt that other resources can be found—a richness that still lives in the genes and psyches of modern Egyptians, and that might offer ancient solutions for modern problems? Is this wishful thinking? The soul of Cairo is definitely connected to the elements of the earth and to the Great Mother. This is what, in my view, makes Cairenes light and resilient, capable of compensating the harshness of their lives with a great sense of humor. Cairo's position at the bifurcation of the Nile before the Delta, at the junction between Upper and Lower Egypt, and the self-explanatory fact that Egyptians fondly call their capital "the Mother of the World," are all elements that point to the positive relation to the Mother in the Cairene psyche. But, with the advent of Islam and with the consolidation of Christianity in what remained of the Roman Empire, patriarchal repression of the feminine worsened. Collective images of the feminine are virtually absent in Islam; the cult of Isis was repressed on all shores of the Mediterranean.

As Iman Hamam reports:

The only existing statue of a twentieth-century Egyptian woman, among a multitude of male writers, engineers, political activists and British colonialists, all of whom have their memorials, is apparently that of the singer Umm Kulthoum (1904-1975) in Cairo. With a roundabout—where her villa once stood in Zamalek—named after her, and a statue beneath some trees outside the Cairo Opera House, Umm Kulthoum's presence extends beyond musical confines. Indeed, like her male peers such as Saad Zaghloul, Mustafa Kamil and Talaat Harb, Umm Kulthoum gave human form to Egypt's nationalist struggle in the last century and to women's role within it. Other women activists, such as Huda Sharawi and Doria Shafik, and prominent actresses such as Aziza Amir and

Fatima (Ruz) al-Yusuf, also made their mark in the public domain. They, however, await memorialisation.[29]

The great twentieth-century diva Umm Kulthoum was beloved by 150 million Arabs, the star of the Middle East; to Cairenes she was simply *al-Sitt*, the Lady. Her funeral in 1975 surpassed President Nasser's, bringing over two million mourners onto the streets of Cairo. A national radio station is entirely dedicated to her songs and only comes second to Qur'anic recitation in popularity, even decades after her death. The rise of this woman—born at the turn of the twentieth century into mud-poverty in a delta village—to unprecedented celebrity could be viewed as a consequence of a compensatory readiness of the people to fill in the void left by the repressed feminine. When, in 1960, her voice trembled at the phrase from the song *"El-Atlal"* ("The Ruins"), "Give me my freedom / let loose my hands," she might have directly expressed the longing and the demands of Egyptian women for equal rights.[30] Significantly, a faceless statue of the Lady (who did not wear the veil) has been placed near the Nilometer on the island of Roda, in the garden right outside the museum dedicated to her. The continuing irony is that the statue sits in one of Cairo's rather hidden spots. A taxi driver complained of how modern musicians are "deforming" her songs, but she is there, near the water of the Nile, expressing in the shade the depth of Cairene men's longing for their anima. The Lady.

Here beauty has remained associated with the longing for reunification with the Great Mother, with a *participation mystique*. I recall deep emotion when, up the minaret of the beautiful Ibn-el-Tulun mosque, I

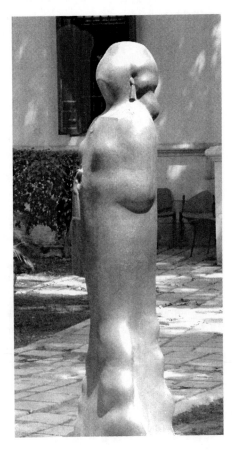

"Umm Kulthoum," by contemporary Christian Adam Henein.

333

heard the music of the Old City's awakening, the progressive spreading of the singing muezzins' voices calling out for prayer from innumerable minarets, and extending it beyond, into the City of the Dead[31] toward the desert, and into modern central Cairo toward the Nile. This phenomenon repeats itself daily. The frame of habit reinforces the sense of the sacred and of beauty. So why is this connection between beauty and its consecration lost to our modern souls? How can we reawaken a modern sense of beauty that connects us to the sacred in the everyday?

Humor may be a partial key to unlocking that door. I once was in Cairo's medieval centre, drinking a *shai* (tea) at the Fishawi coffee house. After some hesitation, I gave my shoes to a shoe shiner, who replaced them with a piece of paper under my feet. Before he left me barefooted, I blocked his way and asked him whether I could trust him to come back with the shoes. He smiled and replied that *he* was the one to worry, because I could run away with his precious piece of paper! This is but one example of Cairene irony, daily renewing itself. Lightness of spirit and a natural propensity for laughter and deflation are a way to open the door to play, common humanity, and the appreciation of beauty in everyday life.

As my half-Egyptian psychotherapist friend Martin Lloyd-Elliott put it,

Cairo carries a particular potency in its capacity to evoke imaginative reaction. I have yet to meet anyone who was indifferent to the city, even if they have never haggled in its *souks* or wiped dust off the glass of the rickety cabinet displaying *that* gold mask. Cairo is a legendary source of the alphabet in our collective imagination because pharaonic Egypt speaks so vividly to our souls through symbol, starting with those monumental and archetypal constructs at Giza.[32]

Egyptians haven't forgotten that only hearts as light as the feather of Maat (and today as the shoe-shiner's piece of paper!) will gain eternal life. So I end this journey through my inner Cairo, along the delicate thread of its oppositions, having recovered some semblance of wholeness through narration, with a prayer: "May the words of the Pharaoh (see the following poem) bless my soul and that of Cairo with their regal wisdom. Let the Mother of the World have a loving, wise Father by her side in the soul of Cairo and of all Egyptians."

AMENEMHET I (1991-1962 BCE)
On the day of his crowning

Fight for happiness
as do worthless men for power
and remember that love is the seed
and the fruit of joy.

Love others
so they may love you,
and love yourselves,
so you may love others.

You will be born fearless
because whoever gives you life
will find joy in being fertile.

You will fear neither
husband nor wife
because love will unite you
and love breeds no enemies.

You will bear no other fetters
than the golden chain of fondness.
Family bonds will not unite brothers
whose only affinity is of the blood.

You will not fear loneliness since
there will never be a lack of friends.
You will not fear idleness
since the New Egypt has need for
idleness as much as work.

You will not fear work
because you will find it congenial.
You might be born a fisherman
and yet become a scribe
or, born a farmer,
choose to become a warrior.

None will be overwhelmed by fields
too vast to till,
nor confined by narrow borders.
You will not suffer hunger
because barns will be filled with bread
for the lean years to come.

You will not be afraid of growing,
because the years will usher in
new horizons.
Nor will you be afraid of ageing
because you will gain new wisdom
at every horizon.

You will have no fear of death
Because you will remember
the other bank of the great river,
where you will be measured
according to the weight
of your hearts.[33]

To Edoardo and Guglielmo: may they discover, one day, their father's Egypt.

My heartfelt thanks to Cristina for her joyful presence and support during this journey across the shadows and the lights of the country of my childhood.

Notes

1   C. P. Cavafy, *Collected Poems*, trans. Edmund Keeley and Philip Sherrard, ed. George Savidis, rev. ed. (Princeton University Press, 1992):

The God Abandons Antony

When suddenly, at midnight, you hear
an invisible procession going by
with exquisite music, voices,

don't mourn your luck that's failing now,
work gone wrong, your plans
all proving deceptive—don't mourn them uselessly.
As one long prepared, and graced with courage,
say goodbye to her, the Alexandria that is leaving.
Above all, don't fool yourself, don't say
it was a dream, your ears deceived you:
don't degrade yourself with empty hopes like these.
As one long prepared, and graced with courage,
as is right for you who were given this kind of city,
go firmly to the window
and listen with deep emotion, but not
with the whining, the pleas of a coward;
listen—your final delectation—to the voices,
to the exquisite music of that strange procession,
and say goodbye to her, to the Alexandria you are losing.

2   Thomas Stern Eliot, "Burnt Norton," *Four Quartets* (London: Faber and Faber, 1983), p. 13.

3   Moloch, "king," the name of the national god of the Ammonites, to whom children were sacrificed by fire. The city's soul is here disfigured in an archaic vision. Moloch-anima is a provocative description of how children in suburban areas are used as "workforce," their childhood being sacrificed to the Moloch of desperate economy.

4   "Cairo is, according to the United Nations, the most densely populated large urban area in the world. Overall, this city packs 70,000 people into each of its 200 square miles, confining its citizens more tightly than does the bristling little island of Manhattan. In central districts like Muski and Bab al-Sha'riyya the density is 300,000 per square mile, a figure that soars in some back streets to a crushing 700,000. By and large, these numbers throng not tower blocks but alleyfuls of low-rise tenements that differ little from the housing stock of, say, a thousand years ago. In such conditions, with three and sometimes five people to a tiny room, families take turns to eat and sleep. Schools operate in up to three shifts, and still have to squeeze fifty, sixty or sometimes eighty students to a class." Max Rodenbeck, *Cairo: The City Victorious* (London: Picador, 1998), p. 16.

5   Henry Miller, *Stand Still Like the Hummingbird* (New York: New Directions, 1962), p. 181.

6   "A vast res extensa of throw-away, suburbs, exurbs, divisions and subdivisions; beltways, strip, squatters, squalor, slums, and smog, choked traffic on clogged arteries," and the homeless, the monstrous bureaucracy embodied in numerous buildings of "faceless offices of restless despair." All of that is also Cairo. James Hillman, *City & Soul*, ed. Robert J. Leaver (Putnam, CT: Spring Publications, 2006), pp. 17-18.

7   The quotations in this paragraph are taken from: *Cairo, A Divided City*. Images and text by photographer Andrew Turner, and audio by reporter Hagar Cohen (Background Briefing, Australian Broadcasting Corporation, ABC Radio National, February 1, 2009). Link: http://www.abc.net.au/rn/backgroundbriefing/stories/2009/2477394.htm.

8   The Beatles, from the album *A Hard Day's Night*, single "Can't Buy Me Love," authors: Lennon/McCartney (recorded at Pathé Marconi Studios, Paris, 1964).

9   Albert Cossery and Michel Mitrani, *Conversation avec Albert Cossery* (Paris: Editions Joelle Losfeld, Diffusion, Harmonia Mundi, 1995).

10   Umberto Galimberti, *Le cose dell'amore*, "Amore e trascendenza" (Milano: Feltrinelli, 2004), pp. 22-23.

11 Luigi Zoja, *Giustizia e Bellezza*, "Il palazzo e la piazza" (Torino: Bollati Boringhieri, 2007), p. 29.

12 A minority of a few million Coptic Christians lives in the country.

13 "Other places may have been neater, quieter and less prone to wrenching change, but they all lacked something. The easy warmth of Cairenes, perhaps, and their indomitable insouciance; the complexities and complicities of their relations; their casual mixing of sensuality with moral rigour, of razor wit with credulity. Or perhaps it was the possibility this city offered of escape in other worlds: into the splendours of its pharaonic and medieval pasts, say, or out of its bruising crowds on to the soft, gentle current of the Nile—even if the tapering lateen sails of the river felucas did now advertise Coca-Cola." Max Rodenbeck, *Cairo*, p. xiii.

14 Gail Thomas, Introduction to James Hillman's *City & Soul*, ed. Robert J. Leaver (Putnam, CT: Spring Publications, 2006), p. 12.

15 Miles Copeland, *The Game of Nations* (New York: Simon and Schuster, NewYork, 1969), p. 174-177.

16 This may hold analogies with the figure of the Caudillo in South America, which, as shown by Octavio Paz, has its roots in Moorish Spain: "En el centro de la familia: el padre. La figura del padre se bifurca en la dualidad de patriarca y de *macho*. El patriarca protege, es bueno, poderoso, sabio. El macho es el hombre terrible, el chingón, el padre que se ha ido, que ha abandonado mujer y hijos. La imagen de la autoridad mexicana se inspira en estos dos extremos: el Señor Presidente y el Caudillo. La imagen del Caudillo no es Mexicana únicamente sino espanola e hispanoamericana. Tal vez es de origen arabe. El mundo islámico se ha caracterizado por su incapacitad para crear sistemas estables de gobierno, es decir, no ha instituido una legitimad suprapersonal. El remedio contra la inestabilidad han sido y son los jefes, los caudillos." Octavio Paz, "Conversacion con Claude Fell," interview in *Plural 50* (1975), reprinted in *Vuelta a El Laberinto de la Soledad y otras obras* (New York: Penguin, 1997), p. 311.

17 Gilles Kepel, *Jihad: The Trail of Political Islam*, "Building Petro-Islam on the Ruins of Arab Nationalism" (London: I.B. Tauris, 2004), p. 61.

18 A sect attributed to Muhammad Ibn Abd-al-Wahhab, an eighteenth-century scholar from what is today known as Saudi Arabia, who advocated purging Islam of what he considered innovations in Islam. In the early twentieth century, the Wahhabist-oriented Al-Saud dynasty conquered and unified the various provinces of the Arabian peninsula, founding the modernday Kingdom of Saudi Arabia in 1932. This provided the movement with a state. Vast wealth from oil discovered in the following decades, coupled with Saudi control of the holy cities of Mecca and Medina, have since provided a base and funding for Wahhabi missionary activity.

19 The English term "sublation" derives from Hegel's German term *Aufhebung*.

20 Wolfgang Giegerich, "Islamic Terrorism," in *Jungian Reflections on September 11 / A Global Nightmare*, ed. Luigi Zoja and Donald Williams (Einsiedeln: Daimon Verlag, 2002), pp. 66-67.

21 In 1979, Sadat issued a strong warning against religious interference in Egypt's political life. There must be, he said in a speech at Alexandria University, "no religion in politics, no politics in religion."

22 The "Khawaga," as my Italian father was called, means Western foreigner, a title of wary respect tinged with ironical contempt.

23 This abysmal nature of the Origin is wonderfully described by Rainer Maria Rilke in his "The Third Elegy," in *Duino Elegies* (Einsiedeln: Schweiz Daimon Verlag, 1997), trans. David Oswald.

24 "The Egyptians of every period in which they are known to us believed that Osiris was of divine origin, that he suffered death and mutilation at the hands of the powers of evil, that after a great struggle with these powers he rose again, that he became henceforth the king of the underworld and judge of the dead, and that because he had conquered death the righteous also might conquer death." Sir E. A. Wallis Budge, *Egyptian Ideas of the Future Life* (Whitefish, MT: Kessinger, 2004), p. 27.

25 It is described in a hymn to Osiris dating from the eighteenth dynasty in the following passage: "She (Isis) sought him without ceasing, she wandered round and round the earth uttering cries of pain, and she rested (or alighted) not until she had found him. She overshadowed him with her feathers, she made air (or wind) with her wings, and she uttered cries at the burial of her brother. She raised up the prostrate form of him whose heart was still, she took from him of his essence, she conceived and brought forth a child, she suckled it in secret, and none knew the place thereof; and the arm of the child hath waxed strong in the great house of Seb." Budge, *Egyptian Ideas of the Future Life*, p. 36. Seb, god of the Earth, has been equated by classical authors with the Greek Titan Cronus or Saturn—meaningfully, the god of patriarchy, later associated with melancholy. See Raymond Klibansky, Erwin Panofsky, and Fritz Saxl, *Saturn and Melancholy: Studies in the History of Natural Philosophy, Religion, and Art* (New York: Basic Books, 1964).

26 Iman Hamam, "The ladies protest," Al Ahram weekly online (20-26 October 2005, Issue No. 765). Link: http://weekly.ahram.org.eg/2005/765/b07.htm.

27 Beth Baron, *Egypt as a Woman: Nationalism, Gender, and Politics* (Los Angeles: University of California Press, 2007), p. 182.

28 Quoted in Sir E. A. Wallis Budge, *Legends of the Gods* (Charleston, SC: Biblio Life, 2007), pp. 160-161.

29 Hamam, "The ladies protest."

30 Descriptions of Umm Kulthoum in this paragraph are freely inspired by Max Rodenbeck, *Cairo*, pp. 328-331.

31 The City of the Dead replicates, after millennia, the dead city of Memphis with its line of pyramids, on the other, eastern, shore of the Nile; the cult of saints and patrons (interestingly, many of them Shiite, while Egyptians define themselves as Sunnis sympathetic to Shiism) and their feasts (*mawlids*) have replaced the ancient pantheon. At the great cemetery of Cairo, generations of guardians actually live with the dead, in houses above the tombs. Ceremonies for the burial and preparation of bodies have maintained a lot of pharaonic tradition. The vicinity of the dead is typically Egyptian, and positively un-Arabic.

32 Martin Lloyd Elliott, personal communication (April 2009).

33 Origin unconfirmed.

17 Arrival in Berlin

JOERG RASCHE

1742

❦ PLAYING OUT OF POCKET ❦

In the summer of 1742, a slim Jewish boy arrived in Berlin. He was poor—hardly a penny to his name. He came by foot along the sandy highway from Dessau, wanting to try his luck in the royal residential town of Berlin. Around the city there was a trench and a wall with gates. Soldiers stood at the gates, wearing colorful uniforms.

The boy was told that he had to enter the city through a special gate, not the famous Brandenburg Gate (which still exists today); Jews were allowed only through the smaller Oranienburg Gate. There the guard asked him what he had learned and how he planned to make a living. The boy answered: "*Ich spiele aus der Tasche*"—"I'm playing out of pocket," which means by juggling or sleight of hand. The guard let him pass—he knew this was one of the few business activities allowed for Jewish people. The clever boy—who, by the way, was a bit crooked—might have had in mind something more with his answer than was apparent. He was none other than Moses Mendelssohn, who was to become one of the most distinguished philosophers of the Age of Enlightenment, and the founder of one of the most respected Jewish family dynasties of Berlin and indeed of Germany. Many years later, facing similar questioning at a city gate in Potsdam, where he had been invited by King Frederick the Great, he is said to have given the soldier the same answer: "*Ich spiele aus der Tasche*." When the king asked him why he

Mofes Mendelsfohns Examen am Berliner Thor zu Potzdam

"Moses Mendelssohn am Rosenthaler Tor," by Daniel Chodowiecki.

responded in that manner, Mendelssohn explained: "Because it is easier for a juggler to gain access to a king than it is for a philosopher."

"Playing out of pocket"—to pretend something, to play with illusions, maybe to build a great structure out of ideas and thoughts, or maybe to cheat somebody—this is a motto that fits Berlin pretty well. Berlin is a city in a region of sand and swamp, erected on marshy ground without mineral resources or any other natural advantages. ("Berlin" is a Slavic word probably meaning "swamp of bears.") The motto of another famous philosopher living in Berlin, Arthur Schopenhauer, elaborated on the theme of "playing out of pocket": "*Die Welt als Wille und Vorstellung*," or " the world as an effort of will and imagination." Without iron acts of volition and imagination, Berlin would never have come into existence. And yet another Berlin philosopher, Georg Friedrich Hegel, took "playing out of pocket" a step further and became a spokesman of the Prussian kingdom by naming the king "Der Weltgeist zu Pferde"—the world's spirit on horseback.

Berlin owes its reputation as a modern and open-minded city to Frederick the Second, also known as "the Great" or "The Old Fritz" (1712–1786). He, too, "played out of pocket" brilliantly in the creation of Berlin, although he preferred to stay in his pastoral idyll of Sanssouci ("without care or worry") in the town of Potsdam, 20 kilometers southwest. He lived on his estate with his dogs, hosting guests such as the French philosopher of the Enlightenment, Voltaire. Frederick played the flute and planned his wars. He didn't like Berlin, where people always seemed to be in a bad mood, and were not so fond of dukes and kings. "Grouse in your homes, but do your duty," he would say to the people. This attitude became a guiding principle of the so-called Prussian Enlightenment. On the one hand, it encouraged free and independent thinking, the "emancipation from self-made minority"; on the other, it insisted on blind obedience to the state, held up as a Prussian virtue and creating the conditions for later disaster when Hitler, claiming to be a follower of King Frederick, led the blinded German people into catastrophe. (Bad moods, by the way, are still characteristic of Berliners today—and it is not hard to pick up the habit. In most cases there is absolutely no reason for it. I'll come to that later.)

One can play "out of pocket" only as long as there is something *in* the pocket—as the world is now learning anew. Old Prussia, like modern Berlin, had its share of illusions coupled with vast pockets. This story goes far back, to the great-grandfather of Frederick the Second, the so-called Great Elector (in Berlin, everything has to be "Great"). The Great Elector lived from 1620 to 1688. He was tolerant in religious affairs, but he used to spend more money than he had (he welcomed the industrious Huguenots into Berlin, for example, but the decision also turned out to be very profitable for him). Much the same was true of his heirs, the kings of Prussia since 1701. They had an expensive hobby: they loved soldiers. This was especially true of the father of Frederick the Great, the so-called *Soldatenkönig* (soldier's king), who would watch soldiers drilling in their colorful uniforms or running and playing hide-and-seek in the forests. He also liked to send them to fight, for example against the Swedish, who in those years occupied the shores of the Baltic Sea. Above all he loved his "long boys" of the garrison in Potsdam, each of whom was at least 180 centimeters in height. He bequeathed this oversized army to his son Frederick the Second, who had to continue financing it.

Although this Frederick the Great preferred to play his flute, he went to war again and again, filling his pockets with booty. Prussia became powerful but disliked, as his successors followed the same course. When Austria was no longer as attractive as a possible enemy, France was given that role (in 1870-1871), and later the role was filled by the entire world (1914-1918 and 1939-1945). Nevertheless, it speaks well for Old Fritz that he also promoted religious tolerance, and that he introduced the potato to Prussia so that people had something to eat. Even today, you can always find fresh potatoes left on his tomb in Potsdam in thankful memory.

1970

⟨ COLD WAR ⟩

When I arrived in Berlin in the summer of 1970, I also had to pass through a city gate. I gained access from West Germany by traveling over the "Transit Highway" through the Soviet sector, known as the German Democratic Republic (GDR), coming through the checkpoint of Dreilinden. The guard here was wearing the uniform of the East German army and spoke with a Saxon accent. He exercised meticulous control and inspected the baggage of everybody who wanted to pass. I was asked whether I was carrying wireless equipment or weapons. In my baggage there were only some books and clothes—a student in the '60s didn't need more. Like Moses Mendelssohn, we were "playing out of pocket" and wanted to change the world.

In fact, it was essential that those who came to Berlin in the 1960s be willing to play "out of pocket." Berlin was in a state of shock, and shocking to behold. An immense grey city, half-dead, cluttered with many ruins from the war. The facades of many houses that had survived the bombings were without balconies and ornaments, because the government had ordered such decoration removed due to the danger of falling parts. This added to the melancholic and ugly look of the streets. In 1970, there were neither new cars nor colorful advertisements to be seen in the streets. Nevertheless, "West Berlin" had a special charm. The old gas lamps were still in the streets, buzzing during the night; there were big, cheap flats to rent; and there was a very lively student scene. Every weekend there was a demonstration. To a 20-year-old dreamer from Bavaria, Berlin seemed gigantic and incredible. It was "the big world" personified, and it was as if the war had ended just the day before. It was a living encounter with the past.

Before I arrived, the wall encircling the western half of the city had been built by the army of the GDR in just a few days in 1961. There were watchtowers, dogs barking, sometimes even shootings. In the districts of Kreuzberg or Grunewald, the border was actually in the middle of the River. GDR navy gun-ships patrolled the water. If you wanted to swim in the summertime, you were not allowed to cross the middle of the river. The ducks didn't care about such imaginary lines.

We adjusted to the existence of the Wall in those years and didn't spend a lot of time thinking about its presence. Living in West Berlin was like living on an island or in a greenhouse. If we wanted to get away for a break, we took an airplane to Greece, which was less expensive and less stressful than traveling on the Transit Highway, with its pot-holed pavement and the provocative soldiers of the GDR.

Nevertheless, for many of us, life in West Berlin remained provisional for a long time. For many years, I felt that I hadn't truly arrived in Berlin. I didn't find rest. I joined those who dressed themselves as working-class people from the 1920s; we wore red flags and promoted world revolution in our leaflets. It was as if we had unknowingly slipped into the costumes of the Weimar period, the time before the Nazi dictatorship. The fact that on the other side of the Wall the grand experiment in communism had failed decades before, and had been transformed into a brutal apparatus of suppression, didn't really interest us. We were much more focused on the current guilt of the United States, which was waging its Vietnam War, and behind that, on the guilt of our parents for their participation in the so-called Third Reich. We regarded it as our duty to be vigilant about militarism and nationalism in the world. The emotions swirling in us were powerful, and sometimes we found ourselves face to face with the horror of the Nazi era in the events happening around us and in our confrontational protests with police. The police became our unwitting partners in an unconscious game—which now seems like a bizarre reenactment of the Nazi rise to power with its paranoid atmosphere and (at that time) the absence of a resistance movement. Ironically, West Berlin, outpost of the United States in the Eastern Bloc, became the stronghold of the student anti-war movement in Germany. But any young person on the other side of the Wall who heard about our protests against the war and tried to do the same was immediately imprisoned in Bautzen and tortured by the Stasi.

1937

{ ARCHETYPES: MARCHING IN THE STREETS? }

When C.G. Jung arrived in Berlin in 1937, he said to his traveling companion, Barbara Hannah, "The archetypes are walking around in the streets here." Jung could be very sarcastic. (He had just published "Wotan," which some read as a statement in favor of Hitler, although just the opposite was the case. Certainly the ironic style of his essay provoked misunderstanding, especially in the German original. But the Nazis marching around shouting *"Sieg Heil!"* were precisely *not* incarnations of the archetypal figure Jung had described in his essay;

they were not the soldiers of the Germanic *Brausegott* or storm god that Jung was fascinated with in those years. Jung knew well the dangers of mixing up the archetypal level of the unconscious with social reality. To conclude that Jung was equating Hitler with the anarchic Wotan remains a profound but not uncommon misinterpretation.)

Beginning in 1933, the National Socialists had established an almost-perfect totalitarian state. All other organizations were either forbidden or *gleich-geschaltet* (streamlined). A system of spies that skillfully used terror tactics to suffocate any public or private resistance to the Nazis was firmly in place. "When the world was the guest" of Hitler as host of the 1936 Olympic Games, the National Socialists didn't want any of their weak spots to be exposed. So in an effort to present themselves as "gentlemanly," they stopped the public terror for a while. One could even listen to jazz music in the bars at Kurfurstendamm (Charlottenburg, the traditional pleasure district of Berlin), even though this form of music had been stigmatized and forbidden as *entartet* (degenerate). The world was willing to accept the illusion because it hoped Hitler would fight Stalin.

The mass events of the Olympic Games were part of the Nazi program of seduction that included the use of archaic images and symbols, of which the *Hakenkreuz*, or swastika, is only one example. Symbolic manipulation also induced a kind of self-hypnosis in the many Germans who were following their "leader." Today it is hard to imagine how this happened. But the misery in Germany after World War I, coupled with the global economic collapse of 1929, were major factors that contributed to the German vulnerability to psychic possession. In addition, the population had become accustomed to a general increase in violence that was part of the disorientation after the collapse of the old patriarchal structures of the German empire in 1918. Democracy was just an infant in Germany, and had not taken hold. Old cultural complexes surfaced in the German psyche again and were used by the Nazis, most notably the projection of the scapegoat onto the Jews. Anti-Semitic propaganda and terror worked closely together. My attempt to understand those connections is not intended to excuse the behavior of most Germans in the years of the "Third Reich." Rather, I want to emphasize how shocking it is to realize how thin the skin of civilization can be in relation to a barbarian monster that lurks not far beneath the surface. As Berliners, we have experienced this shock to our very bones. Unfortunately, we are not the only ones who need to learn this bitter lesson.

Berlin is a city that shows this shadow in many places. One of the most impressive is the memorial for the murdered Jews, the Holocaust Memorial, which is close to the Brandenburg Gate, at the back side of the new US embassy.

The Eisenman memorial.

Photograph by the author

It consists of a field of more than 2,000 blocks of stone that, in their silence, convey a powerful message. One can spend hours here—thinking, remembering, weeping, taking heart. The memorial was designed and built by Peter Eisenman, an American architect who was the son-in-law of Joseph Henderson (the late senior Jungian analyst of San Francisco). It is touching to me that Eisenman quoted Jung in an interview he gave during the construction of the memorial, referring to Jung's statement about the need for mankind to face and integrate the collective shadow, as much as is humanly possible. It was unusual to hear Jung quoted in Berlin, where he is still often viewed as part of the shadow that led to the Holocaust, and not as part of the solution to the problem of violence in the world.

1911

When Sabina Spielrein arrived in 1911, the period of *Gründerzeit* (the Founding Epoch), the city was in full splendor. It was as if Berlin had been conjured up from the ground in only a few decades, mostly with money that France had to pay Germany as "compensation" after its defeat in the war of 1870–1871. (France later took its revenge, after Germany's defeat in 1918.) This French money helped build the newly-founded German Empire in 1871 (the "Second Empire," after the first empire in medieval times). Berlin was built on a large scale with tree-lined avenues, broad alleys, many parks, and grand buildings, behind which were narrow, dark backyards and rear flats for working-class people.

Originally from a Russian-Jewish family from Rostov-on-Don, in southwest Russia, Sabina came to Berlin from Vienna, where she had just passed her medical exams and worked in the circle of Sigmund Freud, beginning to free herself from an intense attachment to C.G. Jung. As a young woman, she had been sent to Switzerland in 1904 for treatment of severe hysteria, becoming a patient of Dr. Jung's at the Burghölzli. Her therapy resulted in the cure of her hysteria, and she was eventually able to study medicine. But her deep relationship with Jung caused a disturbance between the two of them and Jung's wife, and she sought consultation with Dr. Freud in Vienna, after which she moved to Berlin, where she lived until 1914.

In Berlin, Spielrein rented a flat in the Moabit district, close to the Havel River and the Tiergarten. She met the medical doctor Pawel Scheftl, and they married in 1912. In 1913, she gave birth to their first daughter, Renata (the "reborn"), in Berlin; Eva, the second, was born in 1926, after Sabina's final return to Russia.

Sabina Spielrein's influence on the newly emerging form of psychoanalysis was immense. With her Jung experienced, for the first time and with blunt clarity, the power of transference and the entanglements it could engender. She was the first and one of the most important *anima* influences in Jung's life, and it is easy to conjecture that Spielrein was the very source of the notion of the *anima*. I believe that Jung's love of Sabina was as deep and powerful as any he ever experienced, and I imagine that it was as bewildering and impressive as his relationship and break-up with Freud. Just as Spielrein had a profound effect on Jung, however, her later paper on "destruction as a condition for becoming" influenced Freud and may well have been a source of inspiration for his concept of *thanatos*, the death instinct.

Sabina Spielrein was the "first Jungian" in Berlin. The German Association for Analytical Psychology even placed a memorial plaque at her residence at Thomasiusstrasse 2. Today, gazing at the sad postwar façades of Thomasiusstrasse, one can feel the weight of the tragedy of Spielrein's life. With the help of her husband, she left Berlin when World War I began, then worked as an analyst in Lausanne and Geneva (where she became the analyst of Jean Piaget in 1922). In 1923, she decided to return to her homeland, where the Bolsheviks had seized power. In the first years of her return, she was allowed to work as an analyst, but in 1936 psychoanalysis was forbidden by Stalin. Both of Spielrein's brothers disappeared in the gulags. Sabina and her two daughters were murdered in 1942 near Rostov-on-Don by German soldiers, who slaughtered all the Jewish inhabitants of the city.

1933

⁋ EMIGRANTS ⁋

For Sabina Spielrein, Berlin was only one step along her way. Sometimes it seems to me as though her fate may have been that of analytical psychology itself, which has had a difficult time feeling at home in Berlin. Many of the Berlin analysts who followed Jung left the city during the 1930s because of the Nazi rise to power. They lost their permission to work, and their lives were in grave danger. The fact is, there were few Jungians in Berlin during the entire period of the Weimar Republic and the Nazi dictatorship. On the other hand, the Freudian Berlin Psychoanalytic Institute, founded in 1933 out of the Psychoanalytic Policlinic, became home to some of the most well-known Freudians of those times: Karl Abraham, Max Eitingon, Hanns Sachs, Sandor Ferency, Melanie Klein, Siegfried Bernfeld, Otto Fenichel. Nevertheless, the first C.G. Jung Society was founded in Berlin in 1931. Jung himself came to Berlin on occasion to teach seminars. The building that housed the original Jung Society still exists (after World War II it became Harnack House, a mess hall for U.S. officers, and today it is owned by the Max Planck Society).

In 1933, Freud's books were burned in a public square near the university and the Opera House (*Staatsoper*). Psychoanalysis was forbidden. The Psychoanalytic Institute was closed, although some of its equipment was salvaged and shipped to New York. As its replacement, a kind of "mixed institute" was established, the so-called Göring Institute, where a "German psychotherapy" was to be taught. The building doesn't exist anymore.

From among the few Jungians in the city, living and practicing in the Wilmersdorf district in the west part of old Berlin, some later emerged as very important contributors. One was Ernst Bernhard, who was full of enthusiasm for Jung's ideas. He did his training analysis with the Freudians Sandor Rado and Otto Fenichel, but also with Käthe Bügler, a student of Jung. Because of the National Socialists, he emigrated to Italy to work as a Jungian analyst, but eventually still ended up in a concentration camp because he was Jewish. Thanks to the intervention of the indologist Giuseppe Tucci, Bernhard was liberated, but he suffered for many years from his traumatic experiences. He became the founder of analytical psychology in Italy and was the analyst of many important artists, including the famous filmmaker Federico Fellini. A memorial plaque in honor of Bernhard has been placed at Meierottostrasse 7.

Other important Jungians who left Berlin to work elsewhere were Gerhard Adler (who went to England), Werner Engel and Heinz Westmann (New York), Max Zeller (Los Angeles). James Kirsch, who, like his later wife, Hilde, was in personal analysis with Jung in Switzerland in the 1930s, had his psychiatric clinic in Berlin at Olivaer Platz 3. He was famous for his medical work, which led to a saying at the time: "*Sind's die Augen, geh zu Ruhnke, ist's die Birne geh zu Kirsch*" ("If you have problems with your eyes, go to Ruhnke [an ophthalmologist]; if you have problems in your 'bulb' [the word for psyche in Berlin jargon], go to Kirsch"). Kirsch left Berlin in 1933 for Tel Aviv and London, finally settling in Los Angeles.

Erich Neumann, born in Berlin in 1905, also left the city, eventually emigrating to Tel Aviv. He knew Jung in 1933, and was deeply linked to him throughout his lifetime. A memorial plate for Neumann and his wife Julie has been placed in Pariser Strasse 4. Neumann was very critical of Jung's silence about the existential threat to the Jews in Hitler's Germany, especially after 1938. His book, *Depth Psychology and a New Ethic,* published in 1948, is a critique of Jung as well as an encouragement to readers to accept and integrate their own shadows and take responsibility for their own unconscious.

In October 1938 Jung gave a very interesting interview to an American journalist in which he tried to formulate a psychiatric diagnosis of Hitler.[1] He said that Hitler was similar to some of his patients who heard voices and misunderstood reality, and that he was "the voice of the German inferiority complex." It is likely as a result of this interview that Jung's books were forbidden in Germany and the occupied countries, and that he himself was placed on the "blacklist."

During the dictatorship and the war, there was only one Jungian analyst left in Berlin who deeply understood clinical work. Käthe Bügler, who had studied with Jung, unofficially conducted the few training analyses that took place during that time. She herself was classified as "half-Jewish," and lived in a hiding place to avoid being sent to a concentration camp. To get an idea of how crazy and dangerous the situation was, one must try to imagine that Käthe Bügler was protected by her partner, Richard Heyer, himself a member of the Nazi Party. Heyer, too, had been a protégé of Jung's, until Jung discovered Heyer's sympathy for fascist ideology and ended his friendship with Heyer in 1941. Käthe Bügler survived the war.

❧ UNIVERSITY LIFE AND A LOST LIBRARY ☙

After the end of World War II, Berlin became an isolated island in the hostile territory of the so-called socialist state, the German Democratic Republic or GDR (*Deutsche Demokratische Republik*). Surrounded and secluded by the Wall and by the threatening communist bloc, there was no real future for West Berliners, and many who could manage to do so left for West Germany. But while the factories disappeared, the students arrived.

The United States generously gave their front-line German city a new university, the Free University of Berlin (*Freie Universität Berlin*)—although it has not been easy for Berlin to renew its great, pre-1933 scientific tradition. Max Planck had discovered the quantum nature of the radiation of light in Berlin, and Otto Hahn and Lise Meitner had discovered radioactivity here. Albert Einstein had worked in Berlin until the Nazis eliminated his professorship and threatened his life. Scientists such as Hermann von Helmholtz and medical doctors such as Ferdinand Sauerbruch, Rudolf Virchow, Robert Koch and many others had established and sustained the high reputation of the Berlin universities.

The traditional Humboldt University (also known as the *Universität Unter den Linden*), founded in 1810, keeps alive the memory of the brothers Alexander and Wilhelm von Humboldt. Alexander was famous for his discoveries in South America and for his reports from faraway countries; his scientific curiosity and his collections opened the spirit of discovery of the world for Berliners. In a sunny courtyard, a huge ginkgo biloba tree is growing that is said to have been planted by Humboldt himself. In the middle of Unter den Linden ("under the linden trees"), King Frederick the Great rides a horse atop his monument. The entire assembly of squares and buildings, the so-called Forum Fredericianum, was built on his orders. In his lifetime the university had not yet been founded, and the statue looks across to the beautiful building that was the city palace of his happy younger brother, who had not been occupied with the affairs of government, and had plenty of time to play his cello and enjoy long breakfasts. When the monument was erected, it was joked that the busy king liked to look into his brother's window to see if he was still having breakfast.

On the other side of the square is the old opera house of the king (*Staatsoper Unter den Linden*), where the courageous Daniel Barenboim has been the conductor for decades. But the splendor of the site is darkened: in the square next to the opera house, the National Socialists organized the burning of books in 1933 to symbolically bring an end to all "non-German" intellectual life—and this included psychoanalysis. In the very spot where the pyre burned, there is today a subterranean room beneath the pavement. One looks down through a clear pane of glass into an underground "lost library" with empty shelves, created as a memorial by Israeli artist Micha Ullman. Here one can see clearly the loss that Berlin has suffered, and I believe that in this spot, the city is truly rediscovering a sense of itself. Berlin's soul is all about loss.

⟨ MITTE: MIDDLE AND CENTER ⟩

Today, when one arrives by train in Berlin, it is at the new central station—"new" because it was designed and built only after the unification of East and West. Berlin had never had a central station, and it has become a symbol of all that did not exist before.

In Berlin, as in Paris and London, the trains used to arrive from all sides of the city and end outside the center. There was the *Ringbahn*, which encircled the larger center (the so-called *S-Bahn* because of its speed), the dense network of the subway (*U-Bahn*, for underground), and one line of the *S-Bahn* that crossed the city from west to east. Nevertheless, after the *Wende* (the "turning," the coming down of the Wall), officials decided to build a connecting line through the city from north to south with a central station, the Berlin Hauptbahnhof, in the middle. The result is one of the most impressive buildings in the new Berlin, simultaneously a living symbol of the city's rebirth and of an almost archaic meaning. In legend, cities of the ancient world such as old Rome were designed by a founder king, who would make a big circle with his plow. Inside the circle he would plow a cross, and in the middle of the cross he would mark the location of the center of the city.

Berliners say *Mitte* (middle), which in German sounds more neutral than *Zentrum* (center). *Mitte* is an understatement, signifying little more than an almost accidental middle. From its origins, Berlin was a more accidental cluster of dwellings, villages, and little towns like medieval Cologne, Spandau, Charlottenburg, Schöneberg, and so on. But centered in the Mitte area of Berlin, the new cross of the railways and the new central station have created a more formal spatial pattern that overlaps the old irregular patchwork layout of the city. The center now truly functions as a *Zentrum*: not only do trains come and go through the Hauptbahnhof, but it is the government center of a unified Germany. At *its* center is the Reichstag, a postmodern palace for the German chancellor, and the buildings housing the ministries and secretaries of the state. In contrast, the former Federal Republic of Germany had no center. Its capital, Bonn, was little more than a modest seat of administration for a federation. The new Berlin and its Mitte have become the true center of a modern Germany.

{ WHAT IS MITTE? }

While at West Berlin's center are the *Gedächtniskirche*—the ruin of a church built in memory of Emperor Wilhelm II—and the Zoological Garden, East Berlin's Mitte includes the historical area behind the Brandenburg Gate, the famous Unter den Linden boulevard, the noble *Gendarmenmarkt*, and the Isle of the Museums. The baroque castle of the former Prussian kings, which had mostly withstood the bombing of World War II, was demolished by the Stalinist barbarians working with German Communist politician Walter Ulbricht in an attempt to erase the memory of Prussian militarism. It was replaced with a huge, flat processional square, to parade their own army and the armies of the Soviet bloc. The enormous East Berlin television tower, with a rotating restaurant in the middle of a big glass sphere, was built within 1 kilometer of the Brandenburg Gate, the Wall, and West Berlin, as the symbol of the supremacy of socialism. In East Berlin, people used to joke: "What shall we do if the television tower falls down?" Answer: "We can take the elevator to the West." Seen from West Berlin, the East Berlin television tower has a funny characteristic: when the sun shines onto the sphere from the west, the reflection of a huge shining cross appears. West Berliners called it "the revenge of the pope," enjoying the fact that either coincidence or the architect were having their fun with the Communist rulers.

The pope had other, prior reasons to be angry with Berlin. A huge church, the so-called Berliner Dom, stands in Mitte. Emperor Wilhelm the Second (who resigned in 1919, after World War I) built this church to serve as the chapel of his

353

palace, and ordered that it be the same size as St. Peter's Basilica! As emperor, Wilhelm was also the head of the Prussian Lutheran Church (just as the Queen of England is head of the Anglican Church), and he wanted to make Berlin the "Protestant Rome." The result is monstrous, to my taste. Nevertheless, it is worth a visit because it has been perfectly restored. The height of the interior dome is indeed the same as that in Rome, and whereas Peter, Paul, and the other Catholic saints occupy privileged places in the dome of St. Peter's, the protestant heroes Luther, Calvin, Melanchthon, and the Elector of Brandenburg (one of Emperor Wilhelm's ancestors) dwell in the heavens of the Berliner Dom. Today it is hard to believe that this challenge to the Catholic Church was actually constructed and taken seriously.

The cathedral does house a remarkable, romantic pipe organ, which survived the World War II bombing raids because it was protected in its side niche from the collapsing dome. The cathedral itself later escaped the fate of the neighboring Castle of the Kings only because the architect of the parish was able to fool the socialist officials into believing that blowing it up would threaten the surrounding museums with collapse from rising groundwater. Whether this story is true or not, it has become part of the folklore. The organ, still played today, was played by Max Reger in 1909, and in 1935, by a young organist at the wedding of Herman Göring to Emmy Sonnemann, a marriage for which Hitler served as witness. The organist was the famed Heinz Wunderlich, now living in Hamburg, who personally told me his story. He only played the cathedral's organ once more, many decades later, for the reconsecration of the restored church and its dome. On that occasion, he played his own composition, "Sonata Tremolanda Hiroshima," about the horror of the war.

To recover from the hypertrophic splendor of the cathedral, one might have a coffee in the nearby Hackescher Markt Square (a station of the S-Bahn) or visit the Neue Synagogue in Oranienstrasse, an astonishing modern Moorish structure built by the architects Eduard Knoblauch and Friedrich August Stüler (1857–1866). Another option is to drive to Prenzlauer Berg and visit the synagogue in Rykestrasse, which was built at the same time as the cathedral. Its beautiful interiors survived the burning of the synagogues by the Nazis only because they feared the neighboring houses would catch fire, too.

1989

⟨ THE OPENING OF THE WALL ⟩

A Jungian colleague who grew up in East Berlin told me how happy she was to escape to the West. She had fled in the midst of the Cold War, in a very dangerous and carefully arranged operation, with the assistance of a secret organization. If discovered, she would have been killed. One day, she was informed that the next day she had to hide herself in the trunk of a car parked on a quiet side street in East Berlin. Once the trunk was closed, it was not opened again until several hours later. She found herself in Grunewald, a forest district in West Berlin. Everything had gone well. Now she could go on to study and receive her analytical training. Later, when she was able to afford a car, it had to be a sport roadster. I asked her why, and she answered: "Because it has no trunk."

The socialist regime survived for several dark decades until its collapse. But East Berliners did not have to wait until the television tower fell so that they could go to the West "by elevator." On the night of 9 November 1989, an overworked public relations officer in the GDR mistakenly declared in front of live television cameras that the border to West Berlin was now open. It was a slip with gigantic consequences. Immediately a migration started that eventually led to the unification of Germany and the collapse of the Soviet Union. In the preceding months, there had been demonstrations in the bigger cities of the GDR, especially in Leipzig, as well as a mass flight of East Germans to the West German embassy in Hungary, which was on neutral ground (Gorbachev finally agreed to allow them to evacuate to Western Germany).

As an intuitive person, I was not at all surprised by what happened. Two weeks before I had had a daydream in which I saw the former *Potsdamer Platz* (Potsdam Square) as it had looked before the war. In its current reality, it was little more than big, empty space of ruins close to the Wall in Mitte; but I knew how the old square looked from photographs, and in my daydream I saw the old *Normaluhr* (the clock tower) and the tramway as it had existed in the famous "roaring twenties," before the Nazis came to power. My brief vision was like an old movie; and I said to myself: "Everything can change."

I remember that night exactly. I live close to the famous Kurfürstendamm avenue in Charlottenburg, in West Berlin. I was awakened by an unusual noise. When I discovered what was going on, I roused my wife, saying, "The Wall is

open!" She declared me to be crazy and went back to sleep. I got dressed and went down to Ku'damm (as we call the street). At that very moment, the first "Trabbies" (the little cars of the GDR) drove by. They honked, and people cried, roared, and wept. All the nightclubs were open and champagne flowed freely. Spirits were high. There were also many tears. The atmosphere was like a church service and a festival at once. We couldn't believe what had happened. I met some students from Leipzig who by chance had been in East Berlin when the incorrect announcement was made that the Wall was open. We became friends, and they visited us again months later. We were so happy.

With the *Wende*—the turn—of that night, everything changed for us. Instantly many more people were on the streets. Buses coming to West Berlin from Poland were full. The new arrivals looked around in amazement, and bought what they could. Although the Wall was still standing, it was no longer watched over and secured. Every day, more and more of it crumbled as people attacked it with whatever tools they could find. One could hear the picking noise from far away. One day our nine-year-old son called us to say that he was in East Berlin on Alexanderplatz! He had slipped through a self-made hole in the Wall with some friends, and then had gone by tram to the centre of East Berlin, just for fun. It was as if he had called us from the moon. So it began.

❧ A MODERN CITY IN TRANSFORMATION ❧

Today I like to take my Berlin guests for breakfast at the television tower on Alexanderplatz. One needs to get there by nine in the morning to avoid the long lines at the elevator (the famous elevator). Up in the sphere of glass, the restaurant turns slowly and you can take in the whole city quietly while you sip your coffee.

From here, it is as if one is looking toward New York in the West and Moscow in the East. Indeed, while the city was divided, we had regarded West Berlin as more like New York than part of Germany. And East Berlin, the capital of the GDR, looked like any other socialist capital, such as Minsk, Uralsk, or Dnepropetrovsk. One can see all of this very clearly from the television tower as it rotates from west to east. The old districts of Berlin, reconstructed in their former shapes after being demolished in the war, look from above like a chaotic and likable mixture of roofs and yards. The buildings of the socialist capital to the east present a forbidding assembly of monotonous and monstrous rectangular cubes. Further east, at the far end of the former Stalin Alley, one sees two towers with green domes in a modified "gingerbread style" (*Zuckerbäckerstil*), much as in Warsaw or Moscow. From there, the road goes straight on to Warsaw and the former Soviet Union.

As the restaurant continues to turn slowly, the Havel River comes into view, a glittering band of light from the east passing through the city towards the west. A moment later, the beautiful baroque part of the city appears, with its squares and palaces. City officials plan to restore the baroque castle—or at least its façades—and build a modern exposition building behind it. Not long ago, this square was still called the Palace of the Republic, which featured an ugly and ornate prestige project nicknamed *Erichs Lampenladen* (Erich Honnecker's "lamp shop"), which has been recently torn down. Westward, the view continues with the Forum Fridericianum, Unter den Linden, and the Brandenburg Gate. This section also features the Philharmonic, built by Scharoun, with its impressive acoustics and its yellow façade (called "Circus Karajani"). Behind this is the new *Gemäldegalerie* (art gallery), which houses the biggest and best collection of Old Masters in Germany. Next is the *Tiergarten*, a zoological park and the "green lung" of the city. Far on the western horizon lies Charlottenburg, with its tall radio tower (built in 1926, it is the oldest in Europe). Beyond the Brandenburg Gate is the *Reichstag* with its new glass dome, and closer to view is the Berlin Cathedral and Museum Island, with the Pergamon Museum—which houses a fabulous Hellenistic altar of battling giants, and a complete city gate of Babylon.

From the heights of the television tower restaurant, tiny trains go by on their elevated tracks from the Berlin Hauptbahnhof to Friedrichstrasse, Hackescher Markt, and Alexanderplatz. The miraculous Moorish dome of the Neue Synagogue appears nearby, close to an original baroque church tower.

Berlin, a city of four million people, stretches far out in the flat country. And everywhere there are building sites. Berlin is undergoing a rapid and profound transformation; it is becoming one of the most attractive cities in Europe.

Arrival?

{ WHICH BERLIN DO YOU MEAN? }

Today Berlin is a once again a magnet. Out of the capital of the National Socialist nightmare and the ruins of Nazi Germany, out of the divided city of the Cold War, a glittering modern metropolis has appeared as if overnight. The joyous reunification was a miracle that today belongs as much to the myth of Berlin as the memory of the Wall. Many people are attracted to the city—artists, students, criminals. Berlin is the open door to Eastern Europe. Night life goes on around the clock. Never-ending parties for young newcomers sometimes become drug traps. Even though Berlin is one of the safest cities in the world, one should not feel free to go everywhere. There are high unemployment and racial tension, both of which can make for unrest and danger. But Berlin has the second biggest tango scene in the world after Buenos Aires, and is home to the largest Turkish settlement outside of Turkey.

Berlin is not, has never been, and will never be finished. It is a permanent building site. Sometimes it feels like a fiction, existing in a permanent "as if" state, a huge project born out of will and imagination (*Wille und Vorstellung*). Like Moses Mendelssohn, Berlin still can seem as though it was born by "playing out of pocket," or born out of the struggle for power, or even born out of the death instinct (*thanatos* or *Todestrieb*). From the genius of brilliant scientists, artists, and musicians, from the battle of the giants on the Pergamon Gate, to the confusion of Babylonian languages, everything can be found in Berlin. Even love stories (including as my own).

There are special sites that express something of the spirit of Berlin, maybe even something of its soul. For me, there is the square with the "lost library," and the big auditorium of the Philharmonic, built for democracy and for the shared love of music. I also recognize Berlin's soul in the deeply moving field of stone blocks that soberly memorialize the murdered Jews of Europe. Above all, Berlin for me is a challenge. It is open to many things that other cities would not permit—although it is also a metropolis that easily confuses and leads one astray. To arrive at one's own self, one's own *Mitte*, is not so easy in Berlin.

Arriving in Berlin? To go away, maybe to come back?

I have been living in Berlin, where I met my wife, since 1970. It is where we raised our three wonderful children. Often, however, I feel as though I haven't really arrived. No, that is not exactly true; recently I had a feeling of arriving at my *Mitte*—really here, really in Berlin. Not in the way that John F. Kennedy experienced it when he said, "I am a Berliner," but in a very modest way, from inside. It was as if I said to myself, quite simply, "I like this city."

Not long ago, I was on my way to Mitte to give a paper in the Mendelssohn-Remise in Jägerstrasse, close to Gendarmenmarkt, where the Mendelssohn family used to live. The composer Felix Mendelssohn Bartholdy also lived here. He grew up in Berlin, the grandchild of the old philosopher Moses Mendelssohn. I went by U-Bahn to the Stadtmitte station and climbed the stairs. It was dark at the top, and in the cold winter air, I heard the sounds of a Christmas market. Close to the exit of the metro, the baroque columns of the so-called German Cathedral towered into the night. Together with the French Cathedral, it flanks the Gendarmenmarkt—a square that is said to be the most beautiful in old Berlin. The architecture is splendid, solemn, and cheerful, all at the same time. Then my heart opened. I don't have any other way to say it.

After my speech, I went to a wine tavern called Lutter and Wegner at the Gendarmenmarkt. Here in the 1830s, E.T.A. Hoffmann had his wine before he worked on his writing late into the night. I thought of Hoffman's fairy tale, "The Golden Pot" (*"Der Goldene Topf"*), which tells the story of the little snake, Serpentina, and the student Anselmus who comprehends nothing, and of how he finally discovers his great love. And I was happy.

Notes

1. H.R. Knickerbocker, "Diagnosing the Dictators: An Interview with Dr. Jung," *Hearst's International Cosmopolitan* (January 1939). A German translation was published in the Swiss magazine *Traits* in December 1941.

18 Whispers in a Bull's Ear: The Natural Soul of Bangalore

Kusum Dhar Prabhu

I have often been told that Bangalore is seen as the "new India." This is Bangalore's persona, the face it shows the world, but in the last fifteen years I seem to have been slowly becoming an inhabitant of another Bangalore. This other Bangalore has been claiming me, gradually, invisibly.

I have also been awakening to how my own persona relates to how I live; there is much that I keep secret and hidden about my relationship with my city. I share my life in the *"other Bangalore"* with very few people. In conversations with other Bangaloreans, I participate in the collective mourning about the decline of Bangalore, expound on the grand themes that belong to the depressive discourse in a city—traffic jams, pollution, crimes, rising real estate prices, outsiders. There is something addictive in these conversations about the decline of the city. Repeating them often enough, we are convinced that the city has lost its soul and that we know why.

This is archetypal: you find it in every city today. I discover, however, that they said the same thing fifty years ago. In 1961, the *Deccan Herald* writes: "The beauty of the city is already a thing of the past ... New slums ... add to the growing squalour." It speaks of "haphazard growth and the emergence of ugly structures all over the city. Miserable roads, poor lighting, sad state of the parks ... "

I realize that I have never really entirely believed what I and others were saying in these conversations. It was true but not real. I said what was socially appropriate to say, and carried on with my life in the other Bangalore. In this Bangalore, there are other stories and conversations. Today I want to tell some of those stories. Today I feel that, like a map that cannot see itself, this city awaits those who will read it differently to the world.

Shiva in
the tower.

*Photograph
by the author,
digitally
processed by
Paru Ramesh*

The Hound and the Hare:
Nature's Template of Modernity

Each person has a myth, a story that connects to the beyond—in traditional language, something that God wants of them. Each city, each region, too, is carried by a mythological fantasy, a specific form in which the "absolute," the "vast," the unknown wants to be localized, made concrete. All major cities start with a myth.

What happened in Bangalore? Let me begin in the middle.

In 1962, Nehru, then Prime Minister of India, visited Bangalore. Here is part of his speech to the Bangalore Municipal Corporation:

> Most of the cities of India remind one certainly of the present, certainly of the future, but essentially of the past. But Bangalore, as I said, more than any other great cities of India, is a picture of India of the future, more specifically because of the concentration of science, technology and industries in the public sector here. ... Most of the old cities represent ... history whereas your great city represents the future we are moulding ...
>
> It is also one of the most beautiful cities of India.[1]

362

In 2005, Adam Russ has this to say in his travel guide of places not to visit: "Bangalore, a city whose soul has been clinically removed in the name of corporate efficiency. ... Everything about the host culture has been watered down, Westernized or otherwise screwed up ... "[2]

Now let me go back to one of the beginnings.

There are references to Bangalore in inscriptions dating back to the ninth century. One such inscribed stone stands neglected and forgotten in the courtyard of the Shiva temple in Begur, a village off the Hosur road, a six-lane highway leading to Electronic City, the capital of the IT empire of Bangalore.

However, the history of Bangalore as a planned city begins with Kempegowda, its chieftain founder. One day, as Kempegowda walked from Yelahanka, north of Bangalore, in search of a suitable place for the foundation of his new seat of power, he saw the following: A hound was chasing a hare, which stopped running, turned on its pursuer, and started chasing him.

He understood this instantly as a sign that his search was over.

Kempegowda was able to decipher the image that nature showed him and to follow the tracks of this hare into the future city of Bangalore, because this particular image was the equivalent of an "initial dream" for the city-to-be. As in analysis, an initial dream offers a psychic blueprint, a building plan of future developments in the soul.

In the collective memory of those centuries this particular event, the pursued hare turning around and chasing its hunter, happened at places that were destined to be centers of great power.

Kempegowda would have remembered that nearly two hundred years earlier, in the third decade of the fourteenth century, the destiny of Hampi, the capital of one of the greatest empires of the south—the Vijaynagar empire, of which he was a feudatory—was also announced to its founders, Hakka and Bukka, through a similar vision. While out hunting, their dog started chasing a hare. At a certain point, that hare turned around and started pursuing the hound. They reported the incident to Vidyaranya, their guru, who told them that this was nature's voice guiding them to their center of power. That was the beginning of one of the most culturally innovative and vibrant empires of the south.

In India, as in other ancient cultures, the birth and subsequent fate of a city were never products of human desire or rational planning. Larger heavenly forces were seen to play a key role in this process. The creation of a new city under a new dynasty was the start of a new age. It was the expression of cosmic energies finding a new home on earth, an occasion for something eternal to enter human time. In its essence, the foundation of a new city is seen as a reenactment of the creation of the world by Brahma the creator God. A city gives a definite divine impress to the original land, which is the body of the *vastu purusha*, the primal man.

Fantasizing about the site of his new capital, Kempegowda is in a creative reverie that functions like a charged field drawing to itself the spirit of the place. He is on a vision quest in search of the new center that will also be the beginning of a new empire, a quantum leap from feudal consciousness and attitudes to a more independent, self-determined consciousness.

Whatever becomes conscious appears first as an image. Nature offers him the first glimmerings of modernity. The hare pursuing the hound activates his heroic energies, pushes him across a new threshold of consciousness. From hunted hare to chasing hare, nature offers him images of a transformation of energy from feudal vassal to independent ruler. It activates what in Indian psychology we call the *vira bhava*, heroic awareness. Kempegowda is invited to take on his fate as culture hero, the one who will lay the foundations for a new order and power. It is the essence of modernity—a self-conscious break with the past and a search for new forms of expression. From forever being a subject, the hare now turns into an actor, able to turn back, to reflect, to face his fate and even challenge it. It is the irruption of linearity in the eternal cycle.

Kempegowda calls his new capital *gandubhumi*, land of heroes. This is the founding myth of Bangalore. The first rulers of the Vijaynagar empire also had to make a similar leap in consciousness, from an authority derived from vassal-ship to a more autonomous one. This myth, then, shimmers in the background, inviting different and varied reenactments over time.

The first structures of Bangalore, in 1536, are a mud fort and temples. Kempegowda asked for permission to build a fort and was told: mud, not stone. Stone is not allowed by the Vijaynagar rulers as it seems an incitement to grandiose and expansionist energies!

This is probably the first embodied example of the city's motto: *solpa adjust madi*. Over a period of time, outsiders to Bangalore are initiated into this secret of the city's gentle mixture of creativity and conflict. This is the mantra of Bangalore, which non-locals repeat with an ironical half-smile. In Kannada, the official (but not the most widely spoken) language of the state, it has several meanings. Literally: "please adjust a little." Or "I will try and understand where you are coming from, but be patient while I am working on it." Or "I know you would like to murder the so-and-so who parked his car so that you can't get yours out, but if we push and pull the other cars around we will manage to get yours out."

In these three words is expressed a universe of adaptation and balance, a heart that appeals to what is soulful in the other, a readiness to listen, and an invitation to attend to the problem at hand with relatedness. All qualities that will come in handy at the call centers! The fact that the heart of behavioral ethics in this city includes an English word ("adjust") is of course what makes Bangalore what it is, a center of enlightened cosmopolitanism.

From Hare to Bull: The Totem Animal of Bangalore

Along with the mud fort, Kempegowda made sure that the gods were also well housed. Close to where he saw the hare turn on the hound, in a locality called Basavangudi (*basava* is the Kannada word for bull), he constructed a temple dedicated to the bull.

My first visit to the Someshwara temple in Ulsoor, in East Bangalore, was to attend a wedding. The young couple sat on the temple floor. Behind them on a swing sat Shiva and Parvati, the divine couple, reflected to infinity in the mirrors on either side of them. India speaks best in images. This one spoke of the archetypal union that every marriage tries to actualize, with varying degrees of success.

Since I didn't know many people present, I was free to look around. I saw a large bronze Nandi, Shiva's bull, the animal carrier of his being, facing a lingam, as is the case in every Shiva temple. Then, as I watched the file of people streaming into the inner sanctum, I noticed that many of them, on coming out, away from the main image, stopped at the bull, bent down to whisper in his ear, and then moved on—women, men, girls, young boys.

I watched, too, as a woman held her small infant to the bull as if to be blessed by him. I was transported in that moment to the image evoked by Laurens Van der Post's beautiful description of the bush woman holding her infant high up in her arms to the stars. She was asking of the star to take the little heart of her child and give him something of the heart of a star in return. It seemed that this mother was asking for a similar transfer of energy from the bull. Where in our psyche do we take this vulnerable part of ourselves and offer it to the protection of the bull, I wondered? What are people whispering in his ears?

Over the next few years, however, I started noticing that there were many, many bulls in this city—that the bull made house calls, to check on the soul of his people. From afar I would hear the sound of the *nadaswaram*, strident and plaintive in the same breath. A man would then come and stand outside with his bull, adorned with shells and beads and clothed in an intricately embroidered cloth. "Is everything alright with these good people?" the man asks the bull. The bull considers for a moment, then nods. We offer some money, the children stroke the bull, and he moves on to the next house.

Whispering to Nandi.

Photograph by the author

All over the city, at any given point there is a bull visiting a home and offering the blessing of his presence. When he visits in this way, he is considered to be filled with the spiritual essence of Shiva, carrying the god invisibly—god-possessed. When he nods and affirms that the household is doing well, it is Shiva's message he is passing on. In this form, he is called Nandishwar, bull god.

What does this relationship between god and bull offer to those who honor it? Over the years, I have noticed that there are many Shiva temples, more than a hundred, in Bangalore. In every Shiva temple, Nandi is the gatekeeper, facing the image in the innermost chamber. They are never separated from each other. Each sees the other at all moments.

The phrase "limbic resonance" comes to me. It is a complex and constant exchange of information between two beings about their respective states and each's adaptation to the other's state, largely nonverbal. Activated by the intimate gaze, it is what makes looking at another so compelling. It allows for a deep personal connection, well below the conscious level. It facilitates emotional harmony, draws emotions into congruence. It is the mechanism of bonding between mother and child, but also between human and animal. It is the mechanism of love.

This look speaks of their sharing an ancient accord, the hidden but constant relationship between the animal and the divine, between dense matter and condensed spirit. The stories and hopes that are whispered in the bull's ear speak of the need and longing to find a place where feelings can be expressed and accepted by a power larger than us.

In the Indian psyche, it is never really acceptable to feel too strongly. We are told in many different ways that feelings don't really get us anywhere—that because things are not permanent they are somehow not real. In Bangalore, the emotional climate is cool, laid back. We are not encouraged to get too intense about anything. The temperateness of the weather is a geographical clue to the emotional temperature of Bangaloreans.

Nandi, somehow, is the place for expressing all that is not allowed in the collective. Nandi exudes a safe, imperturbable solidity. He will somehow find a way to pass on the whispers of my soul to the transcendence of Shiva—very remote and ascetic; keeping all love and entanglements at a distance; refusing to get into relationship, marriage, partnership of any kind; focused on his inner contemplative experiences.

Here, in the heart of the city, we are being reminded that our human fears, anxieties, and hopes do not fall on deaf ears . They are heard by this magnificent bull, earthed in his body, open to the messages of the instincts. In his presence, our own openness to our instincts and longings comes alive. When we gaze at this image of Shiva and Nandi looking at each other, does it perhaps activate our capacity to hold within ourselves the two ends of this spectrum?

As I reflect on this relationship, I am walking in the park close to home and bump into Yamini, who is a dancer and yoga teacher. She tells me that she is going to be performing Siva's *tandava* dance at a place deep in the interior of Karnataka. "And Nandi?" I ask her, not really expecting an answer. She replies, "Don't you know it is to Nandi's beats that he dances his most inspired dances? The *jathis* composed by Nandi are his favorite ones." (*Jathi* is the sequence of rhythmic syllables that sets the beat for the dancer.) I sense a growing excitement in myself. What is it like to live a life to a rhythm set by a bull?

Rhythm is the natural way in which all life energy develops. Shiva's dance is the most explicit representation of the movement of life and matter, the way planets move at a certain speed and balance, the rotation of the earth, waves, plants, seasons, the rhythmic pulse of nature. Shiva as dancer—his rhythmic play is the source of all movement in the cosmos. The purpose of his dance is to release countless souls from the illusion that only what is "out there" is real. The dance dislodges fixity—fixed ideas, fixed interpretations. We are initiated into the terrifying fluidity of on-the-spot truth. The place of the dance is within the heart. According to a Tamil commentary: "The dance of nature proceeds on one side; the dance of enlightenment on the other. Fix your mind in the center of the latter." I imagine Nandi would have suggested locating ourselves in the center of both!

Through its rhythm, dance brings together the opposites of order and ecstasy. As I reflect more deeply, it comes to me that the image of this relationship could nourish the soul of the city, run like oxygen in its veins. But this is a city where since two years ago dance has been banned, perhaps because a state government intent on asserting the rights of a regional, less Western identity has forgotten the archetypal sacred origins of dance. In identifying dance with "Western culture," the state seems to be experiencing cultural amnesia.

On the twenty-fourth of January 2009, activists of a Hindu fundamentalist organization entered a pub called Amnesia in Mangalore, Bangalore's coastal cousin in the same state, and assaulted young women who were dancing "obscenely." These fundamentalists, too, seem to have forgotten the frenzied, ecstatic dances of the early Indus civilization, when people danced to honor and embody the energy of Shiva, the archetypal dancer. Aggression, among many other factors, belongs to the survival instinct. This aggression seems to be coming from a local identity that feels increasingly unsure of its survival in a globalizing, homogenizing world.

In India, it has come as a shock that Bangalore, that most Western of all cities, is the capital of the first south Indian state to have, since 2008, a Hinducentric government in power, the Indian People's Party (Bharatiya Janata Party, or BJP). I don't pretend to share in the consternation and fear of repressive morality that is being expressed by some sections of Bangalore society. I feel that the rise to power of the BJP in Bangalore is a political expression of the unvoiced longing of many modern Indians to reconnect with their religious roots. Under the spell of secularism—which is indeed an archetype—we lose the sense that religion is an instinct in the human being. And no instinct can be neglected for long without consequences. Unless we address this longing in depth we will swing between religious fundamentalism and secular rootlessness.

The Greedy Bull

But there is a dangerous bull, too, that has something to say about how we live our lives in this city. The legend is as follows.

In the village of Sunkenahalli, close to where Kempegowda saw his hare, people used to grow groundnuts. As the crops ripened, a bull would come and devour them. Angered, a farmer hit the bull, which turned to stone. The shocked farmers then had a temple built in honor of Nandi. To their horror, the granite image kept growing. They turned to Shiva, who told them that there was a trident buried in a nearby field that should be planted on the head of the bull. This was done, and the image stabilized. From then on, a groundnut fair has been held there every year, until today.

To me, this legend speaks above all of things growing dangerously beyond proportion. It speaks of excess, a lack of balance. The bull that eats too much offers us an image of our own overconsumption. It is a greed that leads to unchecked growth. This is the bull that started devouring Bangalore in the 1990s.

Bangalore became global. From being a sedate, dignified "pensioners paradise," it suddenly grew young. In the first manic years of the boom, which began in the 1990s and continued till 2008, everything was about speed: fastest growing city in Asia; fastest population growth, from three to seven million; fastest bandwidth. A devouring bull was eating up every available piece of real estate. Tank beds, which used to be part of a connected system of water tanks for the city, were being appropriated and built on.

The legend, however, also offers an image of the restoration of balance. Shiva's trident (*trishul*), in Hindu symbolic understanding, is a means of dealing with evil. The three prongs are also understood to represent the three qualities of nature, desire, action-and-wisdom. It is a weapon—an instrument of control, which is desperately needed.

The first attempt at dealing with the bull turns it to stone. All growth stops. This is not what the farmer then—or we today—want. It is the first, immediate reaction to this devouring development of the city: stop! But this is not about rational control or repressive denial. The balance we need comes from ancient understanding and wisdom in animal ways, possessed by Shiva as *Pashupatinath*, lord of animals. All drivenness has an unreflecting, compulsive, bestial, matter-only quality. The trident is the power of discriminating thought applied to drivenness. When we ask ourselves what our soul really needs, we have placed Shiva's trident on the bull's head. When we ask where in our city we can create soul-renewing places and activities, then this trident is doing its job.

Perhaps we would consume a little less if the hunger in our soul was being fed. We don't build a temple for those forces that enter our lives only once. The danger of the bull is one we have to tend to many times, and this temple speaks to us of a way of doing so.

Call Centers: Listening to the World

In the 1990s, with the new economic liberalization policy of the Indian government, the representatives of a new empire came to Bangalore: multinational corporations. Newspapers chronicled the arrival of every entrant with great fanfare: Yahoo had set up a design center; Intel unveiled its new chip—the newspaper article showed the manager holding it to the camera like a sacred icon; there was a religious awe in his face as he held it aloft. Microsoft, Lucent, Intel, Texas Instruments, Hewlett Packard, Dell—in addition to the local empires of Infosys and Wipro, these were the names we read about.

Overnight, the architecture of the city changed. If the film *Modern Times* were made today, it would be set in a call center—Chaplin dancing his way through the cubicles, mouthing outrageous disinformation to callers from around the world seeking customer service, now outsourced to India. The identity of modern Bangalore and its international visibility has a lot to do with call centers. Since the 1990s, it is call centers that have dominated the psyche of Bangalore.

Everyone in this city knows someone who knows someone who works in a call center, which have made it possible for large numbers of young people to leave their parental homes in other parts of India and come to Bangalore. They offer the possibility of a huge step towards a new life and a new consciousness, far from the family matrix. It is at this point that the psyche of Bangalore is the most open to the world outside India.

To work in a call center is to submit to an initiatory experience. It is a call to transformation that I don't want to prejudge as only negative. You have to change everything about yourself that has marked your identity. One way to see it is as a *total depersonalization in order to impersonate*. If I work in a call center as an "agent," I have to change my name and the way I speak, learning to speak English in the specific accent of the region of the world where my company does business. What I am and how I speak otherwise are of no value in my workplace; they are indeed disadvantages. I have to change the entire rhythm of my sleeping and waking cycles, because I need to listen to someone in another part of the world. It is about adaptation in every possible way.

This is a far cry from the secrets whispered in Nandi's ears. The call center Nandis have to listen to shouts about computers that don't work, luggage that goes missing. In public consciousness, they have come to symbolize everything that is wrong about the new Bangalore: call center vehicles drive too fast and push all other cars off the road; people who work in call centers lead a promiscuous life; they are the entry point for the "wrong" values that are destroying our culture. Call centers are the new villains in Bangalore culture.

Auto Rickshaws: Carriers of History and Trauma

Each god has its own animal carrier (*vahana*). If you are human and want to move in Bangalore, a three-wheeled vehicle called an auto rickshaw (or auto, for short) is your *vahana*. Everyone in Bangalore seems to have had an encounter with an auto driver. People get emotional when they describe such exchanges. There is rage, outrage, various degrees of irritation, helplessness, and a sense of righteous vindication when they are finally taken to their destination without being overcharged.

Who are these rickshaw drivers, and what—other than you—are they carrying for our city? They carry memories, I discovered. In the *other* Bangalore, auto rickshaw drivers don't only overcharge, drive rashly, or refuse to take you on board; in this *other* city, they reveal themselves in their primal form as Krishnas, driving my chariot in the battlefield of daily life.

In the person of the auto rickshaw driver, I have met beings who responded to my innermost concern of the moment as if I had shouted it aloud. After a Pakistan-India cricket match in 2004, when the whole city, including me, was celebrating India's victory, I saw a procession of Hindu militants marching in their trademark shorts, beating drums and chanting. This troubled me profoundly, and I carried the unease into the next day, when I went into town. On my way back, I had a Muslim auto driver, long beard flowing with tranquil piety from a rectangular face. We stopped at my gate, I opened my purse to pay him, then I just stopped and looked at him. He looked back and, in spite of myself, I heard my voice asking him in Hindi, "What is it like for you to live in this country at this point?" He looked at me—really looked; then he slowly turned off his engine and settled in his seat. He said, "Islam teaches us that whichever country we are born in or choose to live in becomes holy for us."

I insisted. What about the present anti-Muslim signs? Did he not wish to be elsewhere? He quietly repeated that this was his home and that, rather than concern himself with injustices from others, he had to focus on his own struggles. Each day he was reminded that on one shoulder lived a *shaitan* (devil), and on the other, a *farishta* (angel). Each gave different counsel on how to act, and sometimes it was one, sometimes it was the other who proved more persuasive. He spoke of his daily wonder at Allah's creation, at the amazing perfection of every form of new life, from a baby to a plant. For the next forty minutes he spoke of a life lived according to Islam, and it sounded uncannily similar to a life lived listening to soul.

As a Kashmiri Hindu, I can sometimes hear in parts of my psyche the voices of exile, sorrow turning to hate. This auto driver connected me to that part of my psyche that knows of the deep love between Kashmiri Hindus and Muslims, that remembers the common language that once protected both from the assaults of pain-generated violence.

From another Muslim auto driver come memories of the Islamic heritage of Bangalore. There is a sense of pride as he talks of Lal Bagh, one of the finest botanical gardens in the country, set up by the Muslim rulers Hyder Ali and his son Tipu Sultan. Here trees and plants from all over the world testify to Bangalore's botanical cosmopolitanism: Tipu, the great modernist, asked every ambassador to foreign lands to bring back a tree- or flower-spirit. Lal Bagh celebrates global diversity, not a homogenizing global energy. But with this driver's expression of discreet pride comes also pain at the deliberate "forgetting" of Tipu. He remembers from his childhood that Hyder Ali's sword used to be displayed at Lal Bagh, but that today "no one even knows that it was he who started the garden."

He goes on to tell me that Tipu's summer palace in Bangalore has been totally neglected by the state government. For many Muslims in Karnataka, Tipu is the symbol of their community's sense of participation in the history of the land. When he is honored through being remembered, then they as a community also feel they belong, that they are not perpetual "outsiders" or destroyers of a Hindu way of life. They are then not condemned in perpetuity to carry the projected energy of rabid religiosity.

Tipu was an early carrier of the global inclusiveness and openness that marks the Bangalore of today. He was at ease in his faith, and could extend the same ease to other faiths. As the ruler of Mysore, he honored in many ways the Goddess Chamundi, who was the guardian deity of the city. All the important rituals associated with her worship were continued. The tiger that she rode became in many ways Tipu's carrier, too. He was known as the Tiger of Mysore, and was famous for the mechanical tiger—designed for him by French engineers—which devours a British soldier. I remember an older Jungian in Zurich who once spoke of India being the land where Allah and Kali could coexist. My sense is that Tipu was one of the few leaders who made this possible. When he lives in our collective memory, then we are able also to accept that Islam is one of the multiple identities that *all* Indians can draw upon and lay claim to; that the Muslim is an inseparable self for the Hindu, and if we forget this, then we are condemned to violent and traumatic reenactments.

I know the religion of my driver through his visiting card—a large square pasted behind him, facing me, introducing him through his name, address, and blood group. And I see that my consulting room extends to the passenger seat of the auto. In listening to the driver's grief and sense of exclusion, something changes for both of us. I sense that it is important for him to be heard by a "Hindu"; that soul happens when painful feelings are allowed expression between two strangers; that Bangalore is a city where such exchanges are possible between two "outsiders," both of whom now feel more at home. He is one of the many in Bangalore who opens his mouth to speak of a life *beyond, beneath, above,* of another life that is trying to take up existence in this one.

My driver one day is an older man who is driving fast, cursing other drivers, his body angry and twisted. We stop at a traffic light and I ask him how long he's been driving. Thirty years. "You must have seen many changes." He sighs and starts remembering. As this happens, his body becomes less angry, his face loses its aggressive thrust, there is a softening.

He giggles like a schoolboy as he remembers a woman known as the Begum of Ulsoor (a central Bangalore quartier). She sold tickets at the English cinema nearby, and shooed them off when they came near. "These films not for you," she said, "*Your* films are at the Naga theatre."

"This is where we played cricket"—he shows me, pointing to a street overflowing with rush hour traffic. Daily life does not allow them to mourn the loss of their city. They are cut off from their grief—and we know so well what happens when we lose touch with our feelings, are not allowed to feel: the refusal to carry passengers, the overcharging, the rudeness ... the rage.

Boiled Beans and the Earth Mother

At different spots in Bangalore, you come upon two trees tied to each other with threads, as if giant invisible hands were playing cat's cradle with them. As you pause, you notice that images of different gods are placed at the foot of each of the two trees. Then you realize that all these images are damaged in some way—a cemetery or hospital or nursing home of the gods.

Cemetery of the gods.

Photograph by the author

When you ask questions about the place, as I did, you are told that these are places where snakes live under the ground. Over the years, I have noticed that these threaded trees and cemeteries have increased. Why are the broken images not simply put in a plastic bag with the rest of the garbage? They have been placed there with care, not discarded. They testify to the existence of the *other* Bangalore, expressing an important form of collective respect for rituals that have become unimportant in the modern collective. Such places emanate a deep longing: these gods are irreplaceable, and must not be lost.

Tying threads around what is holy is an ancient ritual practice, creating a sacred space, a *temenos*, a vessel that protects and holds together. Snake, tree, and thread belong to the ancient cult of the mother goddess. In this space, people acknowledge the existence of a dark, non-rational energy, which brings protection and relief from a world governed by factual data and technical knowledge. When I linger in such places, I am reminded of humble beginnings.

The most popular and widely accepted origin of the name Bangalore comes from the story of the hero warrior who arrives exhausted and hungry at the house of an old woman. He asks for food, and is told that she has only some boiled beans to offer. "Will you eat?" she asks him. He accepts gratefully, and in honor of this life-saving, soul-restoring food, he names the place *Benda kal uru*, or the town of boiled beans—which became Bengaluru, and later Bangalore. I think this is the preferred version of the city's name because it speaks to our need for nourishment from the old woman, a personification of the earth mother.

Those threaded spaces are charging spots for the psyche. Here, parts of us awaken that know the earth is sacred because it is the body of the goddess; that this goddess is our mother, who nourishes us with the secret of her fecundity and creativity, if we allow ourselves to listen; and that all her creatures teach, if not everyone learns. It is a reminder that the rational mind is an important but miniscule part of our total awareness. Our exhaustion in the business of daily life and our hunger for things of the soul find recognition in this *temenos*.

Here, as in the anthills, which are also tied with threads, the earth listens to us. In the *other* city, anthills are called the ears of the earth. In this space, I can feel the pulse and life of the city as a quiet seer of Bangalore, Amrish Varma, felt it. According to those who knew him, Amrish Varma possessed a sort of clairvoyance about the past and future of Bangalore. The city, he said, was of great spiritual potential because it was situated on an invisible energy grid possessing great power. People like him were able to see through the *maya* of the physical city to the subtle body of Bangalore, the city imagined from beyond this world and dreamed into life and existence. In such a view, Bangalore exists as an archetypal reality, and the actual city is the coming into material existence of the archetype.

The spiritual energy of Bangalore was also fed, according to Amrish Varma and other seers, from the nearby Nandi Hills, which for centuries have been home to meditating *rishis*. Theirs is a map of Bangalore that shows the path taken by the Goddess Chamundi as she chased the buffalo demon Mahishasura to Mysore. The demon is said to have planted explosive energy at a certain point in the center of Bangalore. A very tall building that was to be put up there was originally designed with twenty-five floors, but if that had happened, they would have had to dig to a level at which the explosive energy would be activated. The plan was revised to twenty-four floors, and the underground charges were left undisturbed.

If I share this story with the inhabitants of modern Bangalore, I will get indulgent smiles. The inhabitants of the *other* Bangalore don't smile. They know that under the concrete lie unknown and unpredictable forces, and we can be grateful that the plans were revised. They know about the energy body of Bangalore.

If you look at a map of the city, you will see two major arteries running somewhat parallel to each other—Hosur Road and Kanakpura Road. The former is the "information highway" leading to Electronic City. The second has become a sort of "wisdom highway," as over the years several spiritual centers have been built along it. Perhaps this is what is meant when people speak of South Bangalore as a spiritual magnet. For me, however, it is at these earth altars, found at any point in Bangalore, that I stop and recharge myself. Here certain images and thoughts arise. The water supplied to our city comes from the Cavery River, the most sacred river in the South, and I realize with a sense of wonder that each day the river reaches me through my tap—that I bathe in it every single day.

The Two Cities

In November 2006, Bangalore was renamed Bengaluru, which has always been the Kannada name for Bangalore. This is, understandably, an attempt to reclaim Bangalore as a regional center for the state of Karnataka. "Bangalore" (so called because the British could not pronounce it by its Kannada name, and they had no "Kannada accent training centers") is a global and national city, whereas "Bengaluru" makes the city sink a little deeper into its local earth.

Personally, I like the sound of Bengaluru. It rises and falls like the landscape of the city, its ridges and valleys. It carries the sound "ur," which in German means very old, archaic, and which connects me via German to the archaic soil and topography of the city.

However, for a long time to come there will be two cities, Bangalore and Bengaluru—and this is somehow good. In the future, we might be citizens of both. Indian teachings tell us that, as mortals, we carry within us an immortal, transpersonal nucleus, the Self. This is described as fundamentally unaffected and unmoved by the processes and activities of the more conditioned, active part of ourselves. "Isolated and steeped in beatitude," in Heinrich Zimmer's words. As Indians, we are always asked to live in two worlds, two places—one where we fight with auto drivers, get angry, love, play, grieve, and the other where we partake of the experience of being immaterial, immortal, exalted. As Indians, we often forget one or the other, yet every city offers spaces for the experience of both. Is it in Bangalore or in Bengaluru that we can find spaces that offer freedom from fear of death and narrowness of personality?

Bangalore
Coffee House.

*Photograph by
Martine Meijer*

In moments of reverie, I see the city of the future as arising from a giant churning between the two. In the *samudramanthan*, the Indian creation myth of the churning of the ocean, the gods and the demons pull Vasuki, the serpent, around the mountain as a churning rod—the gods from his tail, the demons from his head. In the myth, both are looking for the elixir of immortality, *amrit*, which has been lost because of the great flood. The myth tells us of a powerful poison that comes up as the churning progresses, threatening to destroy all. Shiva takes on the task of swallowing it, as a result of which his throat turns blue. A few drops fall outside, but Nandi licks those.

In Bangalore today we need a city able to offer itself as Shiva's throat, holding the toxin—whether it be globalization, fundamentalism, or over-consumption. This capacity to hold something difficult, painful, toxic is what makes it possible for something new to happen. New relationships, new values, new forms. It is already happening in Bangalore, through creative couplings between traditional and contemporary forms of dance, music, theatre; through individuals who know how to "convert the outrage of the years into a music, a sound, and a symbol" (Borges).

What is modern comes from the same place as tradition does. In the present political psyche, it would seem that it is the global, techno-savvy, designer-clothed, matter-oriented Bangalore that has been assigned the demonic pole, while the local, more "Indian," more spiritual Bengaluru makes up the godly end. The poles could change, but what will not change is that each needs the other. As inhabitants of this city, we discover perhaps that its soul and our own reside in both.

I asked Kala, who is a teacher and poet, if she could write a poem about the flowering trees of Bangalore. Here is what she offered:

> In this city—
> imagined on the mythboard
> of hare-chasing-hound-daring,
> its margins demarcated by bulls
> whose hooves measure here and also
> in places we think of as immeasurable—
> you always find a map of ways.
>
> Going from my quarters on days when
> no friend is home to let me in,
> I search for crossroads I have mapped in dream.
> Trees by the roads' sides lean out
> of themselves, shedding leaves,
> shedding flowers, telling tales.
>
> It's an old, old story—the
> tale of this city's beginnings—
> standing watch at the boundaries,
> residing where many roads meet.

That hare kicking up dust
with maddened feet
tossed aside obvious measures
and forced the city's impending founder
towards an unlikely courage.

I too am impelled.
Turning onto Cubbon Road, where
pink-flowered trees mark another
spot that sometimes is and sometimes
means,
again I am reminded that
in this city one may say,
I live partly here but also partly in that
other world
where nothing is but anything can be.

Thank you: Kala Ramesh, Martine Meijer, Mich Gupta, Rama Ranee, Ramesh C.V., Sushma Veerappa, Usha Rao, Ruedi Hoegger, for your contribution. You all know how.

Notes

1   Janaki Nair, *The Promise of the Metropolis: Bangalore's Twentieth Century* (New Delhi: Oxford India Paperbacks, 2007), p. 220.

2   Cited in Sugata Srinivasaraju, *Keeping Faith with the Mother Tongue* (Bangalore: Navakarna-taka Publications Private Limited, 2008), p. 227.

3   Ananda K.Coomaraswamy, *The Dance of Siva* (New York: Dover, 1985), p. 58.

PART TWO

Approaches to the City

19 Jane Jacobs, Patron Saint of Cities

CRAIG STEPHENSON

The tradition of hagiography has fallen into disrepute. It is practiced these days most often only in an idealizing parody of its origins, by biographers of celebrity princesses and ghost-writers of memoirs of self-serving politicians, so much so that the word has acquired a derogatory connotation. But I'd like to take back the conventions of the hagiographic tradition and place them in the service of a more worthy subject: in praise of Jane Jacobs, patron saint of cities.

Jane Isabel Butzner was born on 4 May 1916 in Scranton, Pennsylvania, the third child of the physician John Butzner and Bess Robison, a teacher and nurse. They made their home at 1712 Monroe Street, Protestants in a predominantly Catholic town, freethinkers who encouraged their four children to resist conformity, to value experimentation and initiative. Two anecdotes about their daughter's early school experiences demonstrate this. In the first, a teacher invited her students to raise their hands in a promise to brush their teeth every day for the rest of their lives, and having discussed the nature of promises with her father, Jane refused and found herself evicted from the class, walking alone midmorning through the town (Was this a seed moment, when she first observed a street scene with fresh insight, finding herself suddenly "outside" the collective time and space of the school?). In the second, a geography teacher declared that cities grow around waterfalls, and Jane disagreed, pointing out that the economy of Scranton was driven by the coal mines, not by proximity to its waterfall. I retell these anecdotes here because they have been read as significant indications of where Jacobs was heading, that is to say, that she was a voracious reader and observer and thinker and that she was also "cheeky" and "unschooled," in the better sense of both words.

When, in 1934, the mines began to close and the economy of Scranton collapsed (waterfall or no waterfall) during the Depression, Jacobs went to New York City looking for work. She followed her parents' advice to pursue dreams but also to have a practical skill. She worked as a stenographer and freelance writer, living with her older sister Betty in Brooklyn. During her frequent explorations of New York City, she discovered Greenwich Village, and, sensing something that evoked for her a sense of "home," she moved there with her sister just as soon as they were able. In Greenwich Village she met Robert Hyde Jacobs, an architect, whom she married in 1944 and with whom she had three children. They bought a dilapidated building at 555 Hudson Street on which they began to work. And it was from Hudson Street that she performed three small but important miracles for the citizens of New York City.

In 1955, Robert Moses, the most prolific master builder of New York's public works (including the Henry Hudson Bridge, the Cross Bronx Expressway, Lincoln Center, Shea Stadium, and the United Nations) announced, in his capacity as parks commissioner, his intention to extend Fifth Avenue through Washington Square Park. It was part of his plan of "urban renewal" for Greenwich Village, which he had already designated as a "slum" so that, under the Slum Clearance Act, it could be demolished and replaced with Le Corbusier–inspired superblock tower "projects" containing 4,000 apartments. The four-lane roadway through Washington Square Park would function as the gateway to Washington Square Village, the first phase of the Greenwich development projects as well as the continuation of his federally funded work to replace New York's original settlement streets with expressways to accommodate the new age of the automobile.

On 1 June 1955, Jacobs joined the citizens' movement and refocused it against the apparent *fait accompli* of rendering Washington Square Park a derelict space beside a highway. Jane Jacobs strategically reorganized the Greenwich Village Association, the Washington Square Association, and the Fifth Avenue Association under the banner of the Joint Emergency Committee to Close Washington Square to Traffic, a committee that she named to make explicit a common goal and a specific action so that people of different ideologies could back it without compromising their diversity. Recognizing that it was impossible to stop the developers of Washington Square Village, who had the official sanction of the Slum Clearance Act and enough municipal and federal funding to proceed, Jacobs focused for the moment only on the little fight for Washington Square Park; with regard to this specific mandate, she would entertain no negotiations. She engaged in a wily and creative fashion with politicians as well as with the former first lady, Eleanor Roosevelt, and she employed the media mercilessly.

After a three-year struggle, on 25 June 1958, the city agreed to close the park to traffic temporarily. And despite further attempts to reverse this decision, the park was miraculously saved, remained closed to traffic, and is now run by a privately funded conservancy (like Central Park). The defeat, a first for Moses, was as baffling as it was galling: "There is nobody against this," he complained angrily at the site to journalists, "but a bunch of mothers."[1]

Then, on 21 February 1961, *The New York Times* announced that fourteen blocks of Greenwich Village had been chosen for "urban renewal." It included the scene outside her own window onto Hudson Street, the very area that Jacobs had just finished describing as "unslumming" in the manuscript of a book she had submitted to Random House a month before; that is to say, she envisioned how the neighborhood was moving potentially, with the proper stewardship, toward improving itself while maintaining its diversity and affordability. Now, the city mayor, Robert Wagner, Jr., was allotting a budget of $300,000 to make an official determination of whether to designate the area as "blighted." Jacobs had written at length about the consequences of such designations: the area would be subject to a self-fulfilling prophecy of refused bank loans and mortgages, as well as a lack of municipal investment. The buildings would then deteriorate further so that the city could picture itself stepping in heroically to raze and renew, forcing all the businesses and occupants to relocate. Jacobs had completed enough research across America for her book to confirm the extent to which these planned urban projects were producing not so much renewal as "black holes." Jacobs focused on defeating the blight study plan itself and on introducing the notion of the enforced conservation of old buildings. Intuitively she pushed her committee to demand the resignation of the mayor's appointees for unethical conduct; that is, for pushing through plans for redevelopment in the interest of builders while failing to take into account the wishes of the neighborhood, the very citizens for whom they worked as municipal employees. At the same time, Jacobs hired a forensic expert to investigate the City Planning Commission and uncovered the developers' take-over of the entire determination and designation process, including a door-to-door campaign to convince residents to sign a petition supporting redevelopment. On 23 October 1961, in response to these revelations of unethical practice, the Housing and Redevelopment Board announced that it was dropping the West Village blight study plan.

In 1956, President Dwight D. Eisenhower passed his National Interstate and Defense Highways Act, promising America road networks so the military could transport defense systems in the event of a Cold War confrontation with the Soviet Union, and so fathers could transport kids to school before commuting from the suburbs to work in the cities. The Act provided Robert Moses with 90 percent of the budget necessary to complete his New York City plan to construct two major cross-town expressways. For Lower Manhattan, Moses designed an elevated, ten-lane, 350-foot-wide corridor of concrete that would necessitate the demolition of Broome Street and the relocations of 2,200 families, 365 retails stores, and 480 other businesses. Father Gerard La Mountain of the Church of the Most Holy Crucifix approached Jacobs for help with the campaign to save the neighborhood. After attending a community meeting in the church auditorium, she surveyed the working-class area and found a vibrant, diverse community and distinctive historical buildings, many with cast-iron facades. In 1962, she committed herself to a long and complex struggle on their behalf, accepting the position of chairperson of the Joint Committee to Stop the Lower Manhattan Expressway.

In her book *The Death and Life of Great American Cities* (1961), Jacobs defined the problem that she was again politically tackling as a private citizen:

It is understandable that men who were young in the 1920's were captivated by the vision of the freeway Radiant City, with the specious promise that it would be appropriate to an automobile age. At least it was then a new idea; to men of the generation of New York's Robert Moses, for example, it was radical and exciting in the days when their minds were growing and their ideas forming. Some men tend to cling to old intellectual excitements, just as some belles, when they are old ladies, still cling to the fashions and coiffures of their exciting youth. But it is harder to understand why this form of arrested mental development should be passed on intact to succeeding generations of planners and designers. It is disturbing to think that men who are young today, men who are being trained now for their careers, should accept on the grounds that they must be "modern" in their thinking, conceptions of cities and traffic which are not only unworkable, but also to which nothing new of any significance has been added since their fathers were children.[2]

The fight culminated on 10 April 1968, in a hearing for the Lower Manhattan Expressway that had been hurriedly set up at a high school. Under new rules, the New York Department of Transportation was obliged to collect public comments on the project in order to measure its impact on the affected areas. But the officials were only required to record the comments and file a report, not to discuss the feasibility or effects of the project openly. It was Jacobs who rose to the microphone on the floor midway through the meeting and drew to the citizens' attention that it was positioned so that "we've been talking to ourselves all evening" and not to the officials seated at a table on the stage, while a stenotypist merely recorded their comments for the obligatory report. Jacobs announced that in silent protest she would walk up the steps to the stage, march past the officials, and down the other side. Her committee members joined her. And while the chairman of the meeting, the top official from the transportation department, instructed the police to arrest Jacobs for disorderly conduct, the Broome Street residents tore up the stenotype paper. Jacobs announced that the obligatory meeting had been subverted, "There is no record. There is no hearing!" And then she was arrested. It was an audacious tricksterish act performed in the best spirit of American civil disobedience as defined by Thoreau. On July 16, 1969, in response to her arrest and the light this shed on the jaundiced bureaucracy and power brokering associated with the Lower Manhattan Expressway, the mayor declared the project dead.

Jacobs left her beloved New York to protect her two sons from the draft at the time of the Vietnam War. She became a Canadian citizen in 1974 and made a new home with her family at 69 Albany Avenue in a distinctively mixed neighborhood of Toronto. Jacobs was hoping to settle into a life of writing but once again found herself actively engaged in struggles against urban renewal and urban freeways. She helped stop the Toronto Spadina Expressway, promoted the "unslumming" regeneration of the St. Lawrence Market and its neighborhood, and actively opposed the 1997 amalgamation of the cities of Metro Toronto to form a megacity in which individual neighborhoods and districts were rendered increasingly powerless. She raised her family and wrote six more books in Toronto. She died on 25 April 2006, at the age of eighty-nine.

Jungian analyst Jean Kirsch has identified Jacobs's work as Themis-inspired.[3] During the 2009 conference *Ancient Greece, Modern Psyche* at Santorini, Greece, in response to a paper about Themis presented by Thomas Singer, Kirsch described Jacobs as a modern-day Themis. In her most well-known classical Greek form, Themis signified a divine and natural energy of "right order" that applied equally to gods and humans.[4] As a Titan, Themis was a hidden goddess of a race older than the twelve Olympians, the first (or second) wife of Zeus, and one of the original Delphic oracles. Singer emphasizes that Themis, goddess of social order, is mother of Dike, goddess of natural order, a genealogical detail rife with implications.[5] Likewise, Pamela Donleavy and Ann Shearer argue that "her very name means an ancient, divine law, a right order established by nature itself for the living together of gods and humans."[6] Hence, as a mediator between the spiritual and the physical, the individual and the social, the earthly and the divine, Themis can be conceptualized as a particularly feminine incarnation of Jung's notion of the Self (distinctive from the masculine versions most often described in Jungian studies). The energies associated with Themis point to a feminine-based, "powerful and inherent psychological capacity to bring together and contain disparate energies in a work of healing or making more whole."[7]

In describing Jacobs as a contemporary Themis, Kirsch was perhaps recalling the strong and rooted authority with which Jacobs spoke. Architects and urban planners were baffled and angered by the way this housewife and mother wrote disciplined arguments grounded in the real and the particular. Also by what she defended: for instance, in the case of Washington Square Park, the value of unplanned and organic city spaces. According to Jacobs, problems of city planning were most often problems of hubris against the organic nature of city spaces as well as against Time:

> Consider the history of the no-yield space that has recently been rehabilitated by the Arts in Louisville Association as a theater, music room, art gallery, library, bar and restaurant. It started life as a fashionable athletic club, outlived that and became a school, then the stable of a dairy company, then a riding school, then a finishing and dancing school, another athletic club, an artist's studio, a school again, a blacksmith's, a factory, a warehouse, and it is now a flourishing center of the arts. Who could anticipate or provide for such a succession of hopes and schemes? Only an unimaginative man would think he could; only an arrogant man would want to.[8]

It may be difficult for us now to appreciate just how radically subversive Jacobs's position was in 1961 (she was contradicting even her most powerful supporters, such as Lewis Mumford whose masterwork, *The City in History*, had just won the National Book Award),[9] but her words still strike at our hubristic collective one-sidedness when, for instance, she emphasizes that not architects but Time endows the economic value of buildings and how "the economic requisite for diversity is a requisite that vital city neighborhoods can only inherit, and then sustain over the years."[10]

If Kirsch is right, then perhaps we can regard Jacobs's miracles as Themis-inspired and appreciate even more her celebration and defense of cities in that light. In other words, a Jungian perspective would suggest that something useful may emerge from lining up Jacobs's life and work with analogous narratives and images of Themis. In this way (following Singer's lead), we can ask if Jacobs helps us to conceptualize better and "dream onward" the archetype of Themis, making a more conscious place for her in the here and now. At the same time, if we reread the writings of Jacobs that define and value the natural order of cities in a Themis light, not only as political and social texts but as "religious," then her texts may inspire us, like pilgrims, to revisit and immerse ourselves in the bright "healing" particulars of vibrant cities.

Jacobs's first book, *The Death and Life of Great American Cities,* is a contemporary classic. It is utterly grounded in the reality principle. Her definitions are operational and concrete as much as they are conceptual. For instance,

> An effective district has to be large enough to count as a force in the life of the city as a whole. The "ideal" neighborhood of planning theory is useless for such a role. A district has to be big and powerful enough to fight city hall. Nothing less is to any purpose. To be sure, fighting city hall is not a district's only function, or necessarily the most important. Nevertheless, this is a good definition of size, in functional terms, because sometimes a district has to do exactly this, and also because a district lacking the power and will to fight city hall—and to win—when its people feel deeply threatened, is unlikely to possess the power and will to contend with other serious problems.[11]

Jacobs understands that such definitions are problematic, but the more serious problem is to identify clearly whom the act of defining serves:

> Neighborhood planning units that are significantly defined only by their fabric and the life and intricate cross-use they generate, rather than by formalistic boundaries, are of course at odds with orthodox planning conceptions. The difference is the difference between dealing with living, complex organisms, capable of shaping their own destinies, and dealing with fixed and inert settlements, capable merely of custodial care (if that) of what has been bestowed upon them.[12]

In other words, one can define a neighborhood by mapping the "fire" it generates (to use another of Jacobs's metaphors) rather than by mapping its circumference (which is how a municipality usually imposes a definition upon it in order to subjugate it).

The mythopoeic imagination of visionary poet-painter William Blake depicted how a fiery rebel named Orc had to engage over and over in "mental fight" against the petrifying compass-defined orderings of a gray-headed Urizen in order to build the New Jerusalem. To those readers who can track the political argument but find no trace of a religious tone in Jacobs's sentences, consider for a moment, then, how utterly Blakean these metaphors of "fire" and "circumference" sound.

In the stories of Jacobs's miracles, neighborhoods that wanted to survive when their municipal governments fell into betraying and devouring them had to become more conscious of their "fire"; that is to say, of the creative tension between their diversity and their interdependence. With regard to her home on Hudson Street and the threatened Greenwich Village, she writes: "We [residents] possess more convenience, liveliness, variety and choice than we 'deserve' in our own right. The people who work in the neighborhood also possess, on account of us residents, more variety than they 'deserve' in their own right. We support these things together by unconsciously cooperating economically."[13] Rereading Jacobs's arguments from a Jungian perspective, we could say that these living neighborhoods learned to wrestle consciously with their experiences of difference and Otherness and, paradoxically, at the same time came to value the Eros that unified them with an emerging sense of a vital group or collective self. In recounting these experiences, Jacobs emphasizes to young readers that they will need to right the wrongs committed by generations of architects and planners who mistook urban design for a physical science when in fact it is a life science.

Jacobs argues that "urban renewal projects" failed miserably because of another paradox that the planners did not appreciate in their conceptualizing of cities as unified, ordered spaces:

> If the sameness of use is shown candidly for what it is—sameness—it looks monotonous. Superficially, this monotony might be thought of as a sort of order, however dull. But esthetically, it unfortunately also carries with it a deep disorder: the disorder of conveying no direction. In places stamped with monotony and repetition of sameness you move, but in moving you seem to have gotten nowhere. ... Scenes of thoroughgoing sameness lack these natural announcements of direction and movement, or are scantily furnished with them, and so they are deeply confusing. This is a kind of chaos.[14]

These city planners created chaos by overvaluing one kind of order. At the same time, they devalued and undermined the genuine ordering principle behind the regeneration of cities, a principle with its social foundations defined by what early Greek political thinking would have identified as a natural Themis-like dynamic: "Unslumming and its accompanying self-diversification—possibly the greatest regenerative forces inherent in energetic American metropolitan economies—thus appear, in the murky light of conventional planning and rebuilding wisdom, to represent mere social untidiness and economic confusion, and they are so treated."[15]

In her subsequent books, Jacobs worked to describe, revive, and revalue this dynamic for collective consciousness as it manifests in economics. In *The Economy of Cities,* Jacobs argues, from a historical perspective, that cities preceded innovations in agriculture, in the sense that geographically dense cities led to the need for entrepreneurial discoveries and for improvements in the division of labor.[16] In *Cities and the Wealth of Nations,* she argues that cities, not nation-states, define macroeconomics.[17] In *Systems of Survival,* she compares and contrasts two ethical systems that sustain social and economic life.[18] Written in the convention of a Platonic dialogue, her argument differentiates between a commercial moral syndrome (related to what constitutes good business practice) and a guardian moral syndrome (related to how we protect territories and organize courts, legislatures, and religious practices). Jacobs points to the necessity of both systems but demonstrates how conflicts undermine good governance when these two syndromes become undifferentiated or mixed: for example, when policing agencies apply commercial values to their work by setting quotas and rewarding output or when (in Marxist states or in Mafia-controlled neighborhoods, for instance) guardianship takes responsibility for commerce and production.

Concerning the evolution of her work, Jacobs writes:

> At some point along the trail I realized I was engaged in studying the ecology of cities. ... By city ecology I mean something different from, yet similar to, natural ecology as students of wilderness address the subject. A natural ecosystem is defined as "composed of physical-chemical-biological processes active within a space-time unit of any magnitude." A city ecosystem is composed of physical-economic-ethical processes active at a given time within a city and its close dependencies. I've made up this definition, by analogy. ... Both types of ecosystems—assuring they are not barren—require much diversity to sustain themselves.[19]

In *The Nature of Economics,* she again employs the conventions of a Platonic dialogue to discuss the organic nature of ecosystems and economies. Over a series of meals, her characters discuss how economies are governed by the same rules as nature:

> Thinking about development has made me realize how similar economics and ecosystems are. That's to say, principles at work in the two are identical. ... I'm

convinced that universal natural principles limit what we can do economically and how we can do it. Trying to evade overriding principles of development is economically futile. But those principles are solid foundations for economies. My personal biomimicry project is to learn economics from nature.[20]

Grounding her discussions of economic abstractions about development, growth, and stability in earthly realities, Jacobs demonstrates that humans didn't invent and cannot transcend the natural processes that govern economic life.

In 2004, Jacobs published her last book, *Dark Age Ahead*. If we retain Singer's notion of Themis as a social and natural ordering principle and Kirsch's intuition that Jacobs was Themis-inspired, then, in this book, setting aside the conventions of the Platonic dialogue, Jacobs goes deeper, to a singular voice and an emphatic prophecy that is more qualitatively Titanesque. She identifies five pillars on which a vibrant culture depend but that our North American and European societies have seriously eroded almost to the point of irrelevance: community and family, higher education, science and technology, governmental representation, and the self-regulation of learned professionals. For instance, concerning families, she predicts:

If the predicaments of North American families continue mounting and climb further up the income ladder, I have no idea what kinds of households will emerge to deal with needs that families are at a loss to fill. My intuition tells me they will probably be coercive. This is already true of the most swiftly multiplying and rapidly expanding type of American households at the turn of the millennium—prisons.[21]

With regard to the replacing of "educating" with "credentialing," she writes,

My impression is that university-educated parents or grandparents of students presently in university do not realize how much the experience has changed since their own student days, nor do the students themselves, since they have not experienced anything else. Only faculty who have lived through the loss realize what has been lost.[22]

Nor do we realize the extent to which scientific and technological research and innovation are now tied to one-sided ideologies. She decries the weakening of governmental representation in newly formed megacities such as Toronto that undermines the vitality and particularity of neighborhoods. About the fifth pillar, "corporate and professional accountability," we need only recall the case of Bernard Madoff or the bonuses that financiers continue to receive while millions of householders lose their mortgaged homes to the same international banks that their taxes saved from collapse. Jacobs asks the question, "If you allow these pillars to erode further, then who will rebuild them for you?"[23]

We are only now catching up to her. Jacobs mapped the road that many others are now describing in stories of bankrupted, cannibalistic, patriarchal, Chronos-like societies that are devouring their own citizens. But Jacobs's own dark Themis vision also contains an antidote to this paranoid legacy of "every man for himself" and of demonic cities "at the end of things." For humankind, hope resides not in fleeing out into nature or isolationism but in the natural creativity and ingenuity of citizens, in community and social diversity, in the Eros and the Otherness engendered by cities.

I'm not alone in designating Jacobs a saint. In Margaret Atwood's feminine dystopian novel *The Year of the Flood,* the awkward participants in a cultish green-movement commune sing preachy ecological ditties composed to hymntunes from the United Church of Canada and mark their calendar with the names of their saints: one of them is Jane Jacobs.[24] When almost all humankind is destroyed by a virus and many of the remaining survivors prove even more virulent than the disease, the protagonist repeats the names of the saints such as Jacobs (and David Suzuki; not all the saints are women) like touchstones, invoking memories from what now seems a long distant past of those who wrestled with devils and survived.

Likewise, on Jane Jacobs's Day, which the Toronto City Council first designated on May 4, 2007, small groups of citizens, betrayed by their megacities but nevertheless emulating their brave saint on her day, go out walking for the express purpose of reinvesting their city streets with vision by looking to see.[25]

Notes

1   Quoted in Anthony Flint, *Wrestling with Moses: How Jane Jacobs Took on New York's Master Builder and Transformed the American City* (New York: Random House, 2009), p. 87.

2   Jane Jacobs, *The Death and Life of Great American Cities* (1961; repr., New York: Modern Library, 1993), p. 484.

3   Jean Kirsch, correspondence with author, 10 January 2010.

4   The best-known scholarly treatments of the theme of Themis are Jane Ellen Harrison's *Epilegomena to the Study of Greek Religion* and *Themis: A Study of the Social Origins of Greek Religion* (1912; repr., New Hyde Park, NY: University Books, 1962).

5   Thomas Singer, "Themis," paper delivered at the conference Ancient Greece/Modern Psyche, Nomikos Centre, Santorini, Greece, August 2009; publication forthcoming in *Ancient Greece/Modern Psyche* (New Orleans: Spring Journal Books).

6   Pam Donleavy and Ann Shearer, *From Ancient Myth to Modern Healing: Themis: Goddess of Heart-Soul, Justice and Reconciliation* (London: Routledge, 2008), p. 1.

7   *Ibid.*, p. 2.

8   Jacobs, *The Death and Life of Great American Cities*, p. 254.

9   Lewis Mumford, *The City in History: Its Origins, Its Transformations and Its Prospects* (New York: Harcourt Brace Jovanovich, 1961).

10   *Ibid.*, p. 260.

11   *Ibid.*, pp. 159–160.

12   *Ibid.*, p. 173.

13   *Ibid.*, p. 199.

14   *Ibid.*, pp. 291–292.

15   *Ibid.*, p. 369.

16   Jane Jacobs, *The Economy of Cities* (New York: Random House, 1969).

17   Jane Jacobs, *Cities and the Wealth of Nations: Principles of Economic Life* (Toronto: Viking, 1984).

18   Jane Jacobs, *Systems of Survival: A Dialogue on the Moral Foundations of Commerce and Politics* (New York: Random House, 1992).

19   Jacobs, *The Death and Life of Great American Cities*, p. xvi.

20   Jane Jacobs, *The Nature of Economies* (Toronto: Random House Canada, 2000), p. 8.

21   Jane Jacobs, *Dark Age Ahead* (Toronto: Random House Canada, 2004), p. 43.

22   *Ibid.*, p. 63.

23   See *ibid.*, p. 24.

24   Margaret Atwood, *The Year of the Flood* (Toronto: McClelland and Stewart, 2009).

25   For information on how to lead a Jane's Walk and maps of Jane's Walks in urban centers in the United States and Canada, see www.janeswalk.net.

The Remorse of the Sedentary

20

Luigi Zoja

With Baudelaire, Paris for the first time became the subject of lyric poetry.
—Walter Benjamin[1]

Man has been a hunter, a gatherer, and a shepherd, remaining a nomadic wanderer throughout the greater part of human existence. Only during the last few millennia has he become sedentary. In the human being who has a fixed abode, therefore, a great ancestral disquiet hides itself. Just as his body in part preserves the hide and canines of the carnivore, so his psyche preserves the need to pick up and move on, the archetype of the nomad. The human being thus comes into self-contradiction. This is the situation of Cain, the first sedentary, who plotted to kill Abel, the brother who freely went his own way.[2]

Little by little, as agriculture produced a surplus of food, people were able to relocate. By concentrating in cities they could undertake new tasks, generate new wealth, and, as Pericles had already testified, withstand ancient sorrows with new pleasures. The transformation of nature into culture demanded the urban transposition. During the Renaissance, urbanization meant that art, no longer confined to the sacred themes of the monastery, took up the beauties of the natural world. This implied the paradox of the depiction of the Tuscan countryside as seen through a Florentine window casement. This view of the outside world from within the city environment established a tradition that has not yet exhausted itself; romantic poets and composers invoke the world of the forest, but they do business with each other in the city in order to get published and have their works performed.

Most of the growth in today's cities is an affair of the third world, as the migrant poor relocate to cities around the world. These new city-dwellers leave the countryside not because it produces a surplus of food, thus freeing agricultural laborers for other work, as in previous centuries. On the contrary, many rural areas of the globe are now unable to adequately support local populations. Rural migrants today come to the city not in order to live *better* but simply to live. Others come to the city in the hope of escaping the ravages of war. In Colombia, where rural areas have been submerged in war for decades, millions flee to cities simply to avoid being killed. The capital of Angola now resembles a cancerous growth; it harbors over half the country's population.

In 2008, according to the United Nations, more than half of the population of the earth was living in cities.[3] This development is unprecedented, more important than the passing of global hegemony from the United States to China. For even China will put in only a brief appearance on the stage of the eras; other protagonists will rise and fall in the same way as did the empires of Xerxes and Alexander or those of Rome, Spain, and Great Britain. The city, though, will stay. Never again will it cede primacy to the countryside.

Restraining our deeply instinctual impulse toward movement without sacrificing the advantages of stability means returning to the instinctual counterpole of defending our territory. For some, this means projecting the repressed migrant we still carry inside and then trying to eliminate him. We see this in the chauvinism and racism that have inflamed most parts of the developed West in recent years. These irruptions can be explained in part by the psychic history that lives in us. We reject the nomad, yet just yesterday the nomad was us.

Yet there is a third way, one that we find in literature, especially in the writings of Baudelaire and Walter Benjamin—the figure of the *flâneur*. *Flana* is an ancient Scandinavian term that means to wander here and there. It entered the French language by way of the Normans and from there passed into other Western languages. A *flâneur* is someone who strolls through a city with no apparent aim. The *flâneur,* however, is quite different from the loiterer, the *Müssiggänger,* the *vago,* and the *bighellone* or loafer. He also differs from the tourist of the twenty-first century. These figures all travel with no purpose in view. The tourist sprints toward finish lines set up by package tours, Lonely Planet guidebooks, or simply their own ego rationales. But the *flâneur* finds himself propelled by the ancient motive of discovery, and waits for an unconscious drive to emanate from the goal and enthrall him. He doesn't know the points of arrival—the urban destinations—in advance; he keys his itinerary to the soul of the city.

The *flâneur* moves in space but also in time. The street is not the object or means of passage but a subject that determines the route. "It leads downward ... into a past that can be all the more profound because it is not his own, not private."[4] Yet this past perceives him and engulfs him.

The city is mankind as we know it. Without the city, it has been said, human beings possess neither civilization nor history. Mankind is drawn to the city precisely because the city is mankind, because mankind does not want life in the state of nature. But urbanization also contains a threshold. The civic man who crosses that threshold loses a little bit of his soul. He no longer cares about other people. Perhaps his fancy is caught by the crowd, but the individual neighbor does not engage his thoughts or interests. The mass, the crowd, has become the monstrous new anti-human, and in many cases the one who has crossed the urban threshold loses himself in the mass.

The urban crowd became the focus of literary imagination in the nineteenth century. In Edgar Allan Poe's famous story, "The Man of the Crowd" (1840), the throngs of London are atomized by the loneliness of individual haste. His protagonist is "the type and the genius of deep crime. ... He is the man of the crowd." During the same years Poe was writing, a young Friedrich Engels cast a similar gaze, equally horrified, over London.[5] But for our purposes, Baudelaire is the author who wrote most deeply and most subtly about the city of his time.

Baudelaire did not set out to descriptively render either Paris or Parisians. His literary eye could easily have chosen any one of the city's residents, but he chose not to tell their stories. Instead, he allowed himself to wander through the city, looking for what he did not yet know would touch his psyche. He managed to catch himself on the brink of the threshold between the seemingly invincible power of the city to depersonalize and the still-half-animal instinct of the *flâneur,* whose exploration brings him to the margins of the metropolis.[6] Baudelaire paused on the edge of both these worlds, gently holding the city dweller and the nomad who encounters the city as a marvel in delicate equilibrium. He saw the city through both sets of eyes.

The *flâneur* can be enraptured by the rush of the crowd without becoming infected by it. And the poet-vagabond finds glimpses of eternal beauty in the masses he observes. One of Baudelaire's loveliest sonnets, "À une passante," carves the profile of a widow in the instant when she passes by.[7] Her beauty is at once finite and infinite, her agonized *eros* is at one with *thanatos*. The poet's senses are dreamy and vigilant at the same time; he swims in the crowd, yet he snaps alert when he recognizes something of value. His poems reflect this dreamy-watchful state; they begin with a transition from the pure sense of hearing to that of seeing. And from that focused gaze something breaks loose from the mass and lodges in his soul.

La rue assourdissante autour de moi hurlait.
longue, mince, en grand deuil, douleur majesteuse,
Une femme passa, d'une main fasteuse
Soulevant, balançant le feston et l'ourlet . . .
Un éclair, puis la nuit!

All around me, the deafening roar of the street.
Tall, slim, in full mourning, towering grief,
Passed a lady, one glittering hand erect
Lifting and swaying her brocaded hem . . .
A lightning flash, then night!

The final tercet takes leave of the reader and the imagery with the same quick refocusing, returning from an individual object to the whole. It is no longer the gaze, however, that moves through space, but rather the mind through time, tracking how the instant of beauty relates to the observer's life and to eternity.

Ailleur, bien loin d'ici! trop tard! jamais peut-être!
Car j'ignore où tu fuis, tu ne sais où je vais,
Ô toi que j'eusse aimée, ô toi qui le savais!

Elsewhere, far from here, too late! perhaps never!
For I know not where you flee, you know not where I go,
You whom I might have loved, you who indeed know it!

From the archetypal power of Baudelaire's gaze we may take this poetry as a prototype of the experience we are still trying to find in the city, the dreamy-watchful state in which we wait for something that will lodge in our psyches. Even in the twenty-first century it remains the model to follow for keeping a certain balance between the two kinds of seeker-visitors, the pre-modern ones who are still struggling to grasp the metropolis and the postmodern tourists who are unable to achieve an attunement with the soul of the city, the chronic carrier of what twentieth-century writer Walter Benjamin has called "the stigmata which life in an urban metropolis inflicts upon love."[8]

Why didn't the archetype of the *flâneur* emerge in Rome?[9] Because, as we have seen, the verb *flaner* means to be tossed among times as well as places—that is, crossing present with past in an "anamnestic intoxication" (*anamnestische Rausch*).[10] To wander in the past at the behest of the inspiration of the *genius loci* is like going along with a dream. It is no accident that the French *rever*, which today means to dream, used to mean to wander, *esver*, from the Latin *[ex]vagus*. In describing this experience, Benjamin speaks of *Langweile*,[11] a word that is usually badly translated as ennui or boredom. In reality, *Langweile* is above all the absence of temporal containment, an indeterminate relationship to time.

But if Rome is still anticipating the modernization it lacked in the eras of Baudelaire and Benjamin, other cities offer it up: not only American cities, whose *genii loci* instill rapid rhythms, but also London, which provided the model for modernity on both sides of the Atlantic. As much as Baudelaire's writings follow Poe (it was his translations that established Poe's reputation in France), his *flâneur* still has not compromised with modernity, as "the man in the crowd" has. He may strike out into the swirling throng, but he does not associate himself with it. He swims in the mass without getting wet. Because he has kept his distance, when he sees something he can still feel surprise, much like a shock, as with the widow whose profile momentarily crosses Baudelaire's visual field.

During the Second Empire, the first arcades were built in Paris. These forerunners of the department store were enclosed passages whose skylights and shop windows faced inward, secure places halfway between the maternal womb of the house and the mother-city. Silence and slow time lived in this sheltered space. In the arcades one lingered over which elegant objects to choose; it was a drawn-out aesthetic claustrophobia. The degree to which the *flâneur* could remain unaffected by this new consumer world is best illustrated by his habit of walking pet tortoises in the Paris arcades, a fad that began in 1839.[12] In this action he embodied the antithesis of the arcade consumer; he was not looking to buy. Instead, he was there to observe. Walking a leashed tortoise set a slow and deliberate pace that eliminated not only the risk of getting drunk on speed but also the ego: whoever went out for a stroll with this animal knew that it was the tortoise that set the direction, thereby inverting the function of the leash.

Freud has reminded us that great scientific discoveries have reconfigured the egocentrism that stems from taking ourselves to be the darlings of creation.[13] The Earth is only a marginal planet, as Copernicus proved, and man is only one link among many in the evolutionary chain of species, as Darwin demonstrated. According to psychoanalysis, not even the ego is omnipotent but must coexist with unconscious psychic forces that are far greater than it is. That said, however, Freud retreated part way into combative hubris when he asserted that the measure of the success of psychoanalytic work is the replacement of the id, or the unconscious, with the ego.

It was Jung who told us that it is the ego that must retreat, placing itself at the outermost reaches of the psychic field, because the center of that field, the real balance point between ego and unconscious, is the Self. Conscious intentions are not in themselves enough to determine human behavior; they are often clearly counterproductive.

In Jung's wake, Arnold Toynbee has supplied a kindred demonstration in historical studies.[14] Human beings need history; that is, they must do battle with the hubris that would make the present alone seem worthwhile. Respect for people past and gone is necessary if the temporal egocentrism of modernity is to be resisted. Finally, as Claude Lévi-Strauss has taught us, if we wish to understand the different societies of mankind, we westerners must no longer place ourselves at the center of the observational field but instead must step back and turn to look at it with a "view from afar."[15] Only thus, by intentionally marginalizing our viewpoint, may we obtain a comprehensive outlook and grasp relative differences.

One can say that long before these great masters of the non-ego perspective, the *flâneurs* had already struggled against the ego's hubris so they could reconnoiter those uncharted twists and turns of the crowd, the mass, or the soul of the city, what we might today call the city's unconscious.

Millions of vacation trips have been taken in our era. The imperialism of the tourist ego is no less an opponent than the egos that Jung, Toynbee, and Lévi-Strauss fought against. Impatient tourists gaze at cities that are new to them, but their eyes mangle them, unable to know them well at all, because those eyes are infused with Western arrogance: they already know what they want to see. They do not know how to shift their perspective and cannot give themselves over to surprise. They seek but never find. These millions of violent eyes do not impinge without consequences. They disfigure precisely the unviolated beauty they have come to gobble up. If we wish to escape this mentality, we must visit our chosen cities with more than our *Lonely Planet* guidebooks clutched in one hand. We must also imagine in the other hand the leash of the *flâneur,* at whose end a tortoise, heedless of the hour, selects the street for us, inverting one more time the relation between the Self and the ego.

Notes

1   Walter Benjamin, "Paris, Capital of the Nineteenth Century (1939)," in *The Arcades Project*, trans. Howard Eiland and Kevin McLaughlin (Cambridge & London: Belknap Press of Harvard University), p. 880. This is a translation of Walter Benjamin, *Das Passegen-Werk*, vol. 5 of Benjamin's *Gesammelte Werke*.

2   Hans Magnus Enzenberger, *Die Grosse Wanderun: 33 Markierungen* (Frankfurt: M. Suhrkamp, 1992).

3   United Nations Human Settlements Program (UN Habitat), *State of the World's Cities 2008/2009: Harmonious Cities* (London: Earthscan, 2008), p. 1.

4   Walter Benjamin, "The Arcades of Paris," in Benjamin, *The Arcades Project*, p. 880.

5   Friedrich Engels, *The Condition of the Working Class in England in 1844*, trans. Florence Kelley (New York: J. W. Lovell, 1887).

6   Benjamin, "The Arcades of Paris."

7   Baudelaire, "À une passante," in *Le Fleurs du mal*, 2nd ed. (Paris: Poulet-Malassis et de Broise, 1861), section "*Tableaux parisiens.*"

8   Walter Benjamin, "On Some Motifs in Baudelaire," in *Selected Writings*, vol. 4, *1938-1940*, trans. Edmund Jephcott et al., ed. Howard Eiland and Michael W. Jennings (Cambridge & London: Belknap Press of Harvard University Press, 2003), p. 324.

9   Benjamin, "The Arcades of Paris," p. 880. See also Walter Benjamin, "Notes and Materials," in *Gesammelte Schriften*, Bd. I.2 (Frankfurt am Main: Suhrkamp, 1972), p. 525 (hereafter *GS*).

10 Benjamin, "The Arcades of Paris," ibid. Cf. Benjamin, *GS*, Bd. II.3, p. 1053.

11 *Ibid.* (*Weile* means a period of time, *lange* or *kurz*, long or short.)

12 Benjamin, "The Arcades of Paris," p. 881. See also Benjamin, "*Über einige Motive bei Baudelaire,*" in *Charles Baudelaire: Ein Lyriker im Zeitalter des Hochkapitalismus* (Frankfurt am Main: Suhrkamp, 1969); and Benjamin, "*Pariser Passagen,*" in *GS*, Bd. V.2, p. 1054, footnote.

13 Sigmund Freud, *Introductory Lectures on Psychoanalysis* (1915–1917) (London: Liveright, 1989).

14 Arnold Toynbee, *An Historian's Approach to Religion* (Oxford: Oxford University Press, 1956), Chapter 1.

15 Claude Lévi-Strauss, *The View from Afar*, trans. Joachim Neugroschel and Phoebe Hoss (Chicago: University of Chicago Press, 1992). This is a translation of *Le regard eloigné* (1983).

Afterword

THOMAS SINGER

A primary goal of this book is to encourage the reader's own inner and outer excursions into the realms of soul and city. As editor of the book, I was initially relieved that I didn't have to write a chapter, as, frankly, the task seemed overwhelming. I have nothing but admiration for the brave authors who undertook the challenge with grace and courage. But as the chapters began to arrive on my computer from all over the world, I became more and more excited by the different ways each author had gone about the task.

My own reflections were further stimulated by a communication I had with Ann Casement, to whom I sent Antonio LaFranchi's chapter on Cairo after she reminded me of her current explorations of modern and ancient Egypt. She wrote:

Dear Tom,

Thank you for letting me have a preview of Antonio Lanfranchi's chapter, which resonated with me on so many levels.

For one thing, he and I are hybrids who have lived in exile from our home countries for most of our adult lives, which lends itself to a soulful yearning for home. In my case, I was born and brought up in Bombay and then transported to London in my teens. I have never been able to go back and so felt much sympathy for Antonio in being brave enough to do that. Like him, I have fallen in love with other cities over the years—Paris, Venice, New York, Rio, Cairo—as substitutes for the beloved city of childhood. Interestingly enough, my attraction to Ancient Egypt predates my leaving India and has been with me ever since—even thought of reading Egyptology at University College London but then decided the life of an Egyptologist was not for me (for various reasons).

He mentions Naguib Mahfouz in passing and I remember reading the latter's Cairo Trilogy avidly some years ago. I first stopped over in Cairo on the long journey from Bombay to London and have always felt drawn to Egypt but have only started to visit it again in recent years. It is as if my unconscious kept me away, as once I started to explore Egypt in some depth, I realized it was the ultimate to which I shall return from now on as much as possible. There is something archetypal about the Egyptian landscape with the lush oases and tiny villages clustered on the banks of the great river with the desert and pink limestone hills in the background—one could be back four thousand years if it were not for the mosques in each village.

Everything negative Antonio says about Cairo in the chapter is true, but I loved the city from the start—the seemingly utter chaos of the traffic which actually works in what an Egyptian acquaintance calls "typical Egyptian fashion." I feel at home in Arab countries, as I have that English romantic view of Arabs, the desert and the fatalism which is a feature of the Arab psyche—so different to the way we are mollycoddled in England with countless prescriptions and proscriptions. I also love the call of the muezzins at different times of the day (one soon learns to sleep through the one at 5 A.M.) and the way that the sacred and profane are an interwoven part of each day. I don't like the ugly dwellings reaching almost to the pyramids and to the feet of the Sphinx but there is an intriguing paradox in this juxtaposition of ugly modernity with ancient grandeur.

In the last section, I loved the way he linked Maat to modern Egyptians. And, finally, his great-grandmother and mine would have had much in common—mine ending up running her own hospital (obstetrics/gynaecology) in Poona.

As you can see, I got so much from this wonderful chapter.

My best,

Ann

Ann's sensitive and personal comments heightened my awareness of exactly what we hope to achieve with this book—to stimulate in depth readers' own reflections on soul and city. If the book works at all, it should work on that level. In that spirit, I kept coming back to my earliest experiences of growing up in St. Louis, Missouri, as I thought about soul and native place.

As vast and unknown as New York City felt to me as a young man (see the introduction), the opposite was true of the deep, unquestioned soul connection I experienced between myself and the beloved old Midwestern town I grew up in. St. Louis is where my ancestors settled in the 1840s, where my parents lived in the same house for over seventy years, and where I spent the first seventeen years of my life.

By exploring three basic themes that have been particularly meaningful to me and, in some ways, quite different from the perspectives of the other authors who have contributed to *Psyche and City: A Soul's Guide to the Modern Metropolis,* I hope to further encourage the reader to note his or her own way of experiencing soul in familiar and foreign cities.

Mystical Oneness and the Soul of the City

In his paper "Mystical Man," Erich Neumann defines the various stages of mystical experience along a spectrum, moving from undifferentiated (or unconscious) to differentiated (or conscious), from what he calls "uroboric mysticism" to "end stage mysticism."[1] In the stage of "uroboric mysticism," one is unconsciously contained within an experience of wholeness, a kind of unifying *participation mystique*. All is One and one is part of all. It is "uroboric mysticism" that interests me with regard to soul and city, because the experience of oneness between our soul and our city is akin to an unconscious participation in being part of and belonging to a whole.

I have often referred to St. Louis as "the swamp I grew up in," but this description is said with deep affection rather than a sense of negative engulfment. Calling St. Louis "the swamp I grew up in" has been my attempt to describe an early childhood feeling about St. Louis that persists to this day in my feelings about my hometown, even though I haven't lived there for fifty years. "The swamp I grew up in" names my primal, preverbal sense that what is inside of me and outside of me is all part of the same thing, all made of the same stuff that I inhabit and that inhabits me—the very air I breathe and the natural habitat that I "swim" in. The people, the streets, the trees, the houses, the buildings, the river, the sky, the weather—all are continuous with one another and participate in the same being. It is all part of the same stuff, swamp-like.

As a child, I could smell the mystical connection between my self, my family, and St. Louis in the ancient, musty scent of an elevator and its white-gloved old black operator at my grandfathers' apartment building at 709 South Skinker Boulevard. The building still sits directly across from Forest Park, scene of the great 1904 St. Louis World's Fair, commemorated in the wonderful song "Meet Me in St. Louis, Louie." I actually had a long-lost Uncle Louie.

Mystical oneness with St. Louis is embodied in several childhood memories. I had been taken to see the movie *The Wizard of Oz* and then to Peveley Dairy's ice cream store for a treat, where the dazzling, multicolored water shooting up in the fountain merged in my psyche with the film's enchantment—it was Real, I was part of it, I could swim in it! I also knew the shadowy side of mystical connection between my self, my family, and St. Louis in my mother's oft-repeated girlhood tale of when she fell through the ice while skating on the frozen pond across from her grandfather's grand house on Lindell Boulevard. Beside this same pond, again as a young girl, she once saw a "flasher." That small pond still evokes a chilling sense of death and other dangers narrowly averted.

The uncanny sense of mystical oneness extends even into adulthood, for when I meet someone who hails from St. Louis, I believe that I can "see" St. Louisness in their skin. What I "see" in their skin is not skin deep; it is the very essence of shared being. We originated in the same swampy "stuff." They are part of me. I am part of them. We are part of St. Louis. At that level of shared being, there is no separating boundary. Perhaps Walt Whitman said it best and most succinctly in *Leaves of Grass*: "I believe a leaf of grass is no less than the journey-work of the stars."[2]

Soul Dreams and Sports of the City

Citizens dream large when it comes to their aspirations for their cities. And often those dreams revolve around sports teams as the carrier of the city soul. Just as personal soul is often known through our lively connection to instinctual life, our collective soul can come to life in the sports stadiums that provide the communal space for sharing an instinctual part of our human nature as embodied in competitive games. This is underlined by the animal or bird form team mascots and emblems often take, further linking nature, soul, and the spirit of the city.

Linking the themes of mystical oneness and sports teams as carrier of the city soul, I am a devoted baseball fan and have been since childhood. On one occasion, I experienced a sense of mystical oneness with the soul of St. Louis at a hot dog stand directly across from the old Sportsman's Park where the St. Louis Cardinals played baseball many decades ago.

The story unfolds in the following way. Because poor vision disqualified my father from enlisting in the regular armed forces, he served on the city's rationing board during World War II, apportioning food supplies and provisions for the populace. Coupled with his lifelong love for baseball, my father believed that rooting for the home team was good for morale during the difficult war years. Through his position on the ration board, my dad made sure that the hot dog stand had plenty of hot dogs for every baseball game throughout the war. My father was essentially a modest man, and this is one of the few accomplishments that I ever heard him brag about.

Actually, this story really begin in 1917 when my father, as a ten-year-old boy, read about a triple play in the *St. Louis Post Dispatch*—that is, throwing "out" three men of the opposing team with one swift play. He started going to games, became an avid fan, and then spent a lifetime waiting to actually see this rarest of baseball's phenomena. He never did. But as a result of his ability to procure a steady supply of hot dogs for the stand during the war years, my father and I were greeted like royalty when he took me to my first Cardinal's game in 1950, when I was eight. Even that long after the war, the owner's warm expression of his enduring gratitude to my father made me feel that we were an essential part of the city. In a very real sense, my young soul, the soul of my father, and the soul of the city all met that day at that hot dog stand for eight-year-old me. Soul does not need a fancy restaurant, a grand hotel, or a fine museum to find itself.

Most proud cities in the world have their team or teams that carry the soul dreams of their citizens. Most recently, New Orleans experienced profound soul renewal through the Super Bowl football victory of their beloved "Aints," who overnight became "Saints." (It could be a little while before the despairing nickname "Aints" is used again.) In St. Louis, no sports team has generated more reverent affection, devoted concern, or knowledgeable passion among its fans than the Cardinals. Indeed, St. Louis Cardinals fans are often identified by sports commentators as the "best baseball fans" in America, which worries me, because the fans might actually come to believe this good press and become too proud. If nothing else, sports teaches the soulful art of humility, even in an era when consumerism, hype, astronomical players' salaries, and the inflated cost of tickets mock everything that is down to earth about the game.

If you want to learn something about the soul of a city and its inhabitants, ask the natives about their sports teams. Bart Giametti put it this way in *Take Time for Paradise*: "Baseball is the song of homecoming that America sings to herself." Giametti tells us that the ballplayer's goal of scoring a run by rounding the bases to come "home" mirrors the oldest tale of Western civilization, Ulysses' long journey to return home to Ithaca. It is not a stretch of the imagination to think of today's ballpark as the place to which the citizens "march, and rejoice in the dance and song, ... and sing as we come to a stand at thy well-fenced altar."[3] The ballpark is the modern "well-fenced altar" where the citizens of St. Louis and many other cities sing the ancient, Greek leap song of their soul and goodly Themis that serves as the opening anthem of this book.

Soul Values and the Masculine in the City

While that which may be considered feminine contributes a large measure of whatever grace, beauty, and mystery remains in our urban areas, the "feminine" often seems to be at the center of just about every good thing that Jungians and others currently have to say about the world. I have been surprised by the extent to which the masculine is often denigrated, even in our Jungian community, which prides itself on being able to hold the tension between the opposites. Almost anything that has to do with the "masculine" or "the patriarchy" is suspect. But if we had included the proud city of Chicago in this anthology, it would have been difficult to imagine portraying the strength and dynamism of the city without invoking homage to the muscle that is the essence of its almost-steroidal skyline. Brawn and ingenuity built not only the city of Chicago but many others, too, where the philanthropy and civic mindedness of its patriarchs as well as matriarchs contributed to the cultural heritage that is shared by all citizens.

Continuing with the theme of sports, I want to focus on two heroes of St. Louis baseball to highlight the positive values that the "masculine" can bring to psyche and soul in the city. It is fitting that one hero is "Stan the Man" Musial and the other is Albert "el hombre" Pujols. "Stan the Man" is truly beloved among the citizens of St. Louis for the virtues he embodies, and Albert "el Hombre" is carving out a place for himself in that fine tradition. The fact that Stan Musial hit five home runs in one afternoon doubleheader didn't hurt his ascendency to local godhood—a miraculous event that I witnessed firsthand in the same Sportsman's Park across from the hot dog stand. But Musial is remembered for much more than his slugging ability or his spectacular lifetime batting average of .331.

Together, Musial and Pujols represent the continuity of what is most highly valued and symbolic of St. Louis' soul values from the twentieth century and into the twenty-first. Their lineage has created a remarkable pair of noble citizens in St. Louis, one old, the other young. The two are part of a tradition that epitomizes what St. Louis has honored most in its Self-image: excellence in one's craft; decency and fair play in life and in the game; solid consistency in performance over time; gentlemanliness that is far more than public persona and goes to the very heart of one's character; and finally, a spirit of generosity that extends itself to family, neighbors, community, and strangers. Add to those qualities honor and loyalty to others and to the city—all of these qualities add up to what is most highly valued in this quintessentially Midwestern city.

"The Boy and the Man," by Harry Weber.

When I asked my old St. Louis friend, the fine sculptor Harry Weber, if I could use a photo of one of his Stan Musial sculptures in this book, he gave me several images to choose from. The one I chose turned out to be Stan Musial's favorite, too, because it features Stan "the Man" not as a slugger but as a fatherly mentor humanly relating to a young boy. It is the masculine at its best and it captures something of the soul of St. Louis, my hometown.

Only rarely do uroboric mysticism, sports, and the masculine join hands in one's experience of the soul of a city. A major sporting event, such as hosting the Olympics, a World Soccer Cup, or the World Series of baseball, can throw a city into an altered experience of itself when soul, individual citizen, and community come together for a deep celebration of Self and City. Think of the movie *Invictus,* in which Nelson Mandela understood how profoundly interwoven the experience of sports and a city's/nation's soul could be. However, not every day is the World Cup, World Series, or Super Bowl of life, and the intermingling qualities of soul and city are usually much more subtly embodied in one's day-to-day life, contributing to what makes being part of a city or from a city so important to our sense of ourselves as being whole.

Yet, finally, in my hometown of St. Louis, there is the marvelously androgynous landmark that brings the masculine and feminine together in a perfect form. Perhaps no civic monument in the world more fully embodies this union

A tip of the hat from Lewis and Clark, the great early explorers, to the St. Louis Arch, gateway to the West; sculpture by Harry Weber.

than its famous arch, standing on the banks of the Mississippi River. Eero Saarinen's masterpiece joins the soaring spirit of the masculine with the supple curve of the grounded feminine in a *coniunctio,* symbolizing the Self of St. Louis. Just as the arch is a symbolic "Gateway to the West", it may serve as the gateway to this book. It is soaring and circular at the same time; it is inspiring and embracing, aspiring, and containing—and, at their best, that is what we would like all our cities to be.

Notes

1   *The Mystic Vision*, Papers from the Eranos Yearbooks, vol. 6., ed. Joseph Campbell, trans. R. F. Hull and Frank Manheim (Princeton, NJ: Princeton University Press, 1983).

2   Walt Whitman, "Song of Myself," in *Walt Whitman: The Complete Poems* (London: Penguin Books, 2004), p. 63.

3   "The Hymn of the Kouretes," Crete, Greece, 1500 BC, quoted in Jane Ellen Harrison, *Themis: A Study of the Social Origins of Greek Religion* (1912; repr., Glouchester, MA: Peter Smith, 1974), p. 8.

About the Contributors

PAUL ASHTON is a psychiatrist and Jungian analyst in private practice in Cape Town, where he lives with his wife and youngest daughter. He is the author of the monograph *From the Brink: Experiences of the Void from a Depth Psychology Perspective*, published by Karnac, and the contributing editor of *Evocations of Absence: Multidisciplinary Perspectives on Void States*, published by Spring Journal Books. He is a member of the South African Association of Jungian Analysts and is the editor of *Mantis*, the SAAJA journal. Most recently he co-edited and contributed to *Music and Psyche: Contemporary Psychoanalytic Explorations*, to be published by Spring in 2010.

GUSTAVO BARCELLOS is a Jungian analyst in São Paulo, Brazil, and a member of the Associação Junguiana do Brasil-AJB and the International Association for Analytical Psychology-IAAP. Editor of *Cadernos Junguianos*, AJB's yearly journal, and author of books on clinical and cultural issues, Barcellos also writes and teaches in the field of archetypal psychology.

JOHN BEEBE, a psychiatrist who specializes in psychotherapy, is an analyst member of the C.G. Jung Institute of San Francisco. He founded the Institute's quarterly publication, now titled *Jung Journal: Culture and Psyche*, and was the first US co-editor of the London-based *Journal of Analytical Psychology*. He is the author of *Integrity in Depth*, co-author of *The Presence of the Feminine in Film* and the editor of *Terror, Violence, and the Impulse to Destroy* and *C.G. Jung's Aspects of the Masculine*. His lectures on topics related to analytical psychology have taken him to cities throughout the world.

NANCY FURLOTTI, M.A., is a Jungian analyst in private practice in Los Angeles, California. A member of the Inter-Regional Society of Jungian Analysts, she teaches in the Analyst Training Program at the C.G. Jung Institute of Los Angeles, where she is past President of the Board of Directors. Nancy is on the National Board of the Archive for Research in Archetypal Symbolism (ARAS), and has recently assumed the position of Co-President of the Board of Directors of the Philemon Foundation.

JACQUELINE GERSON was born and raised in Mexico City, where she studied dance, Montessori, pedagogy, and obtained a Master's Degree in Psychology. She is a Jungian analyst, an Individual Member of the IAAP, and serves as a supervisor and teacher in the city where she was born. She has published articles in several journals and contributed a chapter to *The Cultural Complex: Contemporary Perspectives on Psyche and Society*, edited by Thomas Singer and Samuel L. Kimbles.

CHRISTOPHER HAUKE is a Jungian analyst in London, and also a writer, film-maker, and Senior Lecturer at Goldsmiths, University of London. He is the author of *Human Being Human: Culture and the Soul* (2005) and *Jung and the Postmodern: The Interpretation of Realities* (2000), and co-editor of *Jung and Film: Post-Jungian Takes on the Moving Image* (2001). He is co-editing the new collection of Jungian film writing: *Jung and Film II: The Return*. His films include the documentaries *One Colour Red* and *Green Ray*. A new short film, *Again*, is to be premiered in Montreal in 2010. See www.christopher-hauke.com.

SHEN HEYONG is a professor of psychology at South China Normal University in Guangzhou and Fudan University in Shanghai. He is a Jungian analyst and a sandplay therapist. He is the President of the Chinese Federation of Analytical Psychology and has been the main organizer of the International Conferences of Analytical Psychology and Chinese Culture held in China for more than a decade. He was also a speaker at the Eranos East and West Round Table in Ascona, Switzerland from 1997-2007.

THOMAS KELLY is a Jungian analyst who completed his training at the C.G. Jung Institute in Zurich in 1986, and is now in private practice in Montreal, Canada. He serves on the editorial board of the *Journal of Analytical Psychology*, *The New York Journal of Jungian Theory and Practice* and *Quadrant*, is a past President of the Inter-Regional Society of Jungian Analysts (IRSJA), as well as past President of the Council of North American Societies of Jungian Analysts (CNASJA). He currently serves as Vice President of the International Association for Analytical Psychology.

THOMAS B. KIRSCH, M.D., is in private practice as a Jungian analyst in Palo Alto, California. He served as President of the C.G. Jung Institute of San Francisco from 1976-1978, and as vice president and then President of the International Association for Analytical Psychology from 1977-1995. Dr. Kirsch is author of *The Jungians*, co-editor of the Jungian section in *International Encyclopedia of Psychiatry, Psychoanalysis, and Neurology*, and co-editor of *Initiation: The Living Reality of an Archetype*. He is Consulting Editor for *The Jung–Kirsch Letters: The Correspondence of C.G. Jung and James Kirsch*, edited by Ann Conrad Lammers, to be published by Routledge in 2011.

ANTONIO KARIM LANFRANCHI is a cardiologist and a trainee at the C.G. Jung Institute in Zurich. Born in Cairo to an Italian father and an Egyptian mother, he moved to Milan at the age of seventeen, where he is now in private practice and works for a university hospital. His interests range from exploring Egypt and the Muslim world from a Jungian perspective, to understanding the founding metaphors of modern medicine and tracking the "reality of the Psyche" in this as well as in other fields of human work.

CHARLOTTE M. MATHES, LCSW, Ph.D., is a certified Jungian analyst, a graduate of the C.G. Jung institute in Zurich, and received her doctoral degree in psychoanalysis from the Union Graduate School in Cincinnati. She is a clinical member of the American Association of Marriage and Family Counselors, and has been in private practice in New

Orleans for twenty years, having recently opened an office in Baton Rouge. She lectures and conducts seminars in Jungian psychology, family therapy, and bereavement. Her book *And a Sword Shall Pierce Your Heart: Moving from Despair to Meaning after the Death of a Child* was published by Chiron in 2006.

ELENA POURTOVA is a Jungian analyst and a member of the International Association of Analytical Psychology and the Russian Society of Analytical Psychology. She is an Assistant Professor and Chair of Consulting Psychology at the High Psychology School in Moscow. She lectures at the Moscow Association of Analytical Psychology and is a teacher of Jungian analysis in Moscow and other Russian cities.

KUSUM DHAR PRABHU, M.Phil., is a graduate of the C.G. Jung Institute in Zurich. Currently the only Jungian analyst in India, she is President of the All India Association of Analytical Psychology as well as the director of the Jung Center Bangalore. She has lived and worked in Bangalore for sixteen years. Nature, poetry, myth, and art are important in her life. Neuroscience research findings are a current interest. Email: dhar.kusum@gmail.com.

JOERG RASCHE is a Child Psychiatrist, Jungian analyst, and sandplay therapist in Berlin where he teaches at the Berlin Jung Institute. He has served as President of the German Jungian Association (DGAP) and is currently Vice President of the International Association of Analytical Psychology. Dr. Rasche is also a trained musician (organ, harpsichord, piano). His publications include books on mythology (*Prometheus*, 1988), sandplay therapy (1992), and music and analytical psychology (*The Song of the Green Lion: Music as a Mirror of the Soul*). He has published many clinical papers and performed Jungian concert-lectures around the world.

CRAIG SAN ROQUE is a community psychologist and Jungian psychotherapist working in Sydney and in central Australia. Previous works have appeared in Thomas Singer's *The Vision Thing* and Singer and Kimbles' *The Cultural Complex*. He has a special interest in environment/psyche conjunctions, influenced by Jung's formative psycho-ecology, Australian eco-philosophers, and his own experience in indigenous Australia. With David Tacey and Amanda Dowd, he is co-editing a forthcoming book on the cultural complex in Australia, to be published by Spring Journal Books.

EREL SHALIT is a training and supervising analyst, past President of the Israel Society of Analytical Psychology, and a past Director of the Shamai Davidson Mental Health Clinic at the Shalvata Psychiatric Centre in Israel. He is the author of several books and professional articles. His most recent books include *Enemy, Cripple & Beggar: Shadows in the Hero's Path* (2008), and a novella, *Requiem: A Tale of Exile and Return* (2010).

THOMAS SINGER, M.D., (Editor) is a psychiatrist and Jungian analyst who lives and practices in the San Francisco Bay Area. He has authored and edited several book and papers, including *A Fan's Guide to Baseball Fever, Who's the Patient Here?*, *The Cultural Com-*

plex, *The Vision Thing*, and *Initiation: The Living Reality of an Archetype*. Dr. Singer is also very active in National ARAS, an archive and online source of archetypal imagery and symbolism.

MURRAY STEIN, Ph.D., is a training analyst at the International School of Analytical Psychology in Zurich, Switzerland, and its President since 2009. He is the author of many articles and several books, including *Jung's Map of the Soul* and *The Principle of Individuation*, and the editor of the recently published works *Symbolic Life 2009* and *Jungian Psychoanalysis*. He was the section editor of Analytical Psychology for the prize-winning *Edinburgh International Encyclopedia of Psychoanalysis*. He presently resides in Goldiwil (Thun), Switzerland and keeps an office in a historic building in the center of old Zurich.

CRAIG E. STEPHENSON is a graduate of the C.G. Jung Institute (Zurich), the Institute for Psychodrama (Zumikon, Switzerland), and the Centre for Psychoanalytic Studies, University of Essex. His books include *Possession: Jung's Comparative Anatomy of the Psyche* (Routledge 2009) and a translation of Luigi Aurigemma's book of essays, *Jungian Perspectives*, from French into English (University of Scranton Press, 2007). He is a Jungian analyst in private practice in Paris, France.

VIVIANE THIBAUDIER is a training analyst at the Société Française de Psychologie Analytique, of which she was President for four years, and also served as Director of the Paris Jung Institute for fourteen years. She has written numerous articles and lectured in many countries around the world, including China. She has translated both James Hillman and C.G. Jung into French, and has co-authored two Jungian dictionaries.

BEVERLEY ZABRISKIE is a Jungian analyst in the borough of Manhattan of the city of New York, where she is a founding member and former President of the Jungian Psychoanalytic Association (JPA). She was the 2002 psychoanalytic educator of the year for the International Federation of Psychoanalytic Education and the 2007 Fay Lecturer at Texas A&M University, where she presented a lecture series on emotion. Her numerous publications include "A Meeting of Rare Minds," which is the Preface to *Atom and Archetype: The Pauli-Jung Correspondence*, Princeton University Press (2001).

LUIGI ZOJA is a Jungian analyst and past President of the International Association of Analytical Psychology. Dr. Zoja practices in Milan where he devotes half his time to writing. His writings have been translated into 14 languages; in English, his books include: *Drugs, Addiction and Initiation* (Sigo, 1989; Daimon, 2000), *Growth and Guilt: Psychology and the Limits of Development* (Routledge, 1995), *The Father: Historical, Psychological and Cultural Perspectives* (Routledge, 2001, Gradiva Award 2002), *Cultivating the Soul* (Free Association, 2005), and *Ethics and Analysis* (Texas A&M University Press, 2007, Gradiva Award 2008); *Violence in History, Culture and the Psyche* (New Orleans: Spring Journal Books, 2009).

Permissions

Images

The editor and Spring Journal Books would like to thank the following for granting permission to reproduce images in this book; any images for which no permission information is provided were either taken by the author of the chapter in question, or are in the public domain. All efforts have been made to contact all copyright holders, but Spring Journal Books would be pleased to correct any errors or omissions in subsequent editions.

37, 43, 48, 50, 63   Erica Cordell
70, 74, 80   Lou Zhengjun
86, 91, 94   Carlos Moreira, www.carlosmoreira.com.br
101, 104, 110 (photo)   David Martinez
110 (painting)   Collection of Diane Johnson and John Murray, San Francisco, CA
115   Gallica, Bibliothèque Nationale de France
118, 120   François Berton, www.berton-photos.eu/
129   Richard Wanderman, www.richardsnotes.org
133   Alexandra Zabriskie
137   Andreas Jung
164, 171, 177   Victoria Grant
189   Alexey Kochemasov
206   Marie-Reine Mattera
215   Hans Boldt and Sylvana Grisonich-Boldt
216   *Le photographe masqué*, www.old.montreal.qc.ca
222   Jacqueline Gerson Cwilich
234   Juan Rulfo Foundation
283, 286-287, 294   Yoram Bouzaglo
299   Africa Dynamics
314   Frances Ashton
322   Cristina Guarneri
324   Paolo Manacorda
356   Ute and Bernd Eickemeyer
377   Martine Meijer
409, 410   Harry Weber

Text

123   Blackmore, A.M.; *Selected Poems of Victor Hugo.* © 2001 by The University of Chicago.
336-337   Keeley, Edmund; *C.P. Cavafy.* © 1975 by Edmund Keeley and Philip Sherrard. Reprinted by permission of Princeton University Press.